PATTERN - ORIENTED
SOFTWARE ARCHITECTURE
A SYSTEM OF PATTERNS

PATTERN - ORIENTED
SOFTWARE ARCHITECTURE

A SYSTEM OF PATTERNS

Frank Buschmann
Regine Meunier
Hans Rohnert
Peter Sommerlad
Michael Stal

of *Siemens AG, Germany*

JOHN WILEY & SONS

Chichester · New York · Brisbane · Toronto · Singapore

Other Wiley Editorial Offices

John Wiley & Sons, Inc., 605 Third Avenue,
New York, NY 10158-0012, USA

Jacaranda Wiley Ltd, 33 Park Road, Milton,
Queensland 4064, Australia

John Wiley & Sons (Canada) Ltd, 22 Worcester Road,
Rexdale, Ontario M9W 1L1, Canada

John Wiley & Sons (Asia) Pte Ltd, 2 Clementi Loop #02-01,
Jin Xing Distripark, Singapore 0512

Cover Illustration: Based upon a photograph of Chartres Cathedral,
© Monique Jacot / Network Photographers Ltd.

British Library Cataloguing in Publication Data

A catalogue record for this book is available from the British Library

ISBN   0 471 95869 7

Produced from camera-ready copy supplied by the authors using FrameMaker
Printed and bound in Great Britain by Bookcraft (Bath) Ltd
This book is printed on acid-free paper responsibly manufactured from sustainable forestation,
for which at least two trees are planted for each one used for paper production.

For Canan

Frank Buschmann

For Michael, Anja and Sandro

Regine Meunier

For Ute

Hans Rohnert

For Andrea

Peter Sommerlad

For Gisela, Macho, Merlin

Michael Stal

Table of Contents

About this Book   xi

Guide to the Reader   xvii

1   **Patterns**   1
1.1   What is a Pattern?   2
1.2   What Makes a Pattern?   8
1.3   Pattern Categories   11
1.4   Relationships between Patterns   16
1.5   Pattern Description   19
1.6   Patterns and Software Architecture   21
1.7   Summary   24

2   **Architectural Patterns**   25
2.1   Introduction   26
2.2   From Mud to Structure   29
        Layers   31
        Pipes and Filters   53
        Blackboard   71
2.3   Distributed Systems   97
        Broker   99
2.4   Interactive Systems 123
        Model-View-Controller 125
        Presentation-Abstraction-Control 145
2.5   Adaptable Systems 169
        Microkernel 171
        Reflection 193

3 **Design Patterns** 221
3.1 Introduction 222
3.2 Structural Decomposition 223
Whole-Part 225
3.3 Organization of Work 243
Master-Slave 245
3.4 Access Control 261
Proxy 263
3.5 Management 276
Command Processor 277
View Handler 291
3.6 Communication 305
Forwarder-Receiver 307
Client-Dispatcher-Server 323
Publisher-Subscriber 339

4 **Idioms** 345
4.1 Introduction 346
4.2 What Can Idioms Provide? 346
4.3 Idioms and Style 348
4.4 Where Can You Find Idioms? 350
Counted Pointer 353

5 **Pattern Systems** 359
5.1 What is a Pattern System? 360
5.2 Pattern Classification 362
5.3 Pattern Selection 368
5.4 Pattern Systems as Implementation Guidelines . 370
5.5 The Evolution of Pattern Systems 374
5.6 Summary 381

6   **Patterns and Software Architecture**   383
6.1   Introduction   384
6.2   Patterns in Software Architecture   391
6.3   Enabling Techniques for Software Architecture .   397
6.4   Non-functional Properties of Software Architecture   404
6.5   Summary   411

7   **The Pattern Community**   413
7.1   The Roots   414
7.2   Leading Figures and their Work   415
7.3   The Community   416

8   **Where Will Patterns Go?**   419
8.1   Pattern Mining   420
8.2   Pattern Organization and Indexing   423
8.3   Methods and Tools   424
8.4   Algorithms, Data Structures and Patterns   426
8.5   Formalizing Patterns   427
8.6   A Final Remark   428

Notations   429

Glossary   433

References   441

Index of Patterns   455

About this Book

This is a book about patterns for software architecture, or simply, patterns. Patterns have been drawing considerable attention over recent years: workshops, tutorials, forums for electronic discussion, papers in journals and whole books are being devoted to patterns. The pattern community has even started its own conference. All this enthusiastic discussion of patterns makes them seem as if they are the climax of the 'object wave'.

What is so exciting about patterns? It is probably the fact that they constitute a 'grass roots' effort to build on the collective experience of skilled designers and software engineers. Such experts already have solutions to many recurring design problems. Patterns capture these proven solutions in an easily-available and, hopefully, well-written form.

We want this book to support both novices and experts in software development. It should help novices to act as if they were—or almost as if they were—experts on modest-sized projects, without having to gain many years of experience. It should support experts in the design of large-scale and complex software systems with defined properties. It should also enable them to learn from the experience of other experts. The book should help both groups to find well-proven solutions, as well as alternatives, to specific design problems.

The book is intended to be both an instructive text and a reference guide. It helps software developers to think about software architecture in a new way, and presents a number of techniques for solving particular recurring design problems. Using this book as a guide in a software engineering course can provide students with an entirely new perspective on the design of large-scale software systems. It can serve as a reference manual, because it presents our techniques comprehensively and ready for use. We include many guidelines and constraints for the practical application of the patterns we include.

The idea of recording design wisdom in a canonical form can be traced to Christopher Alexander[1]. He pioneered patterns in the context of the architecture of buildings. His book *The Timeless Way of Building* shows how patterns can be applied to house construction, as well as to the planning of neighborhoods and whole cities. The underlying theme of his work is the design of living places that are not only functional and fashionable, but also comforting and consoling. Well-designed buildings demonstrate inherent qualities that can be clearly perceived, but are hard to describe or quantify. In short, such buildings possess 'a quality without a name'.

Early experiments in adapting this approach to software engineering leaned heavily on Alexander's style. More recently the software community has been experimenting to find a stylistic form better-suited to software design. Several different description forms for patterns have been tried, but there is no consensus yet.

Although we put considerable effort into finding a good way to describe patterns, developing theories on 'pattern styles' is not the main goal of this book. It was certainly not our initial motivation for starting work on patterns. In 1991 we recorded our first patterns in a straightforward way. While our style of pattern documentation improved slowly, it soon became clear that individual patterns do not stand alone. Instead, patterns reveal a rich set of interrelationships. This was one of the driving forces for producing a book, rather than documenting patterns one at a time and publishing them as a series of papers. The disadvantage of the book approach is the long gestation period before it becomes available. Although this has been well-known for decades, it still astonishes us just how long it takes to come up with good pattern descriptions.

Four other authors experienced the same phenomenon. In the fall of 1994, Erich Gamma, Richard Helm, Ralph Johnson and John Vlissides published the seminal book *Design Patterns – Elements of Reusable Object-Oriented Software*. Although the idea of design

---

1. Christopher Alexander is a practising architect and urban planner, as well as Professor of Architecture at the University of California at Berkeley, and Director of the Center for Environmental Structure. He developed a theory of architecture, building and planning that is based on the construction and use of patterns. The theory itself, the patterns, experiments with his approach, as well as criticisms of the approach are published in a series of books by Oxford University Press.

patterns was no longer novel, the 'GoF' book (named after the 'Gang of Four' in Chinese politics) presented the first catalog of well-described design patterns for object-oriented programs.

Our approach is slightly different to the Gang-of-Four, though there are many similarities and some overlaps. The GoF book concentrates on design-level patterns, whereas our patterns span several levels of abstraction. These range from high-level *architectural patterns* through *design patterns* to low-level *idioms*. We also focus on issues other than object-orientation, and try to incorporate the latest insights into pattern description techniques. Our overall goal is to use patterns to help in the wider context of software architecture. We call this approach *pattern-oriented software architecture*. We talk about *pattern systems,* in which patterns are not just collected into a heterogeneous container, but are also grouped according to appropriate criteria. The GoF book started this categorization effort by dividing patterns into 'creational', 'structural' and 'behavioral' groupings. We try to take the next step by grouping patterns according to finer-grained criteria such as interactive and adaptable systems, organization of work, communication and access control.

We want to encourage users of our pattern system to share it with their colleagues. Pattern-sharing establishes a common vocabulary for design problems. It allows the members of the growing pattern community to identify, name and discuss both problems and solutions more effectively. Getting 'up to speed' in systems design is one of the more important reasons to work with patterns.

Our pattern system is not intended to be complete. There are already so many patterns that it is impossible to record all of them in a single book. With evolving technology new patterns may evolve. We hope you will extend, modify and tailor our pattern system to your specific needs. Missing patterns should be added, those not needed may be ignored and others may be changed.

If you have any comments, criticisms or suggestions for improvement of the style and content of this book, please feel free to make them. We also welcome reports of experiences with the patterns we describe. You can write to us care of John Wiley & Sons Ltd., or send electronic mail to `patterns@zfe.siemens.de`.

Preliminary versions of most of the patterns we include were discussed on the Internet. Our motivation was not to get free advertising or to give away patterns. Instead, we wanted to help a new trend in publishing, that of showing material early on to involve the community before printing, with benefit to all parties. We enjoyed this experience and thank all participants. This does not mean that public electronic discussion of our book is closed, however. The mailing list still exists and readers are welcome to participate. Guidelines for subscription can be found on the patterns home page. Its URL is:

`http://st-www.cs.uiuc.edu/users/patterns/patterns.html`

This URL is also the most important information source for all aspects of patterns, such as available and forthcoming books, conferences on patterns, papers on patterns and so on.

The Structure of the Book

The first chapter systematically introduces the notion of a pattern and discusses the principles of pattern description. Chapters 2 through 4 present our catalog of patterns.

Architectural patterns are the highest-level patterns. They are intended to provide the skeleton of an overall system architecture. Chapter 2 features eight architectural patterns from different application areas.

Chapter 3 presents a collection of eight *design patterns* that address the sort of problems typically encountered after the overall structure of a software system has been specified. Our design patterns deal, for example, with structuring components to handle complexity, distributing workload between components and organizing inter-component communication.

Chapter 4 is the third and last part of the catalog. It deals with *idioms*, the language-dependent patterns. We refer however mainly to other people's work instead of documenting our own idioms, and only present one idiom as a concrete example. The reason for not describing our own set of idioms is simple—a lot of idioms for languages such as C++ and Smalltalk are already available. Instead of just rephrasing these patterns, we choose to refer to the original source.

In Chapter 5 we argue that it is important to organize patterns into *pattern systems*. Such systems should help both writers and users of patterns in several ways: finding the right pattern for the situation at hand, filling gaps in a collection of patterns, understanding the relationships between patterns and evolving pattern systems.

In Chapter 6 we discuss how patterns are embedded in software architecture. In particular we discuss our understanding of software architecture and its underlying principles and we demonstrate how these principles are supported by patterns.

Chapter 7 is about the history of patterns, related work and the pattern community at large. To complete the book, Chapter 8 gives our view of the future of patterns.

The book ends with an appendix on notations, a glossary of frequently used terms, comprehensive references and a pattern index.

Acknowledgments

We wish to thank the many people who helped in different ways with the creation of this book, not just because it is customary, but because we take genuine pleasure in doing so.

We thank Joelle Coutaz, Wilhelm Gruber, Claus Jäkel, Doug Lea, Oscar Nierstrasz, Laurence Nigay, Frances Paulisch, Wolfgang Pree, Uwe Steinmüller, John Vlissides and Walter Zimmer for their discussion and revision of earlier versions of our work. Ralph Johnson and the members of his architecture reading group at the University of Illinois, Urbana-Champaign, namely John Brant, Michael Chung, Brian Foote, Don Roberts and Joseph Yoder carefully reviewed most of our pattern descriptions. They provided us with many useful comments and suggestions for improvement. We also thank the Hillside Group for its support and encouragement.

Acknowledgments to those people who helped with the improvement of specific patterns are given at the end of each pattern description in a separate section.

Special thanks go to James Coplien, Joseph Davison, Neil Harrison, and Douglas Schmidt. Their detailed review of all our material helped us to shape and polish the final contents of this book.

Our summer students Marina Seidl and Martin Botzler suffered with us through some early experiments. Special thanks also go to Franz Kapsner and Hartmut Raffler for their managerial support and backing at the software engineering labs of Corporate Research and Development of Siemens AG, Munich, Germany.

Francis Glassborow and Steve Rickaby attempted to improve upon our limited English writing capabilities, and helped eradicate the worst 'Germanisms'—not an easy task.

Finally, we thank our editor Gaynor Redvers-Mutton and everyone else at John Wiley & Sons who made it possible to meet the tight production schedule for this book.

Guide to the Reader

This book is structured so that it can be read from cover to cover. The following hints are provided in case you want to choose your own route through the book.

Chapter 1, *Patterns* gives an in-depth explanation of patterns for software architecture. Everything that follows builds on this discussion, so you should read this chapter first. The order in which you read individual patterns is up to you. To grasp the key ideas behind a specific pattern, you only need to read its Context, Problem and Solution sections. Extensive cross-referencing will guide you in understanding the relationships between patterns.

If patterns are new to you, we suggest that you read the basic and simple patterns first—patterns that are easy to understand and that appear in many well-structured software systems. Examples are:

- The Pipes and Filters architectural pattern (53)[1]
- The Proxy design pattern (263)
- The Forwarder-Receiver design pattern (307)

You can also use this book to find solutions to design problems you may encounter in your current project. Use the overview of our pattern system in Chapter 5, *Pattern Systems* as a guide in your search, then look up the detailed descriptions of those patterns you have selected as potential solutions.

The other chapters—Chapter 6, *Patterns and Software Architecture*, Chapter 7, *The Pattern Community* and Chapter 8, *Where Will Patterns Go?*—can be read in any order, although the given order will suit most readers best.

---

1. We adopt the page number notation introduced by [GHJV95]. (53) means that the corresponding pattern description starts on page number page 53 of this book.

1   Patterns

*...Somewhere in the deeply remote past it seriously
traumatized a small random group of atoms drifting
through the empty sterility of space and made them cling
together in the most extraordinarily unlikely patterns.
These patterns quickly learnt to copy themselves (this
was part of what was so extraordinary about the
patterns) and went on to cause massive trouble on every
planet they drifted on to.
That was how life began in the Universe ...*

Douglas Adams, *The Hitchhiker's Guide to the Galaxy*

Patterns help you build on the collective experience of skilled software engineers. They capture existing, well-proven experience in software development and help to promote good design practise. Every pattern deals with a specific, recurring problem in the design or implementation of a software system. Patterns can be used to construct software architectures with specific properties.

In this chapter we give an in-depth explanation of what patterns for software architecture are, and how they help you build software.

1.1 What is a Pattern?

When experts work on a particular problem, it is unusual for them to tackle it by inventing a new solution that is completely distinct from existing ones. They often recall a similar problem they have already solved, and reuse the essence of its solution to solve the new problem. This kind of 'expert behavior', the thinking in problem-solution pairs, is common to many different domains, such as architecture [Ale79], economics [Etz64] and software engineering [BJ94]. It is a natural way of coping with any kind of problem or social interaction [NS72].

Here is an elegant and intuitive example of such a problem-solution pair, taken from architecture:

Example   **Window Place** [AIS77]:

Everybody loves window seats, bay windows, and big windows with low sills and comfortable chairs drawn up to them...A room which does not have a place like this seldom allows you to feel comfortable or perfectly at ease...

If the room contains no window which is a "place", a person in the room will be torn between two forces:

1. He wants to sit down and be comfortable.

2. He is drawn toward the light.

Obviously, if the comfortable places—those places in the room where you most want to sit—are away from the windows, there is no way of overcoming this conflict...

Therefore: In every room where you spend any length of time during the day, make at least one window into a "window place"

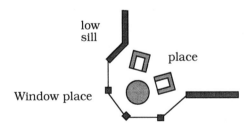

low sill

place

Window place

❏

Abstracting from specific problem-solution pairs and distilling out common factors leads to patterns: 'These problem-solution pairs tend to fall into families of similar problems and solutions with each family exhibiting a pattern in both the problems and the solutions' [Joh94]. In his book *The Timeless Way of Building* [Ale79] (p. 247), the architect Christopher Alexander defines the term *pattern* as follows:

> Each pattern is a three-part rule, which expresses a relation between a certain context, a problem, and a solution.

> As an element in the world, each pattern is a relationship between a certain context, a certain system of forces which occurs repeatedly in that context, and a certain spatial configuration which allows these forces to resolve themselves.

> As an element of language, a pattern is an instruction, which shows how this spatial configuration can be used, over and over again, to resolve the given system of forces, wherever the context makes it relevant.

> The pattern is, in short, at the same time a thing, which happens in the world, and the rule which tells us how to create that thing, and when we must create it. It is both a process and a thing; both a description of a thing which is alive, and a description of the process which will generate that thing.

We also find many patterns in software architecture. Experts in software engineering know these patterns from practical experience and follow them in developing applications with specific properties. They use them to solve design problems both effectively and elegantly. Before discussing this in detail, let us look at a well-known example:

Example   Model-View-Controller (125)

Consider this pattern when developing software with a human-computer interface.

User interfaces are prone to change requests. For example, when extending the functionality of an application, menus have to be modified to access new functions, and user interfaces may have to be adapted for specific customers. A system may often have to be ported to another platform with a different 'look and feel' standard. Even upgrading to a new release of your window system can imply changes to your code. To summarize, the user interface of a long-lived system is a moving target.

Building a system with the required flexibility will be expensive and error-prone if the user interface is tightly interwoven with the functional core. This can result in the development and maintenance of several substantially different software systems, one for each user interface implementation. Ensuing changes then spread over many modules. In summary, when developing such an interactive software system, you have to consider two aspects:

- Changes to the user interface should be easy, and possible at run-time.

- Adapting or porting the user interface should not impact code in the functional core of the application.

To solve the problem, divide an interactive application into three areas: processing, output and input:

- The *model* component encapsulates core data and functionality. The model is independent of specific output representations or input behavior.

- *View* components display information to the user. A view obtains the data it displays from the model. There can be multiple views of the model.

- Each view has an associated *controller* component. Controllers receive input, usually as events that denote mouse movement, activation of mouse buttons or keyboard input. Events are translated to service requests, which are sent either to the model or to the view. The user interacts with the system solely via controllers.

The separation of the model from the view and controller components allows multiple views of the same model. If the user changes the model via the controller of one view, all other views dependent on this data should reflect the change. To achieve this, the model notifies all views whenever its data changes. The views in turn retrieve new data from the model and update their displayed information.

This solution allows you to change a subsystem of the application without causing major effects to other subsystems. For example, you can change from a non-graphical to a graphical user interface without modifying the model subsystem. You can also add support for a new input device without affecting information display or the functional core. All versions of the software can operate on the same model subsystem independently of specific 'look and feel'.

The following OMT class diagram[1] illustrates this solution:

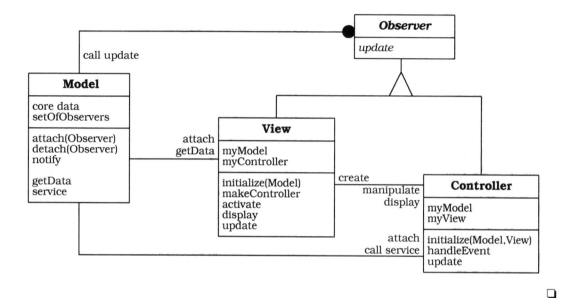

We can derive several properties of patterns for software architecture from this introductory example[2]:

A pattern addresses a recurring design problem that arises in specific design situations, and presents a solution to it. In our example here the problem is supporting variability in user interfaces. This problem may arise when developing software systems with human-computer interaction. You can solve this problem by a strict separation of responsibilities: the core functionality of the application is separated from its user interface.

Patterns document existing, well-proven design experience. They are not invented or created artificially. Rather they 'distill and provide a means to reuse the design knowledge gained by experienced prac-

---

1. For a summary of the analysis and design method Object-Modeling-Technique (OMT) and its notation, see Notations on page 429. For details we refer to [RBPEL91].

2. If not stated otherwise, we use the terms *pattern* and *pattern for software architecture* as synonyms.

titioners' [GHJV93]. Those familiar with an adequate set of patterns 'can apply them immediately to design problems without having to rediscover them' [GHJV93]. Instead of knowledge existing only in the heads of a few experts, patterns make it more generally available. You can use such expert knowledge to design high-quality software for a specific task. The Model-View-Controller pattern, for example, presents experience gained over many years of developing interactive systems. Many well-known applications already apply the Model-View-Controller pattern—it is the classical architecture for many Smalltalk applications, and underlies several application frameworks such as MacApp [Sch86] or ET++ [WGM88].

Patterns identify and specify abstractions that are above the level of single classes and instances, or of components [GHJV93]. Typically, a pattern describes several components, classes or objects, and details their responsibilities and relationships, as well as their cooperation. All components together solve the problem that the pattern addresses, and usually more effectively than a single component. For example, the Model-View-Controller pattern describes a triad of three cooperating components, and each MVC triad also cooperates with other MVC triads of the system.

Patterns provide a common vocabulary and understanding for design principles [GHJV93]. Pattern names, if chosen carefully, become part of a widespread design language. They facilitate effective discussion of design problems and their solutions. They remove the need to explain a solution to a particular problem with a lengthy and complicated description. Instead you can use a pattern name, and explain which parts of a solution correspond to which components of the pattern, or to which relationships between them. For example, the name 'Model-View-Controller' and the associated pattern has been well-known to the Smalltalk community since the early '80s, and is used by many software engineers. When we say 'the architecture of the software follows Model-View-Controller', all our colleagues who are familiar with the pattern have an idea of the basic structure and properties of the application immediately.

Patterns are a means of documenting software architectures. They can describe the vision you have in mind when designing a software system. This helps others to avoid violating this vision when extending and modifying the original architecture, or when modifying the system's code. For example, if you know that a system is structured according to the Model-View-Controller pattern, you also know how to extend it with a new function: keep core functionality separate from user input and information display.

Patterns support the construction of software with defined properties. Patterns provide a skeleton of functional behavior and therefore help to implement the functionality of your application. For example, patterns exist for maintaining consistency between cooperating components and for providing transparent peer-to-peer inter-process communication. In addition, patterns explicitly address non-functional requirements for software systems, such as changeability, reliability, testability or reusability. The Model-View-Controller pattern, for example, supports the changeability of user interfaces and the reusability of core functionality.

Patterns help you build complex and heterogeneous software architectures. Every pattern provides a predefined set of components, roles and relationships between them. It can be used to specify particular aspects of concrete software structures. Patterns 'act as building-blocks for constructing more complex designs' [GHJV93]. This method of using predefined design artifacts supports the speed and the quality of your design. Understanding and applying well-written patterns saves time when compared to searching for solutions on your own. This is not to say that individual patterns will necessarily be better than your own solutions, but, at the very least, a *pattern system* such as is explained in this book can help you to evaluate and assess design alternatives.

However, although a pattern determines the basic structure of the solution to a particular design problem, it does not specify a fully-detailed solution. A pattern provides a scheme for a generic solution to a family of problems, rather than a prefabricated module that can be used 'as is'. You must implement this scheme according to the specific needs of the design problem at hand. A pattern helps with the creation of similar units. These units can be alike in their broad structure, but are frequently quite different in their detailed appearance. Patterns help solve problems, but they do not provide complete solutions.

Patterns help you to manage software complexity. Every pattern describes a proven way to handle the problem it addresses: the kinds of components needed, their roles, the details that should be hidden, the abstractions that should be visible, and how everything works. When you encounter a concrete design situation covered by a pattern there is no need to waste time inventing a new solution to your problem. If you implement the pattern correctly, you can rely on the solution it provides. The Model-View-Controller pattern, for example, helps you to separate the different user interface aspects of a software system and provide appropriate abstractions for them.

We end with the following definition:

A *pattern for software architecture* describes a particular recurring design problem that arises in specific design contexts, and presents a well-proven generic scheme for its solution. The solution scheme is specified by describing its constituent components, their responsibilities and relationships, and the ways in which they collaborate.

1.2   What Makes a Pattern?

The discussion in the previous section leads us to adopt a three-part schema that underlies every pattern:

Context: a situation giving rise to a problem.

Problem: the recurring problem arising in that context.

Solution: a proven resolution of the problem.

The schema as a whole denotes a type of rule that establishes a relationship between a given context, a certain problem arising in that context, and an appropriate solution to the problem. All three parts of this schema are closely coupled. However, to understand the schema in detail, we have to clarify what we mean by *context*, *problem*, and *solution*.

Context   The context extends the plain problem-solution dichotomy by describing situations in which the problem occurs. The context of a pattern may be fairly general, for example 'developing software with a human-computer interface.' On the other hand, the context can tie specific patterns together, such as 'implementing the change-propagation mechanism of the Model-View-Controller triad.'

Specifying the correct context for a pattern is difficult. We find it practically impossible to determine all situations, both general and specific, in which a pattern may be applied. A more pragmatic approach is to list all known situations where a problem that is addressed by a particular pattern can occur. This does not guarantee that we cover every situation in which a pattern may be relevant, but it at least gives valuable guidance.

Problem This part of a pattern description schema describes the problem that arises repeatedly in the given context. It begins with a general problem specification, capturing its very essence—what is the concrete design issue we must solve? The Model-View-Controller pattern, for example, addresses the problem that user interfaces often vary. This general problem statement is completed by a set of *forces*. Originally borrowed from architecture and Christopher Alexander, the pattern community uses the term *force* to denote any aspect of the problem that should be considered when solving it, such as:

- Requirements the solution must fulfil—for example, that peer-to-peer inter-process communication must be efficient.

- Constraints you must consider—for example, that inter-process communication must follow a particular protocol.

- Desirable properties the solution should have—for example, that changing software should be easy.

The Model-View-Controller pattern from the previous section specifies two forces: it should be easy to modify the user interface, but the functional core of the software should not be affected by its modification.

In general, forces discuss the problem from various viewpoints and help you to understand its details. Forces may complement or contradict each other. Two contradictory forces are, for example, extensibility of a system versus minimization of its code size. If you want your system to be extensible, you tend to use abstract superclasses. If you want to minimize code size, for example for embedded applications, you may not be able to afford such a luxury as abstract superclasses. Most importantly, however, forces are the key to solving the problem. The better they are balanced, the better the solution to the problem. Detailed discussion of forces is therefore an essential part of the problem statement.

Solution   The solution part of a pattern shows how to solve the recurring problem, or better, how to balance the forces associated with it. In software architecture such a solution includes two aspects.

Firstly, every pattern specifies a certain structure, a spatial configuration of elements. For example, the description of the Model-View-Controller pattern includes the following sentence: 'Divide an interactive application into the three areas: processing, output, and input.'

This structure addresses the *static* aspects of the solution. Since such a structure can be seen as a micro-architecture [GHJV93], it consists, like any software architecture, of both components and their relationships. Within this structure the components serve as building blocks, and each component has a defined responsibility. The relationships between the components determine their placement.

Secondly, every pattern specifies run-time behavior. For example, the solution part of the Model-View-Controller pattern includes the following statement: 'Controllers receive input, usually as events that denote mouse movement, activation of mouse buttons, or keyboard input. Events are translated to service requests, which are sent either to the model or to the view'.

This run-time behavior addresses the *dynamic* aspects of the solution. How do the participants of the pattern collaborate? How is work organized between them? How do they communicate with each other?

It is important to note that the solution does not necessarily resolve all forces associated with the problem. It may focus on particular forces and leave others half or completely unresolved, especially if forces are contradictory.

As we mentioned in the previous section, a pattern provides a solution schema rather than a fully-specified artifact or blueprint. You should be able to reuse the solution in many implementations, but so that its essence is still retained. A pattern is a *mental* building block. After applying a pattern, an architecture should include a particular structure that provides for the roles specified by the pattern, but adjusted and tailored to the specific needs of the problem at hand. No two implementations of a given pattern are likely to be the same.

The following diagram summarizes the whole schema:

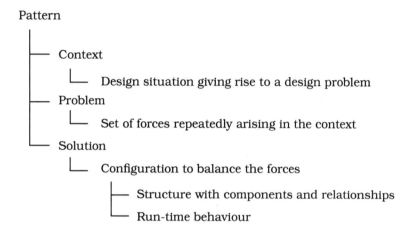

Pattern

—— Context

    └── Design situation giving rise to a design problem

—— Problem

    └── Set of forces repeatedly arising in the context

—— Solution

    └── Configuration to balance the forces

        —— Structure with components and relationships

        └── Run-time behaviour

This schema captures the very essence of a pattern independently of its domain. Using it as a template for describing patterns seems obvious. It already underlies many pattern descriptions, for example those in [AIS77], [BJ94], [Cope94c], [Cun94] and [Mes94]. This gives us confidence that the above form makes it easy to understand, share and discuss a pattern.

1.3 Pattern Categories

A closer look at existing patterns reveals that they cover various ranges of scale and abstraction. Some patterns help in structuring a software system into subsystems. Other patterns support the refinement of subsystems and components, or of the relationships between them. Further patterns help in implementing particular design aspects in a specific programming language. Patterns also range from domain-independent ones, such as those for decoupling interacting components, to patterns addressing domain-specific aspects such as transaction policies in business applications, or call routing in telecommunication.

To refine our classification, we group patterns into three categories:

- Architectural patterns
- Design patterns
- Idioms

Each category consists of patterns having a similar range of scale or abstraction.

Architectural Patterns

Viable software architectures are built according to some overall structuring principle. We describe these principles with *architectural patterns*.

An *architectural pattern* expresses a fundamental structural organization schema for software systems. It provides a set of predefined subsystems, specifies their responsibilities, and includes rules and guidelines for organizing the relationships between them.

Architectural patterns are templates for concrete software architectures. They specify the system-wide structural properties of an application, and have an impact on the architecture of its subsystems. The selection of an architectural pattern is therefore a fundamental design decision when developing a software system.

The Model-View-Controller pattern from the beginning of this chapter is one of the best-known examples of an architectural pattern. It provides a structure for interactive software systems.

Design Patterns

The subsystems of a software architecture, as well as the relationships between them, usually consist of several smaller architectural units. We describe these using *design* patterns.

A *design pattern* provides a scheme for refining the subsystems or components of a software system, or the relationships between them. It describes a commonly-recurring structure of communicating components that solves a general design problem within a particular context [GHJV95].

Design patterns are medium-scale patterns. They are smaller in scale than architectural patterns, but tend to be independent of a particular programming language or programming paradigm. The application of a design pattern has no effect on the fundamental structure of a software system, but may have a strong influence on the architecture of a subsystem.

Many design patterns provide structures for decomposing more complex services or components. Others address the effective cooperation between them, such as the following pattern:

Name   Observer [GHJV95] or Publisher-Subscriber (339)

Context   A component uses data or information provided by another component.

Problem   Changing the internal state of a component may introduce inconsistencies between cooperating components. To restore consistency, we need a mechanism for exchanging data or state information between such components.

Two *forces* are associated with this problem:

- The components should be loosely coupled—the information provider should not depend on details of its collaborators.

- The components that depend on the information provider are not known a priori.

Solution   Implement a change-propagation mechanism between the information provider—the *subject*—and the components dependent on it—the *observers*. Observers can dynamically register or unregister with this mechanism. Whenever the subject changes its state, it starts the change-propagation mechanism to restore consistency with all registered observers. Changes are propagated by invoking a special update function common to all observers. To implement change propagation—the passing of data and state information from the subject to the observers—you can use a *pull-model*, a *push-model*, or a combination of both.

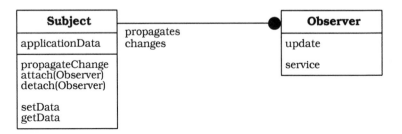

Idioms

Idioms deal with the implementation of particular design issues.

An *idiom* is a low-level pattern specific to a programming language. An idiom describes how to implement particular aspects of components or the relationships between them using the features of the given language.

Idioms represent the lowest-level patterns. They address aspects of both design and implementation.

Most idioms are language-specific—they capture existing programming experience. Often the same idiom looks different for different languages, and sometimes an idiom that is useful for one programming language does not make sense in another. For example, the C++ community uses reference-counting idioms to manage dynamically-allocated resources; Smalltalk provides a garbage collection mechanism, so has no need for such idioms.

The following example deals with a critical operation in C++: assignment. The pattern is called Counted Body. Its description is largely taken from [Cope94a]. We later describe the Counted Pointer pattern (353), which includes the Counted Body pattern as a variant.

Name   Counted Body [Cope94a]

Context   The interface of a class is separated from its implementation. A *handle* class presents the class interface to the user. The other class embodies the implementation, and is called *body*. The handle forwards member function invocations to the body.

Problem   Assignment in C++ is defined recursively as member-by-member assignment, with copying as the termination of the recursion. In Smalltalk, it would be more efficient and more in the spirit of the language if copying were rebinding. In detail, you need to balance three *forces*:

- Copying of bodies is expensive in both storage requirements and processing time.

- Copying can be avoided by using pointers and references, but these leave a problem—who is responsible for cleaning up the object? They also leave a user-visible distinction between built-in types and user-defined types.

- Sharing bodies on assignment is semantically incorrect if the shared body is modified through one of the handles.

Solution   A reference count is added to the body class to facilitate memory management. Memory management is added to the handle class, particularly to its implementations of initialization, assignment, copying and destruction. It is the responsibility of any operation that modifies the state of the body to break the sharing of the body by making its own copy, decrementing the reference count of the original body.

This solution avoids gratuitous copying, leading to a more efficient implementation. Sharing is broken when the body state is modified through any handle. Sharing is preserved in the more common case of parameter passing. Special pointer and reference types are avoided, and Smalltalk semantics are approximated. Garbage collection can be implemented based on this model.

Integration with Software Development

Ideally, our categories help you to preselect potentially useful patterns for a given design problem. They are related to important software development activities. Architectural patterns can be used at the beginning of coarse-grained design, design patterns during the whole design phase, and idioms during the implementation phase. A more detailed discussion of these issues can be found in Section 5.2, *Pattern Classification*, together with a discussion of alternative classification schemas.

1.4 Relationships between Patterns

A close look at many patterns reveals that, despite initial impressions, their components and relationships are not always as 'atomic' as they first appear to be. A pattern solves a particular problem, but its application may raise new problems. Some of these can be solved by other patterns. Single components or relationships inside a particular pattern may therefore be described by smaller patterns, all of them integrated by the larger pattern in which they are contained.

Example   Refinement of the Model-View-Controller pattern

The Model-View-Controller pattern separates core functionality from human-computer interaction to provide adaptable user interfaces. However, applying this pattern introduces a new problem. Views, and sometimes even controllers, depend on the state of the model. The consistency between them must be maintained: whenever the state of the model changes, we must update all its dependent views and controllers. However, we must not lose the ability to change the user interface. The Publisher-Subscriber pattern from the previous section helps us to solve this problem—the model embodies the role of the subject, while views and controllers play the roles of observers.❏

Most patterns for software architecture raise problems that can be solved by smaller patterns. Patterns do not usually exist in isolation. Christopher Alexander puts this in somewhat idealistic terms: 'Each pattern depends on the smaller patterns it contains and on the larger patterns in which it is contained' [Ale79].

A pattern may also be a variant of another. From a general perspective a pattern and its variants describe solutions to very similar problems.

These problems usually vary in some of the forces involved, rather than in general character. This is illustrated in the following example.

Example   The Document-View variant of the Model-View-Controller pattern.

Consider the development of an interactive text editor using the Model-View-Controller pattern. Within such an application it is hard to separate controller functionality from view functionality. Suppose you select text with the mouse and change it from regular to bold face. Text selection is a controller action that does not cause changes to the model. The selected text just serves as input for another controller action, here changing the face of the selected text. However, text selection has a visual appearance—the selected text is highlighted. In a strict Model-View-Controller structure, the controller must either implement this 'view-like' behavior by itself, or must cooperate with the view in which the selected text appears. Both solutions require some unnecessary implementation overhead.

In such a situation it is better to apply the Document-View variant of the Model-View-Controller pattern, which unifies the view and controller functionality in a single component, the view of the Document-View pattern. The document component directly corresponds to the model of the Model-View-Controller triad. When using the Document-View variant, however, we lose the ability to change input and output functionality independently.   ❏

Patterns can also combine in more complex structures at the same level of abstraction. This happens when your original problem includes more forces than can be balanced by a single pattern. In this case, applying several patterns can solve the problem. Each pattern resolves a particular subset of the forces.

Example   Transparent peer-to-peer inter-process communication

Suppose you have to develop a distributed application with high performance peer-to-peer inter-process communication. The following *forces* must be balanced:

- The inter-process communication must be efficient. Spending time searching for the location of remote servers is undesirable.

- Independence from a particular inter-process communication mechanism is desirable. The mechanism must be exchangeable without affecting clients or servers.

- Clients should not be aware of, or dependent on, the name and location of their servers. Instead, they should communicate with each other as if they were in the same process.

This problem cannot be solved by any single pattern in isolation, but two patterns in combination can achieve this. The Proxy pattern (263) resolves the first force, and partly resolves the last force. In this pattern, the client communicates with a representative of the server that is located in the same process. This representative, the *remote proxy*, knows details about the server, such as its name, and forwards every request to it.

The Forwarder-Receiver pattern (307) resolves the second force and the remaining part of the third force. It offers a general interface for sending and receiving messages and data across process boundaries. The pattern hides the details of the concrete inter-process communication mechanism. Replacing this mechanism only affects the forwarders and receivers of the system. In addition, the pattern offers a name-to-address mapping for servers.

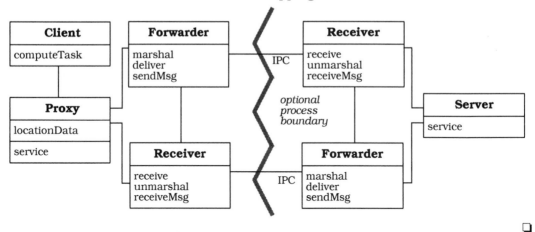

All three kinds of relationship—refinement, variants and combination—help in using patterns effectively. Refinement supports the implementation of a pattern, combination helps you compose complex design structures, and variants help when selecting the right pattern in a given design situation.

You can find complementary discussion of relationships between patterns in [Zim94].

1.5 Pattern Description

Patterns must be presented in an appropriate form if we are to understand and discuss them. A good description helps us grasp the essence of a pattern immediately—what is the problem the pattern addresses, and what is the proposed solution? A good description also provides us with all the details necessary to implement a pattern, and to consider the consequences of its application.

Patterns should also be described uniformly. This helps us to compare one pattern with another, especially when we are looking for alternative solutions to a problem.

The basic Context-Problem-Solution structure we discussed earlier in this chapter provides us with a good starting point for a description format that meets the above requirements. It captures the essential characteristics of a pattern, and provides you with the key ideas. We have therefore based our description template on this structure.

However, describing a pattern based exclusively on a Context-Problem-Solution schema is not enough. A pattern must be named—preferably with an intuitive name—if we are to share it and discuss it. Such a name should also convey the essence of a pattern. A good pattern name is vital, as it will become part of the design vocabulary [GHJV93].

We add an introductory example to the pattern description to help explain the problem and its associated forces. We repeatedly refer to this example when discussing solution and implementation aspects of the general pattern.

We further use diagrams and scenarios to illustrate the static and dynamic aspects of the solution. We also include implementation guidelines for the pattern. These guidelines help us transform a given architecture into one that uses the pattern. We add sample code, and list successful applications of the pattern to enhance its credibility.

We also describe variants of a pattern. Variants provide us with alternative solutions to a problem. However, we do not describe these variants at the same level of detail as the original pattern—we only describe them briefly.

A discussion of the benefits and potential liabilities of a pattern highlight the consequences of its application. This provides us with information to help us decide whether we can use the pattern to provide an adequate solution to a specific problem. We also cross-reference other related patterns, either because they refine the current pattern, or because they address a similar problem.

With all this information available and appropriately laid out, we should be able to understand a pattern, apply and implement it correctly.

Finally we give credits to all who helped to shape a particular pattern. Writing patterns is hard. Achieving a crisp pattern description takes several review and revision cycles. Many experts from all over the world have helped us with this activity, and we owe them our special thanks.

Our pattern description template is therefore as follows:

Name The name and a short summary of the pattern.

Also Known As Other names for the pattern, if any are known.

Example A real-world example demonstrating the existence of the problem and the need for the pattern.

Throughout the description we refer to the example to illustrate solution and implementation aspects, where this is necessary or useful. Text that is specifically about the example is marked by the ➥ symbol at its beginning and by the ❑ symbol at its end.

Context The situations in which the pattern may apply.

Problem The problem the pattern addresses, including a discussion of its associated forces.

Solution The fundamental solution principle underlying the pattern.

We present CRC-cards [BeCu89] (see Notations on page 429) for each participating component.

Structure A detailed specification of the structural aspects of the pattern, including an OMT class diagram [RBPEL91].

Dynamics Typical scenarios describing the run-time behavior of the pattern.

We further illustrate the scenarios with Object Message Sequence Charts (see Notations on page 431).

Implementation Guidelines for implementing the pattern.

These are only a suggestion, not an immutable rule. You should adapt the implementation to meet your needs, by adding different, extra, or more detailed steps, or by re-ordering the steps. We give C++, Smalltalk, Java or pSather code fragments to illustrate a possible implementation, often describing details of the example problem.

Example Resolved Discussion of any important aspects for resolving the example that are not yet covered in the Solution, Structure, Dynamics and Implementation sections.

Variants A brief description of variants or specializations of a pattern.

Known Uses Examples of the use of the pattern, taken from existing systems.

Consequences The benefits the pattern provides, and any potential liabilities.

See Also References to patterns that solve similar problems, and to patterns that help us refine the pattern we are describing.

1.6 Patterns and Software Architecture

An important criterion for the success of patterns is how well they meet the objectives of software engineering. Patterns must support the development, maintenance and evolution of complex, large-scale systems. They must also support effective industrial software production, otherwise they remain just an interesting intellectual concept, but useless for constructing software.

Patterns as Mental Building-Blocks

We have already learned that patterns are useful mental building-blocks for dealing with limited and specific design aspects when developing a software system.

Patterns therefore address an important objective of software architecture—the construction of specific software architectures with defined properties. Consider the Model-View-Controller pattern again. It provides a structure that supports the tailoring of the user interface of an interactive application.

General techniques for software architecture, such as guidelines on using object-oriented features such as inheritance and polymorphism, do not address the solution of specific problems. Most of the existing analysis and design methods also fail at this level. They only provide general techniques for building software, for example 'separate policy from implementation' [RBPEL91]. The creation of specific architectures is still based on intuition and experience.

Patterns effectively complement these general problem-independent architectural techniques with specific problem-oriented ones. Note that patterns do not make existing approaches to software architecture obsolete—instead, they fill a gap that is not covered by existing techniques.

Constructing Heterogenous Architectures

A single heterogenous pattern cannot enable the detailed construction of a complete software architecture—it just helps you to design one aspect of your application. Even if you design one aspect correctly, however, the whole architecture may still fail to meet its desired overall properties. To meet the needs of software architecture 'in the large' we need a rich set of patterns that must cover many different design problems. The more patterns that are available, the more design problems that can be addressed appropriately, and the more we are supported in constructing software architectures with defined properties.

On the other hand, the more patterns that are available, the harder it is to achieve an overview of them. As we have already pointed out, there are many relationships between patterns. When applying one pattern, you want to know which other patterns can help refine the structure it introduces. You also want to know which other patterns you can combine with it.

To use patterns effectively, we therefore need to organize them into *pattern systems*. A pattern system describes patterns uniformly, classifies them, and most importantly, shows how they are interwoven with each other. Pattern systems also help you to find the right pattern to solve a problem or to identify alternative solutions to it. This is in contrast to a *pattern catalog*, where each pattern is described more or less in isolation from other patterns. Pattern systems help us to use the power that the entirety of patterns provides.

Patterns versus Methods

A good pattern description also includes guidelines for its implementation that you can consider as a *micro-method* for creating the solution to a specific problem. These micro-methods complement general but problem-independent analysis and design methods, such as Booch [Boo94] and Object Modeling Technique [RBPEL91], by providing methodological steps for solving concrete recurring problems in software development. Section 5.4, *Pattern Systems as Implementation Guidelines* discusses this issue in detail.

Implementing Patterns

Another aspect that arises from the integration of patterns with software architecture is a paradigm for implementing them. Many current software patterns have a distinctly object-oriented flavor. It is tempting to conclude that the only way we can implement a pattern effectively is in an object-oriented programming language. However, we think such conclusions are false.

On one hand, it is true that many patterns, including those in this book, use object-oriented techniques such as polymorphism and inheritance. Examples of such patterns are the Strategy pattern [GHJV95] and the Proxy pattern (263).

On the other hand, object-oriented features are not essential for implementing these patterns. Proxy, for example, loses only a small fraction of its elegance by giving up inheritance. Strategy can be implemented in C by using function pointers instead of polymorphism and inheritance.

At the design level, most patterns only require certain abstraction facilities of a programming language, such as modules or data abstraction. You can therefore implement patterns with almost any programming paradigm and in almost any programming language. In addition, every programming language has specific patterns of its own, the idioms of that language. They capture existing programming experience with the language and define a programming style for it.

In conclusion, we can say that there is no single paradigm or language for implementing patterns. Patterns can be integrated with every paradigm used for constructing software architectures.

1.7 Summary

Patterns provide a promising approach for developing software with defined properties. They document existing design knowledge and help you find appropriate solutions to design problems. Patterns exist in various ranges of scale and abstraction, and cover many different and important areas of software development. Patterns are interwoven with each other—you can use them to refine other, larger patterns and you can combine them to solve more complex problems. They address important aspects of software architecture and complement existing techniques and methods. You can integrate them with every programming paradigm and implement them in almost any programming language. In summary, the entirety of patterns provides a *mental toolbox* that helps you construct software that meets both the functional and non-functional requirements of an application.

Patterns are already being successfully applied. We find them in applications from the business domain [EKM+94], the automation domain [BM95] and the telecommunication domain [Sch95]. They play an important role in application frameworks such as ET++ [WGM88] or InterViews [LCITV92], as well as in run-time environments like the Meta-Information-Protocol for C++ [BKSP92].

To exploit the full power of patterns, however, we need to provide technical and methodical support that goes beyond the scope of individual patterns. We address some of these aspects in Chapter 5, *Pattern Systems.*

2 Architectural Patterns

Architectural patterns express fundamental structural organization schemas for software systems. They provide a set of predefined subsystems, specify their responsibilities, and include rules and guidelines for organizing the relationships between them.

In this chapter we present the following eight architectural patterns: Layers, Pipes and Filters, Blackboard, Broker, Model-View-Controller, Presentation-Abstraction-Control, Microkernel, and Reflection.

2.1   Introduction

Architectural patterns represent the highest-level patterns in our pattern system. They help you to specify the fundamental structure of an application. Every development activity that follows is governed by this structure—for example, the detailed design of subsystems, the communication and collaboration between different parts of the system, and its later extension.

Each architectural pattern helps you to achieve a specific global system property, such as the adaptability of the user interface. Patterns that help to support similar properties can be grouped into categories. In this chapter we group our patterns into four categories:

- *From Mud to Structure*. Patterns in this category help you to avoid a 'sea' of components or objects. In particular, they support a controlled decomposition of an overall system task into cooperating subtasks. The category includes the Layers pattern (31), the Pipes and Filters pattern (53) and the Blackboard pattern (71).

- *Distributed Systems*. This category includes one pattern, Broker (99), and refers to two patterns in other categories, Microkernel (171) and Pipes and Filters (53). The Broker pattern provides a complete infrastructure for distributed applications. Its underlying architecture is soon to be standardized by the Object Management Group (OMG) [OMG92]. The Microkernel and Pipes and Filters patterns only consider distribution as a secondary concern and are therefore listed under their respective primary categories. Details about distribution aspects of both patterns are discussed in Section 2.3, *Distributed Systems*, however.

- *Interactive Systems*. This category comprises two patterns, the Model-View-Controller pattern (125), well-known from Smalltalk, and the Presentation-Abstraction-Control pattern (145). Both patterns support the structuring of software systems that feature human-computer interaction.

- *Adaptable Systems*. The Reflection (193) pattern and the Microkernel pattern (171) strongly support extension of applications and their adaptation to evolving technology and changing functional requirements.

Note that this categorization is not intended to be exhaustive. It works for the architectural patterns we describe, but it may become necessary to define new categories if more architectural patterns are added—see Chapter 5, *Pattern Systems* for further discussion of this idea.

The selection of an architectural pattern should be driven by the general properties of the application at hand. Ask yourself, for example, whether your proposed system is an interactive system, or one that will exist in many slightly different variants. Your pattern selection should be further influenced by your application's non-functional requirements, such as changeability or reliability.

It is also helpful to explore several alternatives before deciding on a specific architectural pattern. For example, the Presentation-Abstraction-Control pattern (PAC) and the Model-View-Controller pattern (MVC) both lend themselves to interactive applications. Similarly, the Reflection and Microkernel patterns both support the adaptation of software systems to evolving requirements.

Different architectural patterns imply different consequences, even if they address the same or very similar problems. For example, an MVC architecture is usually more efficient than a PAC architecture. On the other hand, PAC supports multitasking and task-specific user interfaces better than MVC does.

Most software systems, however, cannot be structured according to a single architectural pattern. They must support several system requirements that can only be addressed by different architectural patterns. For example, you may have to design both for flexibility of component distribution in a heterogeneous computer network and for adaptability of their user interfaces. You must combine several patterns to structure such systems—in this case, suitable patterns are Broker and Model-View-Controller. The Broker pattern provides the infrastructure for the distribution of components, while the model of the MVC pattern plays the role of a server in the Broker infrastructure. Similarly, controllers take the roles of clients, and views combine the roles of clients and servers, as clients of the model and servers of the controllers.

However, a particular architectural pattern, or a combination of several, is *not* a complete software architecture. It remains a structural framework for a software system that must be further specified and refined. This includes the task of integrating the application's functionality with the framework, and detailing its components and relationships, perhaps with help of design patterns and idioms. The selection of an architectural pattern, or a combination of several, is only the first step when designing the architecture of a software system.

2.2   From Mud to Structure

Before we start the design of a new system, we collect the requirements from the customer and transform them into specifications. Both these activities are more complex than is often believed. A recent book by Michael Jackson [Jac95] illuminates this topic.

Being optimistic, we assume that the requirements for our new system are well-defined and stable. The next major technical task is to define the architecture of the system. At this stage, this means finding a high-level subdivision of the system into constituent parts. We are often aware of a whole slew of different aspects, and have problems organizing the mess into a workable structure. Ralph Johnson calls this situation a 'ball of mud' [Joh96]. This is usually all we have in the beginning, and we must transform it into a more organized structure.

Cutting the ball along lines visible in the application domain won't help, for several reasons. On one hand, the resulting software system will include many components that have no direct relationship to the domain. Manager and helper functionality is a prime example of this. On the other hand, we want more than just a working system—it should possess qualities such as portability, maintainability, understandability, stability, and so forth that are not directly related to the application's functionality.

We describe three architectural patterns that provide high-level system subdivisions of different kinds: Layers, Pipes and Filters, and Blackboard.

- The *Layers* pattern (31) helps to structure applications that can be decomposed into groups of subtasks in which each group of subtasks is at a particular level of abstraction.

- The *Pipes and Filters* pattern (53) provides a structure for systems that process a stream of data. Each processing step is encapsulated in a filter component. Data is passed through pipes between adjacent filters. Recombining filters allows you to build families of related systems.

- The *Blackboard* pattern (71) pattern is useful for problems for which no deterministic solution strategies are known. In

Blackboard several specialized subsystems assemble their knowledge to build a possibly partial or approximate solution.

The Layers pattern describes the most widespread principle of architectural subdivision. Many of the block diagrams we see in system architecture documents seem to imply a layered architecture. However, the real architectures all too often turn out to be either a mix of different paradigms—which by itself cannot be criticized—or concealed collections of cooperating components without clear architectural boundaries between them. To help with the situation, we try to be more rigorous in our description and list the characteristics of truly layered systems.

The Pipes and Filters pattern, in contrast, is less often used, but is attractive in areas where data streams can be processed incrementally. Surprisingly, some system families modelled in this fashion turn out to be poor candidates for this paradigm, neglecting areas where this pattern could be used more beneficially. We expand this topic further in the pattern description.

The Blackboard pattern comes from the Artificial Intelligence community. We describe this paradigm as a pattern since the idea behind it deserves to be seen in a wider context. In poorly-structured—or simply new and immature—domains we often have only patchy knowledge about how to tackle particular problems. The Blackboard pattern shows a method of combining such patchy knowledge to arrive at solutions, even if they are sub-optimal or not guaranteed. When the application domain matures with time, designers often abandon the Blackboard architecture and develop architectures that support closed solution approaches, in which the processing steps are predefined by the structure of the application.

Layers

The *Layers* architectural pattern helps to structure applications that can be decomposed into groups of subtasks in which each group of subtasks is at a particular level of abstraction.

Example Networking protocols are probably the best-known example of layered architectures. Such a protocol consists of a set of rules and conventions that describe how computer programs communicate across machine boundaries. The format, contents, and meaning of all messages are defined. All scenarios are described in detail, usually by giving sequence charts. The protocol specifies agreements at a variety of abstraction levels, ranging from the details of bit transmission to high-level application logic. Therefore designers use several subprotocols and arrange them in layers. Each layer deals with a specific aspect of communication and uses the services of the next lower layer. The International Standardization Organization (ISO) defined the following architectural model, the OSI 7-Layer Model [Tan92]:

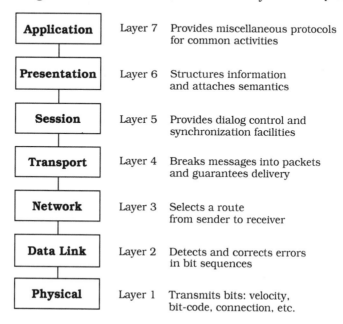

Application	Layer 7	Provides miscellaneous protocols for common activities
Presentation	Layer 6	Structures information and attaches semantics
Session	Layer 5	Provides dialog control and synchronization facilities
Transport	Layer 4	Breaks messages into packets and guarantees delivery
Network	Layer 3	Selects a route from sender to receiver
Data Link	Layer 2	Detects and corrects errors in bit sequences
Physical	Layer 1	Transmits bits: velocity, bit-code, connection, etc.

A layered approach is considered better practice than implementing the protocol as a monolithic block, since implementing conceptually-different issues separately reaps several benefits, for example aiding development by teams and supporting incremental coding and testing. Using semi-independent parts also enables the easier exchange of individual parts at a later date. Better implementation technologies such as new languages or algorithms can be incorporated by simply rewriting a delimited section of code.

While OSI is an important reference model, TCP/IP, also known as the 'Internet protocol suite', is the prevalent networking protocol. We use TCP/IP to illustrate another important reason for layering: the reuse of individual layers in different contexts. TCP for example can be used 'as is' by diverse distributed applications such as telnet or ftp.

Context   A large system that requires decomposition.

Problem   Imagine that you are designing a system whose dominant characteristic is a mix of low- and high-level issues, where high-level operations rely on the lower-level ones. Some parts of the system handle low-level issues such as hardware traps, sensor input, reading bits from a file or electrical signals from a wire. At the other end of the spectrum there may be user-visible functionality such as the interface of a multi-user 'dungeon' game or high-level policies such as telephone billing tariffs. A typical pattern of communication flow consists of requests moving from high to low level, and answers to requests, incoming data or notification about events traveling in the opposite direction.

Such systems often also require some horizontal structuring that is orthogonal to their vertical subdivision. This is the case where several operations are on the same level of abstraction but are largely independent of each other. You can see examples of this where the word 'and' occurs in the diagram illustrating the OSI 7-layer model.

The system specification provided to you describes the high-level tasks to some extent, and specifies the target platform. Portability to other platforms is desired. Several external boundaries of the system are specified a priori, such as a functional interface to which your system must adhere. The mapping of high-level tasks onto the platform is not straightforward, mostly because they are too complex to be implemented directly using services provided by the platform.

In such a case you need to balance the following *forces*:

- Late source code changes should not ripple through the system. They should be confined to one component and not affect others.

- Interfaces should be stable, and may even be prescribed by a standards body.

- Parts of the system should be exchangeable. Components should be able to be replaced by alternative implementations without affecting the rest of the system. A low-level platform may be given but may be subject to change in the future. While such fundamental changes usually require code changes and recompilation, reconfiguration of the system can also be done at run-time using an administration interface. Adjusting cache or buffer sizes are examples of such a change. An extreme form of exchangeability might be a client component dynamically switching to a different implementation of a service that may not have been available at start-up. Design for change in general is a major facilitator of graceful system evolution.

- It may be necessary to build other systems at a later date with the same low-level issues as the system you are currently designing.

- Similar responsibilities should be grouped to help understandability and maintainability. Each component should be coherent—if one component implements divergent issues its integrity may be lost. Grouping and coherence are conflicting at times.

- There is no 'standard' component granularity.

- Complex components need further decomposition.

- Crossing component boundaries may impede performance, for example when a substantial amount of data must be transferred over several boundaries, or where there are many boundaries to cross.

- The system will be built by a team of programmers, and work has to be subdivided along clear boundaries—a requirement that is often overlooked at the architectural design stage.

Solution From a high-level viewpoint the solution is extremely simple. Structure your system into an appropriate number of layers and place them on top of each other. Start at the lowest level of abstraction—call it Layer 1. This is the base of your system. Work your way up the abstraction ladder by putting Layer J on top of Layer J-1 until you reach the top level of functionality—call it Layer N.

Note that this does not prescribe the order in which to actually design layers, it just gives a conceptual view. It also does not prescribe whether an individual Layer J should be a complex subsystem that needs further decomposition, or whether it should just translate requests from Layer J+1 to requests to Layer J-1 and make little contribution of its own. It is however essential that within an individual layer all constituent components work at the same level of abstraction.

Most of the services that Layer J provides are composed of services provided by Layer J-1. In other words, the services of each layer implement a strategy for combining the services of the layer below in a meaningful way. In addition, Layer J's services may depend on other services in Layer J.

Structure An individual layer can be described by the following CRC card:

Class Layer J	*Collaborator* • Layer J-1
Responsibility • Provides services used by Layer J+1. • Delegates subtasks to Layer J-1.	

The main structural characteristic of the Layers pattern is that the services of Layer J are only used by Layer J+1—there are no further direct dependencies between layers. This structure can be compared with a stack, or even an onion. Each individual layer shields all lower layers from direct access by higher layers.

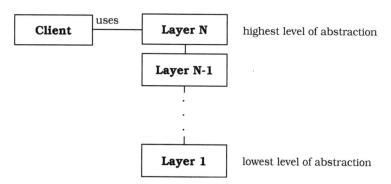

Examining individual layers in more detail may reveal that they are complex entities consisting of different components. In the following figure, each layer consists of three components. In the middle layer two components interact. Components in different layers call each other directly—other designs shield each layer by incorporating a unified interface. In such a design, Component_2.1 no longer calls Component_1.1 directly, but calls a Layer 1 interface object that forwards the request instead. In the Implementation section, we discuss the advantages and disadvantages of direct addressing.

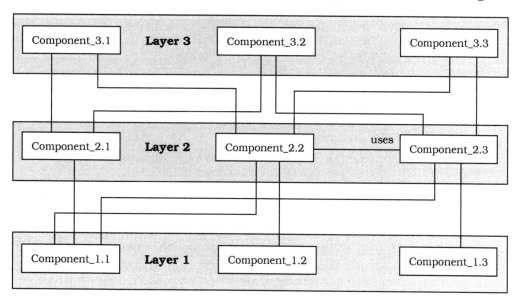

Dynamics   The following scenarios are archetypes for the dynamic behavior of
layered applications. This does not mean that you will encounter
every scenario in every architecture. In simple layered architectures
you will only see the first scenario, but most layered applications
involve Scenarios I and II. Due to space limitations we do not give
object message sequence charts in this pattern.

Scenario I is probably the best-known one. A client issues a request
to Layer N. Since Layer N cannot carry out the request on its own, it
calls the next Layer N-1 for supporting subtasks. Layer N-1 provides
these, in the process sending further requests to Layer N-2, and so
on until Layer 1 is reached. Here, the lowest-level services are finally
performed. If necessary, replies to the different requests are passed
back up from Layer 1 to Layer 2, from Layer 2 to Layer 3, and so on
until the final reply arrives at Layer N. The example code in the
Implementation section illustrates this.

A characteristic of such top-down communication is that Layer J
often translates a single request from Layer J+1 into several requests
to Layer J-1. This is due to the fact that Layer J is on a higher level of
abstraction than Layer J-1 and has to map a high-level service onto
more primitive ones.

Scenario II illustrates bottom-up communication—a chain of actions
starts at Layer 1, for example when a device driver detects input. The
driver translates the input into an internal format and reports it to
Layer 2, which starts interpreting it, and so on. In this way data
moves up through the layers until it arrives at the highest layer. While
top-down information and control flow are often described as
'requests', bottom-up calls can be termed 'notifications'.

As mentioned in Scenario I, one top-down request often fans out to
several requests in lower layers. In contrast, several bottom-up notifications may either be condensed into a single notification higher in
the structure, or remain in a 1:1 relationship.

Scenario III describes the situation where requests only travel
through a subset of the layers. A top-level request may only go to the
next lower level N-1 if this level can satisfy the request. An example
of this is where level N-1 acts as a cache, and a request from level N
can be satisfied without being sent all the way down to Layer 1 and
from here to a remote server. Note that such caching layers maintain

state information, while layers that only forward requests are often stateless. Stateless layers usually have the advantage of being simpler to program, particularly with respect to re-entrancy.

Scenario IV describes a situation similar to Scenario III. An event is detected in Layer 1, but stops at Layer 3 instead of traveling all the way up to Layer N. In a communication protocol, for example, a re-send request may arrive from an impatient client who requested data some time ago. In the meantime the server has already sent the answer, and the answer and the re-send request cross. In this case, Layer 3 of the server side may notice this and intercept the re-send request without further action.

Scenario V involves two stacks of N layers communicating with each other. This scenario is well-known from communication protocols where the stacks are known as 'protocol stacks'. In the following diagram, Layer N of the left stack issues a request. The request moves down through the layers until it reaches Layer 1, is sent to Layer 1 of the right stack, and there moves up through the layers of the right stack. The response to the request follows the reverse path until it arrives at Layer N of the left stack.

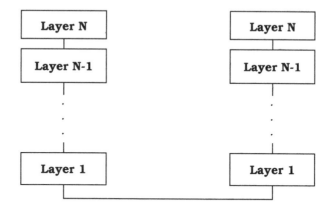

For more details about protocol stacks, see the Example Resolved section, where we discuss several communication protocol issues using TCP/IP as an example.

Implementation The following steps describe a step-wise refinement approach to the definition of a layered architecture. This is not necessarily the best method for all applications—often a bottom-up or 'yo-yo' approach is better. See also the discussion in step 5.

Not all the following steps are mandatory—it depends on your application. For example, the results of several implementation steps can be heavily influenced or even strictly prescribed by a standards specification that must be followed.

1   *Define the abstraction criterion* for grouping tasks into layers. This criterion is often the conceptual distance from the platform. Sometimes you encounter other abstraction paradigms, for example the degree of customization for specific domains, or the degree of conceptual complexity. For example, a chess game application may consist of the following layers, listed from bottom to top:

- Elementary units of the game, such as a bishop

- Basic moves, such as castling

- Medium-term tactics, such as the Sicilian defense

- Overall game strategies

In American Football these levels may correspond respectively to linebacker, blitz, a sequence of plays for a two-minute drill, and finally a full game plan.

In the real world of software development we often use a mix of abstraction criterions. For example, the distance from the hardware can shape the lower levels, and conceptual complexity governs the higher ones. An example layering obtained using a mixed-mode layering principle like this is as follows, ordered from top to bottom:

- User-visible elements

- Specific application modules

- Common services level

- Operating system interface level

- Operating system (being a layered system itself, or structured according to the Microkernel pattern (171))

- Hardware

2 *Determine the number of abstraction levels* according to your abstraction criterion. Each abstraction level corresponds to one layer of the pattern. Sometimes this mapping from abstraction levels to layers is not obvious. Think about the trade-offs when deciding whether to split particular aspects into two layers or combine them into one. Having too many layers may impose unnecessary overhead, while too few layers can result in a poor structure.

3 *Name the layers and assign tasks to each of them.* The task of the highest layer is the overall system task, as perceived by the client. The tasks of all other layers are to be helpers to higher layers. If we take a bottom-up approach, then lower layers provide an infrastructure on which higher layers can build. However, this approach requires considerable experience and foresight in the domain to find the right abstractions for the lower layers before being able to define specific requests from higher layers.

4 *Specify the services.* The most important implementation principle is that layers are strictly separated from each other, in the sense that no component may spread over more than one layer. Argument, return, and error types of functions offered by Layer J should be built-in types of the programming language, types defined in Layer J, or types taken from a shared data definition module. Note that modules that are shared between layers relax the principles of strict layering.

It is often better to locate more services in higher layers than in lower layers. This is because developers should not have to learn a large set of slightly different low-level primitives—which may even change during concurrent development. Instead the base layers should be kept 'slim' while higher layers can expand to cover a broader spectrum of applicability. This phenomenon is also called the 'inverted pyramid of reuse'.

5 *Refine the layering.* Iterate over steps 1 to 4. It is usually not possible to define an abstraction criterion precisely before thinking about the implied layers and their services. Alternatively, it is usually wrong to define components and services first and later impose a layered structure on them according to their usage relationships. Since such a structure does not capture an inherent ordering principle, it is very likely that system maintenance will destroy the architecture. For example, a new component may ask for the services of more than one other layer, violating the principle of strict layering.

The solution is to perform the first four steps several times until a natural and stable layering evolves. 'Like almost all other kinds of design, finding layers does not proceed in an orderly, logical way, but consists of both top-down and bottom-up steps, and certain amount of inspiration...' [Joh95]. Performing both top-down and bottom-up steps alternately is often called 'yo-yo' development, mentioned at the start of the Implementation section.

6   *Specify an interface for each layer.* If Layer J should be a 'black box' for Layer J+1, design a flat interface that offers all Layer J's services, and perhaps encapsulate this interface in a Facade object [GHJV95]. The Known Uses section describes flat interfaces further. A 'white-box' approach is that in which Layer J+1 sees the internals of Layer J. The last figure in the Structure section shows a 'gray-box' approach, a compromise between black and white box approaches. Here Layer J+1 is aware of the fact that Layer J consists of three components, and addresses them separately, but does not see the internal workings of individual components.

Good design practise tells us to use the black-box approach whenever possible, because it supports system evolution better than other approaches. Exceptions to this rule can be made for reasons of efficiency, or a need to access the innards of another layer. The latter occurs rarely, and may be helped by the Reflection pattern (193), which supports more controlled access to the internal functioning of a component. Arguments over efficiency are debatable, especially when inlining can simply do away with a thin layer of indirection.

7   *Structure individual layers.* Traditionally, the focus was on the proper relationships between layers, but inside individual layers there was often free-wheeling chaos. When an individual layer is complex it should be broken into separate components. This subdivision can be helped by using finer-grained patterns. For example, you can use the Bridge pattern [GHJV95] to support multiple implementations of services provided by a layer. The Strategy pattern [GHJV95] can support the dynamic exchange of algorithms used by a layer.

8   *Specify the communication between adjacent layers.* The most often used mechanism for inter-layer communication is the push model. When Layer J invokes a service of Layer J-1, any required information is passed as part of the service call. The reverse is known as the pull model and occurs when the lower layer fetches available information

from the higher layer at its own discretion. The Publisher-Subscriber (339) and Pipes and Filters patterns (53) give details about push and pull model information transfer. However, such models may introduce additional dependencies between a layer and its adjacent higher layer. If you want to avoid dependencies of lower layers on higher layers introduced by the pull model, use callbacks, as described in the next step.

9   *Decouple adjacent layers.* There are many ways to do this. Often an upper layer is aware of the next lower layer, but the lower layer is unaware of the identity of its users. This implies a one-way coupling only: changes in Layer J can ignore the presence and identity of Layer J+1 provided that the interface and semantics of the Layer J services being changed remain stable. Such a one-way coupling is perfect when requests travel top-down, as illustrated in Scenario 1, as return values are sufficient to transport the results in the reverse direction.

For bottom-up communication, you can use callbacks and still preserve a top-down one-way coupling. Here the upper layer registers callback functions with the lower layer. This is especially effective when only a fixed set of possible events is sent from lower to higher layers. During start-up the higher layer tells the lower layer what functions to call when specific events occur. The lower layer maintains the mapping from events to callback functions in a registry. The Reactor pattern [Sch94] illustrates an object-oriented implementation of the use of callbacks in conjunction with event demultiplexing. The Command pattern [GHJV95] shows how to encapsulate functions into first-class objects.

You can also decouple the upper layer from the lower layer to a certain degree. Here is an example of how this can be done using object-oriented techniques. The upper layer is decoupled from specific implementation variants of the lower layer by coding the upper layer against an interface. In the following C++ code, this interface is a base class. The lower-level implementations can then be easily exchanged, even at run-time. In the example code, a Layer 2 component talks to a level 1 provider but does not know which implementation of Layer 1 it is talking to. The 'wiring' of the layers is done here in the main program, but will usually be factored out into a connection-management component. The main program also takes the role of the client by calling a service in the top layer.

```cpp
#include <iostream.h>

class L1Provider {
public:
    virtual void L1Service() = 0;
};
class L2Provider {
public:
    virtual void L2Service() = 0;
    void setLowerLayer(L1Provider *l1) {level1 = l1;}
protected:
    L1Provider *level1;
};
class L3Provider {
public:
    virtual void L3Service() = 0;
    void setLowerLayer(L2Provider *l2) {level2 = l2;}
protected:
    L2Provider *level2;
};

class DataLink : public L1Provider {
public:
    virtual void L1Service(){
        cout << "L1Service doing its job" << endl;}
};
class Transport : public L2Provider {
public:
    virtual void L2Service() {
        cout << "L2Service starting its job" << endl;
        level1->L1Service();
        cout << "L2Service finishing its job" << endl;}
};
class Session : public L3Provider {
public:
    virtual void L3Service() {
        cout << "L3Service starting its job" << endl;
        level2->L2Service();
        cout << "L3Service finishing its job" << endl;}
};

main() {
    DataLink dataLink;
    Transport transport;
    Session session;

    transport.setLowerLayer(&dataLink);
    session.setLowerLayer(&transport);

    session.L3Service();
}
```

The output of the program is as follows:

```
L3Service starting its job
L2Service starting its job
L1Service doing its job
L2Service finishing its job
L3Service finishing its job
```

For communicating stacks of layers where messages travel both up and down, it is often better explicitly to connect lower levels to higher levels. We therefore again introduce base classes, for example classes L1Provider, L2Provider, and L3Provider, as in the code example, and additionally L1Parent, L2Parent, and L1Peer. Class L1Parent provides the interface by which level 1 classes access the next higher layer, for example to return results, send confirmations or pass data streams. An analogous argument holds for L2Parent. L1Peer provides the interface by which a message is sent to the level 1 peer module in the other stack. A Layer 1 implementation class therefore inherits from two base classes: L1Provider and L1Peer. A second-level implementation class inherits from L2Provider and L1Parent, as it offers the services of Layer 2 and can serve as the parent of a Layer 1 object. A third-level implementation class finally inherits from L3Provider and L2Parent.

If your programming language separates inheritance and subtyping at the language level, as for example Sather [Omo93] and Java [AG96] do, the above base classes can be transformed into interfaces by pushing data into subclasses and implementing all methods there.

10 *Design an error-handling strategy.* Error handling can be rather expensive for layered architectures with respect to processing time and, notably, programming effort. An error can either be handled in the layer where it occurred or be passed to the next higher layer. In the latter case, the lower layer must transform the error into an error description meaningful to the higher layer. As a rule of thumb, try to handle errors at the lowest layer possible. This prevents higher layers from being swamped with many different errors and voluminous error-handling code. As a minimum, try to condense similar error types into more general error types, and only propagate these more general errors. If you do not do this, higher layers can be confronted with error messages that apply to lower-level abstractions that the higher layer does not understand. And who hasn't seen totally cryptic error messages being popped up to the highest layer of all—the user?

The most widely-used communication protocol, TCP/IP, does not strictly conform to the OSI model and consists of only four layers: TCP and IP constitute the middle layers, with the application at the top and the transport medium at the bottom. A typical configuration, that for the UNIX `ftp` utility, is shown below:

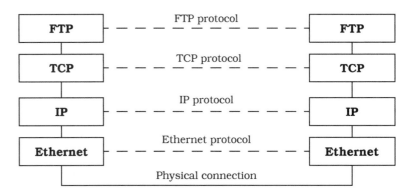

TCP/IP has several interesting aspects that are relevant to our discussion. Corresponding layers communicate in a peer-to-peer fashion using a *virtual protocol*. This means that, for example, the two TCP entities send each other messages that follow a specific format. From a conceptual point of view, they communicate using the dashed line labeled 'TCP protocol' in the diagram above. We refer to this protocol as 'virtual' because in reality a TCP message traveling from left to right in the diagram is handled first by the IP entity on the left. This IP entity treats the message as a data packet, prefixes it with a header, and forwards it to the local Ethernet interface. The Ethernet interface then adds its own control information and sends the data over the physical connection. On the receiving side the local Ethernet and IP entities strip the Ethernet and IP headers respectively. The TCP entity on the right-hand side of the diagram then receives the TCP message from its peer on the left as if it had been delivered over the dashed line.

A notable characteristic of TCP/IP and other communication protocols is that standardizing the functional interface is a secondary concern, partly driven by the fact that TCP/IP implementations from different vendors differ from each other intentionally. The vendors usually do not offer single layers, but full implementations of the protocol suite. As a result, every TCP implementation exports a fixed set of core functions but is free to offer more, for example to increase flexibility or performance. This looseness has no impact on the application developer for two reasons. Firstly, different stacks understand each other because the virtual protocols are strictly obeyed. Secondly, application developers use a layer on top of TCP, or its alternative, UDP. This upper layer has a fixed interface. Sockets and TLI are examples of such a fixed interface.

Assume that we use the Socket API on top of a TCP/IP stack. The Socket API consists of system calls such as `bind()`, `listen()` or `read()`. The Socket implementation sits conceptually on top of TCP/UDP, but uses lower layers as well, for example IP and ICMP. This violation of strict layering principles is worthwhile to tune performance, and can be justified when all the communication layers from sockets to IP are built into the OS kernel.

The behavior of the individual layers and the structure of the data packets flowing from layer to layer are much more rigidly defined in TCP/IP than the functional interface. This is because different TCP/IP stacks must understand each other—they are the workhorses of the increasingly heterogeneous Internet. The protocol rules describe exactly how a layer behaves under specific circumstances. For example, its behavior when handling an incoming re-transmit message after the original has been sent is exactly prescribed. The data packet specifications mostly concern the headers and trailers added to messages. The size of headers and trailers is specified, as well as the meaning of their subfields. In a header, for example, the protocol stack encodes information such as sender, destination, protocol used, time-out information, sequence number, and checksums. For more information on TCP/IP, see for example [Ste90]. For even more detail, study the series started in [Ste94].

Variants *Relaxed Layered System.* This is a variant of the Layers pattern that is less restrictive about the relationship between layers. In a Relaxed Layered System each layer may use the services of all layers below it, not only of the next lower layer. A layer may also be partially opaque— this means that some of its services are only visible to the next higher layer, while others are visible to all higher layers. The gain of flexibility and performance in a Relaxed Layered System is paid for by a loss of maintainability. This is often a high price to pay, and you should consider carefully before giving in to the demands of developers asking for shortcuts. We see these shortcuts more often in infrastructure systems, such as the UNIX operating system or the X Window System, than in application software. The main reason for this is that infrastructure systems are modified less often than application systems, and their performance is usually more important than their maintainability.

Layering Through Inheritance. This variant can be found in some object-oriented systems and is described in [BuCa96]. In this variant lower layers are implemented as base classes. A higher layer requesting services from a lower layer inherits from the lower layer's implementation and hence can issue requests to the base class services. An advantage of this scheme is that higher layers can modify lower-layer services according to their needs. A drawback is that such an inheritance relationship closely ties the higher layer to the lower layer. If for example the data layout of a C++ base class changes, all subclasses must be recompiled. Such unintentional dependencies introduced by inheritance are also known as the *fragile base class problem.*

Known Uses   **Virtual Machines.** We can speak of lower levels as a *virtual machine* that insulates higher levels from low-level details or varying hardware. For example, the Java Virtual Machine (JVM) defines a binary code format. Code written in the Java programming language is translated into a platform-neutral binary code, also called *bytecodes*, and delivered to the JVM for interpretation. The JVM itself is platform-specific—there are implementations of the JVM for different operating systems and processors. Such a two-step translation process allows platform-neutral source code and the delivery of binary code not readable to humans[1], while maintaining platform-independency.

APIs. An Application Programming Interface is a layer that encapsulates lower layers of frequently-used functionality. An API is usually a flat collection of function specifications, such as the UNIX system calls. 'Flat' means here that the system calls for accessing the UNIX file system, for example, are not separated from system calls for storage allocation—you can only know from the documentation to which

---

1. The Java bytecodes can be transformed into an ASCII representation that is a kind of object-oriented assembler code. This code can be read, but only with some pain!

group `open()` or `sbrk()` belong. Above system calls we find other layers, such as the C standard library [KR88] with operations like `printf()` or `fopen()`. These libraries provide the benefit of portability between different operating systems, and provide additional higher-level services such as output buffering or formatted output. They often carry the liability of lower efficiency[2], and perhaps more tightly-prescribed behavior, whereas conventional system calls would give more flexibility—and more opportunities for errors and conceptual mismatches, mostly due to the wide gap between high-level application abstractions and low-level system calls.

Information Systems (IS) from the business software domain often use a two-layer architecture. The bottom layer is a database that holds company-specific data. Many applications work concurrently on top of this database to fulfill different tasks. Mainframe interactive systems and the much-extolled Client-Server systems often employ this architecture. Because the tight coupling of user interface and data representation causes its share of problems, a third layer is introduced between them—the domain layer—which models the conceptual structure of the problem domain. As the top level still mixes user interface and application, this level is also split, resulting in a four-layer architecture. These are, from highest to lowest:

- Presentation
- Application logic
- Domain layer
- Database

See [Fow96] for more information on business modeling.

Windows NT [Cus93]. This operating system is structured according to the Microkernel pattern (171). The NT Executive component corresponds to the microkernel component of the Microkernel pattern. The NT Executive is a Relaxed Layered System, as described in the Variants section. It has the following layers:

- System services: the interface layer between the subsystems and the NT Executive.

---

2. Input/output buffering in higher layers is often intended to have the inverse effect—better performance than undisciplined direct use of lower-level system calls.

- Resource management layer: this contains the modules Object Manager, Security Reference Monitor, Process Manager, I/O Manager, Virtual Memory Manager and Local Procedure Calls.

- Kernel: this takes care of basic functions such as interrupt and exception handling, multiprocessor synchronization, thread scheduling and thread dispatching.

- HAL (Hardware Abstraction Layer): this hides hardware differences between machines of different processor families.

- Hardware

Windows NT relaxes the principles of the Layers pattern because the Kernel and the I/O manager access the underlying hardware directly for reasons of efficiency.

Consequences   The Layers pattern has several **benefits**:

Reuse of layers. If an individual layer embodies a well-defined abstraction and has a well-defined and documented interface, the layer can be reused in multiple contexts. However, despite the higher costs of not reusing such existing layers, developers often prefer to rewrite this functionality. They argue that the existing layer does not fit their purposes exactly, layering would cause high performance penalties—and they would do a better job anyway. An empirical study hints that black-box reuse of existing layers can dramatically reduce development effort and decrease the number of defects [ZEWH95].

Support for standardization. Clearly-defined and commonly-accepted levels of abstraction enable the development of standardized tasks and interfaces. Different implementations of the same interface can then be used interchangeably. This allows you to use products from different vendors in different layers. A well-known example of a standardized interface is the POSIX programming interface [IEEE88].

Dependencies are kept local. Standardized interfaces between layers usually confine the effect of code changes to the layer that is changed. Changes of the hardware, the operating system, the window system, special data formats and so on often affect only one layer, and you can adapt affected layers without altering the remaining layers. This supports the portability of a system. Testability is supported as well, since you can test particular layers independently of other components in the system.

Exchangeability. Individual layer implementations can be replaced by semantically-equivalent implementations without too great an effort. If the connections between layers are hard-wired in the code, these are updated with the names of the new layer's implementation. You can even replace an old implementation with an implementation with a different interface by using the Adapter pattern for interface adaptation [GHJV95]. The other extreme is dynamic exchange, which you can achieve by using the Bridge pattern [GHJV95], for example, and manipulating the pointer to the implementation at run-time.

Hardware exchanges or additions are prime examples for illustrating exchangeability. A new hardware I/O device, for example, can be put in operation by installing the right driver program—which may be a plug-in or replace an old driver program. Higher layers will not be affected by the exchange. A transport medium such as Ethernet could be replaced by Token Ring. In such a case, upper layers do not need to change their interfaces, and can continue to request services from lower layers as before. However, if you want to be able to switch between two layers that do not match closely in their interfaces and services, you must build an insulating layer on top of these two layers. The benefit of exchangeability comes at the price of increased programming effort and possibly decreased run-time performance.

The Layers pattern also imposes **liabilities**:

Cascades of changing behavior. A severe problem can occur when the behavior of a layer changes. Assume for example that we replace a 10 Megabit/sec Ethernet layer at the bottom of our networked application and instead put IP on top of 155 Megabit/sec ATM[3]. Due to limitations with I/O and memory performance, our local-end system cannot process incoming packets fast enough to keep up with ATM's high data rates. However, bandwidth-intensive applications such as medical imaging or video conferencing could benefit from the full speed of ATM. Sending multiple data streams in parallel is a high-level solution to avoid the above limitations of lower levels. Similarly, IP routers, which forward packets within the Internet, can be layered

---

3. ATM (Asynchronous Transfer Mode) provides much higher data rates (ranging from 155Mbps to 2.4Gbps) and functionality (such as quality of service guarantees) than conventional low-speed networks such as Ethernet and Token Ring. In addition, ATM can emulate the behavior of Ethernet in a LAN, which allows it to be integrated seamlessly into existing networks. See [HHS94] for more information on ATM.

to run on top of high-speed ATM networks via multi-CPU systems that perform IP packet processing in parallel [PST96].

In summary, higher layers can often be shielded from changes in lower layers. This allows systems to be tuned transparently by collapsing lower layers and/or replacing them with faster solutions such as hardware. The layering becomes a disadvantage if you have to do a substantial amount of rework on many layers to incorporate an apparently local change.

Lower efficiency. A layered architecture is usually less efficient than, say, a monolithic structure or a 'sea of objects'. If high-level services in the upper layers rely heavily on the lowest layers, all relevant data must be transferred through a number of intermediate layers, and may be transformed several times. The same is true of all results or error messages produced in lower levels that are passed to the highest level. Communication protocols, for example, transform messages from higher levels by adding message headers and trailers.

Unnecessary work. If some services performed by lower layers perform excessive or duplicate work not actually required by the higher layer, this has a negative impact on performance. Demultiplexing in a communication protocol stack is an example of this phenomenon. Several high-level requests cause the same incoming bit sequence to be read many times because every high-level request is interested in a different subset of the bits. Another example is error correction in file transfer. A general purpose low-level transmission system is written first and provides a very high degree of reliability, but it can be more economical or even mandatory to build reliability into higher layers, for example by using checksums. See [SRC84] for details of these trade-offs and further considerations about where to place functionality in a layered system.

Difficulty of establishing the correct granularity of layers. A layered architecture with too few layers does not fully exploit this pattern's potential for reusability, changeability and portability. On the other hand, too many layers introduce unnecessary complexity and overheads in the separation of layers and the transformation of arguments and return values. The decision about the granularity of layers and the assignment of tasks to layers is difficult, but is critical for the quality of the architecture. A standardized architecture can only be used if the scope of potential client applications fits the defined layers.

See Also   *Composite Message.* Aamod Sane and Roy Campbell [SC95b] describe an object-oriented encapsulation of messages traveling through layers. A composite message is a packet that consists of headers, payloads, and embedded packets. The Composite Message pattern is therefore a variation of the Composite pattern [GHJV95].

A *Microkernel* architecture (171) can be considered as a specialized layered architecture. See the discussion of Windows NT in the Known Uses section.

The *PAC* architectural pattern (145) also emphasizes levels of increasing abstraction. However, the overall PAC structure is a tree of PAC nodes rather than a vertical line of nodes layered on top of each other. PAC emphasizes that every node consists of three components, *presentation*, *abstraction*, and *control*, while the Layers pattern does not prescribe any subdivisions of an individual layer.

Credits   This pattern was carefully reviewed by Paulo Villela, who highlighted many dark corners in earlier drafts. Douglas Schmidt gave valuable support in the ATM discussion.

Pipes and Filters

The *Pipes and Filters* architectural pattern provides a structure for systems that process a stream of data. Each processing step is encapsulated in a filter component. Data is passed through pipes between adjacent filters. Recombining filters allows you to build families of related systems.

Example Suppose we have defined a new programming language called Mocha (Modular Object Computation with Hypothetical Algorithms). Our task is to build a portable compiler for this language. To support existing and future hardware platforms we define an intermediate language AuLait (Another Universal Language for Intermediate Translation) running on a virtual machine Cup (Concurrent Uniform Processor). Cup will be implemented by an interpreter or platform-specific backends. The AuLait interpreter simulates Cup in software. A backend will translate AuLait code into the machine instructions of a specific processor for best performance.

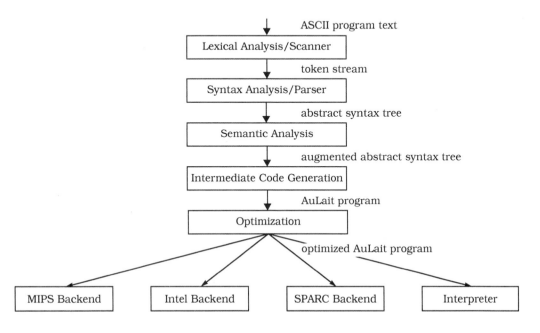

Conceptually, translation from Mocha to AuLait consists of the phases lexical analysis, syntax analysis, semantic analysis, intermediate-code generation (AuLait), and optionally intermediate-code optimization [ASU86]. Each stage has well-defined input and output data. The input to the compilation process is a sequence of ASCII characters representing the Mocha program. The final stage in our system—whether backend or interpreter—takes the binary AuLait code as its input.[4]

Context   Processing data streams.

Problem   Imagine you are building a system that must process or transform a stream of input data. Implementing such a system as a single component may not be feasible for several reasons: the system has to be built by several developers, the global system task decomposes naturally into several processing stages, and the requirements are likely to change.

You therefore plan for future flexibility by exchanging or reordering the processing steps. By incorporating such flexibility, it is possible to build a family of systems using existing processing components. The design of the system—especially the interconnection of processing steps—has to consider the following *forces*:

- Future system enhancements should be possible by exchanging processing steps or by recombination of steps, even by users.

- Small processing steps are easier to reuse in different contexts than large components.

- Non-adjacent processing steps do not share information.

- Different sources of input data exist, such as a network connection or a hardware sensor providing temperature readings, for example.

- It should be possible to present or store final results in various ways.

- Explicit storage of intermediate results for further processing in files clutters directories and is error-prone, if done by users.

- You may not want to rule out multi-processing the steps, for example running them in parallel or quasi-parallel.

---

4. Any similarities in names, persons, or events are coincidental and unintended.

Whether a separation into processing steps is feasible strongly depends on the application domain and the problem to be solved. For example, an interactive, event-driven system does not split into sequential stages.

Solution   The Pipes and Filters architectural pattern divides the task of a system into several sequential processing steps. These steps are connected by the data flow through the system—the output data of a step is the input to the subsequent step. Each processing step is implemented by a *filter* component. A filter consumes and delivers data incrementally—in contrast to consuming all its input before producing any output—to achieve low latency and enable real parallel processing. The input to the system is provided by a *data source* such as a text file. The output flows into a *data sink* such as a file, terminal, animation program and so on. The data source, the filters and the data sink are connected sequentially by *pipes*. Each pipe implements the data flow between adjacent processing steps. The sequence of filters combined by pipes is called a *processing pipeline*.

Structure   *Filter* components are the processing units of the pipeline. A filter enriches, refines or transforms its input data. It enriches data by computing and adding information, refines data by concentrating or extracting information, and transforms data by delivering the data in some other representation. A concrete filter implementation may combine any of these three basic principles.

The activity of a filter can be triggered by several events:

- The subsequent pipeline element pulls output data from the filter.

- The previous pipeline element pushes new input data to the filter.

- Most commonly, the filter is active in a loop, pulling its input from and pushing its output down the pipeline.

The first two cases denote so-called passive filters, whereas the last case is an active filter[5]. An active filter starts processing on its own as a separate program or thread. A passive filter component is activated by being called either as a function (pull) or as a procedure (push).

---

5. Note that all UNIX filters are active by this definition. Passive filters may be an unfamiliar concept. We introduce it to show that the Pipes and Filters pattern can be implemented without the overhead of context switches and data transfers and still remain a viable concept.

Pipes denote the connections between filters, between the data source and the first filter, and between the last filter and the data sink. If two active components are joined, the pipe synchronizes them. This synchronization is done with a first-in-first-out buffer. If activity is controlled by one of the adjacent filters, the pipe can be implemented by a direct call from the active to the passive component. Direct calls make filter recombination harder, however.

Class Filter	*Collaborators* • Pipe	*Class* Pipe	*Collaborators* • Data Source • Data Sink • Filter
Responsibility • Gets input data. • Performs a function on its input data. • Supplies output data.		*Responsibility* • Transfers data. • Buffers data. • Synchronizes active neighbors.	

The *data source* represents the input to the system, and provides a sequence of data values of the same structure or type. Examples of such data sources are a file consisting of lines of text, or a sensor delivering a sequence of numbers. The data source of a pipeline can either actively push the data values to the first processing stage, or passively provide data when the first filter pulls.

The *data sink* collects the results from the end of the pipeline. Two variants of the data sink are possible. An active data sink pulls results out of the preceding processing stage, while a passive one allows the preceding filter to push or write the results into it.

Class Data Source	*Collaborators* • Pipe	*Class* Data Sink	*Collaborators* • Pipe
Responsibility • Delivers input to processing pipeline.		*Responsibility* • Consumes output.	

➥   In our Mocha compiler we use the UNIX tools `lex` and `yacc` to implement the first two stages of the compiler [ASU86]. Both tools generate functions—`yylex()` and `yyparse()`—for embedding in a program. The function `yyparse()` actively controls the frontend of our compiler. It calls `yylex()` whenever further input tokens are needed. The connection to the other frontend stages consists of many procedure calls embedded in the grammar action rules, and not just simple data flow. Such embedded calls are more efficient than creating an explicit abstract syntax tree representation and passing it along a pipe. The backends and interpreter run as separate programs to allow exchangeability. They are connected via a UNIX pipe to the frontend.   ❑

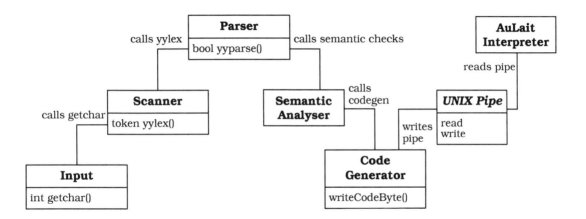

Dynamics   The following scenarios show different options for control flow between adjacent filters. Assume that `Filter1` computes function `f1` on its input data and `Filter2` function `f2`. The first three scenarios show passive filters that use direct calls to the adjacent pipeline components, with different components controlling the activity—no explicit pipe components therefore exist. The last scenario shows the commonest case, in which all filters are active, with a synchronizing pipe between them.

Scenario I shows a push pipeline in which activity starts with the data source. Filter activity is triggered by writing data to the passive filters.

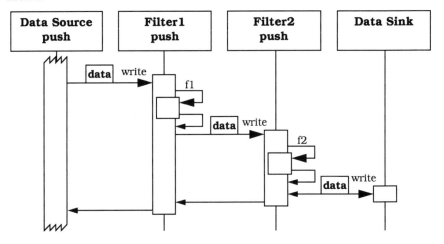

Scenario II shows a pull pipeline. Here control flow is started by the data sink calling for data.

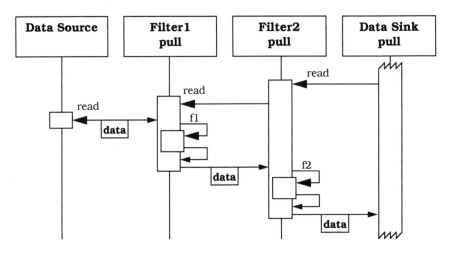

Scenario III shows a mixed push-pull pipeline with passive data source and sink. Here the second filter plays the active role and starts the processing.

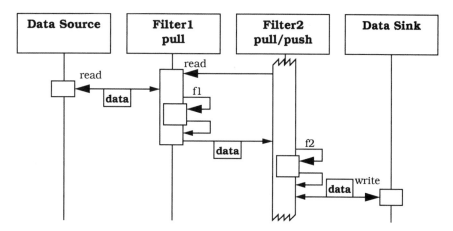

Scenario IV shows a more complex but typical behavior of a Pipes and Filters system. All filters actively pull, compute, and push data in a loop. Each filter therefore runs in its own thread of control, for example as a separate process. The filters are synchronized by a buffering pipe between them. For simplicity we assume that the pipe buffers only a single value. This scenario also shows how you can achieve parallel computing using filters.

The following steps occur in this scenario:

- Filter2 tries to get new data by reading from the pipe. Because no data is available the data request suspends the activity of Filter2—the buffer is empty.

- Filter1 pulls data from the data source and performs function f1.

- Filter1 then pushes the result to the pipe.

- Filter2 can now continue, because new input data is available. Filter1 can also continue, because it is not blocked by a full buffer within the pipe.

- Filter2 computes f2 and writes its result to the data sink.

- In parallel with Filter2's activity, Filter1 computes the next result and tries to push it down the pipe. This call is blocked because Filter2 is not waiting for data—the buffer is full.

- Filter2 now reads new input data that is already available from the pipe. This releases Filter1 so that it can now continue its processing.

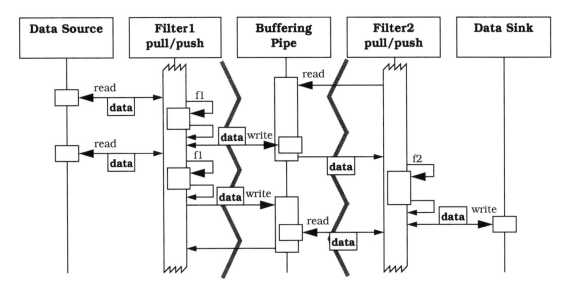

Implementation   Implementing a Pipes and Filters architecture is straightforward. You can use a system service such as message queues or UNIX pipes for pipe connections, or other options like the direct call implementation, as described in steps 3 through 6 below. The design decisions in these steps are closely interrelated, so you may make them in an order other than that given here. The implementation of the data source and data sink is not addressed explicitly, because it follows the guidelines for pipes or filters closely.

1   *Divide the system's task into a sequence of processing stages.* Each stage must depend only on the output of its direct predecessor. All stages are conceptually connected by the data flow. If you plan to develop a family of systems by exchanging processing stages, or if you are developing a toolbox of components, you can consider alternatives or recombinations for some processing stages at this point.

➡   In our Mocha compiler the primary separation is between the AuLait-creating frontend and the backends. Further structuring of the frontend gives us the stages of scanner, parser, semantic analyzer and code generator. We decide not to construct an abstract syntax tree explicitly, to be passed from the parser to the semantic analyzer. Instead we embed calls to the semantic analyzer (sa) and code generator (cg) into yacc's grammar rules:

```
addexpr  :    term
         |    addexpr '+' term
              { sa.checkCompat($1,$3); cg.genAdd($1,$3); }
         |    addexpr '-' term
              { sa.checkCompat($1,$3); cg.genSub($1,$3); }
```

This means that we need to build a filter consisting of the parser, semantic analyzer and code generator stages. The scanner, as a separate filter component, remains passive until called by the parser. We thus link the function yylex() into our frontend program.   ❏

2   *Define the data format to be passed along each pipe.* Defining a uniform format results in the highest flexibility because it makes recombination of filters easy. In most UNIX filter programs the data format is line-structured ASCII text. This may however impose an efficiency penalty. For example, a textual representation of floating-point numbers may be too inefficient to pass along a pipe, because repeated conversion between ASCII and floating-point representations and back is needed. If you both want flexibility and opt for different data representations, you can create transformation filter components to change the data between semantically-equivalent representations.

You must also define how the end of input is marked. If a system service is used for pipe connections an end-of-input error condition may be sufficient. For other pipe implementations you can use a special data value to mark the end of input. The values zero, -1, $, control-D, or control-Z are favored examples of end-of-input markers.

➡   The input to our frontend is a Mocha program, in the form of a stream or file of ASCII characters. The tokens passed from scanner to parser are denoted by integer values. The function yylex() returns either the ASCII code of a character scanned, or a code beyond the ASCII range for tokens, such as a Mocha keyword. The end of input is marked by the value zero. The data format used between the frontend and the backends or interpreter is provided by the definition of the AuLait byte codes.   ❏

3   *Decide how to implement each pipe connection.* This decision directly determines whether you implement the filters as active or passive components. Adjacent pipes further define whether a passive filter is triggered by push or pull of data. The simplest case of a pipe connection is a direct call between adjacent filters to push or pull a data

value, as shown in the first three scenarios of the Dynamics section. If you use a direct call between filters, however, you have to change your code whenever you want to recombine or reuse filter components. Such filters are also harder to develop and test in isolation, due to the need for test frames to call the filter components.

Using a separate pipe mechanism that synchronizes adjacent active filters provides a more flexible solution. If all pipes use the same mechanism, arbitrary recombination of filters becomes possible. A pipe supplies a first-in-first-out buffer to connect adjacent filters that produce and consume unequal amounts of data per computation. Many operating systems provide inter-process communication services such as queues or pipes that you can use to connect active filter programs. If such services are not available, you can implement filters as separate threads, and pipes as queues that synchronize producers and consumers of data.

➡   Because we want flexibility at the backend of our Mocha compiler, we use the UNIX pipe mechanism between frontend and backends. This also allows us to store the intermediate results of our compilation—the AuLait code—in a file for further analysis or translation by another backend.   ❑

4   *Design and implement the filters.* The design of a filter component is based both on the task it must perform and on the adjacent pipes. You can implement passive filters as a function, for pull activation, or as a procedure for push activation. Active filters can be implemented either as processes or as threads in the pipeline program.

The cost of a context switch between processes, and the need to copy data between address spaces, may heavily impact performance. The buffer size of the pipes is an additional parameter you should take into account. A small buffer gives the worst case when combined with the most context switches. You can achieve high flexibility with small active filter components at the price of an overhead for many context switches and data transfers.

If you want to be able to reuse filters easily, it is vital to control their behavior in some way. Several techniques are available for passing parameters to filters. UNIX filter programs, for example, allow many options to be passed on the command line. An alternative method is to use a global environment or repository that is available to filters when they execute. This can be supported by the operating system, the shell or a configuration file. You should think carefully about the trade-off between the flexibility of a filter and its ease of use. As a rule of thumb, a filter should do one thing well.

➡ Our Mocha frontend reads program source code from standard input and creates an AuLait program on its standard output. The stages within the frontend communicate by direct calls. We also create an optimizer for AuLait running as a separate filter program. The AuLait interpreter can be viewed as a data sink, whereas the intended backends are additional filter stages producing object code as output.❑

5 *Design the error handling.* Because pipeline components do not share any global state, error handling is hard to address and is often neglected. As a minimum, error detection should be possible. UNIX defines a specific output channel for error messages, `stderr`, that is used by most provided filter programs for this purpose. Such an approach can denote errors in input data, resource limitations and so on. A single error channel may however mix error messages from different components in a non-obvious and unpredictable way when filters run in parallel.

If a filter detects errors in its input data, it can ignore input until some clearly marked separation occurs. For example, a filter may skip to the next line of input if a line is expected to contain a numerical value and does not. This approach is helpful if incorrect input data is possible and inaccurate results can be tolerated.

It is hard to give a general strategy for error handling with a system based on the Pipes and Filters pattern. For example, consider the case in which a pipeline has consumed three-quarters of its input, already produced half of its output data, and some intermediate filter crashes. In many systems the only solution is to restart the pipeline and hope that it will complete without failure.

Resynchronization of the pipeline can be a goal of an advanced system in which filters process data incrementally. One option is to introduce special marker values to tag the input data stream. These markers are passed unchanged to the output. You can then restart the pipe at the correct stage of the input to continue processing from a failure. Another option is to use pipes to buffer data that has already been consumed, and then use it to restart the pipeline if a filter crashes.

➥ In our simple compiler we send errors to the standard error channel. The parser is designed to skip tokens when it detects a syntax error until the scanner recognizes the ';' statement separator. This is done for example in the following grammar rule, which ignores syntax errors if they occur in an 'import' statement.

```
import   :    FROM identifier objidentlist ';'
         |    FROM error ';'
                { mochaerror(errs[E_IMPRT]); yyerrok; }
```

In this rule yacc's special token error matches all unrecognized tokens until a semicolon is found. The statement yyerrok is a special action that resets the parser into normal mode after the occurrence of a syntax error.   ❏

6   *Set up the processing pipeline.* If your system handles a single task you can use a standardized main program that sets up the pipeline and starts processing. This type of system may benefit from a direct-call pipeline, in which the main program calls the active filter to start processing.

You can increase flexibility by providing a shell or other end-user facility to set up various pipelines from your set of filter components. Such a shell can support the incremental development of pipelines by allowing intermediate results to be stored in files, and supporting files as pipeline input. You are not restricted to a text-only shell such as those provided by UNIX, and could even develop a graphical environment for visual creation of pipelines using 'drag and drop' interaction.

➥ Our compiler is set up by a UNIX shell command that establishes the compilation or interpreter pipeline:

```
# compile and optimize a Mocha program for a Sun
$ Mocha <file.Mocha | optauLait | auLait2SPARC >a.out

# interpret a Mocha program
$ Mocha <file.Mocha | cup
```

Mocha is the frontend program, the optimizer is called optauLait, and the backends follow the naming convention auLait2*machine*. The interpreter is named cup after the virtual machine it implements. ❏

**Example
resolved**   We did not follow the Pipes and Filters pattern strictly in our Mocha
compiler by implementing all phases of the compiler as separate filter
programs connected by pipes. We did this for performance reasons,
and also because, in contrast to the third force, these phases do share
a global state—the symbol table. It is sometimes possible to remove
the need for shared global states by passing global information along
the pipeline as additional data. However, this involves more complex
data structures and an increase in pipeline data volume, imposing a
performance penalty. Where the data being processed consists of
simple types such as lines of text, such complex additional data
structures have to be encoded and decoded by each filter.

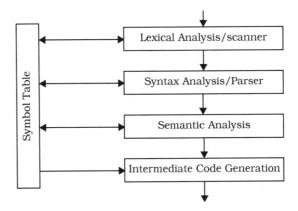

We combined the first four compiler phases into a single program
because they all access and modify the symbol table. This allows us
to implement the pipe connection between the scanner and the parser
as a simple function call. Backends, interpreters or a debugger would
also benefit from access to the symbol table. We therefore follow the
example of many existing compilers by encoding some of the symbol
table information, such as names and source line numbers, into the
binary code for debugging purposes. Note that such symbol table
information can greatly increase the size of compiled programs.

Variants   *Tee and join pipeline systems.* The single-input single-output filter specification of the Pipes and Filters pattern can be varied to allow filters with more than one input and/or more than one output. Processing can then be set up as a directed graph that can even contain feedback loops. The design of such a system, especially one with feedback loops, requires a solid foundation to explain and understand the complete calculation—a rigorous theoretical analysis and specification using formal methods are appropriate, to prove that the system terminates and produces the desired result. If we restrict ourselves to simple directed acyclic graphs, however, it is still possible to build useful systems. The UNIX filter program `tee`, for example, allows you to write data passed along a pipe to a file or to another 'named' pipe. Some filter programs allow the use of files or named pipes as input, as well as standard input. For example, to build a sorted list of all words that occur more than once in a text file, we can construct the following shell program:

```
# first create two auxiliary named pipes to be used
mknod pipeA p
mknod pipeB p
# now do the processing using available UNIX filters
# start side fork of processing in background:
sort pipeA > pipeB &
# the main pipeline
cat file | tee pipeA | sort -u | comm -13 - pipeB
```

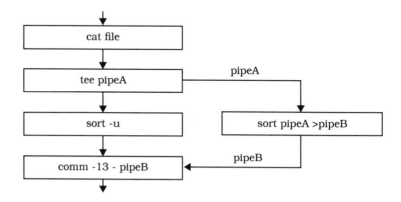

Known Uses **UNIX** [Bac86] popularized the Pipes and Filters paradigm. The command shells and the availability of many filter programs made this approach to system development popular. As a system for software developers, frequent tasks such as program compilation and documentation creation are done by pipelines on a 'traditional' UNIX system. The flexibility of UNIX pipes made the operating system a suitable platform for the binary reuse of filter programs and for application integration.

CMS Pipelines [HRV95] is an extension to the operating system of IBM mainframes to support Pipes and Filters architectures. The implementation of CMS pipelines follows the conventions of CMS, and defines a *record* as the basic data type that can be passed along pipes, instead of a byte or ASCII character. CMS Pipelines provides a reuse and integration platform in the same way as UNIX. Because the CMS operating system does not use a uniform I/O-model in the same way as UNIX, CMS Pipelines defines *device drivers* that act as data sources or sinks, allowing the handling of specific I/O-devices within pipelines.

LASSPTools [Set95] is a toolset to support numerical analysis and graphics. The toolset consists mainly of filter programs that can be combined using UNIX pipes. It contains graphical input devices for analog input of numerical data using knobs or sliders, filters for numerical analysis and data extraction, and data sinks that produce animations from numerical data streams.

Consequences The Pipes and Filters architectural pattern has the following **benefits**:

No intermediate files necessary, but possible. Computing results using separate programs is possible without pipes, by storing intermediate results in files. This approach clutters directories, and is error-prone if you have to set up your processing stages every time you run your system. In addition, it rules out incremental and parallel computation of results. Using Pipes and Filters removes the need for intermediate files, but allows you to investigate intermediate data by using a T-junction in your pipeline.

Flexibility by filter exchange. Filters have a simple interface that allows their easy exchange within a processing pipeline. Even if filter components call each other directly in a push or pull fashion, exchanging a filter component is still straightforward. In our compiler example a scanner generated with lex can easily be replaced by a more efficient hand-coded function yylex() that performs the same task. Filter exchange is generally not possible at run-time due to incremental computation in the pipeline.

Flexibility by recombination. This major benefit, combined with the re-usability of filter components, allows you to create new processing pipelines by rearranging filters or by adding new ones. A pipeline without a data source or sink can be embedded as a filter within a larger pipeline. You should aim to tune the system platform or surrounding infrastructure to support this flexibility, such as is provided by the pipe mechanism and shells in UNIX.

Reuse of filter components. Support for recombination leads to easy reuse of filter components. Reuse is further enhanced if you implement each filter as an active component, while the underlying platform and shell allow easy end-user construction of pipelines.

Rapid prototyping of pipelines. The preceding benefits make it easy to prototype a data-processing system from existing filters. After you have implemented the principal system function using a pipeline you can optimize it incrementally. You can do this, for example, by developing specific filters for time-critical processing stages, or by re-implementing the pipeline using more efficient pipe connections. Your prototype pipeline can however be the final system if it performs the required task adequately. Highly-flexible filters such as the UNIX tools sed and awk reinforce such a prototyping approach.

Efficiency by parallel processing. It is possible to start active filter components in parallel in a multiprocessor system or a network. If each filter in a pipeline consumes and produces data incrementally they can perform their functions in parallel.

Applying the Pipes and Filters pattern imposes some **liabilities**:

Sharing state information is expensive or inflexible. If your processing stages need to share a large amount of global data, applying the Pipes and Filters pattern is either inefficient or does not provide the full benefits of the pattern.

Efficiency gain by parallel processing is often an illusion. This is for several reasons:

- The cost for transferring data between filters may be relatively high compared to the cost of the computation carried out by a single filter. This is especially true for small filter components or pipelines using network connections.

- Some filters consume all their input before producing any output, either because the task, such as sorting, requires it or because the filter is badly coded, for example by not using incremental processing when the application allows it.

- Context-switching between threads or processes is generally an expensive operation on a single-processor machine.

- Synchronization of filters via pipes may stop and start filters often, especially when a pipe has only a small buffer.

Data transformation overhead. Using a single data type for all filter input and output to achieve highest flexibility results in data conversion overheads. Consider a system that performs numeric calculations and uses UNIX pipes. Such a system must convert ASCII characters to real numbers, and vice-versa, within each filter. A simple filter, such as one that adds two numbers, will spend most of its processing time doing format conversion.

Error handling. As we explained in step 5 of the Implementation section, error handling is the Achilles' heel of the Pipes and Filters pattern. You should at least define a common strategy for error reporting and use it throughout your system. A concrete error-recovery or error-handling strategy depends on the task you need to solve. If your intended pipeline is used in a 'mission-critical' system and restarting the pipeline or ignoring errors is not possible, you should consider structuring your system using alternative architectures such as Layers (31).

See Also The *Layers* pattern (31) is better suited to systems that require reliable operation, because it is easier to implement error handling than with Pipes and Filters. However, Layers lacks support for the easy recombination and reuse of components that is the key feature of the Pipes and Filter pattern.

Credits This pattern relies on experience we gained when learning, using, and teaching UNIX. Our thanks therefore go to the designers of the first versions of UNIX, and its predecessors, who invented and established the use of pipes and filters.

The distinction of active and passive pipeline components was influenced by the PLoP'95 paper 'The Pipeline Design Pattern' [VBT95].

We also thank Ken Auer, Norbert Portner, Douglas C. Schmidt, Jiri Soukup, and John Vlissides for their valuable criticism and their suggestions for the improvement of the [PLoP94] version of this pattern.

Blackboard

The *Blackboard* architectural pattern is useful for problems for which no deterministic solution strategies are known. In Blackboard several specialized subsystems assemble their knowledge to build a possibly partial or approximate solution.

Example   Consider a software system for speech recognition. The input to the system is speech recorded as a waveform. The system not only accepts single words, but also whole sentences that are restricted to the syntax and vocabulary needed for a specific application, such as a database query. The desired output is a machine representation of the corresponding English phrases. The transformations involved require acoustic-phonetic, linguistic, and statistical expertise. For example, one procedure divides the waveform into segments that are meaningful in the context of speech, such as *phones*[6]. At the other end of the processing sequence, another procedure checks the syntax of candidate phrases. Both procedures work in different domains.

6. A 'phone' is the smallest unit of sound within a spoken language. This is distinct from 'phoneme', which is the smallest subdivision of a spoken language that conveys a distinct meaning. A phoneme can be represented by different phones. For example, the German hard 'r' sound and the English rolled 'r' sound are different phones, but belong to the same phoneme [Fel84].

This diagram is mostly taken from [EHLR88]. The input is the waveform at the bottom, and the output consists of the phrase 'are any by Feigenbaum'.

For the moment we assume that there is no consistent algorithm that combines all the necessary procedures for recognizing speech—we discuss this topic further in the Consequences section. To make matters worse, the problem is characterized by the ambiguities of spoken language, noisy data, and the individual peculiarities of speakers such as vocabulary, pronunciation, and syntax.

Context An immature domain in which no closed approach to a solution is known or feasible.

Problem The Blackboard pattern tackles problems that do not have a feasible deterministic solution for the transformation of raw data into high-level data structures, such as diagrams, tables or English phrases. Vision, image recognition, speech recognition and surveillance are examples of domains in which such problems occur. They are characterized by a problem that, when decomposed into subproblems, spans several fields of expertise. The solutions to the partial problems require different representations and paradigms. In many cases no predetermined strategy exists for how the 'partial problem solvers' should combine their knowledge. This is in contrast to functional decomposition, in which several solution steps are arranged so that the sequence of their activation is hard-coded.

In some of the above problem domains you may also have to work with uncertain or approximate knowledge. Each transformation step can also generate several alternative solutions. In such cases it is often enough to find an optimal solution for most cases, and a suboptimal solution, or no solution, for the rest. The limitations of a Blackboard system therefore have to be documented carefully, and if important decisions depend on its results, the results have to be verified.

The following *forces* influence solutions to problems of this kind:

- A complete search of the solution space is not feasible in a reasonable time. For example, if you consider phrases of up to ten words using a vocabulary of a thousand words, the number of possible permutations of words is in the order of 1000^{10}.

- Since the domain is immature, you may need to experiment with different algorithms for the same subtask. For this reason, individual modules should be easily exchangeable.

- There are different algorithms that solve partial problems. For example, the detection of phonetic segments in the waveform is unrelated to the generation of phrases based on words and word sequences.

- Input, as well as intermediate and final results, have different representations, and the algorithms are implemented according to different paradigms.

- An algorithm usually works on the results of other algorithms.

- Uncertain data and approximate solutions are involved. For example, speech often includes pauses and extraneous sounds. These significantly distort the signal. The process of interpretation of the signal is also error-prone. Competing alternatives for a recognition target may occur at any stage of the process. For example, it is hard to distinguish between 'till' and 'tell'. The words 'two' and 'too' even have the same pronunciation, as do many others in English.

- Employing disjoint algorithms induces potential parallelism. If possible you should avoid a strictly sequential solution.

Artificial Intelligence (AI) systems have been used with some success for such complex non-deterministic problems. In the 'classical' expert system structure, the input to the system and intermediate results are kept in working memory. The memory contents are used by an inference engine in conjunction with the knowledge base to infer new intermediate results. Such manipulation steps are repeated until some completion condition is fulfilled.

This type of expert system structure is inadequate for a speech recognition system. There are three reasons for this:

- All partial problems are solved using the same knowledge representation. However, the components involved in the speech recognition process work on fields of knowledge that differ as widely as the segmentation of a waveform and the parsing of candidate phrases. They therefore require different representations.

- The expert system structure provides only one inference engine to control the application of knowledge. Different partial problems with different representations require separate inference engines.

- In a 'classical' expert system, control is implicit in the structure of the knowledge base, for example in the ordering of the rules in a rule-based system. This is consistent with the view of many AI systems that 'problem solving is search' and 'knowledge prunes and directs search'. This implies that you search in the search tree for nodes that include the solution for your problem, and use items of knowledge to guide your way from the root of the search tree—where all solutions are possible—to a single leaf.

  For the speech recognition problem, the view 'problem solving is experts assembling their knowledge' is more suitable. In other words, fragments of knowledge have to be applied at an opportune time, rather than in a predetermined order.

Solution The idea behind the Blackboard architecture is a collection of independent programs that work cooperatively on a common data structure. Each program is specialized for solving a particular part of the overall task, and all programs work together on the solution. These specialized programs are independent of each other. They do not call each other, nor is there a predetermined sequence for their activation. Instead, the direction taken by the system is mainly determined by the current state of progress. A central control component evaluates the current state of processing and coordinates the specialized programs. This data-directed control regime is referred to as *opportunistic problem solving*. It makes experimentation with different algorithms possible, and allows experimentally-derived heuristics to control processing.

During the problem-solving process the system works with partial solutions that are combined, changed or rejected. Each of these solutions represents a partial problem and a certain stage of its solution. The set of all possible solutions is called the *solution space*, and is organized into levels of abstraction. The lowest level of solution consists of an internal representation of the input. Potential solutions of the overall system task are on the highest level.

The name 'blackboard' was chosen because it is reminiscent of the situation in which human experts sit in front of a real blackboard and work together to solve a problem. Each expert separately evaluates the current state of the solution, and may go up to the blackboard at any time and add, change or delete information. Humans usually decide themselves who has the next access to the blackboard. In the pattern we describe, a *moderator* component decides the order in which programs execute if more than one can make a contribution.

Structure   Divide your system into a component called *blackboard*, a collection of knowledge *sources*, and a *control* component.

The blackboard is the central data store. Elements of the solution space and control data are stored here. We use the term *vocabulary* for the set of all data elements that can appear on the blackboard. The blackboard provides an interface that enables all knowledge sources to read from and write to it.

All elements of the solution space can appear on the blackboard. For solutions that are constructed during the problem solving process and put on the blackboard, we use the terms *hypothesis* or *blackboard entry*. Hypotheses rejected later in the process are removed from the blackboard.

A hypothesis usually has several attributes, for example its *abstraction level*, that is, its conceptual distance from the input. Hypotheses that have a low abstraction level have a representation that is still similar to input data representation, while hypotheses with the highest abstraction level are on the same abstraction level as the output. Other hypothesis attributes are the estimated degree of truth of the hypothesis or the time interval covered by the hypothesis.

It is often useful to specify relationships between hypotheses, such as 'part-of' or 'in-support-of'.

➥   The solution space for the speech recognition example consists of acoustic-phonetic and linguistic speech fragments. The levels of abstraction are signal parameters, acoustic-phonetic segments, phones, syllables, words, and phrases.

The degree of truth for a syllable is estimated by the quality of the match between the ideal phone sequences for that syllable and the hypothesized phones.

The waveform of the acoustic signal is recorded on a time axis that corresponds to the X-axis in the figure on page 71. Every solution has an attribute that specifies the interval on the X-axis that it describes.

The blackboard can be viewed as a three-dimensional problem space with the time line for speech on the X-axis, increasing levels of abstraction on the Y-axis and alternative solutions on the Z-axis [Nii86]. ❑

Knowledge sources are separate, independent subsystems that solve specific aspects of the overall problem. Together they model the overall problem domain. None of them can solve the task of the system alone—a solution can only be built by integrating the results of several knowledge sources.

➥ In the speech recognition system we specify solutions for the following partial problems: defining acoustic-phonetic segments, and creating phones, syllables, words and phrases. For each of these partial problem we define one or several knowledge sources. One knowledge source at the word level, for example, may create words from adjacent syllables, while another source on the same level verifies words that depend on neighboring words.

Note that the transformation from waveform to phrase is not necessarily a strictly sequential process. The complete waveform is not necessarily first transformed into segments, all segments into phones, then into syllables and words, and phrases then built. A portion of the waveform may have been transformed into words, another may have been rejected at the word level back to the phone level, and a third may not be analyzed at all until enough evidence on the phrase level exists to tackle it. ❑

Knowledge sources do not communicate directly—they only read from and write to the blackboard. They therefore have to understand the vocabulary of the blackboard. We explore the ramifications of this in the Implementation section.

Often a knowledge source operates on two levels of abstraction. If a knowledge source implements forward reasoning, a particular solution is transformed to a higher-level solution. A knowledge source that reasons backwards searches at a lower level for support for a solution, and may refer it back to a lower level if the reasoning did not give support for the solution.

Class	Collaborators	Class	Collaborator
Blackboard	-	Knowledge Source	• Blackboard
Responsibility		**Responsibility**	
• Manages central data		• Evaluates its own applicability • Computes a result • Updates Blackboard	

Each knowledge source is responsible for knowing the conditions under which it can contribute to a solution. Knowledge sources are therefore split into a *condition-part* and an *action-part*. The condition-part evaluates the current state of the solution process, as written on the blackboard, to determine if it can make a contribution. The action-part produces a result that may cause a change to the blackboard's contents.

➡ Our speech recognition system has diverse knowledge sources that transform several hypotheses at the same level and with contiguous time intervals to a single hypothesis on the next higher level. For example, a phrase is built from a selection of words that together span the time interval corresponding to the phrase. Other knowledge sources predict new hypotheses at the same level. For example, one knowledge source predicts possible words that might syntactically precede or follow a given phrase. We also define a knowledge source that verifies the predicted hypotheses based on information at the next lower level. This calculates the consistency between a predicted word and the set of segments that span the same time interval. ❑

The *control* component runs a loop that monitors the changes on the blackboard and decides what action to take next. It schedules knowledge source evaluations and activations according to a knowledge application *strategy*. The basis for this strategy is the data on the blackboard.

The strategy may rely on *control knowledge sources*. These special knowledge sources do not contribute directly to solutions on the blackboard, but perform calculations on which control decisions are made. Typical tasks are the estimation of the potential for progress, or the computational costs for execution of knowledge sources. Their results are called *control data* and are put on the blackboard as well.

Class Control	*Collaborators* • Blackboard • Knowledge Source
Responsibility • Monitors Black-board • Schedules Know-ledge Source acti-vations	

Theoretically, it is possible that the blackboard can reach at state at which no knowledge source is applicable. In this case, the system fails to deliver a result. In practice, it is more likely that each reasoning step introduces several new hypotheses, and that the number of possible next steps 'explodes'. The problem is therefore to restrict the alternatives to be taken rather than to find an applicable knowledge source.

A special knowledge source or a procedure in the control component determines when the system should halt, and what the final result is. The system halts when an acceptable[7] hypothesis is found, or when the space or time resources of the system are exhausted.

The following figure illustrates the relationship between the three components of the Blackboard architecture. The blackboard component defines two procedures: inspect and update. Knowledge sources call inspect to check the current solutions on the blackboard. update is used to make changes to the data on the blackboard.

---

7. We consider the problem of when to accept or reject top-level solutions in the Implementation section.

The Control component runs a loop that monitors changes on the blackboard and decides what actions to take next. We call the procedure responsible for this decision nextSource().

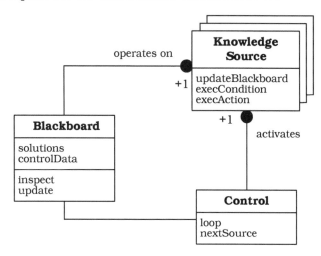

Dynamics The following scenario illustrates the behavior of the Blackboard architecture. It is based on our speech recognition example:

- The main loop of the Control component is started.

- Control calls the nextSource() procedure to select the next knowledge source.

- nextSource() first determines which knowledge sources are potential contributors by observing the blackboard. In this example we assume the candidate knowledge sources are Segmentation, Syllable Creation and Word Creation.

- nextSource() invokes the condition-part of each candidate knowledge source. In the example, the condition-parts of Segmentation, Syllable Creation and Word Creation inspect the blackboard to determine if and how they can contribute to the current state of the solution.

- The Control component chooses a knowledge source to invoke, and a hypothesis or a set of hypotheses to be worked on. In the example the choice is made according to the results of the condition parts. In other cases the selection is also based on control data. It applies the action-part of the knowledge source to the hypotheses. In our speech recognition example, assume that Syllable Creation is the most promising knowledge source. The action-part of Syllable Creation inspects the state of the blackboard, creates a new syllable and updates the blackboard.

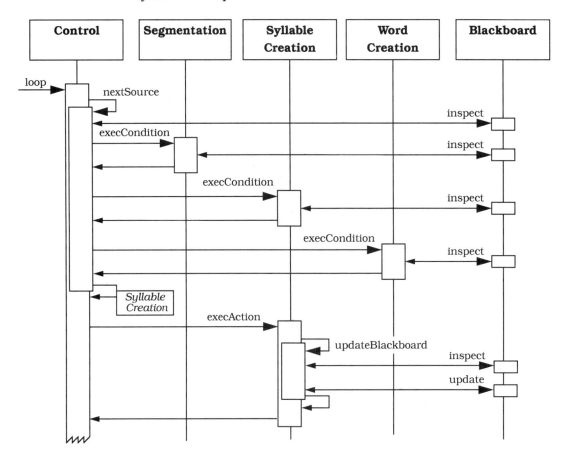

Implementation   To implement the Blackboard pattern, carry out the following steps:

1   *Define the problem:*

   • Specify the domain of the problem and the general fields of knowledge necessary to find a solution.

   • Scrutinize the input to the system. Determine any special properties of the input such as noise content or variations on a theme—that is, does the input contain regular patterns that change slowly over time?

- Define the output of the system. Specify the requirements for correctness and fail-safe behavior. If you need an estimation of the credibility of the results, or if there are cases in which the system should ask the user for further resources, record this.

- Detail how the user interacts with the system.

➡ The fields of knowledge important for a system in the domain of speech recognition are acoustics, linguistics and statistics. The input is a sequence of acoustic signals from a speaker. The data is noisy. If the system allows the speaker to repeat a phrase several times, the input contains 'variations on a theme', as described above. The desired output is a written English phrase corresponding to the spoken phrase. When used for a database query interface, the system can tolerate occasional misinterpretations. If we have to repeat a query in, say, 10% of cases, the system can still be useful. ❏

2 *Define the solution space for the problem.* We distinguish intermediate and top-level solutions on one hand, and partial and complete solutions on the other. A *top-level* solution is at the highest abstraction level. Solutions at other levels are *intermediate* solutions. A *complete* solution solves the whole problem, whereas a *partial* solution solves part of the problem. Note that complete solutions can belong to intermediate levels, and a partial solution may be top-level.

➡ In speech recognition, complete top-level solutions are phrases that are correct with respect to a defined vocabulary and syntax. Complete intermediate solutions are sequences of acoustic-phonetic or linguistic elements that describe the whole spoken phrase. Parts of solutions are the elements themselves. ❏

So, perform the following steps:

- Specify exactly what constitutes a top-level solution.

- List the different abstraction levels of solutions.

- Organize solutions into one or more abstraction hierarchies.

- Find subdivisions of complete solutions that can be worked on independently, for example words of a phrase or regions of a picture or area.

3 *Divide the solution process into steps*:

- Define how solutions are transformed into higher-level solutions.

- Describe how to predict hypotheses at the same abstraction level.

- Detail how to verify predicted hypotheses by finding support for them in other levels.

- Specify the kind of knowledge that can be used to exclude parts of the solution space.

➥ To transform solutions on the syllabic level to solutions on the word level, we provide a dictionary that associates a syllable with all the words whose pronunciation contains the syllable.

Syntactic and statistical knowledge is useful when pruning the search for word sequences. For example, the heuristic that an adjective is normally followed by another adjective or a noun can be used to cut down computing time.   ❏

4 *Divide the knowledge into specialized knowledge sources with certain subtasks.* These subtasks often correspond to areas of specialization. There may be some subtasks for which the system defers to human specialists for decisions about dubious cases, or even to replace a missing knowledge source. Knowledge sources must be complete in the following sense: for most of the input phrases, at least one possible sequence of knowledge source activations that leads to an acceptable solution should exist.

➥ Examples of knowledge sources are segmentation, phone creation, syllable creation, word creation, phrase creation, word prediction and word verification.   ❏

5 *Define the vocabulary of the blackboard.* Elaborate your first definition of the solution space and the abstraction levels of your solutions. Find a representation for solutions that allows all knowledge sources to read from and contribute to the blackboard. This does not mean that each knowledge source must understand every blackboard entry, but each knowledge source must be able to decide whether it can use a blackboard entry. If necessary, provide components that translate between blackboard entries and the internal representations within knowledge sources. This allows knowledge sources to be easily exchanged, to be independent of each other's representation and paradigms, and at the same time use each other's results.

➥   In our speech recognition example, each hypothesis has a uniform attribute-value structure. Some attributes must be included in all hypotheses, while others are optional. The element name, the abstraction level and the time interval covered by the hypothesis are among the required attributes. The estimated degree of truth is optional. For example, the blackboard may contain the following entry:

```
ABOUT+FEIGENBAUM+AND+FELDMAN+] (phrase)(48:225) (83).
```

Depending on the abstraction level, each knowledge source can decide if it is able to work on a hypothesis or not. The knowledge source responsible for segmentation, for example, does not understand the symbols '+' and ']' in the blackboard entry shown here. It knows, by reading the value of the attribute abstraction level, that the hypothesis is a phrase, so it does not check the other attributes.   ❏

To evaluate the contents of the blackboard, the Control component must be able to understand it. The vocabulary of the blackboard cannot therefore be defined once, but evolves in concert with the definition of knowledge sources and the Control component. At some point during design the vocabulary must stabilize, to allow the development of stable interfaces to the knowledge sources.

6   *Specify the control of the system.* The Control component implements an opportunistic problem-solving strategy that determines which knowledge sources are allowed to make changes to the blackboard. The aim of this strategy is to construct a hypothesis that is acceptable as a result. But when is a hypothesis acceptable? Since the correctness of a hypothesis is not verifiable in a strict sense, our goal is to construct the most credible complete, top-level solution possible in the solution space.

The *credibility* of a hypothesis is the likelihood that it is correct. We estimate the credibility of a hypothesis by considering all plausible alternatives to it, and the degree of support each alternative receives from the input data. The credibility rating is, for example, a number on a scale ranging from 0 to 100. A hypothesis is acceptable if it is top-level and complete and if its assessed credibility reaches a threshold value, for example 85. To find an acceptable hypothesis, the system eliminates hypotheses with a low credibility, and detects mutually-supportive clusters of hypotheses that are consistent with the input data.

In the simplest case the control strategy consults the condition-part of all knowledge sources whenever the blackboard is changed, and picks one of the applicable knowledge sources for activation at random. However, this strategy usually is too inefficient, as progress toward an acceptable hypothesis is slow. The design of a good control strategy is the most difficult part of the system design. It often consists of a tedious process of trying combinations of several mechanisms and partial strategies. The Strategy pattern [GHJV95] is useful here to support an exchange of control strategies, even at run-time. Sophisticated control strategies may be implemented by a dedicated knowledge-based system.

The following mechanisms optimize the evaluation of knowledge sources, and so increase the effectiveness and performance of the control strategy:

- Classifying changes to the blackboard into two types. One type specifies all blackboard changes that may imply a new set of applicable knowledge sources, the other specifies all blackboard changes that do not. After changes of the second type, the Control component chooses a knowledge source without another invocation of all condition-parts.

- Associating categories of blackboard changes with sets of possibly applicable knowledge sources.

- Focusing of control. The *focus* contains either partial results on the blackboard that should be worked on next, or knowledge sources that should be preferred over others.

- Creating a queue in which knowledge sources classified as applicable wait for their execution. By using a queue, you save valuable information about knowledge sources rather than discarding it after each change to the blackboard.

Control strategies use *heuristics* to determine which of the applicable knowledge sources to activate. Heuristics are rules based on experience and guesses. Keep in mind that good heuristics work often, but not always. Here are some examples of heuristics that can be used by control strategies:

- Prioritizing applicable knowledge sources. The basis for such a priority calculation is the evaluation of the condition-parts of knowledge sources, and possibly other information such as the potential for making progress using a knowledge source, and the costs of its application. The Control component may consider the contributions of knowledge-sources to decide about prioritization. In this case it must execute the action-parts of all applicable knowledge sources before it can decide which should make a change to the blackboard. If the system uses a queue, the priority of each knowledge source is stored with its entry. A change to the blackboard may result in a change in priorities or the removal of knowledge sources from the queue.

- Preferring low-level or high-level hypotheses. If this is the only strategy used, the control strategy is no longer opportunistic, but rather implements forward- or backward-chaining.

- Preferring hypotheses that cover large parts of the problem.

- 'Island driving'. This strategy involves assuming that a particular hypothesis is part of an acceptable solution, and is considered as an 'island of certainty'. Knowledge source activations that work on this hypothesis are then preferred over others, which removes the need to search constantly for alternative hypotheses with higher priorities.

If the control component displays complex and independent subtasks, define one control knowledge source for each of these subtasks. Treat them like other knowledge sources. For example, the priority calculation for applicable knowledge sources can itself be implemented as a dedicated control knowledge source.

7 *Implement the knowledge sources.* Split the knowledge sources into condition-parts and action-parts according to the needs of the Control component. To maintain the independency and exchangeability of knowledge sources, do not make any assumptions about other knowledge sources or the Control component.

You can implement different knowledge sources in the same system using different technologies. For example, one may be a rule-based system, another a neural net and a third a set of conventional functions. This implies that the knowledge sources themselves may be organized according to diverse architectural or design patterns. For example, one knowledge source may be designed using the Layers pattern (31), while another may be structured according to the Reflection pattern (193). If you intend to develop your system using object-oriented technology, but your knowledge sources are implemented using another paradigm, it makes sense to 'wrap' them using the Facade pattern [GHJV95].

Variants   *Production System.* This architecture is used in the OPS language [FMcD77]. In this variant subroutines are represented as condition-action rules, and data is globally available in working memory. Condition-action rules consist of a left-hand side that specifies a condition, and a right-hand side that specifies an action. The action is executed only if the condition is satisfied and the rule is selected. The selection is made by a 'conflict resolution module'. A Blackboard system can be regarded as a radical extension of the original production system formalism: arbitrary programs are allowed for both sides of the rules, and the internal complexity of the working memory is increased. Complicated scheduling algorithms are used for conflict-resolution.

Repository. This variant is a generalization of the Blackboard pattern. The central data structure of this variant is called a *repository*. In a Blackboard architecture the current state of the central data structure, in conjunction with the Control component, finally activates knowledge sources. In contrast, the Repository pattern does not specify an internal control. A repository architecture may be controlled by user input or by an external program. A traditional database, for example, can be considered as a repository. Application programs working on the database correspond to the knowledge sources in the Blackboard architecture.

Examples of repository systems that are not Blackboard systems are given in [SG96]: 'Programming environments are often organized as a collection of tools together with a shared repository of programs and program fragments. Even applications that have been traditionally viewed as pipeline architectures, may be more accurately interpreted as repository systems...' Compilers, for example, have traditionally been described and sometimes also been implemented as pipelines[8]. Modern compilers have a repository that holds shared information such as symbol tables and abstract syntax trees. The compilation

---

8. For more information on pipeline architectures, refer to the Pipes and Filters pattern (53) where we explain in more detail why building compilers according to Pipes and Filters is usually not a good idea.

phases correspond to knowledge sources operating on the repository. This architecture enables incremental problem solving:

- The *scanner* reads an identifier that is not yet defined.

- The *parser* recognizes the syntactical unit described by the identifier.

- The *code generator* then jumps in and creates the corresponding machine code, if any.

Known uses   **HEARSAY-II.** The first Blackboard system was the HEARSAY-II speech recognition system from the early 1970's. It was developed as a natural language interface to a literature database. Its task was to answer queries about documents and to retrieve documents from a collection of abstracts of Artificial Intelligence publications. The inputs to the system were acoustic signals that were semantically interpreted and then transformed to a database query. [EM88] gives a detailed description and retrospective view of the project. Selected aspects of HEARSAY-II also serve as the running example of this pattern. The following paragraphs discuss its control aspects.

In HEARSAY-II, the condition-part of a knowledge source identifies a configuration of hypotheses on the blackboard appropriate for action by the knowledge source. This subset is called the *stimulus frame*. For example, the condition-part of the knowledge source that generates phrase hypotheses looks for contiguous word or phrase hypotheses. Condition-parts also calculate a formal description of the likely action that the knowledge source will perform, called the *response frame*. For example, a response frame for a word hypothesizer based on syllables indicates that its action will be to generate hypotheses at the word level, and that the interval covered by the hypothesis on the X-axis will include at least the stimulus frame.

The control component of HEARSAY-II consists of the following:

- The *focus-of-control database*, which contains a table of *primitive change types* of blackboard changes, and those condition-parts that can be executed for each change type. Examples of primitive change types are 'new syllable' or 'new word created bottom-up'— indicating that a new word appeared on the blackboard and it was inferred using hypotheses on lower levels.

- The *scheduling queue*, which contains pointers to condition- or action-parts of knowledge sources.[9]

- The *monitor*, which keeps track of each change made to the blackboard. The monitor inserts pointers to applicable condition-parts into the scheduling queue based on the corresponding primitive change types. If a condition-part is actually executed and the calculated response frame is not empty, a pointer to the matching action-part is placed in the scheduling queue.

- The *scheduler*, which uses experimentally-derived heuristics to calculate priorities for the condition- and action-parts waiting in the scheduling queue. This estimation is based on the specific stimulus and response frames. It also takes into account overall blackboard state information, such as which out of several competing hypotheses in the same X-axis interval has highest support from hypotheses on lower levels. The scheduler finally selects the condition- or action-part with the highest priority for execution [LeEr88].

The designers of HEARSAY-II combined several problem-solving techniques for their knowledge application strategy. The first is a bottom-up approach in which interpretations are synthesized directly from the data, working up the abstraction hierarchy. The second is a top-down strategy, in which hypotheses at lower levels are produced recursively until a sequence of hypotheses on the lowest level is produced that can be tested against the original input. Orthogonal to those approaches, HEARSAY-II employs a 'generate-and-test' strategy, in which a knowledge source generates hypotheses, and their validity is evaluated by another knowledge source.

HASP/SIAP. The HASP system was designed to detect enemy submarines. In this system, hydrophone arrays monitor a sea area by collecting sonar signals. A Blackboard system interprets these signals [Nii86]. HASP is an event-based system in the sense that the occurrence of a particular event implies that new information is available. The blackboard is used as a 'situation board' that evolves

---

9. The scheduling queue does not implicitly determine the sequence of elements to be removed, as a LIFO- or FIFO-queue does. Instead the Scheduler determines the sequence by repeatedly calculating priorities. Therefore, according to our terminology, the HEARSAY-II 'scheduling queue' is a container and not a queue.

over time. Since information is collected continuously, there is information redundancy as well as new and different information. HASP deals with multiple input streams. Besides the low-level data from hydrophones, it accepts high-level descriptions of the situation gathered from intelligence or other sources.

CRYSALIS. This system was designed to infer the three-dimensional structure of protein molecules from X-ray diffraction data [Ter88]. The system introduces several features to the Blackboard architecture. The blackboard is divided into several parts called *panels*. Each panel has its own vocabulary and hierarchy. It is possible to restrict access to certain panels by knowledge sources. CRYSALIS uses a data panel and a hypothesis panel. Knowledge sources are organized into levels. Only the lowest level contains knowledge sources that actually create and modify hypotheses. The other levels consist of control knowledge sources. CRYSALIS was the first Blackboard system to use rule-based systems for control.

TRICERO. This system monitors aircraft activities. It extends the Blackboard architecture to distributed computing [Wil84]. Four complete, independent expert systems for partial problems were designed to run on four separate machines.

Generalizations. Between 1977 and 1984 application-oriented Blackboard systems were generalized to produce frameworks intended to ease building Blackboard applications. However, no standard way to do this emerged.

SUS. A recent project called 'Software Understanding System', described in [THG94], is particularly interesting from our point of view as software pattern authors. The aim of SUS is to support understanding of software, and the search for reusable assets. In a matching process the system compares patterns from a pattern base to the system under analysis. SUS incrementally builds a 'pattern map' of the analyzed software that then can be viewed.

Example Resolved

In the following we present an excerpt of the processing steps that HEARSAY-II performs to understand the phrase 'Are any by Feigenbaum and Feldman?', as described in [EHLR88].

To briefly characterize the knowledge sources that are activated in the example:

- RPOL runs as a high-priority task immediately after any knowledge source activity that creates a new hypothesis. RPOL uses rating information on the new hypothesis, as well as rating information on hypotheses to which the new hypothesis is connected, to calculate an overall rating for the new hypothesis.

- PREDICT works on a phrase and generates predictions of all words that can immediately precede or follow the phrase in the language.

- VERIFY tries to verify the existence of, or reject, a predicted word, in the context of the phrase that predicts it. If the word is verified a confidence rating must also be generated for it. This is done by the knowledge source RPOL.

- CONCAT accomplishes the generation of a phrase from a verified word and its predicting phrase. The extended phrase includes a rating that is based on the ratings of the predicting phrase, and the verified word. If a verified word is already associated with some other phrase, CONCAT tries to parse that phrase with the predicting phrase. If successful, a phrase hypothesis is created which represents the merging of the two phrases.

We have simplified the original description for ease of understanding, and have omitted explicit executions of the condition-parts of knowledge sources. Executions of RPOL are also omitted. An execution of the VERIFY knowledge source often immediately follows the execution of the PREDICT knowledge source. The two knowledge source executions are therefore combined into one step.

To help you understand the following sequence of processing steps and the figure, here is an explanation of the notation we have used:

- The number in brackets behind a word or phrase denotes its credibility rating.

- '[' marks the begin of an spoken phrase, and ']' marks its end.

- KS stands for 'knowledge source'.

The highest rated hypotheses on the blackboard are currently:

[ARE+(97), [ARE+REDDY(91), FEIGENBAUM+AND+FELDMAN+](85), and [ARE+ANY(86).

Step 17 is the first step to consider:

```
Step 17: KS PREDICT&VERIFY
Stimulus: FEIGENBAUM+AND+FELDMAN+](85) (phrase).
Action: Predict eight preceding words;
reject one: DISCUSS;
find three already on the blackboard: CITE(70),
ABOUT(75), BY(80);
verify four: CITES(65), QUOTE(70), ED(75), NOT(75).
```

The rating of a hypothesis is not the only parameter the Scheduler uses to assign priorities to waiting knowledge source activations. In particular, the length of a hypothesis is also important. The phrase FEIGENBAUM+AND+FELDMAN+] with a rating of 85 was therefore preferred over the phrases [ARE+REDDY with a rating of 91 and [ARE+ANY with a rating of 86, because it is much longer.

In steps 18 through 24, alternative word extensions of FEIGENBAUM+AND+FELDMAN+](85) are explored. As a result of this exploration, the phrase BY+FEIGENBAUM+AND+FELDMAN+](84) is considered the most credible.

```
Step 18: KS CONCAT
Stimulus: BY(80) (word),
FEIGENBAUM+AND+FELDMAN+](85) (phrase).
Action: Create phrase:
BY+FEIGENBAUM+AND+FELDMAN+](84).

Step 19: KS CONCAT
Stimulus: ABOUT(75) (word),
FEIGENBAUM+AND+FELDMAN+](85) (phrase).
Action: Create phrase:
ABOUT+FEIGENBAUM+AND+FELDMAN+](83)

Step 20: KS PREDICT&VERIFY
Stimulus:
ABOUT+FEIGENBAUM+AND+FELDMAN+](83)(phrase).
Action: Predict one preceding word;
verify: WHAT(10).

Step 21: KS CONCAT
Stimulus: CITE(70)(word),
FEIGENBAUM+AND+FELDMAN+](85)(phrase).
Action: Create phrase:
CITE+FEIGENBAUM+AND+FELDMAN+](83) (phrase).
```

```
Step 22: KS PREDICT&VERIFY
Stimulus: CITE+FEIGENBAUM+AND+FELDMAN+] (83) (phrase).
Action: Predict ten preceding words;
reject five: ABSTRACTS, ARE, BOOKS, PAPERS, REFERENCED;
find two already on the blackboard: ANY(65), THESE(25);
verify three: ARTICLE(25), WRITTEN(25), ARTICLES(10).
```

If all ten word predictions preceding the phrase had been rejected, the phrase hypothesis itself would also be rejected.

```
Step 24: KS CONCAT
Stimulus: NOT(75) (word),
FEIGENBAUM+AND+FELDMAN+] (85).
Action: Create phrase:
NOT+FEIGENBAUM+AND+FELDMAN+] (83).

Step 25 KS CONCAT
Stimulus: ANY(65) (word),
BY+FEIGENBAUM+AND+FELDMAN+] (84) (phrase).
Action: Create phrase:
ANY+BY+FEIGENBAUM+AND+FELDMAN+] (82).
[ARE+ANY+BY+FEIGENBAUM+AND+FELDMAN+] (85)
is also created from [ARE+ANY(86) and
BY+FEIGENBAUM+AND+FELDMAN+] (84).
```

The phrase happens to be a complete sentence, and is therefore a candidate for the interpretation of the spoken input.

In the figure that follows, an arc points from one hypothesis to another if one hypothesis is derived from the other in a single processing step. The arc is labeled with the number of the processing step. Dashed arcs point to hypotheses that were already on the blackboard before step 17.

Consequences   The Blackboard approach to problem decomposition and knowledge application helps to resolve most of the forces listed in the problem section:

Experimentation. In domains in which no closed approach exists and a complete search of the solution space is not feasible, the Blackboard pattern makes experimentation with different algorithms possible, and also allows different control heuristics to be tried.

Support for changeability and maintainability. The Blackboard architecture supports changeability and maintainability because the individual knowledge sources, the control algorithm and the central

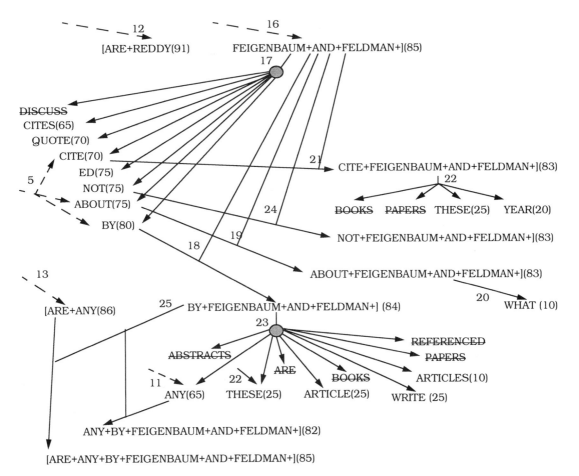

data structure are strictly separated. However, all modules can communicate via the blackboard.

Reusable knowledge sources. Knowledge sources are independent specialists for certain tasks. A Blackboard architecture helps in making them reusable. The prerequisites for reuse are that knowledge source and the underlying Blackboard system understand the same protocol and data, or are close enough in this respect not to rule out adaptors for protocol or data.

Support for fault tolerance and robustness. In a Blackboard architecture all results are just hypotheses. Only those that are strongly supported by data and other hypotheses survive. This provides tolerance of noisy data and uncertain conclusions.

The Blackboard pattern has some **liabilities**:

Difficulty of testing. Since the computations of a Blackboard system do not follow a deterministic algorithm, its results are often not reproducible. In addition, wrong hypotheses are part of the solution process.

No good solution is guaranteed. Usually Blackboard systems can solve only a certain percentage of their given tasks correctly.

Difficulty of establishing a good control strategy. The control strategy cannot be designed in a straightforward way, and requires an experimental approach.

Low Efficiency. Blackboard systems suffer from computational overheads in rejecting wrong hypotheses. If no deterministic algorithm exists, however, low efficiency is the lesser of two evils when compared to no system at all.

High development effort. Most Blackboard systems take years to evolve. We attribute this to the ill-structured problem domains and extensive trial-and-error programming when defining vocabulary, control strategies and knowledge sources.

No support for parallelism. The Blackboard architecture does not prevent the use of a control strategy that exploits the potential parallelism of knowledge sources. It does not however provide for their parallel execution. Concurrent access to the central data on the blackboard must also be synchronized.

To summarize, the Blackboard architecture allows an interpretative use of knowledge. It evaluates alternative actions, chooses the best for the current situation, and then applies the most promising knowledge source. The expense for such deliberation can be justified so long as no adequate explicit algorithm is available for the problem. When such an algorithm emerges, it usually provides higher performance and effectiveness. The Blackboard architecture consequently lends itself best to immature domains in which experimentation is helpful. After research and the gaining of experience, better algorithms may evolve that allow you to use a more efficient architecture.

This occurred in the domain of speech recognition. For example, in the HARPY system, a successor to HEARSAY-II, most of the knowledge is precompiled into a unified structure that represents all possible spoken phrases [EHLR88]. All inter-level substitutions, such as segment to phone, phone to word, and word to phrase are compiled into a single enormous finite-state Markov network. An interpreter then compares segments of the spoken phrase with this structure to find a network path that most closely approximates the segmented speech signal. The search technique used, called *beam search*, combined with word lattices, is a heuristic form of dynamic programming. Acoustical and linguistic knowledge are no longer combined via a blackboard, but rather by a 'maximum likelihood' computation. A window slides over the input and continuously appends new results to the output. This allows speech recognition to be used in a real-time fashion. [Mar95] gives a recent update on simpler speech recognition products. For more details on speech recognition, see [HAJ90], [Rab86] and [Rab89].

Credits Our Blackboard pattern is based mostly on features abstracted from the HEARSAY-II speech recognition system. We found the first reference to the term 'blackboard' in AI literature, in a text by Newell and Simon [NS72] concerned with the organizational problems of checkers-playing, chess-playing and theorem-proving programs. The most comprehensive descriptions and discussions of Blackboard systems are in [EM88] and [Cra95].

We thank Harald Höge from the Siemens speech processing group for explaining recent progress in this domain.

2.3 Distributed Systems

There are two major trends in recent developments in hardware technology:

- Computer systems with multiple CPUs are entering even small offices, notably multiprocessing systems running operating systems such as IBM OS/2 Warp, Microsoft Windows NT, or UNIX.

- Local area networks connecting hundreds of heterogeneous computers have become commonplace.

Nowadays, even small companies are using distributed systems. But what are the advantages of distributed systems that make them so interesting? Tanenbaum [Tan92] suggests the following:

Economics. Computer networks that incorporate both PCs and workstations offer a better price/performance ratio than mainframe computers.

Performance and Scaleability. According to the Sun Microsystems philosophy 'The network is the computer', distributed applications are capable of using resources available on a network. A huge increase in performance can be gained by using the combined computing power of several network nodes. In addition—at least in theory—multiprocessors and networks are easily scalable.

Inherent distribution. Some applications are inherently distributed, for example database applications that follow a Client-Server model.

Reliability. In most cases, a machine on a network or a CPU in a multiprocessor system can crash without affecting the rest of the system. Central nodes such as file servers are notable exceptions to this, but can be protected by backup systems.

Distributed systems, however, have a significant drawback [Tan92]: 'Distributed systems need radically different software than do centralized systems'. This is the major technical reason why consortia such as the Object Management Group (OMG) and companies such as Microsoft have developed their own technologies for distributed computing.

We introduce three patterns related to distributed systems in this category:

- The *Pipes and Filters* pattern (53) provides a structure for systems that process a stream of data. Each processing step is encapsulated in a filter component. Data is passed through pipes between adjacent filters. Recombining filters allows you to build families of related systems.

  This pattern is more often used for structuring the functional core of an application than for distribution, so we describe it in a different category—see Section 2.2, *From Mud to Structure.*

- The *Microkernel* pattern (171) applies to software systems that must be able to adapt to changing system requirements. It separates a minimal functional core from extended functionality and customer-specific parts. The microkernel also serves as a socket for plugging in these extensions and coordinating their collaboration.

  Microkernel systems employ a Client-Server architecture in which clients and servers run on top of the microkernel component. The main benefit of such systems, however, is in design for adaptation and change. We therefore place the pattern description in another category—see Section 2.5, *Adaptable Systems.*

Platforms such as Microsoft OLE (Object Linking and Embedding) [Bro94] and OMG's CORBA (Common Object Request Broker Architecture) [OMG92] share a common software architecture, from which we have abstracted the Broker pattern:

- The *Broker* pattern (99) can be used to structure distributed software systems with decoupled components that interact by remote service invocations. A broker component is responsible for coordinating communication, such as forwarding requests, as well as for transmitting results and exceptions.

There are three groups of developers who can benefit by using the Broker pattern:

- Those working with an existing Broker system who are interested in understanding the architecture of such systems.

- Those who want to build 'lean' versions of a Broker system, without all the bells and whistles of a full-blown OLE or CORBA.

- Those who plan to implement a fully-fledged Broker system, and therefore need an in-depth description of the Broker architecture.

Broker

The *Broker* architectural pattern can be used to structure distributed software systems with decoupled components that interact by remote service invocations. A broker component is responsible for coordinating communication, such as forwarding requests, as well as for transmitting results and exceptions.

Example Suppose we are developing a city information system (CIS) designed to run on a wide area network. Some computers in the network host one or more services that maintain information about events, restaurants, hotels, historical monuments or public transportation. Computer terminals are connected to the network. Tourists throughout the city can retrieve information in which they are interested from the terminals using a World Wide Web (WWW) browser. This front-end software supports the on-line retrieval of information from the appropriate servers and its display on the screen. The data is distributed across the network, and is not all maintained in the terminals.

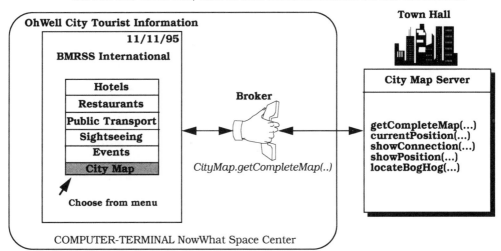

We expect the system to change and grow continuously, so the individual services should be decoupled from each other. In addition, the terminal software should be able to access services without having to know their location. This allows us to move, replicate, or migrate services. One solution is to install a separate network that connects all terminals and servers, leading to an *intranet* system. Such an approach, however, has several disadvantages: not every information provider wants to connect to a closed intranet, and even more importantly, available services should also be accessible from all over the world. We therefore decide to use the Internet as a better means of implementing the CIS system.

Context Your environment is a distributed and possibly heterogeneous system with independent cooperating components.

Problem Building a complex software system as a set of decoupled and inter-operating components, rather than as a monolithic application, results in greater flexibility, maintainability and changeability. By partitioning functionality into independent components the system becomes potentially distributable and scalable.

However, when distributed components communicate with each other, some means of inter-process communication is required. If components handle communication themselves, the resulting system faces several dependencies and limitations. For example, the system becomes dependent on the communication mechanism used, clients need to know the location of servers, and in many cases the solution is limited to only one programming language.

Services for adding, removing, exchanging, activating and locating components are also needed. Applications that use these services should not depend on system-specific details to guarantee portability and interoperability, even within a heterogeneous network.

From a developer's viewpoint, there should essentially be no difference between developing software for centralized systems and developing for distributed ones. An application that uses an object should only see the interface offered by the object. It should not need to know anything about the implementation details of an object, or about its physical location.

Use the Broker architecture to balance the following *forces*:

- Components should be able to access services provided by others through remote, location-transparent service invocations.

- You need to exchange, add, or remove components at run-time.

- The architecture should hide system- and implementation-specific details from the users of components and services.

Solution Introduce a *broker* component to achieve better decoupling of clients and servers. Servers register themselves with the broker, and make their services available to clients through method interfaces. Clients access the functionality of servers by sending requests via the broker. A broker's tasks include locating the appropriate server, forwarding the request to the server and transmitting results and exceptions back to the client.

By using the Broker pattern, an application can access distributed services simply by sending message calls to the appropriate object, instead of focusing on low-level inter-process communication. In addition, the Broker architecture is flexible, in that it allows dynamic change, addition, deletion, and relocation of objects.

The Broker pattern reduces the complexity involved in developing distributed applications, because it makes distribution transparent to the developer. It achieves this goal by introducing an object model in which distributed services are encapsulated within objects. Broker systems therefore offer a path to the integration of two core technologies: distribution and object technology. They also extend object models from single applications to distributed applications consisting of decoupled components that can run on heterogeneous machines and that can be written in different programming languages.

Structure The Broker architectural pattern comprises six types of participating components: *clients*, *servers*, *brokers*, *bridges*, *client-side proxies* and *server-side proxies*.

A *server*[10] implements objects that expose their functionality through interfaces that consist of operations and attributes. These interfaces are made available either through an interface definition language (IDL) or through a binary standard. The Implementation section contains a comparison of these approaches. Interfaces typically

---

10. In this pattern description *servers* are responsible for implementing services. In an object-oriented approach every service is realized by one or more *objects*. We use the term *server object* to emphasize the fact that such a server appears to other components as an object in the object-oriented sense.

group semantically-related functionality. There are two kinds of servers:

- Servers offering common services to many application domains.

- Servers implementing specific functionality for a single application domain or task.

➡   The servers in our CIS example comprise WWW servers that provide access to HTML (Hypertext Markup Language) pages. WWW servers. are implemented as httpd daemon processes (hypertext transfer protocol daemon) that wait on specific ports for incoming requests. When a request arrives at the server, the requested document and any additional data is sent to the client using data streams. The HTML pages contain documents as well as CGI (Common Gateway interface) scripts for remotely-executed operations on the network host—the remote machine from which the client received the HTML-page. A CGI script may be used to allow the user fill out a form and submit a query, for example a search request for vacant hotel rooms. To display animations on the client's WWW browser, Java 'applets' are integrated into the HTML documents. For example, one of these Java applets animates the route between one place and another on a city map. Java applets run on top of a virtual machine that is part of the WWW browser. CGI scripts and Java applets differ from each other: CGI scripts are executed on the server machine, whereas Java applets are transferred to the WWW browser and then executed on the client machine.   ❑

Clients are applications that access the services of at least one server. To call remote services, clients forward requests to the broker. After an operation has executed they receive responses or exceptions from the broker.

The interaction between clients and servers is based on a dynamic model, which means that servers may also act as clients. This dynamic interaction model differs from the traditional notion of Client-Server computing in that the roles of clients and servers are not statically defined. From the viewpoint of an implementation, you can consider clients as applications and servers as libraries—though other implementations are possible. Note that clients do not need to know the location of the servers they access. This is important, because it allows the addition of new services and the movement of existing services to other locations, even while the system is running.

➡　In the context of the Broker pattern, the clients are the available WWW browsers. They are not directly connected to the network. Instead, they rely on Internet providers that offer gateways to the Internet, such as Compuserve. WWW browsers connect to these workstations, using either a modem or a leased line. When connected they are able to retrieve data streams from httpd servers, interpret this data and initiate actions such as the display of documents on the screen or the execution of Java applets.　　　　　　　❏

Class Client	*Collaborators* • Client-side Proxy • Broker	*Class* Server	*Collaborators* • Server-side Proxy • Broker
Responsibility • Implements user functionality. • Sends requests to servers through a client-side proxy.		*Responsibility* • Implements services. • Registers itself with the local broker. • Sends responses and exceptions back to the client through a server-side proxy.	

A *broker* is a messenger that is responsible for the transmission of requests from clients to servers, as well as the transmission of responses and exceptions back to the client. A broker must have some means of locating the receiver of a request based on its unique system identifier. A broker offers APIs (Application Programming Interfaces) to clients and servers that include operations for registering servers and for invoking server methods.

When a request arrives for a server that is maintained by the local broker[11], the broker passes the request directly to the server. If the server is currently inactive, the broker activates it. All responses and exceptions from a service execution are forwarded by the broker to the client that sent the request. If the specified server is hosted by another broker, the local broker finds a route to the remote broker

---

11. In this pattern description we distinguish between *local* and *remote* brokers. A local broker is running on the machine currently under consideration. A remote broker is running on a remote network node.

and forwards the request using this route. There is therefore a need for brokers to interoperate.

Depending on the requirements of the whole system, additional services—such as *name services*[12] or *marshaling support*[13]—may be integrated into the broker.

Class	*Collaborators*
Broker	• Client
	• Server
Responsibility	• Client-side Proxy
• (Un-)registers servers.	• Server-side Proxy
• Offers APIs.	• Bridge
• Transfers messages.	
• Error recovery.	
• Interoperates with other brokers through bridges.	
• Locates servers.	

➥   A broker in our CIS example is the combination of an Internet gateway and the Internet infrastructure itself. Every information exchange between a client and a server must pass through the broker. A client specifies the information it wants using unique identifiers called URLs (Universal Resource Locators). By using these identifiers the broker is able to locate the required services and to route the requests to the appropriate server machines. When a new server machine is added, it must be registered with the broker. Clients and servers use the gateway of their Internet provider as an interface to the broker.   ❑

Client-side proxies represent a layer between clients and the broker. This additional layer provides transparency, in that a remote object appears to the client as a local one. In detail, the proxies allow the hiding of implementation details from the clients such as:

---

12. Name services provide associations between names and objects. To resolve a name, a name service determines which server is associated with a given name. In the context of Broker systems, names are only meaningful relative to a *name space*.

13. Marshaling is the semantic-invariant conversion of data into a machine-independent format such as ASN.1 (Abstract Syntax Notation) or ONC XDR (eXternal Data Representation). Unmarshaling performs the reverse transformation.

- The inter-process communication mechanism used for message transfers between clients and brokers.

- The creation and deletion of memory blocks.

- The marshaling of parameters and results.

In many cases, client-side proxies translate the object model specified as part of the Broker architectural pattern to the object model of the programming language used to implement the client.

Server-side proxies are generally analogous to Client-side proxies. The difference is that they are responsible for receiving requests, unpacking incoming messages, unmarshaling the parameters, and calling the appropriate service. They are used in addition for marshaling results and exceptions before sending them to the client.

Class Client-side Proxy	*Collaborators* • Client • Broker	*Class* Server-side Proxy	*Collaborators* • Server • Broker
Responsibility • Encapsulates system-specific functionality. • Mediates between the client and the broker.		*Responsibility* • Calls services within the server. • Encapsulates system-specific functionality. • Mediates between the server and the broker.	

When results or exceptions are returned from a server, the Client-side proxy receives the incoming message from the broker, unmarshals the data and forward it to the client.

➡   In our CIS example the WWW browsers and httpd servers such as Netscape provide built-in capabilities for communicating with the gateway of the Internet provider, so we do not need to worry about proxies in this case.   ❏

Bridges[14] are optional components used for hiding implementation details when two brokers interoperate. Suppose a Broker system runs on a heterogeneous network. If requests are transmitted over the

---

14. We call these components *Bridges* following the terminology of the OMG in the CORBA 2 specification.

network, different brokers have to communicate independently of the different network and operating systems in use. A bridge builds a layer that encapsulates all these system-specific details.

➡   Bridges are not required in our CIS example, because all httpd servers and WWW browsers implement the protocols necessary for remote data exchange such as http (hypertext transfer protocol) or ftp (file transfer protocol).   ❏

Class	*Collaborators*
Bridge	• Broker
	• Bridge
Responsibility	
• Encapsulates net-work-specific func-tionality.	
• Mediates between the local broker and the bridge of a remote broker.	

There are two different kinds of Broker systems: those using direct communication and those using indirect communication. To achieve better performance, some broker implementations only establish the initial communication link between a client and a server, while the rest of the communication is done directly between participating components—messages, exceptions and responses are transferred between client-side proxies and server-side proxies without using the broker as an intermediate layer. This direct communication approach requires that servers and clients use and understand the same protocol. In this pattern description we focus on the Indirect Broker variant, where all messages are passed through the broker. The Client-Dispatcher-Server pattern (323) describes the important aspects of the direct variant of the Broker pattern.

➡   Our CIS example implements the indirect communication variant, because browsers and servers can only collaborate using Inter-net gateways. There is one place in CIS however where we use the direct communication variant instead—Java applets loaded from the network may connect directly to the WWW server from which they came using a socket connection.   ❏

The following diagram shows the objects involved in a Broker system:

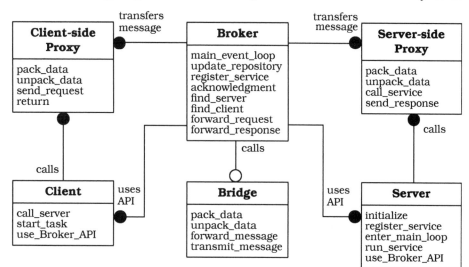

Dynamics   This section focuses on the most relevant scenarios in the operation of a Broker system.

Scenario I illustrates the behavior when a server registers itself with the local broker component:

- The broker is started in the initialization phase of the system. The broker enters its event loop and waits for incoming messages.

- The user, or some other entity, starts a server application. First, the server executes its initialization code. After initialization is complete, the server registers itself with the broker.

- The broker receives the incoming registration request from the server. It extracts all necessary information from the message and stores it into one or more repositories. These repositories are used to locate and activate servers. An acknowledgment is sent back.

- After receiving the acknowledgment from the broker, the server enters its main loop waiting for incoming client requests.

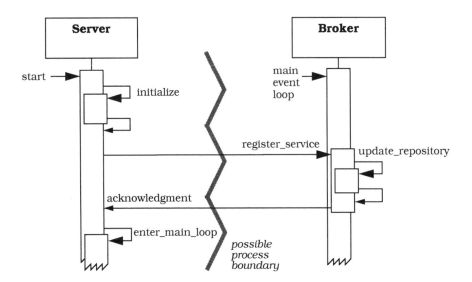

Scenario II illustrates the behavior when a client sends a request to a local server. In this scenario we describe a synchronous invocation, in which the client blocks until it gets a response from the server. The broker may also support asynchronous invocations, allowing clients to execute further tasks without having to wait for a response.

- The client application is started. During program execution the client invokes a method of a remote server object.

- The client-side proxy packages all parameters and other relevant information into a message and forwards this message to the local broker.

- The broker looks up the location of the required server in its repositories. Since the server is available locally, the broker forwards the message to the corresponding server-side proxy. For the remote case, see the following scenario.

- The server-side proxy unpacks all parameters and other information, such as the method it is expected to call. The server-side proxy invokes the appropriate service.

- After the service execution is complete, the server returns the result to the server-side proxy, which packages it into a message with other relevant information and passes it to the broker.

- The broker forwards the response to the client-side proxy.
- The client-side proxy receives the response, unpacks the result and returns to the client application. The client process continues with its computation.

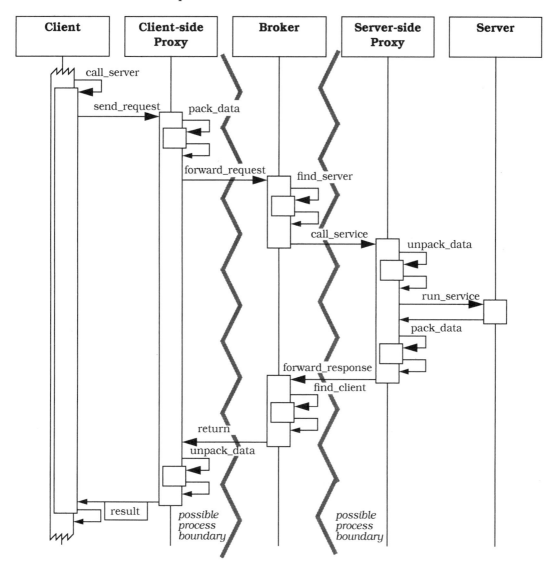

Scenario III illustrates the interaction of different brokers via bridge components:

- Broker A receives an incoming request. It locates the server responsible for executing the specified service by looking it up in the repositories. Since the corresponding server is available at another network node, the broker forwards the request to a remote broker.

- The message is passed from Broker A to Bridge A. This component is responsible for converting the message from the protocol defined by Broker A to a network-specific but common protocol understood by the two participating bridges. After message conversion, Bridge A transmits the message to Bridge B.

- Bridge B maps the incoming request from the network-specific format to a Broker B-specific format.

- Broker B performs all the actions necessary when a request arrives, as described in the first step of this scenario.

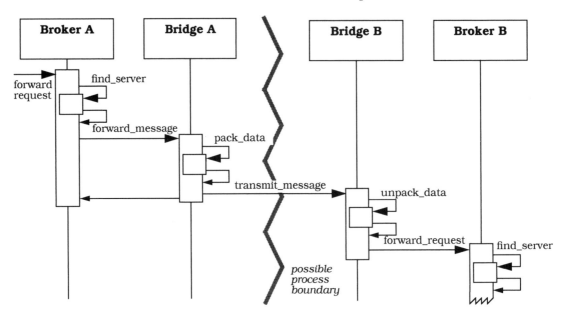

Implementation   To implement this pattern, carry out the following steps:

1   *Define an object model, or use an existing model.* Your choice of object model has a major impact on all other parts of the system under development. Each object model must specify entities such as object names, objects, requests, values, exceptions, supported types, type extensions, interfaces and operations. In this first step you should only consider semantic issues. If the object model has to be extensible, prepare the system for future enhancements. For example, specify a basic object model and how it can be refined systematically using extensions. More information on this topic is available in [OMG92].

The description of the underlying computational model is a key issue in designing an object model. You need to describe definitions of the state of server objects, definitions of methods, how methods are selected for execution and how server objects are generated and destroyed. The state of server objects and their method implementations should not be directly accessible to clients. Clients may only change or read the server's state indirectly by passing requests to the local broker. With this separation of interfaces and server implementations the so-called 'remoting' of interfaces becomes possible—clients use the client-side proxies as server interfaces that are completely decoupled from the server implementations, and thus from the concrete implementations of the server interfaces.

2   *Decide which kind of component-interoperability the system should offer.* You can design for interoperability either by specifying a binary standard or by introducing a high-level interface definition language (IDL). An IDL file contains a textual description of the interfaces a server offers to its clients. The binary approach needs support from your programming language. For example, binary method tables are available in Microsoft Object Linking and Embedding (OLE) [Bro94]. These tables consist of pointers to method implementations, and enable clients to call methods indirectly using pointers. Access to OLE objects is only supported by compilers or interpreters that know the physical structure of these tables.

In contrast to the binary approach, the IDL approach is more flexible in that an IDL mapping may be implemented for any programming language. Sometimes both approaches are used in combination, as in IBM's System Object Model (SOM) [Cam94].

An IDL compiler uses an IDL file as input and generates programming-language code or binary code. One part of this generated code is required by the server for communicating with its local broker, another part is used by the client for communicating with its local broker. The broker may use the IDL specification to maintain type information about existing server implementations.

Whenever interoperability is provided as a binary standard, every semantic concept of the object model must be associated with a binary representation. However, if you supply an interface definition language for interoperability, you can map the semantic concepts to programming language representations. For example, object handles may be represented by C++ pointers and data types may be mapped to appropriate C++ types.

One question remains—when should a Broker system expose interfaces with an interface definition language, and when by a binary standard? The rationale for the first approach is to gain more flexibility for the broker's implementation—every implementation of the Broker architecture may define its own protocol for the interaction between the broker and other components. It is the task of the IDL to provide a mapping to the local broker protocol. When following a binary approach, you need to define binary representations such as method tables for invoking remote services. This often leads to greater efficiency, but requires all brokers to implement the same kind of protocol when communicating with clients and servers.

3   *Specify the APIs the broker component provides for collaborating with clients and servers.* On the client side, functionality must be available for constructing requests, passing them to the broker and receiving responses. Decide whether clients should only be able to invoke server operations statically, allowing clients to bind the invocations at compile-time. If you want to allow dynamic invocations[15] of servers as well, this has a direct impact on the size or number of APIs. For example, you need some way of asking the broker about existing server objects. You can implement this with the help of a meta-level schema, as described in the Reflection pattern (193).

---

15. Dynamic invocations are method calls that are dynamically constructed at runtime using API functions as well as type information. In contrast, static invocations are hard-coded into the source code.

You have to offer operations to clients, so that they are capable of constructing requests at run-time. The server implementations use API functions primarily for registering with the broker. Brokers use repositories to maintain the information. These repositories may be available as external files, so that servers can register themselves before system start-up. Another approach is to implement the repository as an internal part of the broker component. Here, the broker must offer an API that allows servers to register at run-time. Since the broker needs to identify these servers when requests arrive, an appropriate identification mechanism is necessary. In other words, the broker component is responsible for associating server object identifiers with server object implementations. The server-side API of the broker must therefore be able to generate system-unique identifiers.

If clients, servers and the broker are running as distinct processes, the API functions need to be based on an efficient mechanism for inter-process communication between clients, servers and the local broker.

4   *Use proxy objects to hide implementation details from clients and servers.* On the client side, a local proxy (263) object represents the remote server object called by the client. On the server side, a proxy is used for playing the role of the client. Proxy objects have the following responsibilities:

- Client-side proxies package procedure calls into messages and forward these messages to the local broker component. In addition, they receive responses and exceptions from the local broker and pass them to the calling client. You must specify an internal message protocol for communication between proxy and broker to support this.

- Server-side proxies receive requests from the local broker and call the methods in the interface implementation of the corresponding server. They forward server responses and exceptions to the local broker after packaging them, according to an internal message protocol.

Note that proxies are always part of the corresponding client or server process.

Proxies hide implementation details by using their own inter-process communication mechanism to communicate with the broker component. They may also implement the marshaling and unmarshaling of parameters and results into/from a system-independent format.

If you follow the IDL approach for interoperability, proxy objects are automatically available, because they can be generated by an IDL compiler. If you use a binary approach, the creation and deletion of proxy objects can happen dynamically.

5   *Design the broker component* in parallel with steps 3 and 4. In this step we describe how to develop a broker component that acts as a messenger for every message passed from a client to a server and vice-versa. To increase the performance of the whole system, some implementations do not transmit messages via the broker. In these systems most of the work is done by the proxies, while the broker is still responsible for establishing the initial communication link between clients and servers. A direct communication between client and server is only possible when both of them can use the same protocol. We call such systems *Direct Communication Broker systems* (see Variants section).

During design and implementation, iterate systematically through the following steps:

5.1   Specify a detailed *on-the-wire* protocol for interacting with client-side proxies and server-side proxies. Plan the mapping of requests, responses, and exceptions to your internal message protocol. In an on-the-wire protocol, the internal message protocol handles the mapping of higher-level structures such as parameter values, method names and return values to corresponding structures specified by the underlying inter-process communication mechanism.

5.2   A local broker must be available for every participating machine in the network. If requests, responses or exceptions are transferred from one network node to another, the corresponding local brokers must communicate with each other using an on-the-wire protocol. Use bridges to hide details such as network protocols and operating system specifics from the broker. The broker must also maintain a repository to locate the remote brokers or gateways to which it forwards messages. You may encode the routing information for finding remote brokers as a part of the server or client identifier. Broadcast communication is another (potentially inefficient) way to locate the network node where a server or client resides.

5.3   When a client invokes a method of a server, the Broker system is responsible for returning all results and exceptions back to the original client. In other words, the system must remember which client has sent the request. In the *Direct Communication variant* (see the Variants section) there is no need to remember the originator of an invocation, because the client and the server are directly connected through a communication channel. In Indirect Broker systems you can choose between different means of remembering the sender of a request. For example, you may specify the client's address as an additional, invisible parameter of the request or message.

5.4   If the proxies (see step 4) do not provide mechanisms for marshaling and unmarshaling parameters and results, you must include that functionality in the broker component.

5.5   If your system supports asynchronous communication between clients and servers, you need to provide *message buffers* within the broker or within the proxies for the temporary storage of messages.

5.6   Include a *directory service* for associating local server identifiers with the physical location of the corresponding servers in the broker. For example, if the underlying inter-process communication protocol is based on TCP/IP, you could use an Internet port number as the physical server location.

5.7   When your architecture requires system-unique identifiers to be generated dynamically during server registration, the broker must offer a *name service* for instantiating such names.

5.8   If your system supports *dynamic method invocation* (see step 3), the broker needs some means for maintaining type information about existing servers. A client may access this information using the broker APIs to construct a request dynamically. You can implement such type information by instantiating the Reflection pattern (193). In this, metaobjects maintain type information that is accessible by a metaobject protocol.

5.9   Consider the case in which something fails. In a distributed system two levels of errors may occur:

- A component such as a server may run into an error condition. This is the same kind of error you encounter when executing conventional non-distributed applications.

- The communication between two independent processes may fail. Here the situation is more complicated, since the communicating components are running asynchronously.

Plan the broker's actions when the communication with clients, other brokers or servers fails. For example, some brokers resend a request or response several times until they succeed. If you use an *at-most-once semantic*[16], you have to make sure that a request is only executed once even if it is resent. Do not forget the case in which a client tries to access a server that either does not exist, or which the client is not allowed to access. Error handling is an important topic when implementing a distributed system. If you forget to handle errors in a systematic way, testing and debugging of client applications and servers becomes an extremely tedious job.

6   *Develop IDL compilers.* Whenever you implement interoperability by providing an interface definition language, you need to build an *IDL compiler* for every programming language you support. An IDL compiler translates the server interface definitions to programming language code. When many programming languages are in use, it is best to develop the compiler as a *framework* that allows the developer to add his own code generators.

Example Resolved   Our example CIS system offers different kinds of services. For example, a separate server workstation provides all the information related to public transport. Another server is responsible for collecting and publishing information on vacant hotel rooms. A tourist may be interested in retrieving information from several

---

16. When supporting at-most-once semantics your system has to guarantee that any request either fails, or is executed only once. If you implement other semantics instead such as *at-least-once*, the same request may be resent and executed several times. This strategy is only applicable to *idempotent* services, where overall consistency is not damaged by executing a service more than once. A typical example of an idempotent service is a function that assigns an initial value to a variable.

hotels, so we decide to provide this data on a single workstation. Every hotel can connect to the workstation and perform updates.

A tourist is capable of booking hotel rooms on-line from anywhere in the Internet using CGI scripts. Payments for hotel reservations are charged on-line by credit card. For security reasons we include encryption mechanisms for such transactions. Additional httpd servers are available to provide extra services such as flight booking or train reservations, the ordering of tickets or the retrieval of information about museums and other places of interest.

Each CIS terminal executes a WWW browser. This allows use to use inexpensive PCs and Internet PCs as terminals. The httpd servers run on fast UNIX and Windows NT workstations to guarantee short response times.

Variants *Direct Communication Broker System.* You may sometimes choose to relax the restriction that clients can only forward requests through the local broker for efficiency reasons. In this variant clients can communicate with servers directly. The broker tells the clients which communication channel the server provides. The client can then establish a direct link to the requested server. In such systems, the proxies take over the broker's responsibility for handling most of the communication activities. A similar argument applies to *off-board* communication: here clients address the remote broker directly, using bridges when appropriate, as opposed to sending requests to their local broker for forwarding to the remote server's broker.

Message Passing Broker System. This variant is suitable for systems that focus on the transmission of data, instead of implementing a Remote Procedure Call abstraction[17]. Using this variant, servers use the type of a message to determine what they must do, rather than offering services that clients can invoke. In this context, a message is a sequence of raw data together with additional information that specifies the type of a message, its structure and other relevant attributes.

Trader System. A client request is usually forwarded to exactly one uniquely-identified server. In some circumstances, services and not

---

17. Brokers offering RPC (Remote Procedure Call) interfaces are typically built using message-passing interfaces.

servers are the targets to which clients send their requests. In a Trader system, the broker must know which server(s) can provide the service, and forward the request to an appropriate server. Client-side proxies therefore use *service identifiers* instead of server identifiers to access server functionality. The same request might be forwarded to more than one server implementing the same service.

Adapter Broker System. You can hide the interface of the broker component to the servers using an additional layer, to enhance flexibility. This *adapter* layer is a part of the broker and is responsible for registering servers and interacting with servers. By supplying more than one adapter, you can support different strategies for server granularity and server location. For example, if all the server objects accessed by an application are located on the same machine and are implemented as library objects, a special adapter could be used to link the objects directly to the application. Another example is the use of an object-oriented database for maintaining objects. Since the database is responsible for providing methods and storing objects, there may be no need to register objects explicitly. In such a scenario, you could provide a special database adapter. See also [OMG92].

Callback Broker System. Instead of implementing an active communication model in which clients produce requests and servers consume them, you can also use a *reactive* model. The reactive model is event-driven, and makes no distinction between clients and servers. Whenever an event arrives, the broker invokes the callback method of the component that is registered to react to the event. The execution of the method may generate new events that in turn cause the broker to trigger new callback method invocations. For more details on this variant, see [Sch94].

There are several ways of combining the above variants. For example, you can implement a Direct Communication Broker system and combine it with the Trader variant. In such a system an incoming client request causes the broker to select one server among those that provide the requested service. The broker then establishes a direct link between the client and the selected server.

Known Uses   **CORBA**. The Broker architectural pattern was used to specify the Common Object Request Broker Architecture (CORBA) defined by the Object Management Group. CORBA is an object-oriented technology for distributing objects on heterogeneous systems. An interface definition language is available to support the interoperability of client and server objects [OMG92]. Many CORBA implementations realize the *Direct Communication Broker System* variant, for example IONA Technologies' Orbix [Iona95].

IBM **SOM/DSOM**. [Cam94] represents a CORBA-compliant Broker system. In contrast to many other CORBA implementations, it implements interoperability by combining the CORBA interface definition language with a binary protocol. SOM's binary approach supports subclassing from existing binary parent classes. You can implement a class in SOM in one programming language and derive a subclass from it in another language.

Microsoft's **OLE 2.x** technology provides another example of the use of the Broker architectural pattern. While CORBA guarantees interoperability using an interface definition language, OLE 2.x defines a binary standard for exposing and accessing server interfaces [Bro94].

The **World Wide Web** is the largest available Broker system in the world. Hypertext browsers such as HotJava, Mosaic, and Netscape act as brokers and WWW servers play the role of service providers.

ATM-P. We implemented the *Message Passing Broker System* variant [ATM93] in a Siemens in-house project to build a telecommunication switching system based on ATM (Asynchronous Transfer Mode).

Consequences The Broker architectural pattern has some important **benefits**:

Location Transparency. As the broker is responsible for locating a server by using a unique identifier, clients do not need to know where servers are located. Similarly, servers do not care about the location of calling clients, as they receive all requests from the local broker component.

Changeability and extensibility of components. If servers change but their interfaces remain the same, it has no functional impact on clients. Modifying the internal implementation of the broker, but not the APIs it provides, has no effect on clients and servers other than performance changes. Changes in the communication mechanisms used for the interaction between servers and the broker, between clients and the broker, and between brokers may require you to recompile clients, servers or brokers. However, you will not need to change their source code. Using proxies and bridges is an important reason for the ease with which changes can be implemented.

Portability of a Broker system. The Broker system hides operating system and network system details from clients and servers by using indirection layers such as APIs, proxies and bridges. When porting is required, it is therefore sufficient in most cases to port the broker component and its APIs to a new platform and to recompile clients and servers. Structuring the broker component into layers is recommended, for example according to the Layers architectural pattern (31). If the lower-most layers hide system-specific details from the rest of the broker, you only need to port these lower-most layers, instead of completely porting the broker component.

Interoperability between different Broker systems. Different Broker systems may interoperate if they understand a common protocol for the exchange of messages. This protocol is implemented and handled by bridges, which are responsible for translating the broker-specific protocol into the common protocol, and vice versa.

Reusability. When building new client applications, you can often base the functionality of your application on existing services. Suppose you are going to develop a new business application. If components that offer services such as text editing, visualization, printing, database access or spreadsheets are already available, you do not need to implement these services yourself. It may instead be sufficient to integrate these services into your applications.

The Broker architectural pattern imposes some **liabilities**:

Restricted efficiency. Applications using a Broker implementation are usually slower than applications whose component distribution is static and known. Systems that depend directly on a concrete mechanism for inter-process communication also give better performance than a Broker architecture, because Broker introduces indirection layers to enable it to be portable, flexible and changeable.

Lower fault tolerance. Compared with a non-distributed software system, a Broker system may offer lower fault tolerance. Suppose that a server or a broker fails during program execution. All the applications that depend on the server or broker are unable to continue successfully. You can increase reliability through replication of components.

The following aspect gives **benefits** as well as **liabilities**:

Testing and Debugging. A client application developed from tested services is more robust and easier itself to test. However, debugging and testing a Broker system is a tedious job because of the many components involved. For example, the cooperation between a client and a server can fail for two possible reasons—either the server has entered an error state, or there is a problem somewhere on the communication path between client and server.

See also The *Forwarder-Receiver* pattern (307) encapsulates inter-process communication between two components. On the client side a *forwarder* receives a request and addressee from the client and handles the mapping to the IPC (inter-process communication) facility used. The receiver on the server side unpacks and delivers the message to the server. There is no broker component in this pattern. It is simpler to implement and results in smaller implementations than the Broker pattern, but is also less flexible.

The *Proxy* pattern (263) comes in several flavors, the *remote* case being one of them. A remote proxy is often used in conjunction with a forwarder. The proxy encapsulates the interface and remote address of the server. The forwarder takes the message and transforms it into IPC-level code.

The *Client-Dispatcher-Server* pattern (323) is a lightweight version of the Direct Communication Broker variant. A *dispatcher* allocates, opens and maintains a direct channel between client and server.

The *Mediator* design pattern [GHJV95] replaces a web of inter–object connections by a star configuration in which the central *mediator* component encapsulates collective behavior by defining a common interface for communicating with objects. As with the Broker pattern, the Mediator pattern uses a hub of communication, but it also has several major differences. The Broker pattern is a large-scale infra-structure paradigm—it is not used for building single applications, but rather serves as a platform for whole families of applications. It is not restricted to processing local computation, and dispatches and monitors requests without regard to the sender or the content of the request. In contrast, the Mediator pattern encapsulates application semantics by checking what a request is about and possibly where it came from—only then does it decide what to do. It may return a message to the sender, fulfill the request on its own, or involve more than one other component.

Credits   We wish to thank the participants of the workshop on patterns for concurrent and distributed systems at OOPSLA '95 for reviewing the Broker pattern. Special credit is due to Jim Coplien, David DeLano, Doug Schmidt and Steve Vinoski, who reviewed early version of the Broker description and contributed several fruitful suggestions and hints.

2.4 Interactive Systems

Today's systems allow a high degree of user interaction, mainly achieved with help of graphical user interfaces. The objective is to enhance the usability of an application. Usable software systems provide convenient access to their services, and therefore allow users to learn the application and produce results quickly.

When specifying the architecture of such systems, the challenge is to keep the functional core independent of the user interface. The core of interactive systems is based on the functional requirements for the system, and usually remains stable. User interfaces, however, are often subject to change and adaptation. For example, systems may have to support different user interface standards, customer-specific 'look and feel' metaphors, or interfaces that must be adjusted to fit into a customer's business processes. This requires architectures that support the adaptation of user interface parts without causing major effects to application-specific functionality or the data model underlying the software.

We describe two patterns that provide a fundamental structural organization for interactive software systems:

- The *Model-View-Controller* pattern (MVC) (125) divides an interactive application into three components. The model contains the core functionality and data. Views display information to the user. Controllers handle user input. Views and controllers together comprise the user interface. A change-propagation mechanism ensures consistency between the user interface and the model.

- The *Presentation-Abstraction-Control* pattern (PAC) (145) defines a structure for interactive software systems in the form of a hierarchy of cooperating agents. Every agent is responsible for a specific aspect of the application's functionality and consists of three components: presentation, abstraction, and control. This subdivision separates the human-computer interaction aspects of the agent from its functional core and its communication with other agents.

MVC provides probably the best-known architectural organization for interactive software systems. It was pioneered by Trygve Reenskaug [RWL96] and first implemented within the Smalltalk-80 environment [KP88]. It underlies many interactive systems and application frameworks for software systems with graphical user interfaces, such as MacApp [App89], ET++ [Gam91], and of course the Smalltalk libraries. Even Microsoft's Foundation Class Library [Kru96] follows the principles of MVC.

However, it is not our intention to explain the Smalltalk MVC implementation—many details of Smalltalk's MVC implementation are left out to give a clearer understanding of the underlying principles. Few readers will create a new framework for MVC, but are more likely to use an existing framework, or to partition their application following the key principles of MVC.

PAC is not used as widely as MVC, but this does not mean that it is not worth describing. As an alternative approach for structuring interactive applications, PAC is especially applicable to systems that consist of several self-reliant subsystems. PAC also addresses issues that MVC leaves unresolved, such as how to effectively organize the communication between different parts of the functional core and the user interface. PAC was first described by Joelle Coutaz [Cou87]. The first application of PAC was in the area of Artificial Intelligence [Cro85].

Model-View-Controller

The *Model-View-Controller* architectural pattern (MVC) divides an interactive application into three components. The model contains the core functionality and data. Views display information to the user. Controllers handle user input. Views and controllers together comprise the user interface. A change-propagation mechanism ensures consistency between the user interface and the model.

Example   Consider a simple information system for political elections with proportional representation. This offers a spreadsheet for entering data and several kinds of tables and charts for presenting the current results. Users can interact with the system via a graphical interface. All information displays must reflect changes to the voting data immediately.

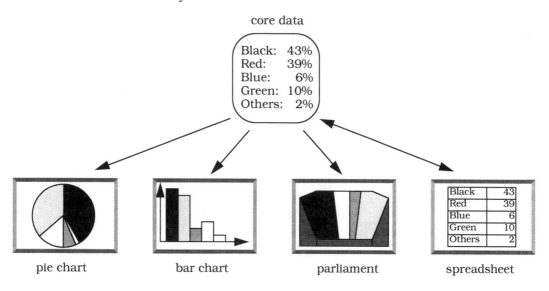

It should be possible to integrate new ways of data presentation, such as the assignment of parliamentary seats to political parties, without major impact to the system. The system should also be portable to platforms with different 'look and feel' standards, such as workstations running Motif or PCs running Microsoft Windows 95.

Context Interactive applications with a flexible human-computer interface.

Problem User interfaces are especially prone to change requests. When you extend the functionality of an application, you must modify menus to access these new functions. A customer may call for a specific user interface adaptation, or a system may need to be ported to another platform with a different 'look and feel' standard. Even upgrading to a new release of your windowing system can imply code changes. The user interface platform of long-lived systems thus represents a moving target.

Different users place conflicting requirements on the user interface. A typist enters information into forms via the keyboard. A manager wants to use the same system mainly by clicking icons and buttons. Consequently, support for several user interface paradigms should be easily incorporated.

Building a system with the required flexibility is expensive and error-prone if the user interface is tightly interwoven with the functional core. This can result in the need to develop and maintain several substantially different software systems, one for each user interface implementation. Ensuing changes spread over many modules. The following *forces* influence the solution:

- The same information is presented differently in different windows, for example, in a bar or pie chart.

- The display and behavior of the application must reflect data manipulations immediately.

- Changes to the user interface should be easy, and even possible at run-time.

- Supporting different 'look and feel' standards or porting the user interface should not affect code in the core of the application.

Solution Model-View-Controller (MVC) was first introduced in the Smalltalk-80 programming environment [KP88]. MVC divides an interactive application into the three areas: *processing*, *output*, and *input*.

The *model* component encapsulates core data and functionality. The model is independent of specific output representations or input behavior.

View components display information to the user. A view obtains the data from the model. There can be multiple views of the model.

Each view has an associated *controller* component. Controllers receive input, usually as events that encode mouse movement, activation of mouse buttons, or keyboard input. Events are translated to service requests for the model or the view. The user interacts with the system solely through controllers.

The separation of the model from view and controller components allows multiple views of the same model. If the user changes the model via the controller of one view, all other views dependent on this data should reflect the changes. The model therefore notifies all views whenever its data changes. The views in turn retrieve new data from the model and update the displayed information. This change-propagation mechanism is described in the Publisher-Subscriber pattern (339).

Structure The *model* component contains the functional core of the application. It encapsulates the appropriate data, and exports procedures that perform application-specific processing. Controllers call these procedures on behalf of the user. The model also provides functions to access its data that are used by view components to acquire the data to be displayed.

The change-propagation mechanism maintains a registry of the dependent components within the model. All views and also selected controllers register their need to be informed about changes. Changes to the state of the model trigger the change-propagation mechanism. The change-propagation mechanism is the only link between the model and the views and controllers.

Class	*Collaborators*
Model	• View
	• Controller
Responsibility	
• Provides functional core of the application.	
• Registers dependent views and controllers.	
• Notifies dependent components about data changes.	

View components present information to the user. Different views present the information of the model in different ways. Each view defines an update procedure that is activated by the change-propagation mechanism. When the update procedure is called, a view retrieves the current data values to be displayed from the model, and puts them on the screen.

During initialization all views are associated with the model, and register with the change-propagation mechanism. Each view creates a suitable controller. There is a one-to-one relationship between views and controllers. Views often offer functionality that allows controllers to manipulate the display. This is useful for user-triggered operations that do not affect the model, such as scrolling.

The *controller* components accept user input as events. How these events are delivered to a controller depends on the user interface platform. For simplicity, let us assume that each controller implements an event-handling procedure that is called for each relevant event. Events are translated into requests for the model or the associated view.

If the behavior of a controller depends on the state of the model, the controller registers itself with the change-propagation mechanism and implements an update procedure. For example, this is necessary when a change to the model enables or disables a menu entry.

Class View	*Collaborators* • Controller • Model
Responsibility • Creates and initializes its associated controller. • Displays information to the user. • Implements the update procedure. • Retrieves data from the model.	

Class Controller	*Collaborators* • View • Model
Responsibility • Accepts user input as events. • Translates events to service requests for the model or display requests for the view. • Implements the update procedure, if required.	

An object-oriented implementation of MVC would define a separate class for each component. In a C++ implementation, view and controller classes share a common parent that defines the update interface. This is shown in the following diagram. In Smalltalk, the class Object defines methods for both sides of the change-propagation mechanism. A separate class Observer is not needed.

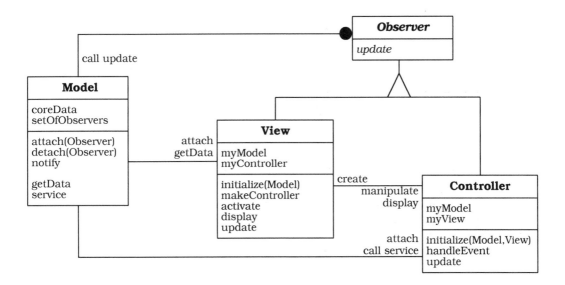

➥   In our example system the model holds the cumulative votes for each political party and allows views to retrieve vote numbers. It further exports data manipulation procedures to the controllers.

We define several views: a bar chart, a pie chart and a table. The chart views use controllers that do not affect the model, whereas the table view connects to a controller used for data entry.   ❑

You can also use the MVC pattern to build a framework for interactive applications, as within the Smalltalk-80 environment [KP88]. Such a framework offers prefabricated view and controller subclasses for frequently-used user interface elements such as menus, buttons, or lists. To instantiate the framework for an application, you can combine existing user interface elements hierarchically using the Composite pattern [GHJV95].

Dynamics   The following scenarios depict the dynamic behavior of MVC. For simplicity only one view-controller pair is shown in the diagrams.

Scenario I shows how user input that results in changes to the model triggers the change-propagation mechanism:

- The controller accepts user input in its event-handling procedure, interprets the event, and activates a service procedure of the model.

- The model performs the requested service. This results in a change to its internal data.

- The model notifies all views and controllers registered with the change-propagation mechanism of the change by calling their update procedures.

- Each view requests the changed data from the model and re-displays itself on the screen.

- Each registered controller retrieves data from the model to enable or disable certain user functions. For example, enabling the menu entry for saving data can be a consequence of modifications to the data of the model.

- The original controller regains control and returns from its event-handling procedure.

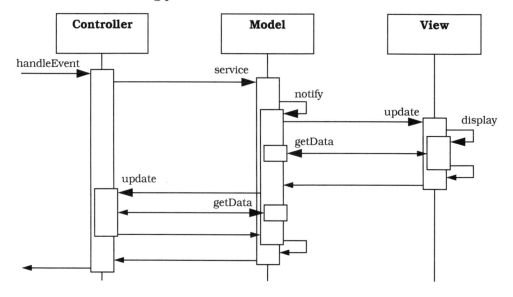

Scenario II shows how the MVC triad is initialized. This code is usually located outside of the model, views and controllers, for example in a main program. The view and controller initialization occurs similarly for each view opened for the model. The following steps occur:

- The model instance is created, which then initializes its internal data structures.

- A view object is created. This takes a reference to the model as a parameter for its initialization.

- The view subscribes to the change-propagation mechanism of the model by calling the attach procedure.

- The view continues initialization by creating its controller. It passes references both to the model and to itself to the controller's initialization procedure.

- The controller also subscribes to the change-propagation mechanism by calling the attach procedure.

- After initialization, the application begins to process events.

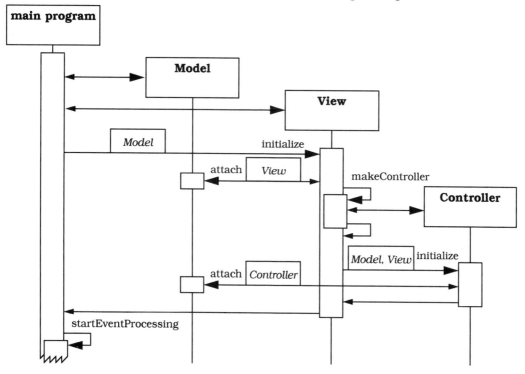

Implementation   Steps 1 through 6 below are fundamental to writing an MVC-based application. Steps 7 through 10 describe additional topics that result in higher degrees of freedom, and lend themselves to highly flexible applications or application frameworks.

1   *Separate human-computer interaction from core functionality.* Analyze the application domain and separate the core functionality from the desired input and output behavior. Design the model component of your application to encapsulate the data and functionality needed for the core. Provide functions for accessing the data to be displayed. Decide which parts of the model's functionality are to be exposed to the user via the controller, and add a corresponding interface to the model.

➡   The model in our example stores the names of the political parties and the corresponding votes in two lists of equal length[18]. Access to the lists is provided by two methods, each of which creates an iterator. The model also provides methods to change the voting data.

```
class Model{
    List<long>   votes;
    List<String> parties;
public:
    Model(List<String> partyNames);

// access interface for modification by controller
    void clearVotes(); // set voting values to 0
    void changeVote(String party, long vote);

// factory functions for view access to data
    Iterator<long>   makeVoteIterator(){
        return Iterator<long>(votes);
    }
    Iterator<String> makePartyIterator(){
        return Iterator<String>(parties);
    }
// ... to be continued
}                                                                              ❏
```

2   *Implement the change-propagation mechanism.* Follow the Publisher-Subscriber design pattern (339) for this, and assign the role of the publisher to the model. Extend the model with a registry that holds references to observing objects. Provide procedures to allow views and

---

18. An associative array with party names as keys and votes as the information would be a more realistic implementation but would bloat the example code.

controllers to subscribe and unsubscribe to the change-propagation mechanism. The model's notify procedure calls the update procedure of all observing objects. All procedures of the model that change the model's state call the notify procedure after a change is performed.

➥ Proper C++ usage suggests that one should define an abstract class Observer to hold the update interface. Both views and controllers inherit from Observer. The Model class from step 1 is extended to hold a set of references to current observers, and two methods, attach() and detach(), to allow observing objects to subscribe and unsubscribe. The method notify() will be called by methods that modify the state of the model.

```
class Observer{ // common ancestor for view and controller
public:
    virtual void update() { }
// default is no-op
};

class Model{
// ... continued
public:
    void attach(Observer *s) { registry.add(s); }
    void detach(Observer *s) { registry.remove(s); }
protected:
    virtual void notify();
private:
    Set<Observer*> registry;
};
```

Our implementation of the method notify() iterates over all Observer objects in the registry and calls their update method. We do not provide a separate function to create an iterator for the registry, because it is only used internally.

```
void Model::notify(){
    // call update for all observers
    Iterator<Observer*> iter(registry);
    while (iter.next()){
        iter.curr()->update();
    }
}
```

The methods changeVote() and clearVotes() call notify() after the voting data is changed. ❏

3   *Design and implement the views.* Design the appearance of each view. Specify and implement a draw procedure to display the view on the screen. This procedure acquires the data to be displayed from the model. The rest of the draw procedure depends mainly on the user interface platform. It would call, for example, procedures for drawing lines or rendering text.

Implement the update procedure to reflect changes to the model. The easiest approach is to simply call the draw procedure. The draw procedure goes ahead and fetches data needed for the view. For a complex view requiring frequent updates, such a straightforward implementation of update can be inefficient. Several optimization strategies exist in this situation. One is to supply additional parameters to the update procedure. The view can then decide if a re-draw is needed. Another solution is to schedule, but not perform, the re-draw of the view when it is likely that further events also require it. The view can then be redrawn when no more events are pending.

In addition to the update and draw procedures, each view needs an initialization procedure. The initialization procedure subscribes to the change-propagation mechanism of the model and sets up the relationship to the controller, as shown in step 5. After the controller is initialized, the view displays itself on the screen. The platform or the controller may require additional view capabilities, such as a procedure to resize a view window.

➡   For all the views used by the election system we define a common base class View. The relationships to model and controller are represented by two member variables with corresponding access methods. The constructor of View establishes the relationship to the model by subscribing to the change-propagation mechanism. The destructor removes it again by unsubscribing. View also provides a simple non-optimized update() implementation.

```
class View : public Observer {
public:
    View(Model *m) : myModel(m), myController(0)
        { myModel->attach(this); }
    virtual ~View() { myModel->detach(this); }
    virtual void update() { this->draw(); }
    // abstract interface to be redefined:
    virtual void initialize() ;// see below
    virtual void draw() ;      // (re-)display view
// ... to be continued below
```

```
      Model *getModel() { return myModel; }
      Controller *getController() { return myController; }
protected:
      Model          *myModel;
      Controller     *myController; // set by initialize
};

class BarChartView : public View {
public:
      BarChartView(Model *m) : View(m) { }
      virtual void draw();
};

void BarChartView::draw(){
      Iterator<String> ip = myModel->makePartyIterator();
      Iterator<long> iv = myModel->makeVoteIterator();
      List<long> dl; //for scaling values to fill screen
      long      max = 1;// maximum for adjustment

      // calculate maximum vote count
      while (iv.next()) {
          if (iv.curr() > max ) max = iv.curr();
      }
      iv.reset();
      // now calculate screen coordinates for bars
      while (iv.next()) {
          dl.append((MAXBARSIZE * iv.curr())/max);
      }

      // reuse iterator object for new collection:
      iv = dl; // assignment rebinds iterator to new list
      iv.reset();

      while (ip.next() && iv.next()) {
          // draw text: cout << ip.curr() << " : " ;
          // draw bar: ... drawbox(BARWIDTH, iv.curr());...
      }
}
```

The class definition of BarChartView demonstrates a specific view of our system. It redefines draw() to show the voting data as a bar chart.   ❑

4   *Design and implement the controllers.* For each view of the application, specify the behavior of the system in response to user actions. We assume that the underlying platform delivers every action of a user as an event. A controller receives and interprets these events using a dedicated procedure. For a non-trivial controller, this interpretation depends on the state of the model.

The initialization of a controller binds it to its model and view and enables event processing. How this is achieved depends on the user-interface platform. For example, the controller may register its event-handling procedure with the window system as a callback.

➡   Most views in our example do not require any specific event processing—they are only used for display. We therefore define a base class `Controller` with an empty `handleEvent()` method. The constructor attaches the controller to its model and the destructor detaches it again.

```cpp
class Controller : public Observer {
public:
    virtual void handleEvent(Event *) { }
        // default = no op

    Controller( View *v) : myView(v) {
        myModel = myView->getModel();
        myModel->attach(this);
    }

    virtual ~Controller() { myModel->detach(this); }
    virtual void update() { } // default = no op
protected:
    Model    *myModel;
    View     *myView;
};
```

We omit a separate controller initialization method, because the relationship to the view and the model is already set up by its constructor.   ❑

Calling the functional core closely links a controller with the model, since the controller becomes dependent on the application-specific model interface. If you plan to modify functionality, or if you want to provide reusable controllers and therefore would like the controller to be independent of a specific interface, apply the Command Processor (277) design pattern. The model takes the role of the supplier of the Command Processor pattern. The command classes and the command processor component are additional components between controller and model. The MVC controller has the role of controller in Command Processor.

5   *Design and implement the view-controller relationship.* A view typically creates its associated controller during its initialization. When you build a class hierarchy of views and controllers, apply the Factory Method design pattern [GHJV95] and define a method makeController() in the view classes. Each view that requires a controller that differs from its superclass redefines the factory method.

➥   In our C++ example the View base class implements a method initialize() that in turn calls the factory method makeController(). We cannot put the call to makeController() into the constructor of the View class, because then a subclass' redefined makeController() would not be called as desired. The only View subclass that requires a specific controller is TableView. We redefine makeController() to return a TableController to accept data from the user.

```cpp
class View : public Observer {
// ... continued
public:
//C++ deficit: use initialize to call right factory method
    virtual void initialize()
        { myController = makeController();}
    virtual Controller *makeController()
        { return new Controller(this); }
};

class TableController : public Controller {
public:
    TableController(TableView *tv) : Controller(tv) {}
    virtual void handleEvent(Event *e) {
    // ... interpret event e,
    //      for instance, update votes of a party
        if(vote && party){ // entry complete:
            myModel->changeVote(party,vote);
        }
    }
};
class TableView : public View {
public:
    TableView(Model *m) : View(m) { }
    virtual void draw();
    virtual Controller *makeController()
        { return new TableController(this); }
};
```
❑

6   *Implement the set-up of MVC.* The set-up code first initializes the model, then creates and initializes the views. After initialization, event processing is started, typically in a loop, or with a procedure that includes a loop, such as XtMainLoop() from the X Toolkit. Because the model should remain independent of specific views and controllers, this set-up code should be placed externally, for example, in a main program.

➥   In our simple example the main function initializes the model and several views. The event processing delivers events to the controller of the table view, allowing the entry and change of voting data.

```
main() {
    // initialize model
    List<String> parties;       parties.append("black");
    parties.append("blue ");  parties.append("red  ");
    parties.append("green");  parties.append("oth. ");
    Model m(parties);

    // initialize views
    TableView *v1 = new TableView(&m);
    v1->initialize();
    BarChartView *v2 = new BarChartView(&m);
    v2->initialize();
    // now start event processing ...                        ❑
```

7   *Dynamic view creation.* If the application allows dynamic opening and closing of views, it is a good idea to provide a component for managing open views. This component, for example, can also be responsible for terminating the application after the last view is closed. Apply the View Handler (291) design pattern to implement this view management component.

8   *'Pluggable' controllers.* The separation of control aspects from views supports the combination of different controllers with a view. This flexibility can be used to implement different modes of operation, such as casual user versus expert, or to construct read-only views using a controller that ignores any input. Another use of this separation is the integration of new input and output devices with an application. For example, a controller for an eye-tracking device for disabled people can exploit the functionality of the existing model and views, and is easily incorporated into the system.

➥   In our example only the class TableView supports several controllers. The default controller TableController allows the user to enter voting data. For display-only purposes, `TableView` can be configured with a controller that ignores all user input. The code below shows how a controller is substituted for another controller. Note that `setController` returns the previously-used controller object. Here the controller object is no longer used and so it is deleted immediately.

```
class View : public Observer{
// ... continued
public:
    virtual Controller *setController(Controller *ctlr);
};

main()
// ...
    // exchange controller
    delete v1->setController(
        new Controller(v1)); // this one is read only
// ...
    // open another read-only table view;
    TableView *v3 = new TableView(&m);
    v3->initialize();
    delete v3->setController(
        new Controller(v3)); // make v3 read-only
    // continue event processing
// ...
}                                                                            ❑
```

9   *Infrastructure for hierarchical views and controllers.* A framework based on MVC implements reusable view and controller classes. This is commonly done for user interface elements that are applied frequently, such as buttons, menus, or text editors. The user interface of an application is then constructed largely by combining predefined view objects. Apply the Composite pattern [GHJV95] to create hierarchically composed views. If multiple views are active simultaneously, several controllers may be interested in events at the same time. For example, a button inside a dialog box reacts to a mouse click, but not to the letter 'a' typed on the keyboard. If the parent dialog view also contains a text field, the 'a' is sent to the controller of the text view. Events are distributed to event-handling routines of all active controllers in some defined sequence. Use the Chain of Responsibility pattern [GHJV95] to manage this delegation of events. A controller will pass an unprocessed event to the controller of the parent view or to the controller of a sibling view if the chain of responsibility is set up properly.

10 *Further decoupling from system dependencies.* Building a framework with an elaborate collection of view and controller classes is expensive. You may want to make these classes platform independent. This is done in some Smalltalk systems. You can provide the system with another level of indirection between it and the underlying platform by applying the Bridge pattern [GHJV95]. Views use a class named *display* as an abstraction for windows and controllers use a *sensor* class.

The abstract class *display* defines methods for creating a window, drawing lines and text, changing the look of the mouse cursor and so on. The *sensor* abstraction defines platform-independent events, and each concrete *sensor* subclass maps system-specific events to platform-independent events. For each platform supported, implement concrete *display* and *sensor* subclasses that encapsulate system specifics.

The design of the abstract classes *display* and *sensor* is non-trivial, because it impacts both the efficiency of the resulting code, and the efficiency with which the concrete classes can be implemented on the different platforms. One approach is to use *sensor* and *display* abstractions with only the very basic functionality that is provided directly by all user-interface platforms. The other extreme is to have *display* and *sensor* offer higher-level abstractions. Such classes need greater effort to port, but use more native code from the user-interface platform. The first approach leads to applications that look similar across platforms, while the second results in applications that conform better to platform-specific guidelines.

Variants *Document-View.* This variant relaxes the separation of view and controller. In several GUI platforms, window display and event handling are closely interwoven. For example, the X Window System reports events relative to a window. You can combine the responsibilities of the view and the controller from MVC in a single component by sacrificing exchangeability of controllers. This kind of structure is often called a Document-View architecture [App89], [Gam91], [Kru96]. The document component corresponds to the model in MVC, and also implements a change-propagation mechanism. The view component of Document-View combines the responsibilities of controller and view in MVC, and implements the user interface of the system. As in MVC, loose coupling of the document and view components enables multiple simultaneous synchronized but different views of the same document.

Known Uses   **Smalltalk** [GR83]. The best-known example of the use of the Model-View-Controller pattern is the user-interface framework in the Smalltalk environment [LP91], [KP88]. MVC was established to build reusable components for the user interface. These components are shared by the tools that make up the Smalltalk development environment. However, the MVC paradigm turned out to be useful for other applications developed in Smalltalk as well. The VisualWorks Smalltalk environment supports different 'look and feel' standards by decoupling view and controllers via *display* and *sensor* classes, as described in implementation step 10.

MFC [Kru96]. The Document-View variant of the Model-View-Controller pattern is integrated in the Visual C++ environment—the Microsoft Foundation Class Library—for developing Windows applications.

ET++ [Gam91]. The application framework ET++ also uses the Document-View variant. A typical ET++-based application implements its own document class and a corresponding view class. ET++ establishes 'look and feel' independence by defining a class `WindowPort` that encapsulates the user interface platform dependencies, in the same way as do our *display* and *sensor* classes.

Consequences   The application of Model-View-Controller has several **benefits**:

Multiple views of the same model. MVC strictly separates the model from the user-interface components. Multiple views can therefore be implemented and used with a single model. At run-time, multiple views may be open at the same time, and views can be opened and closed dynamically.

Synchronized views. The change-propagation mechanism of the model ensures that all attached observers are notified of changes to the application's data at the correct time. This synchronizes all dependent views and controllers.

'Pluggable' views and controllers. The conceptual separation of MVC allows you to exchange the view and controller objects of a model. User interface objects can even be substituted at run-time.

Exchangeability of 'look and feel'. Because the model is independent of all user-interface code, a port of an MVC application to a new platform does not affect the functional core of the application. You only need suitable implementations of view and controller components for each platform.

Framework potential. It is possible to base an application framework on this pattern, as sketched in implementation steps 7 through 10. The various Smalltalk development environments have proven this approach.

The **liabilities** of MVC are as follows:

Increased complexity. Following the Model-View-Controller structure strictly is not always the best way to build an interactive application. Gamma [Gam91] argues that using separate model, view and controller components for menus and simple text elements increases complexity without gaining much flexibility.

Potential for excessive number of updates. If a single user action results in many updates, the model should skip unnecessary change notifications. It may be that not all views are interested in every change-propagated by the model. For example, a view with an iconized window may not need an update until the window is restored to its normal size.

Intimate connection between view and controller. Controller and view are separate but closely-related components, which hinders their individual reuse. It is unlikely that a view would be used without its controller, or vice-versa, with the exception of read-only views that share a controller that ignores all input.

Close coupling of views and controllers to a model. Both view and controller components make direct calls to the model. This implies that changes to the model's interface are likely to break the code of both view and controller. This problem is magnified if the system uses a multitude of views and controllers. You can address this problem by applying the Command Processor pattern (277), as described in the Implementation section, or some other means of indirection.

Inefficiency of data access in view. Depending on the interface of the model, a view may need to make multiple calls to obtain all its display data. Unnecessarily requesting unchanged data from the model weakens performance if updates are frequent. Caching of data within the view improves responsiveness.

Inevitability of change to view and controller when porting. All dependencies on the user-interface platform are encapsulated within view and controller. However, both components also contain code that is independent of a specific platform. A port of an MVC system thus requires the separation of platform-dependent code before rewriting. In the case of an MVC framework or a large composed application, an additional encapsulation of platform dependencies may be required.

Difficulty of using MVC with modern user-interface tools. If portability is not an issue, using high-level toolkits or user interface builders can rule out the use of MVC. It is usually expensive to retrofit toolkit components or the output of user interface layout tools to MVC. Additional wrapping would be the minimum requirement. In addition, many high-level tools or toolkits define their own flow of control and handle some events internally, such as displaying a pop-up menu or scrolling a window. Finally, a high-level user interface platform may already interpret events and offer callbacks for each kind of user activity. Most controller functionality is therefore already provided by the toolkit, and a separate component is not needed.

See Also The Presentation-Abstraction-Control pattern (145) takes a different approach to decoupling the user-interface aspects of a system from its functional core. Its abstraction component corresponds to the model in MVC, and the view and controller are combined into a presentation component. Communication between abstraction and presentation components is decoupled by the control component. The interaction between presentation and abstraction is not limited to calling an update procedure, as it is within MVC.

Credits Trygve Reenskaug created MVC and introduced it to the Smalltalk environment [RWL96].

Presentation-Abstraction-Control

The *Presentation-Abstraction-Control* architectural pattern (PAC) defines a structure for interactive software systems in the form of a hierarchy of cooperating agents. Every agent is responsible for a specific aspect of the application's functionality and consists of three components: presentation, abstraction, and control. This subdivision separates the human-computer interaction aspects of the agent from its functional core and its communication with other agents.

Example Consider a simple information system for political elections with proportional representation. This offers a spreadsheet for entering data and several kinds of tables and charts for presenting current standings. Users interact with the software through a graphical interface.

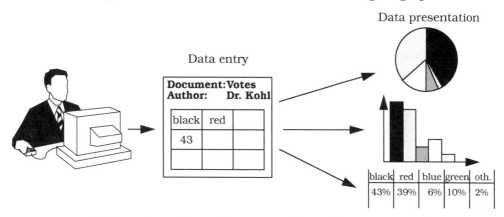

Different versions, however, adapt the user interface to specific needs. For example, one version supports additional views of the data, such as the assignment of parliament seats to political parties.

Context Development of an interactive application with the help of agents[19].

19. In the context of this pattern an *agent* denotes an information-processing component that includes event receivers and transmitters, data structures to maintain state, and a processor that handles incoming events, updates its own state, and that may produce new events [BaCo91]. Agents can be as small as a single object, but also as complex as a complete software system. We use the terms *agent* and *PAC agent* as synonyms in this pattern description.

Problem   Interactive systems can often be viewed as a set of cooperating agents. Agents specialized in human-computer interaction accept user input and display data. Other agents maintain the data model of the system and offer functionality that operates on this data. Additional agents are responsible for diverse tasks such as error handling or communication with other software systems. Besides this horizontal decomposition of system functionality, we often encounter a vertical decomposition. Production planning systems (PPS), for example, distinguish between production planning and the execution of a previously specified production plan. For each of these tasks separate agents can be defined.

In such an architecture of cooperating agents, each agent is specialized for a specific task, and all agents together provide the system functionality. This architecture also captures both a horizontal and vertical decomposition. The following *forces* affect the solution:

- Agents often maintain their own state and data. For example, in a PPS system, the production planning and the actual production control may work on different data models, one tuned for planning and simulation and one performance-optimized for efficient production. However, individual agents must effectively cooperate to provide the overall task of the application. To achieve this, they need a mechanism for exchanging, data, messages, and events.

- Interactive agents provide their own user interface, since their respective human-computer interactions often differ widely. For example, entering data into spreadsheets is done using keyboard input, while the manipulation of graphical objects uses a pointing device.

- Systems evolve over time. Their presentation aspect is particularly prone to change. The use of graphics, and more recently, multimedia features, are examples of pervasive changes to user interfaces. Changes to individual agents, or the extension of the system with new agents, should not affect the whole system.

Solution   Structure the interactive application as a tree-like hierarchy of *PAC agents*. There should be one top-level agent, several intermediate-level agents, and even more bottom-level agents. Every agent is responsible for a specific aspect of the application's functionality, and consists of three components: presentation, abstraction, and control.

The whole hierarchy reflects transitive dependencies between agents. Each agent depends on all higher-level agents up the hierarchy to the top-level agent.

The agent's *presentation* component provides the visible behavior of the PAC agent. Its *abstraction* component maintains the data model that underlies the agent, and provides functionality that operates on this data. Its *control* component connects the presentation and abstraction components, and provides functionality that allows the agent to communicate with other PAC agents.

The *top-level PAC agent* provides the functional core of the system. Most other PAC agents depend or operate on this core. Furthermore, the top-level PAC agent includes those parts of the user interface that cannot be assigned to particular subtasks, such as menu bars or a dialog box displaying information about the application.

Bottom-level PAC agents represent self-contained semantic concepts on which users of the system can act, such as spreadsheets and charts. The bottom-level agents present these concepts to the user and support all operations that users can perform on these agents, such as zooming or moving a chart.

Intermediate-level PAC agents represent either combinations of, or relationships between, lower-level agents. For example, an intermediate-level agent may maintain several views of the same data, such as a floor plan and an external view of a house in a CAD system for architecture.

➡   Our information system for political elections defines a top-level PAC agent that provides access to the data repository underlying the system. The data repository itself is not part of the application. At the bottom level we specify four PAC agents: one spreadsheet agent for entering data, and three view agents for each type of diagram for representing the data. The application has one intermediate-level PAC agent. This coordinates the three bottom-level view agents and keeps them consistent. The spreadsheet agent is directly connected to the top-level PAC agent. Users of the system only interact with bottom-level agents.

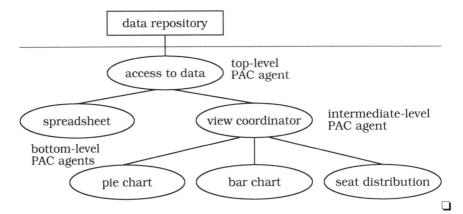

Structure The main responsibility of the top-level PAC agent is to provide the global data model of the software. This is maintained in the abstraction component of the top-level agent. The interface of the abstraction component offers functions to manipulate the data model and to retrieve information about it. The representation of data within the abstraction component is media-independent. For example, in a CAD system for architecture, walls, doors, and windows are represented in centimeters or inches that reflect their real size, not in pixels for display purposes. This media-independency supports adaptation of the PAC agent to different environments without major changes in its abstraction component.

The presentation component of the top-level agent often has few responsibilities. It may include user-interface elements common to the whole application. In some systems, such as the network traffic manager [TS93], there is no top-level presentation component at all.

The control component of the top-level PAC agent has three responsibilities:

- It allows lower-level agents to make use of the services of the top-level agents, mostly to access and manipulate the global data model. Incoming service requests from lower-level agents are forwarded either to the abstraction component or the presentation component.

- It coordinates the hierarchy of PAC agents. It maintains information about connections between the top-level agent and lower-level agents. The control component uses this information to ensure correct collaboration and data exchange between the top-level agent and lower-level agents.

- It maintains information about the interaction of the user with the system. For example, it may check whether a particular operation can be performed on the data model when triggered by the user. It may also keep track of the functions called to provide history or undo/redo services for operations on the functional core.

➠ In our example information system for political elections, the abstraction component of the top-level PAC agent provides an application-specific interface to the underlying data repository. It implements functions for reading and writing election data. It also implements all functions that operate on the election data, such as algorithms for calculating projections and seat distributions. It further includes functions for maintaining data, such as those for updating and consistency checking. The control component organizes communication and cooperation with lower-level agents, namely the view coordinator and spreadsheet agents. This top-level PAC agent does not include a presentation component. ❑

Bottom-level PAC agents represent a specific semantic concept of the application domain, such as a mailbox in a network traffic management system [TS93] or a wall in a mobile robot system [Cro85]. This semantic concept may be as low-level as a simple graphical object such as a circle, or as complex as a bar chart that summarizes all the data in the system.

The presentation component of a bottom-level PAC agent presents a specific view of the corresponding semantic concept, and provides access to all the functions users can apply to it. Internally, the presentation component also maintains information about the view, such as its position on the screen.

The abstraction component of a bottom-level PAC agent has a similar responsibility as the abstraction component of the top-level PAC agent, maintaining agent-specific data. In contrast to the abstraction component of the top-level agent, however, no other PAC agents depend on this data.

The control component of a bottom-level PAC agent maintains consistency between the abstraction and presentation components, thereby avoiding direct dependencies between them. It serves as an adapter and performs both interface and data adaptation.

The control component of bottom-level PAC agents communicates with higher-level agents to exchange events and data. Incoming events—such as a 'close window' request—are forwarded to the presentation component of the bottom-level agent, while incoming data is forwarded to its abstraction component. Outgoing events and data, for example error messages, are sent to the associated higher-level agent.

Concepts represented by bottom-level PAC agents, such as the bar and pie charts in the example, are atomic in the sense that they are the smallest units a user can manipulate. For the election system this means that users can only operate on the bar chart as a whole, for instance by changing the scaling factor of the y-axis. They cannot, for example, resize an individual bar of a bar chart.

Bottom-level PAC agents are not restricted to providing semantic concepts of the application domain. You can also specify bottom-level agents that implement system services. For example, there may be a communication agent that allows the system to cooperate with other applications and to monitor this cooperation.

➡   Consider a bar-chart agent in our information system for political elections. Its abstraction component saves the election data presented in the chart, and maintains chart-specific information such as the order of presentation for the data. The presentation component is responsible for displaying the bar chart in a window, and for providing all the functions that can be applied to it, such as zooming, moving, and printing. The control component serves as a level of indirection between the presentation and abstraction components. The control component is also responsible for the bar-chart agent's communication with the view coordinator agent.   ❏

Intermediate-level PAC agents can fulfill two different roles: *composition* and *coordination*. When, for example, each object in a complex graphic is represented by a separate PAC agent, an intermediate-level agent groups these objects to form a composite graphical object. The intermediate-level agent defines a new abstraction, whose behavior encompasses both the behavior of its components and the new characteristics that are added to the composite object. The second role of an intermediate-level agent is to maintain consistency between lower-level agents, for example when coordinating multiple views of the same data.

The abstraction component maintains the specific data of the intermediate-level PAC agent. The presentation component implements its user interface. The control component has the same responsibilities of the control components of bottom-level PAC agents and of the top-level PAC agent.

➡ Our example information system for political elections defines one intermediate-level PAC agent. Its presentation component provides a palette that allows users to create views of the election data, such as bar or pie charts. The abstraction component maintains data about all currently-active views, each of which is realized by its own bottom-level agent. The main responsibility of the control component is to coordinate all subordinate agents. It forwards incoming notifications about data model changes taking place in the top-level agent to the bottom-level agents, and organizes their update. It also includes functionality to create and delete bottom-level agents on user request. ❑

Class Top-level Agent	*Collaborators*
Responsibility • Provides the functional core of the system. • Controls the PAC hierarchy.	• Intermediate-level Agent • Bottom-level Agent

Class Interm. -level Agent	*Collaborators*
Responsibility • Coordinates lower-level PAC agents. • Composes lower-level PAC agents to a single unit of higher abstraction.	• Top-level Agent • Intermediate-level Agent • Bottom-level Agent

Class Bottom-level Agent	*Collaborators*
Responsibility • Provides a specific view of the software or a system service, including its associated human-computer interaction.	• Top-level Agent • Intermediate-level Agent

The following OMT diagram illustrates the PAC hierarchy of the information system for political elections. However, it only lists those functions that are necessary for controlling and coordinating the PAC hierarchy, or which are accessible to other PAC agents or to the user. We keep the interfaces of PAC agents small by applying the Composite Message pattern [SC95b]. All incoming service requests, events, and data are handled by a single function called `receiveMsg()`. This interprets messages and routes them to their intended recipient, which may be the abstraction or presentation components of the agent, or of another agent. Similarly, the function `sendMsg()` is used to pack and deliver service requests, events, and data to other agents. Another approach would be to provide an agent-specific interface that includes all the services the agent offers. The consequences of both these approaches are discussed in the Implementation section.

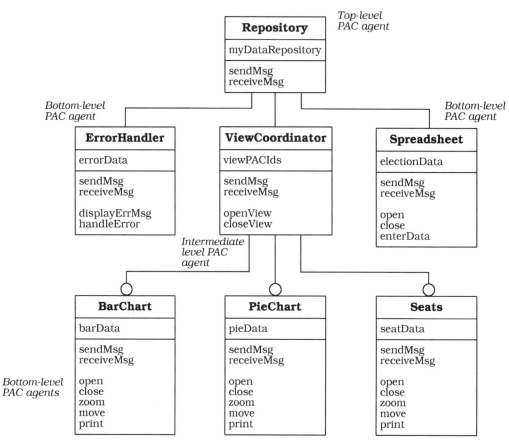

The internal structure of a PAC agent is shown below, using the bar-chart agent from our example:

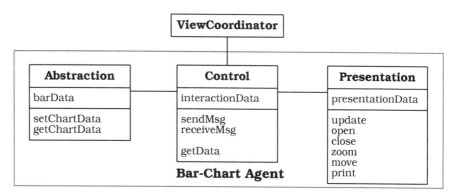

Dynamics   We will illustrate the behavior of a PAC architecture with two scenarios, both based on our election system example.

Scenario I describes the cooperation between different PAC agents when opening a new bar-chart view of the election data. The scenario also includes a more detailed description of the internal behavior of the bar-chart agent. It is divided into five phases:

- A user asks the presentation component of the view coordinator agent to open a new bar chart.

- The control of the view coordinator agent instantiates the desired bar-chart agent.

- The view coordinator agent sends an 'open' event to the control component of the new bar-chart agent.

- The control component of the bar-chart agent first retrieves data from the top-level PAC agent. The view coordinator agent mediates between bottom and top-level agents. The data returned to the bar-chart agent is saved in its abstraction component. Its control component then calls the presentation component to display the chart.

- The presentation component creates a new window on the screen, retrieves data from the abstraction component by requesting it from the control component, and finally displays it within the new window.

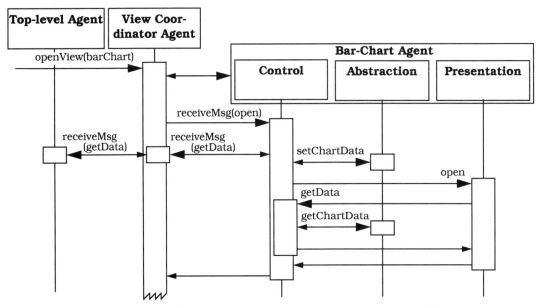

There are obvious optimizations possible here, such as caching top-level data in the view coordinator, or calling the bottom-level presentation component first and then storing the data. At this point, however, our emphasis is on explaining the basic ideas of the pattern.

Scenario II shows the behavior of the system after new election data is entered, providing a closer look at the internal behavior of the top-level PAC agent. It has five phases:

- The user enters new data into a spreadsheet. The control component of the spreadsheet agent forwards this data to the top-level PAC agent.

- The control component of the top-level PAC agent receives the data and tells the top-level abstraction to change the data repository accordingly. The abstraction component of the top-level agent asks its control component to update all agents that depend on the new data. The control component of the top-level PAC agent therefore notifies the view coordinator agent.

- The control component of the view coordinator agent forwards the change notification to all view PAC agents it is responsible for coordinating.

- As in the previous scenario, all view PAC agents then update their data and refresh the image they display.

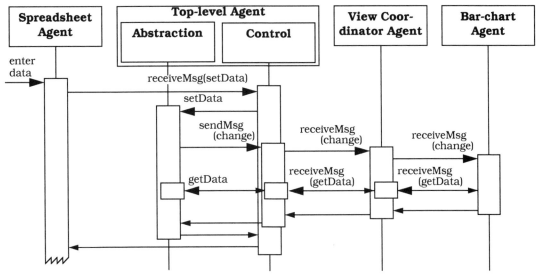

Implementation   To implement a PAC architecture, carry out the following ten steps, repeating any step or group of steps as necessary.

1   *Define a model of the application.* Analyze the problem domain and map it onto an appropriate software structure. Do not consider the distribution of components to PAC agents when performing this step. Concentrate on finding a proper decomposition and organization of the application domain. To this end, answer the following questions:

- Which services should the system provide?

- Which components can fulfill these services?

- What are the relationships between components?

- How do the components collaborate?

- What data do the components operate on?

- How will the user interact with the software?

Follow an appropriate analysis method when specifying the model.

2   *Define a general strategy for organizing the PAC hierarchy.* At this point we have not yet defined individual agents, but can specify general guidelines for organizing the hierarchy of cooperating agents.

One rule to follow is that of 'lowest common ancestor'. When a group of lower-level agents depends on the services or data provided by another agent, we try to specify this agent as the root of the subtree formed by the lower-level agents. As a consequence only agents that provide global services rise to the top of the hierarchy. For example, all agents in the election system depend on the central data repository. This is therefore provided by the top-level PAC agent. If only a fraction of all agents depend on the repository, we would try to group them into a subtree and define an agent holding the repository at the root of that subtree.

A second aspect to consider is the depth of the hierarchy. Most PAC architectures comprise several intermediate levels of PAC agents. In the Mobile Robot system [Cro85], for example, bottom-level agents are composed to environments which again are composed to workspaces —this is covered in more detail in the description of the Mobile Robot system in the Known Uses section. The deeper the hierarchy, the better it often reflects the decomposition of an application into self-contained concepts. On the other hand, deep hierarchies tend to be inefficient at run-time, and also hard to maintain. Finding the appropriate decomposition of a system into PAC agents is important to be able to gain the benefits of this architecture.

3   *Specify the top-level PAC agent.* Identify those parts of the analysis model that represent the functional core of the system. These are mostly components that maintain the global data model of the system, and components directly operating on this data. Identify also all user interface elements that are common to the whole application, such as menu bars or dialogs with information about the system. All components identified in this step will be part of the top-level agent.

4   *Specify the bottom-level PAC agents.* Identify those components of the analysis model that represent the smallest self-contained units of the system on which the user can perform operations or view presentations. In our example system, these units are the various diagrams and charts presenting election data, and the spreadsheet for entering this data.

For each of these units, identify those components that provide the human-computer interaction associated with them. The bar chart in our example requires a window in which the diagram is displayed, and functionality to manipulate the diagram, such as zooming and printing. Each semantic concept such as a bar chart and its user interface components together form a separate bottom-level agent.

5 *Specify bottom-level PAC agents for system services.* Often an application includes additional services that are not directly related to its primary subject. In our example system we define an error handler. Other systems may provide services for communicating with other systems or for configuration purposes. Each of these services, including their human-computer interaction, can be implemented as a separate bottom-level agent [BaCo91].

6 *Specify intermediate-level PAC agents to compose lower-level PAC agents.* Often, several lower-level agents together form a higher-level semantic concept on which users can operate.

In the mobile robot system described in [Cro85], several wall, place, and route PAC agents form an environment. Users of the system can specify new environments, and missions for robots within environments. Environments are displayed on the screen, and users perform actions such as scrolling and zooming on these presentations. An environment is therefore a higher-level concept with its own functionality and human-computer interaction. Such concepts are implemented as separate agents. They provide their own human-computer interaction, and operate on their constituent lower-level agents.

➥ Our election example does not provide semantic concepts above individual charts, diagrams, and spreadsheets. Therefore we do not define PAC agents for composing other PAC agents. ❏

7 *Specify intermediate-level PAC agents to coordinate lower-level PAC agents.* Many systems offer multiple views of the same semantic concept. For example, in text editors you find 'layout' and 'edit' views of a text document. When the data in one view changes, all other views must be updated. Such coordination components, which you may have identified when modeling the analysis model, provide their own human-computer interaction; for example, menu entries and associated callback functions. The view coordinator agent of our example system is such an intermediate-level agent. To implement agents that coordinate multiple views you may apply the View Handler pattern (291).

Note that views are not the only aspect of an application that must be coordinated. The network traffic management system described in the

Known Uses section [TS93], for example, implements an agent that coordinates the different concurrent jobs the system performs in a telecommunication network.

8   *Separate core functionality from human-computer interaction.* For every PAC agent, introduce presentation and abstraction components. All components that provide the user interface of the agent, such as graphical images presented to the user, presentation-specific data like screen coordinates, or menus, windows, and dialogs form the presentation part. All components that maintain core data or operate on them form the abstraction.

You can provide a unified interface to the abstraction and presentation components of a PAC agent by applying the Facade pattern [GHJV95]. The control component exports those parts of the abstraction and presentation interfaces that other components can use.

For some PAC agents it may be hard to specify presentation or abstraction parts. For example, top-level PAC agents often do not provide a presentation component. [BaCo91] suggest the implementation of the top-level presentation as a general geometry manager that maintains spatial relationships between the presentation components of lower-level PAC agents. You can apply the Command Processor pattern (277) to further organize the presentation component. This allows you to schedule user requests for deferred or prioritized execution, and to provide agent-specific undo/redo services.

Some abstraction components, especially those in lower-level agents, often operate on data provided by other PAC agents. In this case, you may either not specify an abstraction component, or design the application such that the abstraction component just serves as a data cache. In the first case, you save all the effort of implementing components to keep replica data, and the functionality to keep these replica consistent. In the latter case, you save additional communication effort between PAC agents, for example when refreshing a view after a window is moved.

Finally, introduce the control component to mediate between the abstraction and presentation components, and to avoid direct dependencies between them. The control component is implemented as an Adapter [GHJV95]. It links the presentation and abstraction components together by performing interface and data adaptation between them. In this step, do not consider the parts of the control component that deal with the communication between the agent and other PAC agents. That is a different role of the control component, and should therefore be separated from the mediation between the agent internal abstraction and presentation components.

➡ To illustrate this step in our example, we refine the bar-chart agent from the example, as described in the Structure section. The abstraction component keeps a copy of the election data displayed in the bar chart.

The presentation component is structured into components that provide the functionality of windowing, menus, dialogs, and of maintaining presentation-specific data. To shield clients from this structure we provide a Facade [GHJV95].

The control component of the pie chart PAC agent is simple. It just forwards data read requests from the presentation component to the abstraction component. Communication with higher-level agents is handled in the next step.

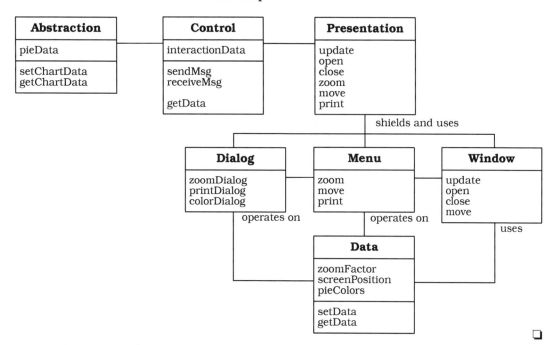

9   *Provide the external interface.* To cooperate with other agents, every PAC agent sends and receives events and data. Implement this functionality as part of the control component.

Within an agent, incoming events or data are forwarded to their intended recipient. The recipient may be the abstraction or the presentation component of the agent, but may also be lower or higher-level agents. For example, the view coordinator agent of our information system regularly receives change notifications from the top-level PAC agent and forwards them to the view agents. It also receives requests from lower-level agents that are forwarded to the top-level agent. In other words, the control component is a mediator—you may use the Mediator pattern [GHJV95] to implement this role.

One way of implementing communication with other agents is to apply the Composite Message pattern [SC95b]. This keeps the interface of an agent small. It also allows agents to be independent of the specific interfaces of other agents, and also of particular data formats, marshaling, unmarshaling, fragmentation and re-assembling methods. Applying the Composite Message pattern requires, however, that the control component interprets incoming messages. It must decide what to do with them—calling the abstraction or presentation components, or forwarding the message to another agent. This functionality is usually very complex and hard to implement.

A second option is to provide a public interface that offers every service of an agent as a separate function. These functions 'know' how to handle data and events when called. Compared to the Composite Message solution, this reduces the inner complexity of the control component, but introduces additional dependencies between agents—they depend on the specific interfaces of other agents. In addition, in this approach the interface of an agent can 'explode'. For example, an intermediate-level agent must offer all the functions of the top-level agent that are called by its associated lower-level agents. Vice versa, the intermediate-level agent must offer all the services of its associated lower-level agents that are called by the top-level agent. The interface of an agent may become complex and hard to maintain as a result.

A PAC agent can be connected to other PAC agents in a flexible and dynamic way by using *registration functionality*, as introduced by the Publisher-Subscriber pattern (339). For example, if a new instance of the bar-chart agent in our election system is created, it is dynamically registered with the view coordinator agent.

If a PAC agent depends on data or information maintained by other PAC agents, you should provide a change-propagation mechanism. Such a mechanism should involve all agents and all levels of the hierarchy and work in both directions. When changes to data occur within an agent, its abstraction component starts the change propagation. The control component forwards change notifications to all dependent PAC agents, but often also to the presentation component. Incoming change notifications from other agents cause the abstraction and presentation components to update their internal states. One way to implement such a change-propagation mechanism is to use the Publisher-Subscriber pattern (339). Another way is to integrate change propagation with the general functionality for sending and receiving events, messages, and data; see the example code below.

The interface for these communication and cooperation functions should be the same for all PAC agents. This supports re-configuration and reuse of PAC agents, and the extension of the application with new PAC agents.

➡ The control component of the view coordinator PAC agent in our election example provides the following interface:

```
enum ViewKind { barChart, pieChart, seats };
    // type of available views of election data
class DataSetInterface { /* ... */ };
    // Common interface for datasets, messages, and
    // events, according to the specifications of the
    // Composite Message pattern [SC95b]
class PACId { /* ... */ };
    // Provides a handle to a PAC agent
class VCControl {
    // Data member specifications
    PACId        parent;  // higher-level agent
    List<PACId>  children;// lower-level agents
    // More data member specifications ...
private:
    void attach(PACId agent, parentAgent = 0);
    void detach(PACId agent);
        // Registration functionality for connecting
        // dependent view agents and the top-level agent
        // with the view coordinator agent.
```

```
        DataSetInterface sendMsg(DataSetInterface data);
                // Sending events, messages, or data to other PAC
                // agents including change notifications
        void openView(ViewKind kind);
        void closeView(PACId agent);
                // Opening and closing views including
                // creation, registration,and deletion
                // of bottom-level agents displaying charts
    public:
        DataSetInterface receiveMsg(DataSetInterface data);
                // Receiving events, messages, or data from other
                // PAC agents including change notifications
    };
```

sendMsg() and receiveMsg() return objects for holding answers to
the messages sent and received.   ❑

10   *Link the hierarchy together.* After implementing the individual PAC
      agents you can build the final PAC hierarchy. Connect every PAC
      agent with those lower-level PAC agents with which it directly
      cooperates.

      Provide the PAC agents that dynamically create and delete lower-level
      PAC agents with functionality to dynamically extend or reduce the
      PAC hierarchy. For example, the view coordinator agent in our
      information system creates a new view PAC agent if the user wants to
      open a particular view, and deletes this agent when the user closes
      the window in which the view is displayed.

Variants   Many large applications—especially interactive ones—are multi-user
      systems. Multi-tasking is thus a major concern when designing such
      software systems. The following two variants of PAC address this
      force.

      PAC agents as active objects. Many applications, especially interactive
      ones, benefit from multi-threading. The mobile robot system [Cro85]
      is an example of a multi-threaded PAC architecture. Every PAC agent
      can be implemented as an active object that lives in its own thread of
      control. Design patterns like Active Object and Half-Sync/Half-Async
      [Sch95] can help you implement such an architecture.

      PAC agents as processes. To support PAC agents located in different
      processes or on remote machines, use proxies (263) to locally
      represent these PAC agents and to avoid direct dependencies on their
      physical location. Use the Forwarder-Receiver pattern (307) or the

Client-Dispatcher-Server pattern (323) to implement the inter-process communication (IPC) between PAC agents.

Since IPC is inefficient, you can also consider organizing coherent subtrees of the PAC hierarchy within different processes. Agents that cooperate closely in carrying out a particular task are then located within the same process. IPC between PAC agents is minimized, and is only necessary for coordinating different subtrees, as well as for accessing the services of the top-level PAC agent.

Known Uses   **Network Traffic Management**. This system is described in [TS93]. It displays the traffic in telecommunication networks. Every fifteen minutes all monitored switching units report their current traffic situation to a control point where the data is stored, analyzed and displayed. This helps with identification of potential bottlenecks and in preventing traffic overload. The system includes functions for:

- Gathering traffic data from switching units.

- Threshold checking and generation of overflow exceptions.

- Logging and routing of network exceptions.

- Visualization of traffic flow and network exceptions.

- Displaying various user-configurable views of the whole network.

- Statistical evaluations of traffic data.

- Access to historic traffic data.

- System administration and configuration.

The design and implementation of the system follows the Presentation-Abstraction-Control pattern. Every function of the system is represented by its own bottom-level PAC agent. There are dedicated agents for each view of the network, for the jobs the system can perform, and for the additional services the system offers, such as mail or help. Three intermediate-level PAC agents coordinate these bottom-level PAC agents, one for each of the three categories of application functionality: view, jobs, and additional services. In the diagram below, they are denoted by the agents NetEnv, JobEnv, and RegieEnv. An additional intermediate PAC agent organizes user sessions. The top-level PAC agent coordinates individual user sessions, and communicates with the functional core of the system. The core is implemented separately from the PAC hierarchy, probably because it incorporates legacy software. The PAC agent hierarchy of the system is dynamic. If, for example, a user starts a new session, a corresponding UISession agent is created and registered with the top-level agent. At the end of the session this agent is deleted.

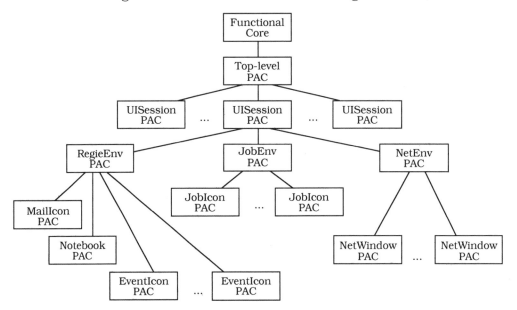

Mobile Robot. This system [Cro85] allows an operator to interact with a mobile robot that navigates within a closed and hazardous environment consisting of walls, equipment and people, either intruders or accident victims. The robot navigates using its own sensors and information from the system operator. The software allows the operator to:

- Provide the robot with a description of the environment it will work in, places in this environment, and routes between places.

- Subsequently modify the environment.

- Specify missions for the robot.

- Control the execution of missions.

- Observe the progress of missions.

Each wall, route and place within an environment is represented by its own bottom-level PAC agent. These agents together visualize the environment. Environments are represented by intermediate-level

PAC agents. They control the constituent wall, route and place PAC agents. The control users can exert on an environment is implemented in a 'palette' PAC agent, which is also at the bottom level of the hierarchy. The environment PAC agent and the palette PAC agent form a workspace for the robot. This workspace is represented by its own intermediate-level PAC agent. To support multiple views of the same environment, a multi-workspace PAC agent coordinates the different views of the same workspace. The PAC agent at the top level of the hierarchy encapsulates the functional core of the application, which is a rule-based intelligent supervisor for navigating and controlling the robot.

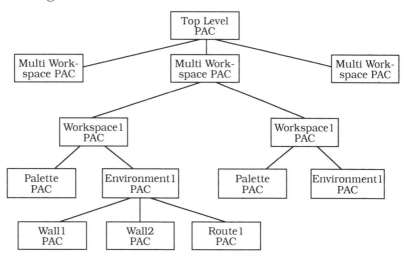

Consequences   The Presentation-Abstraction-Control architectural pattern has several **benefits**:

Separation of concerns. Different semantic concepts in the application domain are represented by separate agents. Each agent maintains its own state and data, coordinated with, but independent of other PAC agents. Individual PAC agents also provide their own human-computer interaction. This allows the development of a dedicated data model and user interface for each semantic concept or task within the application, independently of other semantic concepts or tasks.

Support for change and extension. Changes within the presentation or abstraction components of a PAC agent do not affect other agents in the system. This allows you to individually modify or tune the data model underlying a PAC agent, or to change its user interface, for example from command shells to menus and dialogs.

New agents are easily integrated into an existing PAC architecture without major changes to existing PAC agents. All PAC agents communicate with each other through a pre-defined interface. In addition, existing agents can dynamically register new PAC agents to ensure communication and cooperation. To add, for example, a new view PAC agent to our information system for political elections, we only need to extend the presentation of the view coordinator PAC agent with an appropriate palette field that allows users to create this new view. The functionality for handling this new PAC agent, for registering it with the view coordinator PAC agent, and for propagating changes and events to it is already available.

Support for multi-tasking. PAC agents can be distributed easily to different threads, processes, or machines. Extending a PAC agent with appropriate IPC functionality only affects its control component.

Multi-tasking also facilitates multi-user applications. For example, in our information system a newscaster can present the latest projection while data entry personnel update the data base with new election data. All that is necessary is for the shared data repository, or its control component, to take care of serialization or synchronization.

The **liabilities** of this pattern are as follows:

Increased system complexity. The implementation of every semantic concept within an application as its own PAC agent may result in a complex system structure. For example, if every graphical object such as a circle or square within a graphics editor is implemented as its own PAC agent, the system would drown in a sea of agents. Agents must also be coordinated and controlled, which requires additional coordination agents. Think carefully about the level of granularity of your design, and where to stop refining agents into more and more bottom-level agents.

Complex control component. In a PAC system, the control components are the communication mediators between the abstraction and presentation parts of an agent, and between different PAC agents. The quality of the control component implementations is therefore crucial to an effective collaboration between agents, and therefore for the overall quality of the system architecture. The individual roles of control components should be strongly separated from each other. The implementation of these roles should not depend on specific details of other agents, such as their concrete names or physical locations in a distributed system. The interface of the control components should be independent of internal details, to ensure that an agent's collaborators do not depend on the specific interface of its presentation or abstraction components. It is the responsibility of the control component to perform any necessary interface and data adaptation.

Efficiency. The overhead in the communication between PAC agents may impact system efficiency. For example, if a bottom-level agent retrieves data from the top-level agent, all intermediate-level agents along the path from the bottom to the top of the PAC hierarchy are involved in this data exchange. If agents are distributed, data transfer also requires IPC, together with marshaling, unmarshaling, fragmentation and re-assembling of data.

These are serious potential pitfalls. We take them into account in the following discussion about when to use, and when not to use, the Presentation-Abstraction-Control pattern.

Applicability. The smaller the atomic semantic concepts of an application are, and the greater the similarity of their user interfaces, the less applicable this pattern is. For example, a graphical editor in which every individual object in a document is represented by its own PAC agent will probably result in a complex fine-grain structure which is hard to maintain. On the other hand, if the atomic semantic concepts are substantially larger, and require their own human-computer interaction, PAC provides a maintainable and extensible structure with clear separation of concerns between different system tasks.

See also   The *Model-View-Controller* pattern (125) also separates the functional core of a software system from information display and user input handling. MVC, however, defines its controller as the entity responsible for accepting user input and translating it into internal semantics. This means that MVC effectively divides the user-accessible part—the presentation in PAC—into view and control. It lacks mediating control components. Furthermore, MVC does not separate self-reliant subtasks of a system into cooperating but loosely- coupled agents.

Credits PAC was originally described in [Cou87] by Joelle Coutaz. One of the first systems to be implemented based on PAC was the mobile robot application [Cro85]. Further valuable guidelines for implementing PAC can be found in [BaCo91] and [CNS95].

We thank Joelle Coutaz and Laurence Nigay for fruitful discussions and valuable input that helped us to shape the description of this pattern. Steve Berczuk, Brian Foote, Ralph Johnson, Tim Ottinger, David E. DeLano and Linda Rising carefully reviewed an earlier version of PAC and provided us with detailed feedback for improvement.

2.5 Adaptable Systems

Systems evolve over time—new functionality is added and existing services are changed. They must support new versions of operating systems, user-interface platforms or third-party components and libraries. Adaptation to new standards or hardware platforms may also be necessary. During system design and implementation, customers may request new features, often urgently and at a late stage. You may also need to provide services that differ from customer to customer.

Design for change is therefore a major concern when specifying the architecture of a software system. An application should support its own modification and extension a priori. Changes should not affect the core functionality or key design abstractions, otherwise the system will be hard to maintain and expensive to adapt to changing requirements.

This section describes two patterns that help when designing for change:

- The *Microkernel* pattern (171) applies to software systems that must be able to adapt to changing system requirements. It separates a minimal functional core from extended functionality and customer-specific parts. The microkernel also serves as a socket for plugging in such extensions and coordinating their collaboration.

- The *Reflection* pattern (193) provides a mechanism for changing structure and behavior of software systems dynamically. It supports the modification of fundamental aspects, such as type structures and function call mechanisms. In this pattern, an application is split into two parts. A meta level provides information about selected system properties and makes the software self-aware. A base level includes the application logic. Its implementation builds on the meta level. Changes to information kept in the meta level affect subsequent base-level behavior.

The Microkernel pattern was developed to support the design of small, efficient and portable operating systems, and to support their extension with new services. It serves as the base architecture for several modern operating systems such as Chorus [Cho90], Mach [Tan92] and Windows NT [Cus93]. The Microkernel pattern provides a 'plug'n play' software environment, allowing you to connect extensions easily and to integrate them with the core services of the system. Specific components are used to encapsulate platform dependencies. Although only a few applications outside the domain of operating systems apply the principles of this pattern today, we believe that the Microkernel structure is very attractive, and that it lends itself to many systems that require a high degree of adaptability to different platforms and customer-specific requirements.

The Reflection pattern takes a different approach. A system designed using Reflection maintains information about itself and uses this information to remain changeable and extensible. In particular, a Reflection system opens its implementation to support adaptation, change, and extension of specific structural and behavioral aspects such as type structures, function call mechanisms or implementations of particular services. The principles of reflection are supported by various programming languages, such as CLOS [Kee89] and Smalltalk [GR83], operating systems such as Apertos [Yok92], and even large-scale industrial applications. Modern platforms such as CORBA [OMG92] and Microsoft's OLE [Bro94] also make use of some of the principles of the Reflection pattern.

Microkernel

The *Microkernel* architectural pattern applies to software systems that must be able to adapt to changing system requirements. It separates a minimal functional core from extended functionality and customer-specific parts. The microkernel also serves as a socket for plugging in these extensions and coordinating their collaboration.

Example

Suppose we intend to develop a new operating system for desktop computers called Hydra. Our development team has elaborated a list of design goals to achieve this. One requirement is that this innovative operating system must be easily portable to the relevant hardware platforms, and must be able to accommodate future developments easily. It must also be able to run applications written for other popular operating systems such as NeXTSTEP, Microsoft Windows and UNIX System V. A user should be able to choose which operating system he wants from a pop-up menu before starting an application. Hydra will display all the applications currently running within its main window:

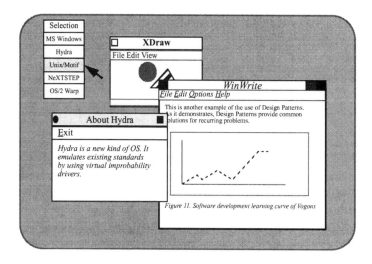

Figure 11. Software development learning curve of Vogons

To emulate all these operating systems, Hydra will integrate special servers that implement specific views of Hydra's functional core. A view denotes a layer of abstraction built on top of the core functionality. The emulation of Microsoft Windows by a server process is an example of such a view. Since several new technologies such as multimedia, pen-based computing and the World Wide Web are likely to increase in importance, Hydra should be designed for their easy integration, as well as for adaptation, evolution and enhancement of its overall functionality.

Context The development of several applications that use similar programming interfaces that build on the same core functionality.

Problem Developing software for an application domain that needs to cope with a broad spectrum of similar standards and technologies is a non-trivial task. Well-known examples are *application platforms* such as operating systems and graphical user interfaces[20]. Such systems often have a long life-span, sometimes ten years or more. Over time periods of this length, new technologies emerge and old ones change. The following *forces* therefore need particular consideration when designing such systems:

- The application platform must cope with continuous hardware and software evolution.

- The application platform should be portable, extensible and adaptable to allow easy integration of emerging technologies.

The success of such application platforms further depends on their capability to run applications written for existing standards. To support a broad range of applications, there is a need for more than one view of the functionality of the underlying application platform. In other words, an application platform such as an operating system or a database should also be able to emulate other application platforms that belong to the same application domain.

---

20. In the existing literature Microkernel systems have mainly been described in relation to the design of operating systems. Nonetheless, we believe this pattern is also applicable to several other domains, for example that of financial applications or database systems [Woo96]. Due to the wide knowledge available about implementing operating systems using microkernels, our example will focus on this specific domain.

➥ For example, Hydra is designed to run applications that were originally developed for popular operating systems such as Microsoft Windows or OS/2 Warp. ❑

This leads to the following *forces*:

- The applications in your domain need to support different, but similar, application platforms.

- The applications may be categorized into groups that use the same functional core in different ways, requiring the underlying application platform to emulate existing standards.

An application platform that provides the functional core of a domain is an exclusive resource for its clients. To avoid performance problems and to guarantee scaleability, your solution must take an additional force into account:

- The functional core of the application platform should be separated into a component with minimal memory size, and services that consume as little processing power as possible.

Solution Encapsulate the fundamental services of your application platform in a *microkernel* component. The microkernel includes functionality that enables other components running in separate processes to communicate with each other. It is also responsible for maintaining system-wide resources such as files or processes. In addition, it provides interfaces that enable other components to access its functionality.

Core functionality that cannot be implemented within the microkernel without unnecessarily increasing its size or complexity should be separated in *internal servers*.

External servers implement their own view of the underlying microkernel. To construct this view, they use the mechanisms available through the interfaces of the microkernel. Every external server is a separate process that itself represents an application platform. Hence, a Microkernel system may be viewed as an application platform that integrates other application platforms.

Clients communicate with external servers by using the communication facilities provided by the microkernel.

Structure   The Microkernel pattern defines five kinds of participating components:

- *Internal servers*
- *External servers*
- *Adapters*
- *Clients*
- *Microkernel*

The *microkernel* represents the main component of the pattern. It implements central services such as communication facilities or resource handling. Other components build on all or some of these basic services. They do this indirectly by using one or more interfaces that comprise the functionality exposed by the microkernel.

Many system-specific dependencies are encapsulated within the microkernel. For example, most of the hardware-dependent parts are hidden from other participants. Clients of the microkernel only see particular views of the underlying application domain and the platform specifics.

The microkernel is also responsible for maintaining system resources such as processes or files. It controls and coordinates the access to these resources.

In summary, a microkernel implements *atomic* services, which we refer to as *mechanisms*. These mechanisms serve as a fundamental base on which more complex functionality, called *policies*, are constructed.

Class Microkernel	*Collaborators* • Internal Server
Responsibility • Provides core mechanisms. • Offers communication facilities. • Encapsulates system dependencies. • Manages and controls resources.	

➥ In Hydra we want to support UNIX System V and OS/2 Warp, amongst other operating systems. We face a problem when implementing Hydra's process model. A system call such as that to create a new child process is implemented in UNIX by cloning an existing process, copying the whole address space. OS/2 Warp handles process creation totally differently, in that it does not copy the address space of the parent process. In other words, OS/2 Warp and UNIX offer different policies for processes. Hydra is therefore designed to supply basic services such as mechanisms for creating processes as well as mechanisms for cloning existing process spaces. These are combined in various ways for implementing both the process model of UNIX System V and the process model of OS/2 Warp. ❏

An *internal server*—also known as a *subsystem*—extends the functionality provided by the microkernel. It represents a separate component that offers additional functionality. The microkernel invokes the functionality of internal servers via service requests. Internal servers can therefore encapsulate some dependencies on the underlying hardware or software system. For example, device drivers that support specific graphics cards are good candidates for internal servers.

Class Internal Server	*Collaborators* • Microkernel
Responsibility • Implements additional services. • Encapsulates some system specifics.	

One of the design goals should be to keep the microkernel as small as possible to reduce memory requirements. Another goal is to provide mechanisms that execute quickly, to reduce service execution time. Additional and more complex services are therefore implemented by internal servers that the microkernel activates or loads only when necessary. You can consider internal servers as extensions of the microkernel. Note that internal servers are only accessible by the microkernel component.

An *external server*—also known as a *personality*—is a component that uses the microkernel for implementing its own view of the underlying application domain. As already mentioned, a view denotes a layer of abstraction built on top of the atomic services provided by the microkernel. Different external servers implement different policies for specific application domains.

External servers expose their functionality by exporting interfaces in the same way as the microkernel itself does. Each of these external servers runs in a separate process. It receives service requests from client applications using the communication facilities provided by the microkernel, interprets these requests, executes the appropriate services and returns results to its clients. The implementation of services relies on microkernel mechanisms, so external servers need to access the microkernel's programming interfaces.

Class External Server	*Collaborators* • Microkernel
Responsibility • Provides programming interfaces for its clients.	

➥   In Hydra we want to implement an OS/2 Warp external server and a UNIX System V external server. Both these servers use the mechanisms of the underlying microkernel to implement a complete set of OS/2 Warp and UNIX System V system calls.   ❏

A *client* is an application that is associated with exactly one external server. It only accesses the programming interfaces provided by the external server.

A problem arises if a client needs to access the interfaces of its external server directly. Each client has to use the available communication facilities to interoperate with the external servers.

Every communication with an external server must therefore be hard-coded into the client code. Such a tight coupling between clients and servers, however, leads to various disadvantages:

- Such a system does not support changeability very well.

- If external servers emulate existing application platforms, client applications developed for these platforms will not run without modification.

We therefore introduce interfaces between clients and their external servers to protect clients from direct dependencies. *Adapters*—also known as *emulators*—represent these interfaces between clients and their external servers, and allow clients to access the services of their external server in a portable way. They are part of the client's address space. If the external server implements an existing application platform, the corresponding adapter mimics the programming interfaces of that platform. Clients written for the emulated platform can therefore be compiled and run without modification. Adapters also protect clients from the specific implementation details of the microkernel.

Whenever a client requests a service from an external server, it is the task of the adapter to forward the call to the appropriate server. For this purpose the adapter uses the communication services provided by the microkernel.

Class Client	*Collaborators* • Adapter	*Class* Adapter	*Collaborators* • External Server • Microkernel
Responsibility • Represents an application.		*Responsibility* • Hides system dependencies such as communication facilities from the client. • Invokes methods of external servers on behalf of clients.	

➥ Due to encapsulation by an adapter, a Hydra client associated with the OS/2 Warp external server does not know whether it is running on a native OS/2 Warp system or on a Microkernel system that provides an OS/2 Warp external server. It just uses the OS/2 system calls as before. What happens 'behind the scenes' is hidden by the adapter.   ❏

The following OMT diagram shows the static structure of a Microkernel system. Its central component, the microkernel, collaborates with external servers, internal servers and adapters. Each client is associated with an adapter used as a bridge between the client and its external server. Internal servers are only accessible by the microkernel component.

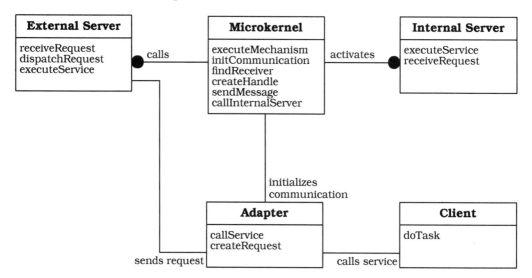

Dynamics   The dynamic behavior of a Microkernel system depends on the functionality it provides for inter-process communication. In the following scenarios we assume the availability of remote procedure calls. The first scenario also assumes that the external server does not access the microkernel interfaces—this latter case is illustrated in the second scenario.

Scenario I demonstrates the behavior when a client calls a service of its external server:

- At a certain point in its control flow the client requests a service from an external server by calling the adapter.

- The adapter constructs a request and asks the microkernel for a communication link with the external server.

- The microkernel determines the physical address of the external server and returns it to the adapter.

- After retrieving this information, the adapter establishes a direct communication link to the external server.

- The adapter sends the request to the external server using a remote procedure call.

- The external server receives the request, unpacks the message and delegates the task to one of its own methods. After completing the requested service, the external server sends all results and status information back to the adapter.

- The adapter returns to the client, which in turn continues with its control flow.

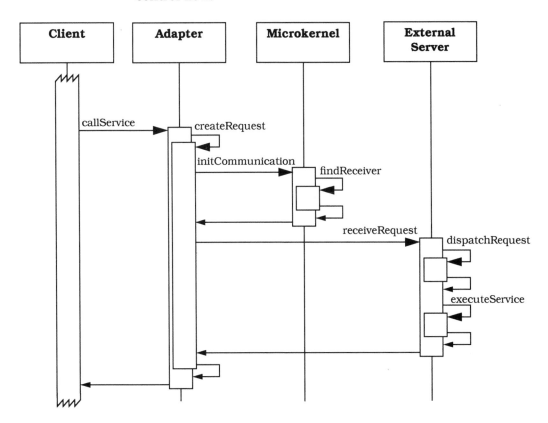

Scenario II illustrates the behavior of a Microkernel architecture when an external server requests a service that is provided by an internal server. In this scenario we assume that the internal server is implemented as a separate process. It could alternatively be implemented as a shared library that is dynamically linked to the microkernel.

- The external server sends a service request to the microkernel.

- A procedure of the programming interface of the microkernel is called to handle the service request. During method execution the microkernel sends a request to an internal server.

- After receiving the request, the internal server executes the requested service and sends all results back to the microkernel.

- The microkernel returns the results back to the external server.

- Finally, the external server retrieves the results and continues with its control flow.

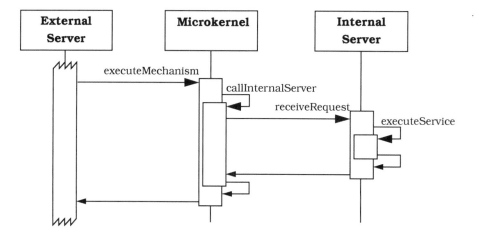

Implementation   To implement a Microkernel system, carry out the following steps:

1   *Analyze the application domain.* If you already know the policies your external servers need to offer, or if you have a detailed knowledge about the external servers you are going to implement, continue with step 2. If not, perform a domain analysis and identify the core functionality necessary for implementing external servers, then continue with step 3.

2   *Analyze external servers.* Analyze the policies external servers are going to provide. You should then be able to identify the functionality you require within your application domain.

➥   For Hydra we already know which external servers have to be implemented: UNIX System V, OS/2 Warp, Microsoft Windows and NeXTSTEP. We therefore analyze their programming interfaces to determine the services they provide. This requirement analysis results in the list of services and service categories necessary for implementing desktop operating systems.   ❑

3   *Categorize the services.* Whenever possible, group all the functionality into semantically-independent categories.

Build categories of operations that are not directly related with the application domain, but are necessary to implement the system infrastructure. Some of these operations may be candidates for migration to internal servers.

➥   For example, in Hydra the core categories that are predefined by the domain of operating systems are memory management, process management, low-level services for I/O and communication services.

The following categories are not directly related to the core concepts of the application domain: page-handler processes, file systems, hardware and software drivers. We need these categories in our Hydra implementation, but they may be migrated to internal servers.   ❑

4   *Partition the categories.* Separate the categories into services that should be part of the microkernel, and those that should be available as internal servers. You need to establish criteria for this separation. For example, it is best to implement time-critical, frequently-used or hardware-dependent operations within the microkernel component.

➥   In Hydra the microkernel provides services such as process management, memory management, communication and low-level I/O. This functionality is time-critical, used by all other components, and also encapsulates system dependencies. It should therefore be part of the microkernel. All additional services such as page fault handlers, drivers or file systems are implemented by internal servers.   ❑

5   *Find a consistent and complete set of operations and abstractions* for every category you identified in step 1. Remember that the microkernel provides mechanisms, not policies. Each policy an external server provides must be implemented through use of the services the microkernel offers through its interfaces.

➡   Operations such as the creation of processes or threads are handled differently by operating systems like UNIX or Microsoft Windows. In Hydra we need to support both. We therefore provide a complete set of basic mechanisms for managing processes and threads. For example, we provide services for:

- Creating and terminating processes and threads.

- Stopping and restarting them.

- Reading from or writing to process address spaces.

- Catching and handling exceptions.

- Managing relationships between processes or threads.

- Synchronizing and coordinating threads.   ❑

6   *Determine strategies for request transmission and retrieval.* Specify the facilities the microkernel should provide for communication between components. You can choose among several alternatives, for example, asynchronous communication versus synchronous communication. The relationship between communicating components may be a one-to-one, a many-to-one or a many-to-many relationship. The communication strategies you integrate depend on the requirements of the application domain. In many cases low-level communication facilities such as message-passing or shared memory are available, and you can build more complex communication mechanisms on top of them. Compare design patterns such as Forwarder-Receiver (307) and Client-Dispatcher-Server (323) for more information on the implementation of communication mechanisms.

➡   Hydra provides two basic communication facilities:

- Synchronous Remote Procedure Calls (RPCs). RPCs enable a client to invoke the services of a remote server as if they were implemented by local procedure calls. The mechanisms necessary for supporting RPCs, for example the packing and unpacking of requests or the transmission of messages across process boundaries, are hidden from the caller and the server called.

- Asynchronous Mailboxes. A *mailbox* is a type of message buffer. A set of components is allowed to read messages from the mailbox, another set of components has permission to write messages to it. A component may be allowed to perform both activities. ❏

7 *Structure the microkernel component.* If possible, design the microkernel using the Layers pattern (31) to separate system-specific parts from system-independent parts of the microkernel. Place the services that the microkernel exposes to other components in the uppermost layer, and use the lower layers to hide system dependencies from higher layers.

➥   In our Hydra project we decide to use object-oriented techniques to implement the microkernel:

- The lowermost layer consists of low-level objects that hide hardware-specific details such as the bus architecture from other parts of the microkernel.

- In the intermediate layers the primary services are provided by system objects, such as objects responsible for memory management and objects used for managing processes.

- The uppermost layer comprises all the functionality that the microkernel exposes publicly, and represents the gateway to the microkernel services for any process. ❏

8 To *specify the programming interfaces* of the microkernel, you need to decide how these interfaces should be accessible externally. You must obviously take into account whether the microkernel is implemented as a separate process or as a module that is physically shared by other components. In the latter case, you can use conventional method calls to invoke the methods of the microkernel.

If you implement the microkernel as a separate process, existing communication facilities are required for transmitting requests from components to the microkernel. In this case you need to be aware that the kernel represents an exclusive resource, and can therefore be a bottleneck. To increase overall performance you could provide multiple threads within the microkernel that wait for incoming requests, and use the same, or other, threads to execute the appropriate services. If you design such a multi-threaded system, make sure that the consistency of internal data is guaranteed.

➡   Since Hydra represents an operating system, its microkernel component is part of each user process. Services are therefore accessible by conventional system calls. These functions are logically grouped into APIs (Application Programming Interfaces) that support functionality such as file system operations or process management.

Invoking a Hydra system call results in a system trap. Software exceptions are handled by a special trap handler routine in the microkernel. The trap handler analyzes the type of interrupt that led to the system trap, and delegates the work to one of its internal service objects. After the service is completed, a scheduling object decides which available thread should be executed next and assigns a processing unit to it.   ❏

9   The microkernel is responsible for *managing all system resources* such as memory blocks, devices or *device contexts*—a handle to an output area in a graphical user interface implementation. The microkernel maintains information about resources and allows access to them in a coordinated and systematic way. If components want to access a resource, they use a unique identifier (handle) rather than accessing the resource directly. The microkernel has the task of creating these handles and providing a mapping between handles and resources. This mapping can be implemented using hash tables. As resource management involves more than just providing a mapping, the microkernel must also implement strategies for the sharing, locking, allocation and deallocation of resources.

➡   Within Hydra, handles refer to objects that are instances of a resource class. Each of these objects offers a uniform interface to control access to a specific resource.

Our resource objects expose the following interface, which follows the Windows NT approach:

```
class Resource {
    String name;             // Name of object
    void OpenHandle();       // open handle to object
    Handle IterateHandles(); // iterate over handles
    Body pointerToObject;    // pointer to real object
    ...                      // (much, much more ...)
}                                                          ❏
```

10   *Design and implement the internal servers* as separate processes or shared libraries. Perform this step in parallel with steps 7–9, because some of the microkernel services need to access internal servers. It is helpful to distinguish between *active* and *passive* servers:

- Active servers are implemented as processes

- Passive servers as shared libraries

While passive servers are always invoked by directly calling their interface methods, active servers need different treatment. The active server process waits in an event loop for incoming requests. If it receives a request via the available communication facilities, it interprets and executes a service on behalf of the caller. Note that internal servers are accessed exclusively by the microkernel—no other component is permitted to invoke the services of internal servers.

➥   In Hydra we provide device drivers, authentication servers and page fault handlers, among other components, by implementing them as internal servers.

Graphics card drivers are developed as shared libraries because they only act on behalf of clients. In contrast, page fault handlers are separate processes. They always have to remain in main memory and cannot be swapped to external storage.   ❑

11   *Implement the external servers.* All the policies the external servers include are based on the services available in the programming interfaces of the microkernel. An external server receives requests, analyzes them, executes the appropriate services and sends the results back to the caller. When executing services, the external server may call operations in the microkernel.

Each external server is therefore implemented as a separate process that provides its own service interface. The internal architecture of an external server depends on the policies it comprises.

Specify how external servers dispatch requests to their internal procedures. For example, they may integrate a dispatcher component that executes a main event loop and waits for incoming requests. When a request arrives, the dispatcher unpacks it, interprets the request and calls the appropriate procedure via a callback mechanism. This is particularly useful if you design external servers as application frameworks. See the Reactor pattern [Sch94] for a description of this event-driven approach.

➥   We want to develop the following external servers for Hydra:

• A full implementation of Microsoft's Win32 and Win16 APIs, to allow users to run Windows NT, Windows 3.11 and Windows 95 applications.

• The complete functionality provided by IBM OS/2 Warp 2.0.

• An implementation of OpenStep.

• All relevant UNIX System V interfaces specified by X/Open.   ❑

12   *Implement the adapters.* The primary task of an adapter is to provide operations to its clients that are forwarded to an external server. Whenever the client calls a function of the external server, the adapter packages all relevant information into a request and forwards the request to the appropriate external server. The adapter then waits for the server's response and finally returns control to the client, using the facilities for inter-component communication.

You can design the adapter either as a conventional library that is statically linked to the client during compilation, or as a shared library dynamically linked to the client on demand. You can view an adapter as a proxy that represents exactly one external server. You could therefore use the Proxy pattern (263) to implement an adapter. You could optimize the adapter by allowing it to execute some of the API operations on its own instead of forwarding requests to the external server, or by storing several client requests in a cache before forwarding them. Answers to common requests could also be stored here. See the Proxy pattern (263) for benefits and pitfalls of caching.

You must decide whether one adapter should be available for all clients, or if every client is associated with its own adapter. The first approach results in less memory contention, while the second can lead to better response times.

➥   If we design Hydra with a Microsoft Windows external server, all client applications associated with this server use the Win16 or Win32 APIs. In a native Windows 3.11 system all APIs are available as a set of shared libraries. In Hydra, however, Windows clients and the Windows server are separate processes. Since we want to be able to run a Windows-application on Hydra without modification, we need to supply the same environment. We therefore implement an adapter to work as a bridge between a Windows client and the Windows server. When the client calls a Win16 or Win32 API function, the call is handled by the adapter, which forwards a request to the Windows external server. Existing Windows clients can therefore be compiled and executed on the Hydra system.   ❏

13 *Develop client applications* or use existing ones for the ready-to-run Hydra system. When creating a new client for a specific external server, its architecture is only limited by the constraints imposed by the external server. That is, clients depend on the policies implemented by their external server.

➥ In Hydra we can develop Microsoft Windows applications by accessing the services of the Microsoft Windows external server via the Microsoft Windows adapter.   ❏

Example resolved Shortly after the development of Hydra has been completed, we are asked to integrate an external server that emulates the Apple MacOS operating system. To provide a MacOS emulation on top of Hydra, the following activities are necessary:

Building an external server on top of the Hydra microkernel that implements all the programming interfaces provided by MacOS, including the policies of the Macintosh user interface. In its main loop the MacOS server waits for incoming requests, which are stored in a message port specifically assigned to the MacOS server. The server pulls these requests out of the message port, interprets them and dispatches them to internal procedures. These procedures emulate the policies that are typical of the MacOS environment.

Providing an adapter that is designed as a library, dynamically linked to clients. For every API function available in a native MacOS system, a syntactically-identical procedure must be provided by the library. Each of these procedures is responsible for packaging the type of request, the arguments, and the identifiers of sender and receiver into a message. It then calls the procedure `sendMessage` in the microkernel, which in turn stores the message in the message port of the MacOS server.

Implementing the internal servers required for MacOS. For example, one internal server provides the network protocol AppleTalk. The microkernel must be modified to invoke these additional internal servers on behalf of the MacOS server.

Variants   *Microkernel System with indirect Client-Server connections.* In this variant, a client that wants to send a request or message to an external server asks the microkernel for a communication channel. After the requested communication path has been established, client and server communicate with each other indirectly using the microkernel as a message backbone. Using this variant leads to an architecture in which all requests pass through the microkernel. You can apply it, for example, when security requirements force the system to control all communication between participants.

Distributed Microkernel System. In this variant a microkernel can also act as a message backbone responsible for sending messages to remote machines or receiving messages from them. Every machine in a distributed system uses its own microkernel implementation. From the user's viewpoint the whole system appears as a single Microkernel system—the distribution remains transparent to the user. A distributed Microkernel system allows you to distribute servers and clients across a network of machines or microprocessors. To achieve this the microkernels in a distributed implementation must include additional services for communicating with each other.

Known Uses   The **Mach** operating system [Tan92] was developed at Carnegie-Mellon-University, and its first version was released in 1986. The Mach microkernel is intended to form a base on which other operating systems can be emulated. One of the commercially-available operating systems that use Mach as its system kernel is NeXTSTEP.

The operating system **Amoeba** [Tan92] consists of two basic elements: the microkernel itself and a collection of servers (subsystems) that are used to implement the majority of Amoeba's functionality. The kernel provides four basic services: the management of processes and threads, the low-level-management of system memory, communication services, both for point-to-point-communication as well as group-communication, and low-level I/O-services. Services not provided by the kernel must be implemented by server processes. This leads to a reduction in kernel size and increases flexibility.

Chorus [Cho90] is a commercially-available Microkernel system that was originally developed by the French research institute INRIA specifically for real-time applications. UNIX System V is available as an external server.

Windows NT [Cus93] was developed by Microsoft as an operating system for high-performance servers. From an architectural point of view Windows NT is definitely a Microkernel system. It offers three external servers, an OS/2 1.x server, a POSIX server and a Win32 server.

The **MKDE** (Microkernel Datenbank Engine) system [Woo96] introduces an architecture for database engines that follows the Microkernel pattern. In this system the microkernel is responsible for providing fundamental services such as physical data access, caching of data and transaction management. Various external servers run on top of the microkernel and provide different conceptual views of the underlying microkernel. A conceptual view denotes a data abstraction according to a given data model, for example the data model of a relational SQL database. Applications such as accounting systems can use the external servers to access databases. MKDE implements the Distributed Microkernel variant to support distributed environments.

Consequences The Microkernel pattern offers some important **benefits**:

Portability. A Microkernel system offers a high degree of portability, for two reasons:

- In most cases you do not need to port external servers or client applications if you port the Microkernel system to a new software or hardware environment.

- Migrating the microkernel to a new hardware environment only requires modifications to the hardware-dependent parts.

Flexibility and Extensibility. One of the biggest strengths of a Microkernel system is its flexibility and extensibility. If you need to implement an additional view, all you need to do is add a new external server. Extending the system with additional capabilities only requires the addition or extension of internal servers.

Separation of policy and mechanism. The microkernel component provides all the mechanisms necessary to enable external servers to implement their policies. This strict separation of policies and mechanisms increases the maintainability and changeability of the whole system. It also allows you to add new external servers that implement their own specialized views. If the microkernel component were to implement policies, this would unnecessarily limit the views that could be implemented by external servers.

If we consider the Distributed Microkernel variant of the Microkernel architecture, further benefits appear:

Scaleability. A distributed Microkernel system is applicable to the development of operating systems or database systems for computer networks, or multiprocessors with local memory. If your Microkernel system works on a network of machines, it is easy to scale the Microkernel system to the new configuration when you add a new machine to the network.

Reliability. Two issues are important in achieving reliability: availability and fault tolerance [Tan92]. A distributed Microkernel architecture supports availability, because it allows you to run the same server on more than one machine, increasing availability. If a server or a machine fails, therefore, the failure does not necessarily have an impact on an application. Fault tolerance may be easily supported because distributed systems allow you to hide failures from a user.

Transparency. In a distributed system components can be distributed over a network of machines. In such a configuration, the Microkernel architecture allows each component to access other components without needing to know their location. All details of inter-process communication with servers are hidden from clients by the adapters and the microkernel.

The Microkernel architectural framework also has **liabilities**:

Performance. If we compare a monolithic software system designed to offer a specific view with a Microkernel system supporting different views, the performance of the former will be better in most cases. We therefore have to pay a price for flexibility and extensibility. If the communication within the Microkernel system is optimized for performance, however, this price can be overlooked[Tan92].

Complexity of design and implementation. Developing a Microkernel-based system is a non-trivial task. For example, it can sometimes be very difficult to analyze or predict the basic mechanisms a micro-kernel component must provide. In addition, the separation between mechanisms and policies requires in-depth domain knowledge and considerable effort during requirements analysis and design.

See also   The *Broker* pattern (99) is suitable for distributed software systems that consist of interacting and decoupled components. In the Broker pattern clients access the services provided by servers using remote procedure calls or message-passing. In contrast to the Microkernel architectural framework, the Broker pattern focuses on distribution over a network. A further difference between these patterns is that the coupling of components within a Broker system is not normally as tight as it is within a Microkernel system. You can however combine both patterns when developing a distributed Microkernel system.

The *Reflection* pattern (193) provides a two-tiered architecture. A base level corresponds to a combination of microkernel and internal servers. A meta level enables the behavior of base-level functionality to be changed dynamically, for example changing the strategies for resource management or communication between components. In addition, the meta level allows integration of customer-specific exten-sions to the base-level services. This corresponds to the provision of external servers in a Microkernel architecture. In contrast to the Microkernel pattern, the adaptation of the meta level is performed indirectly with help of a specific interface, the Metaobject Protocol (MOP). This allows users to specify a change, checks its correctness, and automatically integrates the change into the meta level. In recent developments of operating systems, the Reflection pattern and the Microkernel pattern are often combined [Zim96].

The relationship between the *Layers* (31) and the Microkernel pattern is twofold. Firstly, a Microkernel system may also be considered as a variant of the Layers pattern. The microkernel implements a virtual machine, relying on internal servers to do this. The internal servers are the lowest layer and also belong to the virtual machine. The applications executed by the virtual machine include external servers and adapters, representing the layer on top of the virtual machine. One external server and one adapter together can be considered as a second virtual machine on top of the microkernel. Each personality offered corresponds to a single second-level virtual machine. Client applications make up the highest layer in this hierarchy, and use specific personalities.

Secondly, for some application domains both patterns may be applied alternatively. Consider architectures for business applications [Fow96]. A very common approach is to separate these systems into three tiers:

- The lowest layer includes the database management system.

- The middle layer contains the business logic.

- The highest layer comprises different business applications.

If these applications can be grouped into different categories, you could instead introduce a microkernel responsible for implementing the core business logic. This microkernel could additionally encapsulate the functionality for accessing the DBMS into internal servers. External servers would provide different views of the microkernel mechanisms, covering the business logic in different ways to capture functionality specific to a particular business category. The actual business applications are then the clients. If, however, all clients build upon the same view of the underlying business logic, the Microkernel pattern should not be applied.

Reflection

The *Reflection* architectural pattern provides a mechanism for changing structure and behavior of software systems dynamically. It supports the modification of fundamental aspects, such as type structures and function call mechanisms. In this pattern, an application is split into two parts. A meta level provides information about selected system properties and makes the software self-aware. A base level includes the application logic. Its implementation builds on the meta level. Changes to information kept in the meta level affect subsequent base-level behavior.

Also Known As Open Implementation, Meta-Level Architecture

Example Consider a C++ application that needs to write objects to disk and read them in again. Since persistence is not a built-in feature of C++, we must specify how to store and read every type in the application. Many solutions to this problem, such as implementing type-specific store and read methods, are expensive and error-prone. For example, whenever we change the class structure of the application, we must modify these methods as well.

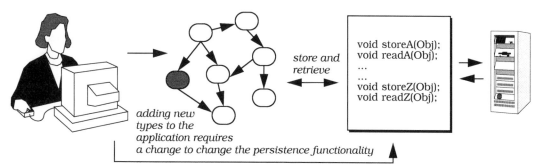

store and retrieve

```
void storeA(Obj);
void readA(Obj);
...
...
void storeZ(Obj);
void readZ(Obj);
```

adding new types to the application requires a change to change the persistence functionality

Other solutions to the lack of persistence raise other problems. For example, we could provide a special base class for persistent objects from which application classes are derived, with inherited store and read methods overridden. Changes to the class structure require us to modify these methods within existing application classes. Persistence and application functionality are strongly interwoven.

Instead we want to develop a persistence component that is independent of specific type structures. However, to store and read arbitrary C++ objects, we need dynamic access to their internal structure.

Context   Building systems that support their own modification a priori.

Problem   Software systems evolve over time. They must be open to modifications in response to changing technology and requirements. Designing a system that meets a wide range of different requirements a priori can be an overwhelming task. A better solution is to specify an architecture that is open to modification and extension. The resulting system can then be adapted to changing requirements on demand. In other words, we want to design for change and evolution. Several *forces* are associated with this problem:

- Changing software is tedious, error prone, and often expensive. Wide-ranging modifications usually spread over many components and even local changes within one component can affect other parts of the system. Every change must be implemented and tested carefully. Software which actively supports and controls its own modification can be changed more effectively and more safely.

- Adaptable software systems usually have a complex inner structure. Aspects that are subject to change are encapsulated within separate components. The implementation of application services is spread over many small components with different interrelationships [GHJV95]. To keep such systems maintainable, we prefer to hide this complexity from maintainers of the system.

- The more techniques that are necessary for keeping a system changeable, such as parameterization, subclassing, mix-ins, or even copy and paste, the more awkward and complex its modification becomes. A uniform mechanism that applies to all kinds of changes is easier to use and understand.

- Changes can be of any scale, from providing shortcuts for commonly-used commands to adapting an application framework for a specific customer.

- Even fundamental aspects of software systems can change, for example the communication mechanisms between components.

Solution   Make the software self-aware, and make selected aspects of its structure and behavior accessible for adaptation and change. This leads to an architecture that is split into two major parts: a *meta level* and a *base level*.

The meta level provides a self-representation of the software to give it knowledge of its own structure and behavior, and consists of so-called *metaobjects*. Metaobjects encapsulate and represent information about the software. Examples include type structures, algorithms, or even function call mechanisms.

The base level defines the application logic. Its implementation uses the metaobjects to remain independent of those aspects that are likely to change. For example, base-level components may only communicate with each other via a metaobject that implements a specific user-defined function call mechanism. Changing this metaobject changes the way in which base-level components communicate, but without modifying the base-level code.

An interface is specified for manipulating the metaobjects. It is called the *metaobject protocol* (MOP), and allows clients to specify particular changes, such as modification of the function call mechanism metaobject mentioned above. The metaobject protocol itself is responsible for checking the correctness of the change specification, and for performing the change. Every manipulation of metaobjects through the metaobject protocol affects subsequent base-level behavior, as in the function call mechanism example.

➡   For the persistence component, located at the base level of our example application, we specify metaobjects that provide run-time type information. For example, to store an object, we must know its internal structure and also the layout of all its data members. With this information available we can recursively iterate over any given object structure to break it down into a sequence of built-in types. The persistence component 'knows' how to store these. If we change the run-time type information we also modify the behavior of the store method. For example, objects of classes that are no longer persistent are no longer stored. Following similar strategies for every method, we can construct a persistence component that is able to read and store arbitrary data structures.   ❑

Structure   The *meta level* consists of a set of *metaobjects*. Each metaobject encapsulates selected information about a single aspect of the structure, behavior, or state of the base level. There are three sources for such information:

- It can be provided by the run-time environment of the system, such as C++ type identification objects [DWP95].

- It can be user-defined, such as the function call mechanism in the previous section.

- It can be retrieved from the base level at run-time, for example information about the current state of computation.

All metaobjects together provide a self-representation of an application. Metaobjects make information, which is otherwise only implicitly available, explicitly accessible and modifiable. Almost every system internal can be described in this way. For example, in a distributed system there may be metaobjects that provide information about the physical location of base-level components. Other base-level components can use these metaobjects to determine whether their communication partners are local or remote. They can select the most efficient function call mechanism to communicate with them. The function call mechanisms themselves may be provided by other metaobjects. Further examples include type structures, real-time constraints, inter-process communication mechanisms and transaction protocols.

However, what you represent with metaobjects depends on what should be adaptable. Only system details that are likely to change or which vary from customer to customer should be encapsulated by metaobjects. System aspects that are expected to stay stable over the lifetime of an application should not be.

The interface of a metaobject allows the base level to access the information it maintains or the service it offers. For example, a metaobject that provides location information about a distributed component will provide functions to access the name and identifier of the component, information about the process in which it is located, and information about the host on which the process runs. A metaobject that implements a function call mechanism will offer a method of activating a specific function of a specific addressee, including input and output parameter passing. A metaobject does not allow the base level to modify its internal state. Manipulation is possible only through the metaobject protocol or by its own computation.

The *base level* models and implements the application logic of the software. Its components represent the various services the system offers as well as their underlying data model. The base level also specifies the fundamental collaboration and structural relationships between the components it includes. If the software includes a user interface, this is also part of the base level.

The base level uses the information and services provided by the metaobjects, such as location information about components and function call mechanisms. This allows the base level to remain flexible—its code is independent of aspects that may be subject to change and adaptation. Using the metaobject's services, base-level components do not need to hard-code information about the concrete locations of communication partners—they consult appropriate metaobjects for this information.

Base-level components are either directly connected to the metaobjects on which they depend, or submit requests to them through special retrieval functions. These functions are also part of the meta level. The first type of connection is preferred if the relationship between the base level and the metaobject is relatively static. The base-level component always consults the same metaobject, for example if an object needs type information about itself. The second type of connection is used if the metaobjects used by the base level vary dynamically, as in the case of the store procedure of our persistence component.

Class Base Level	*Collaborators* • Meta Level	*Class* Meta Level	*Collaborators* • Base Level
Responsibility • Implements the application logic. • Uses information provided by the meta level.		*Responsibility* • Encapsulates system internals that may change. • Provides an interface to facilitate modifications to the meta-level.	

The *metaobject protocol* (MOP) serves as an external interface to the meta level, and makes the implementation of a reflective system accessible in a defined way. Clients of the metaobject protocol, which may be base-level components, other applications, or privileged human users, can specify modifications to metaobjects or their relationships using the base level. The metaobject protocol itself is responsible for performing these changes. This provides a reflective application with explicit control over its own modification.

To continue our example above, a user may specify a new function call mechanism to be used for communication between base-level components. As a first step, the user provides the metaobject protocol with the code of this new function call mechanism. The metaobject protocol then performs the change. It may do this, for example, by generating an appropriate metaobject that includes the user-defined code for the new mechanism, compiling the generated metaobject, dynamically linking it with the application, and updating all references of the 'old' metaobject to the 'new' one.

The metaobject protocol is usually designed as a separate component. This supports the implementation of functions that operate on several metaobjects. For example, modifying metaobjects that encapsulate location information about distributed components eventually requires an update of the corresponding function call mechanism metaobjects. If we delegate the responsibility for such changes to the metaobjects themselves, consistency between them is hard to maintain. The metaobject protocol has a better control over every modification that is performed, because it is implemented separately from the metaobjects.

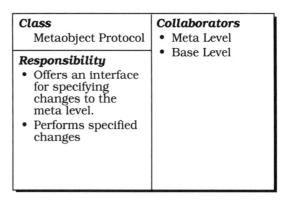

To perform changes, the metaobject protocol needs access to the internals of both the metaobjects and the base-level components. One way of providing this access is to allow the metaobject protocol to directly operate on their internal states. Another safer but more inefficient, way of providing it is for metaobjects and base-level components to provide a special interface for their manipulation, only accessible by the metaobject protocol.

Since the base-level implementation explicitly builds upon information and services provided by metaobjects, changing them has an immediate effect on the subsequent behavior of the base level. In our example, we changed the way base-level components communicate. However, in contrast to a conventional modification, the system was changed without modifying base-level code.

The general structure of a reflective architecture is very much like a Layered system (31). The meta level and base level are two layers, each of which provides its own interface. The base-level layer specifies the user interface for exploiting application functionality. The meta-level layer defines the metaobject protocol to modify the metaobjects.

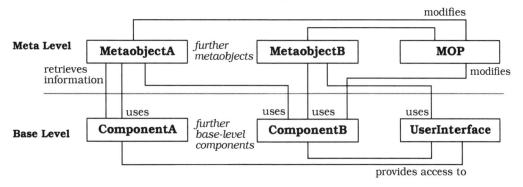

However, in contrast to a layered architecture, there are mutual dependencies between both layers. The base level builds on the meta level, and vice-versa. An example of the latter occurs when metaobjects implement behavior that is executed in case of an exception. The kind of exception procedure that must be executed often depends on the current state of computation. The meta level retrieves this information from the base level, often from different components to those providing the interrupted service. In a pure layered architecture, these bidirectional dependencies between layers are not allowed. Every layer only builds upon the layers below.

➡   For our persistence component example we specify metaobjects that provide *introspective access* to the type structure of our application—that is, they can access information about the application's structure or behavior, but cannot modify it. We can obtain information about the name, size, data members and superclasses of a given type or object. An additional metaobject specifies a function that allows a client to instantiate objects of arbitrary types. We use this function, for example, when restoring an object structure from a data file. The metaobject protocol includes functions for adding new, and modifying existing, run-time type information.

The body of the persistence component is independent of the concrete type structure of our application. For example, the store procedure only implements the general algorithm for recursively breaking down a given object structure into a sequence of built-in types. If it needs information about the inner structure of user-defined types, it consults the meta level. Data members with built-in types are directly stored. All other data members are further decomposed.   ❏

Dynamics   It is almost impossible to describe the dynamic behavior of reflective systems in general. We therefore present two scenarios based on the persistence component example. See the Implementation section for details of the metaobject protocol and metaobjects involved.

Scenario I illustrates the collaboration between base level and meta level when reading objects stored in a disk file. All data is stored in an appropriate order, and a type identifier proceeds every object. The scenario further abstracts from special cases, such as reading strings, static members, and restoring cycles in the object structure. The scenario is divided into six phases:

- The user wants to read stored objects. The request is forwarded to the read() procedure of the persistence component, together with the name of the data file in which the objects are stored.

- Procedure read() opens the data file and calls an internal readObject() procedure which reads the first type identifier.

- Procedure readObject() calls the metaobject that is responsible for the creation of objects. The 'object creator' metaobject instantiates an 'empty' object of the previously-determined type. It returns a handle to this object and a handle to the corresponding run-time type information (RTTI) metaobject.

- Procedure `readObject()` requests an iterator over the data members of the object to be read from its corresponding metaobject. The procedure iterates over the data members of the object.

- Procedure `readObject()` reads the type identifier for the next data member. If the type identifier denotes a built-in type—a case we do not illustrate—the `readObject()` procedure directly assigns the next data item from the file to the data member, based on the data member's size and offset within the object. Otherwise `readObject()` is called recursively. This recursion starts with the creation of an 'empty' object if the data member is a pointer. If not, the recursively called `readObject()` operates on the existing layout of the object that contains the data member.

- After reading the data, the `read()` procedure closes the data file and returns the new objects to the client that requested them.

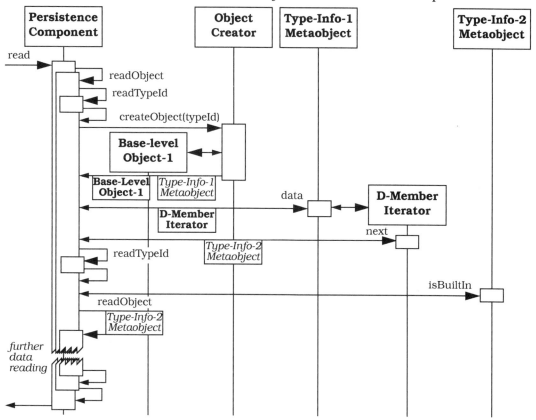

Scenario II illustrates the use of the metaobject protocol when adding type information to the meta level. Consider a class library used by the application that changes to a new version with new types. To store and read these types, we must extend the meta level with new metaobjects. Adding this information can be performed by the user, or automatically, using a tool. For reasons of simplicity we unify the classes `type_info` and `extTypeInfo` as specified in the Implementation section. The scenario is divided into six phases which are performed for every new type:

- A client invokes the metaobject protocol to specify run-time type information for a new type in the application. The name of the type is passed as an argument.

- The metaobject protocol creates a metaobject of class `type_info` for this type. This metaobject also serves as a type identifier.

- The client calls the metaobject protocol to add extended type information. This includes setting the size of the type, whether or not it is a pointer, and its inheritance relationships to other types. To handle the inheritance relationship, the metaobject protocol creates metaobjects of class `baseInfo`. These maintain a handle to the `type_info` object for a particular base class and its offset within the new type.

- In the next step, the client specifies the inner structure for the new type. The metaobject protocol is provided with the name and type of every data member. For every data member the metaobject protocol creates an object of class `dataInfo`. It maintains a handle to the `type_info` object for the type of the member, its name, and whether or not it is a static data member. The `dataInfo` object also maintains the absolute address of the data member if it is static, otherwise its offset within the new type.

- The client invokes the metaobject protocol to modify existing types that include the new type as a data member. Appropriate data member information is added for every type. Since this step is very similar to the previous one, we do not illustrate it in the object message sequence chart that follows.

- Finally, the client calls the metaobject protocol to adapt the 'object creator' metaobject. The persistence component must be able to instantiate an object of the new type when reading persistent data.

The metaobject protocol automatically generates code for creating objects of the new type, based on the previously-added type information. It further integrates the new code with the existing implementation of the 'object creator' metaobject, compiles the modified implementation, and links it with the application.

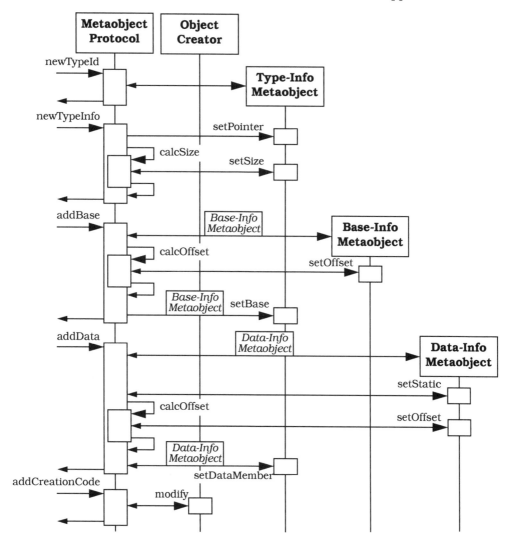

Implementation The following guidelines help with implementing a Reflection architecture. Iterate through any subsequence if necessary.

1 *Define a model of the application.* Analyze the problem domain and decompose it into an appropriate software structure. Answer the following questions:

- Which services should the software provide?

- Which components can fulfil these services?

- What are the relationships between the components?

- How do the components cooperate or collaborate?

- What data do the components operate on?

- How will the user interact with the software?

Follow an appropriate analysis method when specifying the model.

➡ The persistence component in our C++ disk-storage example is part of a warehouse management application [Coad95]. We identify components that represent physical storage, such as warehouses, aisles and bins. We also identify components for orders and items. It is a requirement that we can resume computation with a valid state after system crashes. Both the physical structure of the warehouse and its current population of items must therefore be made persistent. We need two components to achieve this. A persistence component provides the functionality for storing and reading objects. A file handler is responsible for locking, opening, closing, unlocking and deleting files, as well as for writing and reading data. ❑

2 *Identify varying behavior.* Analyze the model developed in the previous step and determine which of the application services may vary and which remain stable. There are no general rules for specifying what can alter in a system. Whether a certain aspect varies depends on many factors such as the application domain, the environment of the application and its customers and users. An aspect that is likely to vary in one system may stay stable in others. The following are examples of system aspects that often vary:

- Real-time constraints [HT92], such as deadlines, time-fence protocols and algorithms for detecting deadline misses.

- Transaction protocols [SW95], for example optimistic and pessimistic transaction control in accounting systems.

- Inter-process communication mechanisms [CM93], such as remote procedure calls and shared memory.

- Behavior in case of exceptions [EKM+94], [HT92], for example the handling of deadline misses in real-time systems.

- Algorithms for application services [EKM+94], such as country-specific VAT calculation.

The Open Implementation Analysis and Design Method [KLLM95] helps with this step.

➥ To keep the persistence component example simple, we do not consider an adaptation of application behavior. ❏

3 *Identify structural aspects* of the system, which, when changed, should not affect the implementation of the base level. Examples include the type structure of an application [BKSP92], its underlying object model [McA95], or the distribution of components [McA95] in a heterogenous network.

➥ Our implementation of the persistence component must be independent of application-specific types. This requires access to run-time type information, such as the name, size, inheritance relationships and internal layout of each type, as well as the types, order and names of their data members. ❏

4 *Identify system services* that support both the variation of application services identified in step 2 and the independence of structural details identified in step 3. For example, implementing resumable exceptions in C++ requires explicit access to the exception handling mechanism of the language. Other examples of basic system services are:

- Resource allocation

- Garbage collection

- Page swapping

- Object creation

➥ The persistence component must instantiate arbitrary classes when reading persistent objects. ❏

5   *Define the metaobjects.* For every aspect identified in the three previous steps, define appropriate metaobjects. Encapsulating behavior is supported by several domain-independent design patterns, such as Objectifier [Zim94], Strategy, Bridge, Visitor, and Abstract Factory [GHJV95]. For example, metaobjects for function call mechanisms can be implemented as strategy objects, and multiple implementations of components can be implemented with the Bridge pattern. Visitor allows you to integrate new functionality without modifying existing structures. Sometimes you may find appropriate domain-specific patterns that support this step, for example the Acceptor and Connector patterns for developing distributed systems [Sch95]. Another example is the Detachable Inspector pattern [SC95a], which supports the addition of run-time facilities such as debuggers and inspectors. Detachable Inspector builds on the Visitor pattern. Encapsulating structural and state information is supported by design patterns like Objectifier [Zim94] and State [GHJV95].

➡   The metaobjects that provide the run-type information for our persistence component are organized as follows:

The C++ standard library class `type_info` is used for identifying types [DWP95]. Its interface offers functions for accessing the name of a type, for comparing two types, and for determining their system internal order. Every type in the application is represented by an instance of class `type_info`.

```
class type_info {
    //...
private:
    type_info(const type_info& rhs);
    type_info& operator=(const type_info& rhs);
public:
    virtual      ~type_info();
    int          operator==(const type_info& rhs) const;
    int          operator!=(const type_info& rhs) const;
    int          before(const type_info& rhs) const;
    const char*  name() const;
};
```

None of the other classes of the run-time type information system are part of the C++ standard.

A class `extTypeInfo` provides access to information about the size, superclasses, and data members of a class. Clients can also determine whether the type is built-in or a pointer.

```
class extTypeInfo {
    // ...
public:
    const bool     isBuiltIn() const;
    const bool     isPointer() const;
    const size_t   size() const;
    baseIter*      bases(int direct = 0) const;
    dataIter*      data(int direct = 0) const;
};
```

The method bases() returns an object of class baseIter, which is an iterator over either all base classes of a given type or just its direct base classes. If the type is built-in, the method returns a NULL iterator. Analogously, the method data() returns an object of class dataIter. It iterates either over all data members of a given type, including inherited ones, or just the data members declared specifically for this type. If the type is built-in, the method returns a NULL iterator.

A class BaseInfo offers functions for accessing type information about a base class of a class, as well as to determine its offset in the class layout.

```
class BaseInfo {
    // ...
public:
    const type_info*  type() const;
    const long        offset() const;
};
```

A class DataInfo includes functions that return the name of a data member, its offset and its associated type_info object.

```
class DataInfo {
    // ...
public:
    const char*       name() const;
    const type_info*  type() const;
    const bool        isStatic() const;
    const long        offset() const;
    const long        address() const;
};
```

❏

6 *Define the metaobject protocol.* Support a defined and controlled modification and extension of the meta level, and also a modification of relationships between base-level components and metaobjects.

There are two options for implementing the metaobject protocol:

- Integrate it with the metaobjects. Every metaobject provides those functions of the metaobject protocol that operate on it.

- Implement the metaobject protocol as a separate component.

An advantage of the latter approach is that the control of every modification of the reflective application is localized at a central point. Functions that operate on several metaobjects are easier to implement. In addition, a separate component can shield metaobjects from unauthorized access and modification, if its implementation follows patterns such as Facade [GHJV95] or Whole-Part (225). The Singleton idiom [GHJV95] helps ensure that the metaobject protocol can only be instantiated once.

If implemented as a separate component, the metaobject protocol usually does not serve as a base class for classes that define metaobjects—it just operates on them. It only makes sense to specify the metaobject protocol as a base class from which concrete metaobject classes are derived if it applies to every metaobject.

➡ We provide a class MOP which defines the metaobject protocol for the meta level of our persistence component example. It is implemented as a singleton and operates directly on the internal structure of all classes declared in the previous step.

Type information is accessible by two functions.

```
const type_info* getInfo(char* typeName) const;
const extTypeInfo* getExtInfo(char* typeName) const;
```

The first function allows clients to access the standard type information about an object. The second function accesses the extended type information that we defined specifically for our run-time type information system. We need this function because objects of the standard class type_info do not provide access to user-defined information. All other type information—such as that about base classes—is accessible through the extTypeInfo object.

New type information metaobjects can be initialized with two functions, one for instantiating `type_info` objects and one for creating `extTypeInfo` objects.

```
void newTypeId(char* typeName);
void newTypeInfo(char* typeName,
            bool builtIn, bool pointer);
```

The `newTypeInfo()` function also calculates and sets the size of a type. The function `deleteInfo()` deletes all available information about a type, but only if no other class of the system contains a reference to an object of that type.

```
void deleteInfo(char* typeName);
```

We define four functions for adding new or modifying existing type information. The functions `addBase()` and `deleteBase()` respectively add and remove base class information, while the functions `addData()` and `deleteData()` respectively add and delete data member information.

```
void addBase(char* typeName, char* baseName);
void addData(char* typeName,
            char* memberType, char* memberName);
void deleteBase(char* typeName, char* baseName);
void deleteData(char* typeName, char* memberName);
```

Before executing changes, all functions perform consistency checks. For example, to set base class information, corresponding `type_info` and `extTypeInfo` objects must be available.

Two functions support modification of the 'object creator' metaobject.

```
void addCreationCode(char* typeName);
void deleteCreationCode(char* typeName);
```

Internally, the metaobject protocol needs functions for calculating type sizes and offsets of base classes and data members. These functions are compiler-dependent and must therefore be changed when using a different compiler. One way to support changing these functions is provided by the Strategy pattern [GHJV95]. To maintain `type_info` and `extTypeInfo` objects, the metaobject protocol maintains two maps, `tMap` and `eMap`. These maps offer functions to add, remove and find elements.

Most functions of the metaobject protocol can be implemented straightforwardly. Calculating offset and sizes and manipulating the 'object creator' metaobject requires higher implementation effort. The following code defines the `addBase()` function.

```
void MOP::addBase(char* typeName, char* baseName) {
    BaseInfo* base;
    // Is extended type information for type typeName
    // and type information for type baseName available?
    if ((!eMap.element(typeName)) ||
                        (!tMap.element(baseName)))
        // error handling ...

    // Instantiate the baseInfo object for type baseName
    base = new BaseInfo(tMap[baseName]);
    // Calculate the offset of the base class.
    base->baseOffset = calcOffset(typeName, baseName);
    // Add the new baseInfo object to the list of
    // bases within the extTypeInfo object for
    // type typeName
    eMap[typeName]->baseList.add(base);
}
```

Robustness is a major concern when implementing the metaobject protocol. Errors in change specifications should be detected wherever possible. Changes should also be reliable. The metaobject protocol described above, for example, checks the availability of appropriate type information metaobjects when adding new base class and data member information. Before deleting its type information, it also checks whether a type is used as a base class or data member.

Robustness also means maintaining consistency. For example, if we add a data member to a specific type, we must recalculate the size of all types that include the changed type as a base class or a data member. In addition, any modification should only affect those parts of the system that are subject to change. Finally, clients of the metaobject protocol should not take responsibility for integrating changes into the meta level. Ideally, a client only specifies a change, and the metaobject protocol is responsible for its integration. This avoids direct manipulation of source code.

7   *Define the base level.* Implement the functional core and user interface of the system according to the analysis model developed in step 1.

Use metaobjects to keep the base level extensible and adaptable. Connect every base-level component with metaobjects that provide system information on which they depend, such as type information, or which offer services they need, such as object creation in our persistence component. To handle system services, use design patterns such as Strategy, Visitor, Abstract Factory and Bridge [GHJV95], or idioms like Envelope-Letter [Cope92]. For example, the context class component of the Strategy pattern represents the base-level component, and the strategy class hierarchy the metaobjects. When applying the Visitor pattern, the metaobjects are the visitors, and the object structure represents the base-level components.

Provide base-level components with functions for maintaining the relationships with their associated metaobjects. The metaobject protocol must be able modify every relationship between the base level and the meta level. For example, when replacing a metaobject with a new one, the metaobject protocol must update all references to the replaced metaobject. The metaobject protocol operates either directly on internal data structures of base-level components, or uses a special interface the base-level components provide.

If the metaobjects to be used are not known a priori, provide the meta level or the metaobject protocol with appropriate retrieval functions, such as the `getInfo()` and `getExtInfo()` functions in the persistence component example.

Metaobjects often need information about the current state of computation. For example, the 'object creator' in our persistence component example must know what type it should instantiate. This information can either be passed as a parameter to the metaobjects, the metaobjects can retrieve it from other metaobjects, or the metaobjects can retrieve it from appropriate base-level components.

Changes to metaobjects affect the subsequent behavior of base-level components to which they are connected. Changing a relationship between the base level and the meta level affects only a specific base-level component, the one that maintains the modified relationship.

➡️   The implementation of the `read()` method of our persistence component follows the first scenario depicted in the Dynamics section. The method implements a general recursive algorithm for reading objects from a data file. The method consults the meta level to get information about how to read user-defined types. Reading built-in types or strings is hard-coded within its implementation. To obtain information about types, `read()` consults the `getInfo()` and `getExtInfo()` functions of the metaobject protocol. For creating objects of arbitrary types, `read()` is directly connected with the 'object creator' metaobject.

The structure of the `store()` method is similar to that of the `read()` method. It first opens the data file to be read, then calls an internal `storeObject()` method that stores the object structure. Finally, `store()` closes the data file.

The most challenging part of implementing `store()` is the detection of cycles in the object structure to be stored—it is essential to avoid storing duplicates and running into infinite recursion. To achieve this, the method marks the structure with a unique identifier which is also stored, before storing the object. If we return to an object that is so marked, we then just store its identifier.

The following simplified code illustrates the structure of the `storeObject()` method. It abstracts from several details, such as the storage of static data members.

```
void Persistence::storeObject
                   (void* object, char* typeName) {
    type_info*       objectId;
    extTypeInfo*     objectInfo;
    baseIter*        iterator;

    // Get type information about the object to be stored
    objectId    = mop->getInfo(typeName);
    objectInfo  = mop->getExtInfo(typeName);
    iterator    = objectInfo->data();

    // Mark the object to avoid storing duplicates
    markObject(object);

    // Object is of built-in type?
    if (objectInfo->isBuiltIn())
        storeBuiltIn(object, objectId);
```

```
                // Object is of type char*?
                else if (!strcmp("char*", objectId->name()))
                    storeString(object);

                // Object is a pointer != NULL?
                // *(char**)object means that we interpret the
                // generic pointer object as a pointer to an address
                else if ((objectInfo->isPointer()) &&
                                    (!(*(char**)object)))
                    // Dereference the pointer
                    storeObject(*(char**)object,
                        iterator->curr()->type()->name());

                // Object is a user-defined type with data members
                else while (!iterator->atEnd()) {
                    // If not marked, store the data member,
                    // else store the marker
                    if (!marked((char*)object +
                            iterator->curr()->offset()))
                        storeObject((char*)object +
                            iterator->curr()->offset(),
                            iterator->curr()->type()->name());
                    else
                        storeMarker((char*)object +
                            iterator->curr()->offset());

                    iterator->next();
                };
                delete iterator;
            };                                                      ❏
```

Example Resolved

In the previous sections we explained the Reflection architecture of our persistence component example. How we provide run-time type information is still an open issue.

Unlike languages like CLOS or Smalltalk, C++ does not support reflection very well—only the standard class `type_info` provides reflective capabilities: we can identify and compare types. One solution for providing extended type information is to include a special step in the compilation process. In this, we collect type information from the source files of the application, generate code for instantiating the metaobjects, and link this code with the application. Similarly, the 'object creator' metaobject is generated. Users specify code for instantiating an 'empty' object of every type, and the toolkit generates the code for the metaobject. Some parts of the system are compiler-dependent, such as offset and size calculation.

As illustrated in the code examples, we use pointer and address arithmetic, offsets, and sizes of types and data members to read and store objects. Since these features are considered harmful, for example by incurring the danger of overwriting object code, the persistence component must be implemented and tested very carefully.

Variants *Reflection with several meta levels.* Sometimes metaobjects depend on each other. For example, consider the persistence component. Changes to the run-time type information of a particular type requires that you update the 'object creator' metaobject. To coordinate such changes you may introduce separate metaobjects, and—conceptually—a meta level for the meta level, or in other words, a meta meta level. In theory this leads to an infinite tower of reflection. A software system has an infinite number of meta levels in which each meta level is controlled by a higher one, and where each meta level has its own metaobject protocol. In practice, most existing reflective software comprises only one or two meta levels.

An example of a programming language with several meta levels is RbCl [IMY92]. RbCl is an interpreted language. RbCl base-level objects are represented by several meta-level objects. These are interpreted by an interpreter that resides at the meta metal level of RbCl. The metaobject protocol of RbCl allows users to modify the metaobjects that represents RbCl base-level objects, the metaobject protocol of the meta meta level the behavior of the RbCl metaobject interpreter.

Known Uses **CLOS**. This is the classic example of a reflective programming language [Kee89]. In CLOS, operations defined for objects are called *generic functions,* and their processing is referred to as generic function *invocation.* Generic function invocation is divided into three phases:

- The system first determines the methods that are applicable to a given invocation.

- It then sorts the applicable methods in decreasing order of precedence.

- The system finally sequences the execution of the list of applicable methods. Note that in CLOS more than one method can be executed in response to a given invocation.

The process of generic function invocation is defined in the metaobject protocol of CLOS [KRB91]. Basically, it executes a certain sequence of meta-level generic functions. Through the CLOS metaobject protocol users can vary the behavior of an application by modifying these generic functions or the generic functions of the metaobjects they call.

MIP [BKSP92] is a run-time type information system for C++. It is mainly used for introspective access to the type system of an application. Every type of a C++ software system is represented by a set of metaobjects that provide general information about that type, its relationships to other types, and its inner structure. All information is accessible at run-time. The functionality of MIP is separated into four layers:

- The first layer includes information and functionality that allows software to identify and compare types. This layer corresponds to the standard run-time type identification facilities for C++ [SL92].

- The second layer provides more detailed information about the type system of an application. For example, clients can obtain information about inheritance relationships for classes, or about their data and function members. This information can be used to browse type structures.

- The third layer provides information about relative addresses of data members, and offers functions for creating 'empty' objects of user-defined types. In combination with the second layer, this layer supports object I/O.

- The fourth layer provides full type information, such as that about friends of a class, protection of data members, or argument and return types of function members. This layer supports the development of flexible inter-process communication mechanisms, or of tools such as inspectors, that need very detailed information about the type structure of an application.

The metaobject protocol of MIP allows you to specify and modify the metaobjects that provide run-time type information. It offers appropriate functions for every layer of the MIP functionality.

MIP is implemented as a set of library classes. It also includes a toolkit for collecting type information about an application, and to generate code for instantiating the corresponding metaobjects. This code is linked to the application that uses MIP and is executed at the beginning of the main program. The toolkit can be integrated with the 'standard' compilation process for C++ applications. A special interface allows users to scale the available type information for every individual class or type.

PGen [THP94] is a persistence component for C++ that is based on MIP. It allows an application to store and read arbitrary C++ object structures.

The example used to explain the Reflection pattern is based mainly on MIP and PGen. Although simplified, the description of the persistence component, the class declarations for the metaobjects and the metaobject protocol widely reflect the original structure of MIP and PGen.

NEDIS. The car-dealer system NEDIS [EKM+94] uses reflection to support its adaptation to customer- and country-specific requirements. NEDIS includes a meta level called *run-time data dictionary*. It provides the following services and system information:

- Properties for certain attributes of classes, such as their allowed value ranges.

- Functions for checking attribute values against their required properties. NEDIS uses these functions to evaluate user input, for example to validate a date.

- Default values for attributes of classes, used to initialize new objects.

- Functions specifying the behavior of the system in the event of errors, such as invalid input or unexpected 'null' values of attributes.

- Country-specific functionality, for example for tax calculation.

- Information about the 'look and feel' of the software, such as the layout of input masks or the language to be used in the user interface.

The run-time data dictionary is implemented as a persistent database. A special interface allows users to modify any information or service it provides. Whenever the run-time data dictionary changes, special tools check and eventually restore its consistency. The run-time data dictionary is loaded when starting the software. For reasons of safety it cannot be modified while NEDIS is running.

OLE 2.0 [Bro94] provides functionality for exposing and accessing type information about OLE objects and their interfaces. The information can be used to dynamically access structural information about OLE objects, and to create invocations of OLE interfaces. For example, the run-time environment of Visual Basic [Mic95] checks the correctness of method calls to an object before dynamically invoking it. A similar concept is specified for Corba [OMG92].

Further examples of languages and systems that use a Reflection architecture include Open C++ [CM93], RbCl [IMY92], AL-1/D [OIT92], R2 [HT92], Apertos [Yok92] and CodA [McA95]. Even more examples can be found in [IMSA92], but note that although all examples provide reflective facilities, not all of them really implement a Reflection architecture as described by this pattern.

Consequences   A Reflection architecture provides the following **benefits**:

No explicit modification of source code. You do not need to touch existing code when modifying a reflective system. Instead, you specify a change by calling a function of the metaobject protocol. When extending the software, you pass the new code to the meta level as a parameter of the metaobject protocol. The metaobject protocol itself is responsible for integrating your change requests: it performs modifications and extensions to meta-level code, and if necessary re-compiles the changed parts and links them to the application while it is executing.

Changing a software system is easy. The metaobject protocol provides a safe and uniform mechanism for changing software. It hides all specific techniques such as the use of visitors, factories and strategies from the user. It also hides the inner complexity of a changeable application. The user is not confronted with the many metaobjects that encapsulate particular system aspects. The metaobject protocol also takes control over every modification. A well-designed and robust metaobject protocol helps prevent undesired changes of the fundamental semantics of an application [Kic92].

Support for many kinds of change. Metaobjects can encapsulate every aspect of system behavior, state and structure. An architecture based on the Reflection pattern thus potentially supports changes of almost any kind or scale. Even fundamental system aspects can be changed, such as function call mechanisms or type structures. With the help of reflective techniques it is also possible to adapt software to meet specific needs of the environment or to integrate customer-specific requirements.

However, a Reflection architecture has some significant **liabilities**:

Modifications at the meta level may cause damage. Even the safest metaobject protocol does not prevent users from specifying incorrect modifications. Such modifications may cause serious damage to the software or its environment. Examples of dangerous modifications include changing a database schema without suspending the execution of the objects in the application that use it, or passing code to the metaobject protocol that includes semantic errors. Similarly, bugs in pointer arithmetic can cause object code to be overwritten.

The robustness of a metaobject protocol is therefore of great importance [Kic92]. Potential errors within change specifications should be detected before the change is performed. Each change should only have a limited effect on other parts of the software.

Increased number of components. It may happen that a reflective software system includes more metaobjects than base-level components. The greater the number of aspects that are encapsulated at the meta level, the more metaobjects there are.

Lower efficiency. Reflective software systems are usually slower than non-reflective systems. This is caused by the complex relationship between the base level and the meta level. Whenever the base level is unable to decide how to continue with computation, it consults the meta level for assistance. This reflective capability requires extra processing: information retrieval, changing metaobjects, consistency checking, and the communication between the two levels decrease the overall performance of the system. You can partly reduce this performance penalty by optimization techniques, such as injecting meta-level code directly into the base level when compiling the system.

Not all potential changes to the software are supported. Although a Reflection architecture helps with the development of changeable software, only changes that can be performed through the metaobject protocol are supported. As a result, it is not possible to integrate easily all unforeseen changes to an application, for example changes or extensions to base-level code.

Not all languages support reflection. A Reflection architecture is hard to implement in some languages, such as C++, which offers little or no support for reflection. C++ only provides type identification. Reflective applications in C++ often build on language constructs such as pointer arithmetic to handle arbitrary objects, and need tool support for dynamically modifying meta-level code. This is, however, tedious and error-prone. In such languages it is also impossible to exploit the full power of reflection, such as adding new methods to a class dynamically. However, even in languages that do not provide reflective capabilities, it is possible to build reflective systems that are changeable and extensible, such as the C++ systems NEDIS [EKM+94], MIP [BKSP92] and Open C++ [CM93].

See Also The *Microkernel* architectural pattern (171) supports adaptation and change by providing a mechanism for extending the software with additional or customer-specific functionality. The central component of this architecture—the *microkernel*—serves as a socket for plugging in such extensions and for coordinating their collaboration. Modifications can be made by exchanging these 'pluggable' parts.

An earlier version of this pattern appeared in [PLoP95].

Credits One of the first works on reflection is the Ph.D. thesis by Brian Cantwell Smith [Smi82]. This describes reflection in the context of procedural languages. An overview of reflective concepts can be found in [Mae87].

We thank the members of PLoP'95 Working Group 1 for their valuable criticism and suggestions for improvement of an earlier version of this pattern, especially Douglas C. Schmidt and Aamod Sane. Special thanks also go to Linda Rising and David E. DeLano from AG Communication Systems, and Brian Foote and Ralph Johnson from the University of Illinois at Urbana Champaign. Their detailed review of an earlier version of this pattern helped to shape this description.

3 Design Patterns

We all know the value of design experience. How many times you had design dejá-vu—that feeling that you've solved a problem before but not knowing exactly where or how? If you could remember the details of the previous problem and how you solved it, then you could reuse the experience instead of rediscovering it.

The Gang-of-Four, Design Patterns – Elements of
Reusable Object-Oriented Software

A design pattern describes a commonly-recurring structure of communicating components that solve a general design problem in a particular context [GHJV95].

In this chapter we present eight design patterns: Whole-Part, Master-Slave, Proxy, Command Processor, View Handler, Forwarder-Receiver, Client-Dispatcher-Server and Publisher-Subscriber.

3.1   Introduction

Design patterns are medium-scale patterns. They are smaller in scale than architectural patterns, but are at a higher level than the programming language-specific idioms. The application of a design pattern has no effect on the fundamental structure of a software system, but may have a strong influence on the architecture of a subsystem.

We group design patterns into categories of related patterns, in the same way as we did for architectural patterns:

- *Structural Decomposition.* This category includes patterns that support a suitable decomposition of subsystems and complex components into cooperating parts. The Whole-Part pattern (225) is the most general pattern we are aware of in this category. It has wide applicability for structuring complex components.

- *Organization of Work.* This category comprises patterns that define how components collaborate together to solve a complex problem. We describe the Master-Slave pattern (245), which helps you to organize the computation of services for which fault tolerance or computational accuracy is required. It also supports the splitting of services into independent parts and their execution in parallel.

- *Access Control.* Such patterns guard and control access to services or components. We describe the Proxy pattern (263) here. Proxy lets clients communicate with a representative of a component, rather than to the component itself.

- *Management.* This category includes patterns for handling homogenous collections of objects, services and components in their entirety. We describe two patterns: the Command Processor pattern (277) addresses the management and scheduling of user commands, while the View Handler pattern (291) describes how to manage views in a software system.

- *Communication.* Patterns in this category help to organize communication between components. Two patterns address issues of inter-process communication: the Forwarder-Receiver pattern (307) deals with peer-to-peer communication, while the Client-

Dispatcher-Server pattern (323) describes location-transparent communication in a Client-Server structure.

The Publisher-Subscriber pattern (339) helps with the task of keeping data consistent between cooperating components. Publisher-Subscriber corresponds directly to the Observer pattern in [GHJV95]. We therefore only present the essence of this pattern, and focus on describing an important variant of Publisher-Subscriber, the Event Channel.

The design patterns included in this chapter only cover a small range of the problems that can occur when designing a software system. The collection can and should be extended with further design patterns, for example those in [GHJV95]. If more design patterns are added, it may also become necessary to define new categories for organizing them. We expand on this topic in Chapter 5, *Pattern Systems*.

An important property of all design patterns is that they are independent of a particular application domain. They deal with the structuring of application functionality, not with the implementation of the application functionality itself.

Most design patterns are independent of a particular programming paradigm. Usually they can be implemented easily in an object-oriented fashion, but all our design patterns are general enough to be adapted to more traditional programming practices, such as a procedural style.

3.2 Structural Decomposition

Subsystems and complex components are handled more easily if structured into smaller independent components, rather than remaining as monolithic blocks of code. Changes are easier to perform, extensions are easier to integrate and your design is much easier to understand.

In this section we describe a design pattern that supports the structural decomposition of components:

- The *Whole-Part* design pattern (225) helps with the aggregation of components that together form a semantic unit. An aggregate component, the whole, encapsulates its constituent components, the parts, organizes their collaboration, and provides a common interface to its functionality. Direct access to the parts is not possible.

The Whole-Part pattern has wide applicability. Almost every software system includes components or even whole subsystems that can be organized using this pattern. Hierarchical structures with containment relationships are especially suitable for the application of Whole-Part in one of its variants.

Another well-known pattern that helps with structural decomposition is Composite [GHJV95].

- The *Composite* pattern organizes objects into tree structures that represent part-whole hierarchies. Composite allows clients to interact with individual objects and compositions of objects uniformly.

Note that patterns such as Whole-Part and Composite do not provide the structural decomposition of a specific subsystem or component. You still need to specify the participants in a component structure according to the requirements of the application you are developing.

Such patterns do however provide general techniques for decomposing subsystems and complex components. Composite, for example, describes how to build hierarchical structures that allow clients to ignore the difference between compositions of objects and the individual objects in the hierarchies.

Patterns in this category also specify how to implement specific relationships between components, such as assembly-parts or container-contents. They also specify the general kinds of responsibilities particular components in such structures should have.

Whole-Part

The *Whole-Part* design pattern helps with the aggregation of components that together form a semantic unit. An aggregate component, the Whole[1], encapsulates its constituent components, the Parts, organizes their collaboration, and provides a common interface to its functionality. Direct access to the Parts is not possible.

Example A computer-aided design (CAD) system for 2-D and 3-D modeling allows engineers to design graphical objects interactively. In such systems most graphical objects are modeled as compositions of other objects. For example, a car object aggregates several smaller objects such as wheels and windows, which themselves may be composed of even smaller objects such as circles and polygons. It is the responsibility of the car object to implement functionality that operates on the car as a whole, such as rotating or drawing.

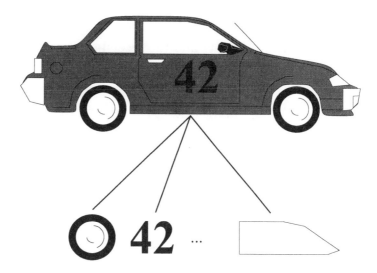

---

1. In this description the names of pattern participants start with a leading uppercase letter to distinguish between the word 'whole' and the component called 'Whole'.

Context   Implementing aggregate objects.

Problem   In almost every software system objects that are composed of other objects exist. For example, consider a molecule object in a chemical simulation system—it can be implemented as a graph of separate atom objects. Such aggregate objects do not represent loosely-coupled sets of components. Instead, they form units that are more than just a mere collection of their parts. In this example, a molecule object would have attributes such as its chemical properties, and methods, such as rotation. These attributes and methods refer to the molecule as a semantic unit, and not to the individual atoms of which it is composed. The molecules example illustrates the typical case in which aggregates reveal behavior that is not obvious or visible from their individual parts—the combination of parts makes new behavior emerge. Such behavior is called *emergent behavior*. Consider, for example, the chemical reactions in which a molecule can participate—these cannot be determined by only analyzing its individual atoms.

We need to balance the following *forces* when modeling such structures:

- A complex object should either be decomposed into smaller objects, or composed of existing objects, to support reusability, changeability and the recombination of the constituent objects in other types of aggregate.

- Clients should see the aggregate object as an atomic object that does not allow any direct access to its constituent parts.

Solution   Introduce a component that encapsulates smaller objects, and prevents clients from accessing these constituent parts directly. Define an interface for the aggregate that is the only means of access to the functionality of the encapsulated objects, allowing the aggregate to appear as a semantic unit.

The general principle of the Whole-Part pattern is applicable to the organization of three types of relationship:

- An *assembly-parts* relationship, which differentiates between a product and its parts or subassemblies—such as the relationship of a molecule to its atoms in our previous example. All parts are tightly integrated according to the internal structure of the assembly. The amount and type of subassemblies is predefined and does not vary.

- A *container-contents* relationship, in which the aggregated object represents a container. For example, a postal package can include different contents such as a book, a bottle of wine, and a birthday card. These contents are less tightly coupled than the parts in an assembly-parts relationship. The contents may even be dynamically added or removed.

- The *collection-members* relationship, which helps to group similar objects—such as an organization and its members. The collection provides functionality, such as iterating over its members and performing operations on each of them. There is no distinction between individual members of a collection—all of them are treated equally.

These relationships mimic relationships between objects in the real world. When modeling them with software entities, it is not always obvious which kind of relationship is appropriate. A molecule may be considered as an assembly composed of different atoms, but also as a container with atoms as its contents. Which relationship is most appropriate depends on the desired use of the aggregate.

It is important to note that these categorizations define relationships between objects, and not between data types.

Structure   The Whole-Part pattern introduces two types of participant:

A *Whole* object represents an aggregation of smaller objects, which we call *Parts*. It forms a semantic grouping of its Parts in that it coordinates and organizes their collaboration. For this purpose, the Whole uses the functionality of Part objects for implementing services.

Some methods of the Whole may be just placeholders for specific Part services. When such a method is invoked the Whole only calls the relevant Part service, and returns the result to the client.

➡   Each graphical object in a CAD system may contain a Part that provides version information to the user. When a client invokes the method `getVersion()`, the request is forwarded to the appropriate method of the Part.   ❏

Other services of the Whole implement complex strategies that build on several smaller services offered by Parts.

➥   Consider zooming a group of 2-D objects. To achieve this, the smallest surrounding rectangles of all group members are determined. Calculating the union of these rectangles leads to the smallest surrounding rectangle of the group itself. Its center represents the center of the zoom operation. To complete the execution of the zoom method, the group object invokes the zoom operations of all its Parts, passing the center and the percentage zoom as arguments.   ❏

The Whole may additionally provide functionality that does not invoke any Part service at all.

➥   Consider the implementation of collections such as sets. Set objects offer functions like `getSize()` for returning the current number of contained elements. For performance reasons, `getSize()` can be implemented by introducing caching strategies. An additional data member `size` stores the current sizes of elements within the set. Whenever elements are removed or added, the value of `size` is updated accordingly. If a client invokes `getSize()`, the function returns the value of `size` without needing to access any elements of the set.   ❏

Only the services of the Whole are visible to external clients. The Whole also acts as a wrapper around its constituent Parts and protects them from unauthorized access.

Each Part object is embedded in exactly one Whole. Two or more Wholes cannot share the same Part. Each Part is created and destroyed within the life-span of its Whole.

Class Whole	*Collaborators* • Part	*Class* Part	*Collaborators* -
Responsibility • Aggregates several smaller objects. • Provides services built on top of part objects. • Acts as a wrapper around its constituent parts.		*Responsibility* • Represents a particular object and its services.	

The static relationships between a Whole and its Parts are illustrated in the OMT diagram below:

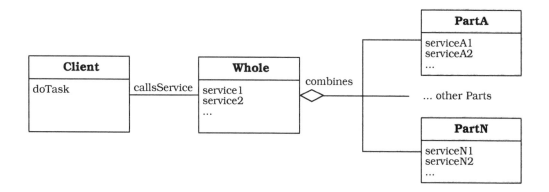

Dynamics   The following scenario illustrates the behavior of a Whole-Part structure. We use the two-dimensional rotation of a line within a CAD system as an example. The line acts as a Whole object that contains two points p and q as Parts. A client asks the line object to rotate around the point c and passes the rotation angle as an argument. Since the rotation of a line can be based on the rotation of single points, it is sufficient for the line object to call the rotate methods of its endpoints. After rotation, the line redraws itself on the screen. For brevity, the scenario does not demonstrate how the old line is deleted from the screen, nor how the drawLine method retrieves the coordinates of the new endpoints.

The rotation of a point p around a center c with an angle a can be calculated using the following formula:

$$p' = \begin{bmatrix} \cos a & -\sin a \\ \sin a & \cos a \end{bmatrix} \cdot (p - c) + c$$

In the diagram below the rotation of the line given by the points p and q is illustrated.

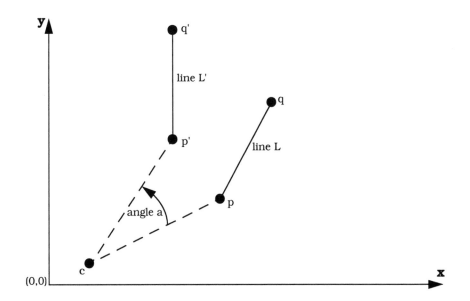

The scenario consists of four phases:

- A client invokes the rotate method of the line L and passes the angle a and the rotation center c as arguments.

- The line L calls the rotate method of the point p.

- The line L calls the rotate method of the point q.

- The line L redraws itself using the new positions of p' and q' as endpoints.

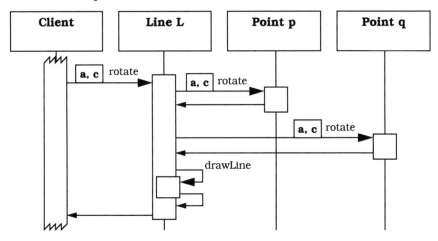

Implementation To implement a Whole-Part structure, apply the following steps:

1 *Design the public interface of the Whole.* Analyze the functionality the Whole must offer to its clients. Only consider the client's viewpoint in this step. Think of the Whole as an atomic component that is not structured into Parts, and compile a list of methods that together comprise the public interface of the Whole.

2 *Separate the Whole into Parts, or synthesize it from existing ones.* There are two approaches to assembling the Parts you need—either assemble a Whole 'bottom-up' from existing Parts, or decompose it 'top-down' into smaller Parts:

• The bottom-up approach allows you to compose Wholes from loosely-coupled Parts that you can later reuse when implementing other types of Whole. A liability of this approach is the difficulty of covering all aspects of the required functionality of the Whole using existing Parts. As a result, you often have to implement 'glue' to bridge the gap between the composition of Parts and the interface provided by the Whole.

• The top-down approach makes it is possible to cover all of the Whole's functionality. Partitioning into Parts is driven by the services the Whole provides to its clients, freeing you from the requirement to implement glue code. However, strictly applying the top-down approach often leads to Parts that are tightly coupled and not reusable in other contexts as a result.

A mixture of both approaches is often applied. For example, you may follow the top-down approach until the resulting structure allows you to reuse existing Parts.

3 *If you follow a bottom-up approach,* use existing Parts from component libraries or class libraries and specify their collaboration. If you cannot cover all the Whole's functionality with existing Parts, specify additional ones and their integration with the remaining Parts. You may need to use the top-down approach to implement such missing Parts.

4   *If you follow a top-down approach, partition the Whole's services into smaller collaborating services* and map these collaborating services to separate Parts. For example, in the Forwarder-Receiver design pattern (307) a forwarder component is responsible for marshaling an IPC message and delivering it to the receiver. You can therefore decompose a forwarder into two Parts, one responsible for marshaling and another responsible for message delivery.

Note that there are often several ways to decompose a Whole into Parts. For example, a triangle can be specified by three points that are not co-linear, or by three lines, or by a line and a point. As a rule of thumb, select the decomposition strategy that provides the easiest way of implementing the services of the Whole. If, for example, hidden-line algorithms are going to be applied to triangles, you should implement them as compositions of lines.

5   *Specify the services of the Whole in terms of services of the Parts.* In the structure you found in the previous two steps, the Whole is represented as a set of collaborating Parts with separate responsibilities. You need to specify which Part functionality the Whole uses for servicing client requests, and which requests it executes on its own.

Two are two possible ways to call a Part service:

- If a client request is forwarded to a Part service, the Part does not use any knowledge about the execution context of the Whole, relying on its own environment instead. Such forwarding leads to a loose coupling between the Whole and its Parts—they may even be implemented as active objects running in different processes.

- A delegation approach requires the Whole to pass its own context information to the Part. Delegation is useful when the Part should be tightly embedded in the Whole's environment. For example, delegation is required if implementation inheritance between a Part and the Whole must be simulated.

Decide whether all Part services are called only by their Whole, or if Parts may also call each other. Usually Parts are activated by their Whole. Sometimes, however, it is necessary for Parts to interact. For example, consider a simulation object such as a Whole that represents a set of astronomical galaxies. If you need to determine the movements of such galaxies, it is not sufficient to just consider the effects of the 'Big Bang'—you also have to take the gravitation attraction between galaxies into account. The solution to this problem requires numerical methods in which Parts interact with each other. Another example is provided by linked lists in which elements contain references to their neighbors.

You can find further discussion about interaction between Parts in the Mediator design pattern [GHJV95].

6 *Implement the Parts.* If the Parts are Whole-Part structures themselves, design them recursively starting with step 1. If not, reuse existing Parts from a library, or just implement them if their implementation is straightforward and further decomposition is not necessary.

7 *Implement the Whole.* Implement the Whole's services based on the structure you developed in the preceding steps. Implement services that depend on Part objects by invoking their services from the Whole. You also need to implement those services that do not depend on a Part object in this step.

When implementing the Whole, you need to take any given constraints into account, such as cardinality properties. For example, a water molecule consists of exactly two hydrogen atoms and one oxygen atom. Constraints may also exist between parts. Consider a postal package object and its contents—the size of the contents cannot exceed the size of the package.

You also need to manage the life cycle of Parts. Since a Part lives and must therefore die with its Whole, the Whole must be responsible for creating and deleting the Part.

The Example Resolved section presents a concrete example of an implementation of the Whole-Part pattern.

Variants *Shared Parts.* This variant relaxes the restriction that each Part must be associated with exactly one Whole by allowing several Wholes to share the same Part. The life-span of a shared Part is then decoupled from that of its Whole. For example, consider an electronic mail message that consists of a header and several attachments. The receiver of such a message could extract the attachments and package them into a new message. Even if the original message is deleted, its Parts—the attachments—may still exist. In such cases the Part itself, or a central administration component, is responsible for managing the Part's life cycle. In programming languages such as C++ you can use reference-counting strategies for this purpose—this is explained in the Counted Pointer idiom (353).

The next three variants describe the implementation of the Whole-to-Parts relationships we introduced in the Solution section:

Assembly-Parts. In this variant the Whole may be an object that represents an assembly of smaller objects. For example, a CAD representation of a car might be assembled from wheels, windows, body panels and so on. Constituent Parts could follow the assembly-parts relationship recursively—a wheel may itself be a Whole consisting of Parts such as circles. Recursively applying whole-part relationships leads to trees, and may also lead to directed acyclic graphs if shared Parts are allowed. Assembly-Parts structures are fixed, in that they do not support the addition or removal of Parts at run-time. They only allow you to exchange Parts with other Parts of the same type.

Container-Contents. In this variant a container is responsible for maintaining differing contents. For example, an electronic mail message may contain a header, the message body, and optional attachments. In contrast to the Assembly-Parts variant, a container component allows you to add or remove its contents dynamically.

The *Collection-Members* variant is a specialization of Container-Contents, in that the Part objects all have the same type. Parts are usually not coupled to or dependent on each other. You can apply this variant when implementing collections such as sets, lists, maps, and arrays. In addition, this pattern supports the inclusion of functionality for iterating over all members, and for executing operations on some or all members.

The *Composite* pattern was introduced in [GHJV95]. It is applicable to Whole-Part hierarchies in which the Wholes and their Parts can be treated uniformly—that is, in which both implement the same abstract interface.

Example Resolved   In our CAD system we decide to define a Java package that provides the basic functionality for graphical objects. The class library consists of atomic objects such as circles or lines that the user can combine to form more complex entities. We implement these classes directly instead of using the standard Java package awt (Abstract Windowing Toolkit) because awt does not offer all the functionality we need.

Objects use virtual coordinates instead of physical screen coordinates to hide system dependencies such as screen resolution. The abstract base class GraphicsObject defines common methods such as draw, rotate and dump. All other classes are either derived from Graphics-Object or one of its subclasses. The implementation of classes that provide a particular type of graphical objects such as Triangle uses the Assembly-Parts variant.

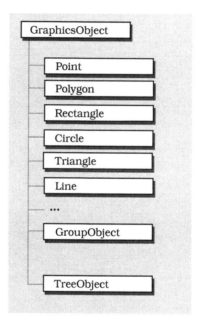

```
abstract class GraphicsObject {
    abstract public void dump();
    abstract public void
                rotate(int xc, int yc, double angle);
    // much more ...
}
```

The class Triangle is an example of a subclass of GraphicsObject. Each triangle is assembled from exactly three cartesian points that are not co-linear. A triangle object therefore acts as a Whole that contains three points as Part objects. The implementation of the class Triangle, therefore, is based on the implementation of the class Point. For example, the rotation of a triangle can be performed by rotating its corners. The rotate method is therefore an example of a service of the Whole that uses operations provided by the Parts. The Assembly-Parts relationship between a triangle and its corners is illustrated in the following diagram:

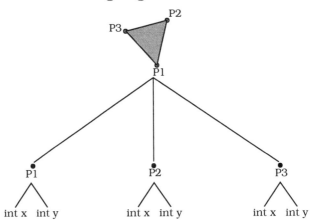

When the method rotate is invoked for a point, the center of rotation is passed as an argument. If the center and the point are the same, the method does nothing, otherwise it rotates the point around the center using the specified angle:

```java
class Point extends GraphicsObject {
    int x;
    int y;

    public static double dist(Point p, Point q) {
        double res = 0;
        if (p.x == q.x)
            res = Math.abs(p.y - q.y);
        else {
            double dx = p.x - q.x;
            double dy = p.y - q.y;
            res = Math.sqrt(dx*dx + dy*dy);
        }
        return res;
    }
    public static boolean isCollinear
        (Point p, Point q, Point r) {
        double tmp = dist(p,q) - (dist(p,r) + dist(r,q));
        if (Math.abs(tmp) < EPSILON) return true;
            else return false;
    }
```

```
public Point(int xCoord, int yCoord) {
    x = xCoord;
    y = yCoord;
}
public void dump() {
    System.out.print("POINT ");
    System.out.println("(" + x + "/" + y + ")");
}
public boolean isEqual(Point aPoint) {
    return ( (x == aPoint.x) &&
             (y == aPoint.y));
}
public void rotate(int xc, int yc, double angle) {
    if (isEqual(new Point(xc,yc)))
        return;
    else {
        double cosA = Math.cos(angle);
        double sinA = Math.sin(angle);
        double dx = x - xc;
        double dy = y - yc;
        x = (int) Math.round( cosA * dx -
                              sinA * dy +
                              xc         );

        y = (int) Math.round( sinA * dx +
                              cosA * dy +
                              yc         );
    }
}
}
```

The constructor of `Triangle` must check that the three points passed as arguments are not co-linear. Three points p, q, and r are co-linear if and only if the distance between p and q (`Point.dist(p,q)`) is equal to the sum of the distances between p and r (`Point.dist(p,r)`) and between r and q (`Point.dist(r,q)`). If this is the case, the constructor raises an exception. This is an example of constraint checking of the triangle as a Whole.

```
class PointsAreCollinear extends Exception {}
class Triangle extends GraphicsObject {
    Point p1;
    Point p2;
    Point p3;
```

```
public Triangle(Point po1, Point po2, Point po3)
    throws PointsAreCollinear
{   // check if these points are collinear.
    // If yes, raise an exception
    if (Point.isCollinear(po1, po2, po3))
        throw new PointsAreCollinear();
    p1 = po1; p2 = po2; p3 = po3;
}
public void dump() {
    System.out.println("TRIANGLE");
    System.out.print("Point 1: ");
    p1.dump();
    System.out.print("Point 2: ");
    p2.dump();
    System.out.print("Point 3: ");
    p3.dump();
}
public void rotate(int xc, int yc, double angle) {
    p1.rotate(xc, yc, angle);
    p2.rotate(xc, yc, angle);
    p3.rotate(xc, yc, angle);
}
}
```

We implement groups of different graphics objects using the Collection-Member variant. We can use this variant because a group does not need to know the concrete subtypes of its members—it can handle each of its members as an instance of class GraphicsObject instead. The class GroupObject comprises functionality such as the addition of graphical objects, and the iteration through all group members. Note that the class GroupObject does not comply exactly with the Composite variant [GHJV95]. The reason for this is that Part objects have a type different from the Whole. Whereas the Whole is an instance of GroupObject, the Parts are not—we have introduced the class GroupObject for this purpose. The alternative would have been to extend GraphicsObject with functionality for adding elements, regardless whether derived classes implement group objects or not.

If a method such as rotate is invoked for such a group, the group recursively invokes the method on all its members.

```
class GroupObject extends GraphicsObject {

    private Vector members = new Vector();

    public int size() { // number of members
        return members.size();
    }
```

```
public GraphicsObject objectAt(int pos) {
    return (GraphicsObject)(members.elementAt(pos));
}
public void addObject(GraphicsObject aShape) {
    members.addElement(aShape);
}
public void rotate(int xc, int yc, double angle) {
    for (int i = 0; i < members.size(); i++) {
        objectAt(i).rotate(xc, yc, angle);
    }
}
public void dump() {
    System.out.println("GROUP with " + size() +
                        " members: ");
    for (int i = 0; i < members.size(); i++) {
        objectAt(i).dump();
    }
}
}
```

Imagine that a user creates different graphics objects, selects them with the mouse, inserts them into a group, and tells the object editor to rotate the group around $(0,0)$ with an angle of $\pi/4$. The editor will execute a code sequence similar to that listed below:

```
Point p1 = new Point(10,10);
Point p2 = new Point(10,20);
Point p3 = new Point(20,10);
Triangle t = new Triangle(p1,p2,p3);
Circle  c = new Circle(new Point(0,0), 10);
Rectangle r = new Rectangle(new Point(-5,-5),
                            new Point(+5,+5));
Line l = new Line(new Point(1,1), new Point(10,5));
GroupObject g = new GroupObject();
g.addObject(t);
g.addObject(c);
g.addObject(r);
g.addObject(l);
g.rotate(0,0,java.lang.Math.PI/4);
```

The classes we have already introduced support simple shapes such as circles or triangles, as well as the grouping of such graphics objects. To create more complex shapes, instances of the class TreeObject support the composition of graphics objects using operators. For example, a circle with a rectangular hole may be represented by a binary tree. The left child specifies the circle, the right child the rectangle, and the node consists of the operator SUB as well as additional data. SUB is defined as subtraction of one figure from another. In this example, the rectangle is geometrically subtracted from the circle, resulting in a circle with a hole.

Tree objects implement the Container-Contents variant of Part-Whole. The Whole is given by the complex shape that is calculated from simpler shapes using a geometrical formula. The graphics objects and the operator in this formula represent the Parts. When an operation such as move is invoked on the `TreeObject` instance, the Whole forwards the request to all the sub-shapes of which it is composed.

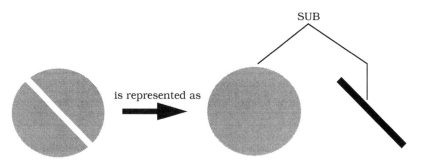

Known Uses The key abstractions of many **object-oriented applications** follow the Whole-Part pattern. For example, some graphical editors support the combination of different types of data to form multimedia documents. These are often implemented according to the Composite design pattern [GHJV95]. In CAD or animation systems, items under construction are represented by Assembly-Part structures. Almost all aspects of an application that can be hierarchically structured and can represent semantic units may be a subject for the application of the Whole-Part pattern in one of its variants.

Most **object-oriented class libraries** provide collection classes such as lists, sets, and maps. These classes implement the Collection-Member and Container-Contents variants. See [SNI94] and [Lea96] for examples.

Graphical user interface toolkits such as Fresco or ET++ [Gam91] use the Composite variant of the Whole-Part pattern.

Consequences The Whole-Part pattern offers several **benefits**:

Changeability of Parts. The Whole encapsulates the Parts and thus conceals them from its clients. This makes it possible to modify the internal structure of the Whole without any impact on clients. Part implementations may even be completely exchanged without any need to modify other Parts or clients.

Separation of concerns. A Whole-Part structure supports the separation of concerns. Each concern is implemented by a separate Part. It therefore becomes easier to implement complex strategies by composing them from simpler services than to implement them as monolithic units.

Reusability. The Whole-Part pattern supports two aspects of reusability. Firstly, Parts of a Whole can be reused in other aggregate objects. Secondly, the encapsulation of Parts within a Whole prevents a client from 'scattering' the use of Part objects all over its source code—this supports the reusability of Wholes.

The Whole-Part pattern suffers from the following **liabilities**:

Lower efficiency through indirection. Since the Whole builds a wrapper around its Parts, it introduces an additional level of indirection between a client request and the Part that fulfils it. This may cause additional run-time overhead compared with monolithic structures, especially when Parts are themselves implemented as Whole-Part structures.

Complexity of decomposition into Parts. An appropriate composition of a Whole from different Parts is often hard to find, especially when a bottom-up approach is applied. This is because an optimal partitioning into Parts depends on many issues, such as the given application domain, the structure to be modeled and the functionality to be provided by the Whole.

See also According to [GHJV95] the *Composite* design pattern is applicable when:

> You want to represent whole-part hierarchies of objects.

> You want clients to be able to ignore the difference between compositions of objects and individual objects. Clients will treat all objects in the composite structure uniformly.

Composite is a variant of the Whole-Part design pattern that you should consider when facing these two requirements.

The *Facade* design pattern [GHJV95] helps to provide a simple interface to a complex subsystem. A client uses this interface instead of accessing different Parts of the subsystem directly. However, a Facade structure does not enforce the encapsulation of Parts—clients may also access them directly. Another difference from Whole-Part structures is that facades do not compose complex services from simpler Part services—they only perform necessary interface translations and forward client requests to the appropriate Parts.

Credits   We thank our colleague Peter Graubmann for all his fruitful suggestions and comments regarding this pattern description.

3.3 Organization of Work

The implementation of complex services is often solved by several components in cooperation. To organize work optimally within such structures you need to consider several aspects. For example, each component should have a clearly-defined responsibility, and the basic strategy for providing the service should not be spread over many different components.

Several general principles apply when organizing the implementation of complex services. Examples are the separation of concerns, the separation of policy and implementation, and the 'divide and conquer' approach (see Chapter 6, *Patterns and Software Architecture*). Patterns that address the organization of work for particular kinds of services build on such enabling techniques.

In this section we describe one pattern for organizing work within a system:

- The *Master-Slave* pattern (245) supports fault tolerance, parallel computation and computational accuracy. A master component distributes work to identical slave components and computes a final result from the results these slaves return.

Master-Slave applies the 'divide and conquer' principle. Work is partitioned into several subtasks that are processed independently. The result of the whole service is calculated using the results that each partial processing operation provides. The Master-Slave pattern is widely applied in the areas of parallel and distributed computing.

Another example of the application of Master-Slave is the implementation of the so-called 'triple modular redundancy' principle. In this approach the execution of a service is delegated to three independent components, at least two of which must provide the same result for it to be considered valid.

The Chain of Responsibility, Command and Mediator patterns [GHJV95] also belong to this category:

- The *Chain of Responsibility* pattern avoids coupling the sender of a request to its receiver by giving more than one object the chance to handle the request. The receiving objects are chained and the request is passed along the chain until an object can handle it.

- The *Command* pattern encapsulates a request as an object, allowing you to parameterize clients with different requests, to queue or log requests and to support undoable operations.

- The *Mediator* pattern defines an object that encapsulates the way in which a set of objects interact. Mediator promotes loose coupling by preventing objects from referring to each other explicitly, and allows you to vary their interaction independently.

Patterns like Master-Slave (245), Chain of Responsibility and Mediator provide general collaboration techniques and structural frameworks for organizing work, analogously to patterns that address the structural decomposition of subsystems and components (see Section 3.2, *Structural Decomposition*).

Adapting these patterns for solving a specific problem, for example using Master-Slave for matrix multiplication, is still subject to the concrete design activities for the application under development.

Master-Slave

The *Master-Slave* design pattern supports fault tolerance, parallel computation and computational accuracy. A master component distributes work to identical slave components and computes a final result from the results these slaves return.

Example The traveling-salesman problem is well-known in graph theory. The task is to find an optimal round trip between a given set of locations, such as the shortest trip that visits each location exactly once.

The solution to this problem is of high computational complexity—there are approximately $6.0828 * 10^{62}$ different trips that connect the state capitals of the United States! Generally, the solution to the traveling-salesman problem with n locations is the best of $(n-1)!$ possible routes. Since the traveling-salesman problem is NP-complete [GJ79], there is no way to circumvent this high complexity if the optimal solution must be found.

Most existing implementations of the traveling-salesman problem therefore approximate the optimal solution by only comparing a fixed number of routes. One of the simplest approaches is to select routes to compare at random, and hope that the best route found approximates the optimal route sufficiently. We should make sure however that the routes to be investigated are chosen in a random and independent fashion, and that the number of selected routes is sufficiently large.

Context   Partitioning work into semantically-identical sub-tasks.

Problem   'Divide and conquer' is a common principle for solving many kinds of problem. Work is partitioned into several equal sub-tasks that are processed independently. The result of the whole calculation is computed from the results provided by each partial process. Several *forces* arise when implementing such a structure:

- Clients should not be aware that the calculation is based on the 'divide and conquer' principle.

- Neither clients nor the processing of sub-tasks should depend on the algorithms for partitioning work and assembling the final result.

- It can be helpful to use different but semantically-identical implementations for processing sub-tasks, for example to increase computational accuracy.

- Processing of sub-tasks sometimes needs coordination, for example in simulation applications using the finite element method.

Solution   Introduce a coordination instance between clients of the service and the processing of individual sub-tasks.

A *master* component divides work into equal sub-tasks, delegates these sub-tasks to several independent but semantically-identical *slave* components, and computes a final result from the partial results the slaves return.

This general principle is found in three application areas:

- *Fault tolerance*. The execution of a service is delegated to several replicated implementations. Failure of service executions can be detected and handled.

- *Parallel computing*. A complex task is divided into a fixed number of identical sub-tasks that are executed in parallel. The final result is built with the help of the results obtained from processing these sub-tasks.

- *Computational accuracy.* The execution of a service is delegated to several different implementations. Inaccurate results can be detected and handled.

Provide all slaves with a common interface. Let clients of the overall service communicate only with the master.

➡ We decide to approximate the solution to the traveling-salesman problem by comparing a fixed number of trips. Our strategy for selecting trips is simple—we just pick them randomly. This simple-minded implementation uses an early version of the object-oriented parallel programming language pSather [MFL93]. The program is tuned for a CM5 computer from Thinking Machines Corporation with sixty-four processors.

To take advantage of the CM-5 multi-processor architecture, the lengths of different trips are calculated in parallel. We therefore implement the trip length calculation as a slave. Each slave takes a number of trips to be compared as input, randomly selects these trips and returns the shortest trip found. A master determines a priori the number of slaves that are to be instantiated, specifies how many trips each slave instance should compare, launches the slave instances, and selects the shortest trip from all trips returned. In other words, the slaves provide local optima that the master resolves to a global optimum. ❑

Structure The *master* component provides a service that can be solved by applying the 'divide and conquer' principle. It offers an interface that allows clients to access this service. Internally, the master implements functions for partitioning work into several equal sub-tasks, starting and controlling their processing, and computing a final result from all the results obtained. The master also maintains references to all slave instances to which it delegates the processing of sub-tasks.

The *slave* component provides a sub-service that can process the sub-tasks defined by the master. Within a Master-Slave structure, there are several instances of the slave component connected to the master.

Class	Collaborators
Master	• Slave
Responsibility	
• Partitions work among several slave components • Starts the execution of slaves • Computes a result from the sub-results the slaves return.	

Class	Collaborators
Slave	-
Responsibility	
• Implements the sub-service used by the master.	

The structure defined by the Master-Slave patterns consists of one master and at least two slaves.

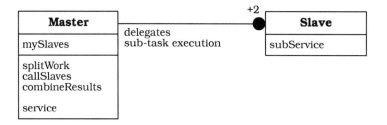

Dynamics   In the following scenario we assume, for simplicity, that slaves are called one after the other. However, the Master-Slave pattern unleashes its full power when slaves are called concurrently, for example by assigning them to several separate threads of control. The scenario comprises six phases:

- A client requests a service from the master.

- The master partitions the task into several equal sub-tasks.

- The master delegates the execution of these sub-tasks to several slave instances, starts their execution and waits for the results they return.

- The slaves perform the processing of the sub-tasks and return the results of their computation back to the master.

- The master computes a final result for the whole task from the partial results received from the slaves.

- The master returns this result to the client.

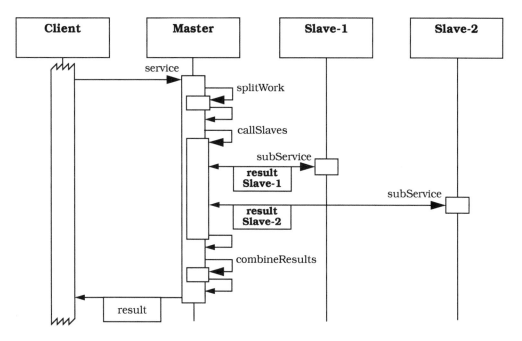

Implementation   The implementation of the Master-Slave pattern follows five steps. Note that these steps abstract from specific issues that need to be considered when supporting the application of the pattern to the special cases of fault tolerance, parallel computation, and computational accuracy, or when distributing slaves to several processes or threads. These aspects are addressed in the Variants section.

1   *Divide work.* Specify how the computation of the task can be split into a set of equal sub-tasks. Identify the sub-service that is necessary to process a sub-task.

➠   For our parallel traveling-salesman program we could partition the problem so that a slave is provided with one round trip at time and computes its cost. However, for a machine like the CM5 with SPARC node processors, such a partitioning might be too fine-grained. The costs for monitoring these parallel executions and for passing parameters to them decreases the overall performance of the algorithm instead of speeding it up.

A more efficient solution is to define sub-tasks that identify the shortest trip of a particular subset of all trips. This solution also takes account of the fact that there are only sixty-four processors available on our CM5. The number of available processors limits the number of sub-tasks that can be processed in parallel. To find the number of trips to be compared by each sub-task, we divide the number of all trips to be compared by the number of available processors.   ❏

2   *Combine sub-task results.* Specify how the final result of the whole service can be computed with the help of the results obtained from processing individual sub-tasks.

➡   Each sub-task returns only the shortest trip of a subset of all trips to be compared. We must still identify the shortest trip of these.❏

3   *Specify the cooperation between master and slaves.* Define an interface for the sub-service identified in step 1. It will be implemented by the slave and used by the master to delegate the processing of individual sub-tasks.

One option for passing sub-tasks from the master to the slaves is to include them as a parameter when invoking the sub-service. Another option is to define a repository where the master puts sub-tasks and the slaves fetch them. When processing a sub-task, individual slaves can work on separate data structures, or all slaves can share a single data structure. Slaves may return the result of their processing explicitly as a return parameter, or they may write it to a separate repository from which the master retrieves it.

Which of these options are best depends on many factors; for example, the costs of passing sub-tasks to slaves, of duplicating data structures, and of operating on a shared data structure with several slaves. The original problem also influences the decisions to be made. When slaves modify the data on which they operate, you need to provide each slave with its own copy of the original data structure. If they do not modify data, all slaves can work on a shared data structure, for example when implementing matrix multiplication.

➡   For the traveling-salesman program we let each slave operate on its own copy of the graph that represents all cities and their connections. We will create these copies when instantiating the slaves. The alternative—having the slaves read from one shared graph representation—was not chosen since such a communication load on the CM5 internal network would reduce the performance of our application considerably.

The interface of the slave to the master is defined by a function that takes the number of random routes to be evaluated as an input parameter. The function returns the optimal route found, which is represented by an instance of class TOUR.

```
random_perms(numberPerms : INT) : TOUR
```

The term perms in random_perms() stands for permutations, since we represent round trips as permutations of the n nodes that stand for the n cities to be visited. ❑

4 *Implement the slave components* according to the specifications developed in the previous step.

➥ The class TSP is the design center of our small applications. It includes a constructor, functions to create a random trip and to update the shortest trip found so far, and the random_perms() function specified in the previous step. The class COMPLETE_GRAPH represents the graph structure on which instances of TSP operate. The class RANDOM represents a random number generator. The code is not complete, but is an excerpt from a working application.

```
class TSP is
    -- Data structures
    best_tour, current_tour   : TOUR;
    graph                     : COMPLETE_GRAPH;
    random                    : RANDOM;
    -- Constructor for the slave that initializes
    -- the return value, creates the graph structure,
    -- and creates the random number generator.
    create() : TSP is
        res          := new;
        res.graph    := COMPLETE_GRAPH::create;
        res.random   := RANDOM::create;
    end; -- create
    -- Construct a number of randomly selected tours and
    -- return the tour with the lowest costs
    random_perms(numberPerms : INT) : TOUR is
        i : INT := 1;
        while i <= numberPerms loop
            construct_random_tour;
            update_optimum;
            i := i+1;
        end; -- loop
        res := best_tour;
    end; -- random_perms
    -- Construct a new random tour and calculate its costs
    construct_random_tour is -- not shown here
    end; -- construct_random_tour
```

```
            -- Update the optimal tour if the currently evaluated
            -- tour is better than the current optimum
        update_optimum is
            if current_tour.cost < best_tour.cost then
                best_tour      := current_tour;
            end; -- if
        end; -- update_optimum
    end; -- class TSP
```

Note that the assignment in `update_optimum` assumes either deep-copy semantics, or that `current_tour` will refer to a new TOUR object after the assignment. Otherwise, `construct_random_tour()` corrupts `best_tour` when modifying `current_tour`. The original program solved the problem by swapping the two TOUR objects to which `best_tour` and `current_tour` referred.   ❏

5   *Implement the master* according to the specifications developed in step 1 to 3.

There are two options for dividing a task into sub-tasks. The first is to split work into a fixed number of sub-tasks. This is most applicable if the master delegates the execution of the complete task to the slaves. This might typically occur when the Mater-Slave pattern is used to support fault tolerance or computational accuracy applications, or if the amount of parallel work is always fixed and known a priori. The second option is to define as many sub-tasks as necessary, or possible. For example, the master component in our traveling-salesman program could define as many sub-tasks as there are processors available.

The exchange of algorithms for subdividing a task can be supported by applying the Strategy pattern [GHJV95]. We discuss further issues you should consider in the Variants section.

The code for launching the slaves, controlling their execution and collecting their results depends on many factors. Are the slaves executed sequentially, or do they run concurrently in different processes or threads? Are slaves independent of each other, or do they need coordination? We give more details about this in the Variants section.

The master computes a final result with help of the results collected from the slaves. This algorithm may follow different strategies, as described in the Variants section. To support its dynamic exchange and variation, you can again apply the Strategy pattern [GHJV95].

You also must deal with possible errors, such as failure of slave execution or failure to launch a thread. Details are discussed in the Variants section.

There is only one master component within a Master-Slave structure. You can apply the Singleton pattern [GHJV95] to ensure this property.

➡   In the traveling salesman program we represent the master with an object of class CM5_TSP. It offers a function best_tour() to its clients which returns the best round trip visited by the whole Master-Slave structure. The best_tour() function takes the number of routes to be generated and the number of processors to use as parameters.

The function distribute() copies the graph and some additional data structures to all processors. The implementation we show works sequentially. '@j' means 'do this operation on processor j'. The function distribute() creates as many new slaves as there are processors available. The function random_perms() launches the slaves. The function update_optimum() selects the optimal route from the local optima returned by the slaves.

Our strategy for coordinating the slaves is to start them asynchronously and to synchronize them later, in particular when we want to select the best trip found. To implement this behavior we use the 'future' principle. A future is a variable that defines a value that is computed asynchronously in a different process or thread of control. Synchronization is achieved when the variable is accessed later. Since pSather supports futures, we use an array of futures for slaves to coordinate their parallel execution. For reasons of brevity we do not illustrate object creation. For more details on the pSather version we use in our example, see [Lim93].

```
class CM5_TSP is
    -- Data structures. Shared variables in pSather
    -- correspond to static members in C++
    shared n : INT              -- Number of Cities
    shared P : INT;             -- Number of processors
    shared T : ARRAY{TSP};      -- The slave array
    shared best_tour : TOUR     -- The best round trip
```

```
                     -- Assign a slave to each available processor
                 distribute is
                     -- Create the slave instances
                     i : INT := 1;
                     while i <= P loop
                         -- initializes T[j];
                         copy_graph()@j;
                         i := i+1;
                     end; -- loop
                 end; -- distribute
                 -- Launch the slaves      .
                 random_perms(t : INT) is
                     i, j, jobs_per_proc : INT;
                     -- Calculate how many tours each slave must visit
                     -- Assume that P divides t
                     jobs_per_proc      := t/P;
                     -- Define a monitor
                     m := MONITOR{TOUR}:=MONITOR{TOUR}::new;
                     -- Launch each slave at its processor
                     i := 1;
                     while i <= P loop
                         m :- T[i].random_perms(jobs_per_proc)@i;
                         i := i + 1;
                     end; -- loop
                     -- wait until the slaves finish with their
                     -- computation and take the results of the slaves
                     -- in whatever order they are returned
                     j := 1;
                     while j <= P loop
                         current_tour := m.take;
                         update_optimum();
                     end; -- loop
                 end; -- random_perms
                 -- Select the optimal tours from the trips the slaves
                 -- returned
                 update_optimum is -- not shown here
                 end; -- update_optimum
                 -- Return the optimal tour from t randomly created
                 -- ones with help of P slaves.
                 best_tour(t, p : INT): TOUR is
                     P := p;
                     -- Create the slaves, launch them, determine
                     -- the best trip visited, and return this tour
                     -- to the client calling the master
                     distribute;
                     random_perms(t);
                     update_optimum;
                     res := best_tour;
                 end; -- best_tour

         end; -- class CM5_TSP                                        ❏
```

Variants   There are three application areas for the Master-Slave pattern:

Master-Slave for fault tolerance. In this variant the master just delegates the execution of a service to a fixed number of replicated implementations, each represented by a slave. As soon as the first slave terminates, the result produced is returned to the client of the master. Fault tolerance is supported by the fact that as long as at least one slave does not fail, the client can be provided with a valid result. The master can handle the situation in which all slaves fail, for example by raising an exception or by returning a special 'Exceptional Value' [Cun94] with which the client can operate. The master may use time-outs to detect slave failure. However, this variant does not help with the situation in which the master itself fails—it is the critical component that must 'stay alive' to make this structure work.

Master-Slave for parallel computation. The most common use of the Master-Slave pattern is for the support of parallel computation. In this variant the master divides a complex task into a number of identical sub-tasks, each of which is executed in parallel by a separate slave. The master builds the final result from the results obtained from the slaves. The master contains the strategies for dividing the overall task and for computing the final result.

The algorithm for sub-dividing the task and for coordinating the slaves is strongly dependent on the hardware architecture of the machine on which the program runs. On distributed memory machines with general-purpose processors, for example, the granularity is usually larger than on SIMD (single instruction multiple data) machines. Other aspects that govern the algorithm are the machine's topology and the speed of its processor interconnections. The cooperation between the master and the slaves also depends on aspects such as the existence of shared or distributed memory for machines. The division of work is further influenced by issues listed in the *Slave as Threads variant* (see below), and the cooperation between master and slaves by issues listed in step 3 of the Implementation section.

Before the master can compute the final result it must wait for all slaves to finish executing their sub-tasks. To free the master from the task of synchronizing each slave individually, [KSS96] introduces the concept of a *barrier*. A barrier is initialized with the slaves on whose termination the master waits. It then suspends the execution of the master until all the slaves it controls have terminated. Our pSather example, in contrast, works in an incremental fashion—whenever a slave terminates the random_perms() method takes its result.

Master-Slave for computational accuracy. In this variant the execution of a service is delegated to at least three different implementations, each of which is a separate slave. The master waits for all slaves to complete, and votes on their results to detect and handle inaccuracies. This voting may follow different strategies. Examples include that in which the master selects the result that is returned by the greatest number of slaves, the average of all results, or the use of an Exceptional Value [Cun94] in the case in which all slaves produce different results.

To provide different slave implementations, we can extend the structure of the Master-Slave pattern with an additional abstract class. This defines an interface common to all slave implementations. Different slave implementations are then derived from this abstract base.

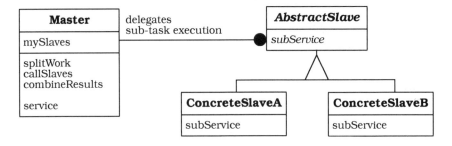

Further variants exist for implementing slaves:

Slaves as Processes. To handle slaves located in separate processes, you can extend the original Master-Slave structure with two additional components [Bro96]. The master includes a *top component* that keeps track of all slaves working for the master. To keep the master and the top component independent of the physical location of distributed slaves, remote proxies (263) represent each slave in the master process. You can apply the Forwarder-Receiver (307) or Client-Dispatcher-Server pattern (323) to implement the interprocess communication.

Slaves as Threads. In this variant, every slave is implemented within its own thread of control [KSS96]. In this variant the master creates the threads, launches the slaves, and waits for all threads to complete before continuing with its own computation. The Active Object pattern [Sch95] helps in implementing such a structure.

In this variant the master must deal with two problems: what happens if a thread cannot be created, and how many threads should be created? A solution to the first problem is to call the slave's services directly, without launching them in a separate thread. Performance will suffer, but the result will be correct. The optimal number of threads depends on the number of processors available and on the amount of work required from each thread. Too many threads incur overheads in their creation and destruction, as well as in memory consumption. [KSS96] suggests experimenting with different strategies, starting with 'a few more threads than the number of processors'.

Master-Slave with slave coordination. The computation of a slave may depend on the state of computation of other slaves, for example when performing simulation with finite elements. In this case the computation of all slaves must be regularly suspended for each slave to coordinate itself with the slaves on which it depends, after which the slaves resume their individual computation.

There are two ways of implementing such a behavior. Firstly, you can include the control logic for slave coordination within the slaves themselves. This frees the master from the task of implementing this coordination, but may decrease the performance of the overall structure. Slaves will stop their execution independently and may idle until the slaves on which they depend are ready for coordination.

The second option is to let the master maintain dependencies between slaves and to control slave coordination. At regular time intervals the master suspends all slaves, retrieves the current state of their computation, forwards this data to all slaves that depend on this data, and resumes the execution of all slaves.

Known Uses   [KSS96] lists three concrete examples of the application of the Master-Slave pattern for parallel computation:

- Matrix multiplication. Each row in the product matrix can be computed by a separate slave.

- Transform-coding an image, for example in computing the discrete cosine transform (DCT) of every 8×8 pixel block in an image. Each block can be computed by a separate slave.

- Computing the cross-correlation of two signals. This is done by iterating over all samples in the signal, computing the mean-square distance between the sample and its correlate, and summing the distances. We can partition the iteration over the samples into several parts and compute the square distance and its sums separately for each partition. The final sum is computed by summing all sums from these partitions. Each partial summing can be performed by a separate slave. A master component defines the partitions, launches the slaves, and computes the final sum.

The **workpool model** described in [KR96] applies the Master-Slave pattern to implement process control for parallel computing, based on the principles of Linda [Gel85]. A programmer can assign a number of so-called workers to a workpool. Each worker offers the same services and is implemented in a separate process or thread. Clients send requests to the workpool, which handles these requests with help of its associated workers. The request itself is a function whose execution should be parallelized with help of the workers, such as matrix multiplication. This function corresponds to the master component in the Master-Slave pattern.

The concept of **Gaggles** [BI93] builds upon the principles of the Master-Slave pattern to handle 'plurality' in an object-oriented software system. A *gaggle* represents a set of replicated service objects. When receiving a service request from a client, the gaggle forwards this request to one of the service objects it includes. Each of these service objects can be atomic, which means it executes the service and delivers a result, or another gaggle which itself represents a set of replicated service objects.

[Bro96] lists several applications of the Master-Slave design pattern, all of which focus on distributed slaves. These include the distributed design rule checking system **Calibre™ DRC-MP** and the **CheckMate** IC verification tool, both from Mentor Graphics.

Factoring large numbers into **prime factors** can also be done in a 'divide and conquer' fashion. As this problem is central to cryptography, of great interest to governments, and requires vast computing resources, it has been carried out over the Internet. One site did the subdivision and sent sub-tasks to people willing to provide computing time and the use of their machines.

Consequences   The Master-Slave design pattern provides several **benefits**:

Exchangeability and extensibility. By providing an abstract slave class, it is possible to exchange existing slave implementations or add new ones without major changes to the master. Clients are not affected by such changes. If they are implemented with the Strategy pattern [GHJV95], the same holds true when changing the algorithms for allocating sub-tasks to slaves and for computing the final result.

Separation of concerns. The introduction of the master separates slave and client code from the code for partitioning work, delegating work to slaves, collecting the results from the slaves, computing the final result and handling slave failure or inaccurate slave results.

Efficiency. The Master-Slave pattern for parallel computation enables you to speed up the performance of computing a particular service when implemented carefully. However, you must always consider the costs of parallel computation (see below).

The Master-Slave pattern suffers from three **liabilities**:

Feasibility. A Master-Slave architecture is not always feasible. You must partition work, copy data, launch slaves, control their execution, wait for the slave's results and compute the final result. All these activities consume processing time and storage space.

Machine dependency. The Master-Slave pattern for parallel computation strongly depends on the architecture of the machine on which the program runs—see the Variants section for details. This may decrease the changeability and portability of a Master-Slave structure.

Hard to implement. Implementing Master-Slave is not easy, especially for parallel computation. Many different aspects must be considered and carefully implemented, such as how work is subdivided, how master and slaves should collaborate, and how the final result should be computed. You also must deal with errors such as the failure of slave execution, failure of communication between the master and slaves, or failure to launch a parallel slave. Implementing the Master-Slave pattern for parallel computation usually requires sound knowledge about the architecture of the target machine for the system under development.

Portability. Because of the potential dependency on underlying hardware architectures, Master-Slave structures are difficult or impossible to transfer to other machines. This is especially true for the Master-Slave pattern for parallel computation , and similarly for our simple traveling-salesman program tuned for the CM5 computer.

See also An earlier version of this pattern appeared in [PLoP94].

The *Master-Slave Pattern for Parallel Compute Services* [Bro96] provides additional insights for implementing a Master-Slave structure. It differs from the structure described here, as it concentrates on describing the *Slaves as Processes* variant.

The book *Programming with Threads* [KSS96] describes the Slaves as Threads variant in detail.

Object Group [Maf96] is a pattern for group communication and support of fault tolerance in distributed applications. It corresponds to the *Master-Slave for fault tolerance* variant and provides additional details for its implementation. The Object Group pattern provides a local surrogate for a group of replicated objects distributed across networked machines. A request is broadcast to all objects of the group. The request will succeed as long as one group member terminates successfully.

Credits We thank Ken Auer, Norbert Portner, Douglas C. Schmidt, Jiri Soukup, and John Vlissides for their valuable criticism and suggestions for improvement of the [PLoP94] version of this pattern. Special thanks go to Phil Brooks and Jürgen Knopp for their contribution to this new version.

3.4 Access Control

Sometimes a component or even a whole subsystem cannot or should not be accessible directly by its clients. For example, not all clients may be authorized to use the services of a component, or to retrieve particular information that a component supplies.

In this section we describe one design pattern that helps to protect access to a particular component:

- The *Proxy* design pattern (263) makes the clients of a component communicate with a representative rather than to the component itself. Introducing such a placeholder can serve many purposes, including enhanced efficiency, easier access and protection from unauthorized access.

[GHJV95] also describes the Proxy pattern. Our description differs in that it separates the general principle that underlies the pattern from its concrete application cases, which we describe as variants. We also provide several new variants of Proxy that are not covered by the Gang-of-Four version.

The Proxy pattern is widely applicable. Almost every distributed system or infrastructure for distributed systems uses the pattern to represent remote components locally, for example OMG-Corba [OMG92]. A more recent application of Proxy is the World Wide Web [LA94], where it is used to implement the proxy servers.

Two other patterns described in [GHJV95] also belong to this category—Facade and Iterator:

- The *Facade* pattern provides a uniform interface to a set of interfaces in a subsystem. Facade defines a higher-level interface that makes the subsystem easier to use.

- The *Iterator* pattern provides a way to access the elements of an aggregate object sequentially without exposing its underlying representation.

Like the Proxy pattern, both the Facade and Iterator patterns are widely applicable.

Facade shields the components of a subsystem from direct access by their clients. Vice-versa, clients do not depend on the internal structure of the subsystem. A facade component routes incoming service requests to the subsystem component that implements the service. Facade is therefore of larger granularity than Proxy, which guards access to single component.

Iterators are offered by almost every container class in an object-oriented program or class library. An iterator defines the order in which clients can traverse and access the elements of a container. For example, to access all elements in a binary tree, you can define iterators for pre-order, in-order and post-order traversal.

Proxy

The *Proxy* design pattern makes the clients of a component communicate with a representative rather than to the component itself. Introducing such a placeholder can serve many purposes, including enhanced efficiency, easier access and protection from unauthorized access.

Example Company engineering staff regularly consult databases for information about material providers, available parts, blueprints, and so on. Every remote access may be costly, while many accesses are similar or identical and are repeated often. This situation clearly offers scope for optimization of access time and cost. However, we do not want to burden the engineer's application code with such optimization. The presence of optimization and the type used should be largely transparent to the application user and programmer.

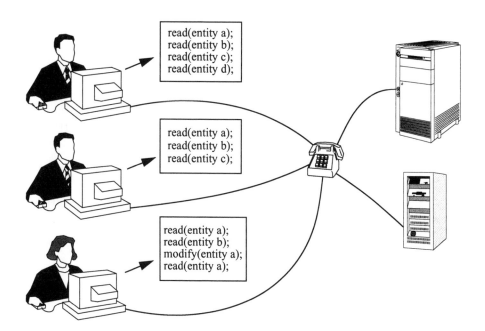

Context   A client needs access to the services of another component[2]. Direct access is technically possible, but may not be the best approach.

Problem   It is often inappropriate to access a component directly. We do not want to hard-code its physical location into clients, and direct and unrestricted access to the component may be inefficient or even insecure. Additional control mechanisms are needed. A solution to such a design problem has to balance some or all of the following *forces*:

- Accessing the component should be run-time-efficient, cost-effective, and safe for both the client and the component.

- Access to the component should be transparent and simple for the client. The client should particularly not have to change its calling behavior and syntax from that used to call any other direct-access component.

- The client should be well aware of possible performance or financial penalties for accessing remote clients. Full transparency can obscure cost differences between services.

Solution   Let the client communicate with a representative rather than the component itself. This representative—called a *proxy*—offers the interface of the component but performs additional pre- and post-processing such as access-control checking or making read-only copies of the original—see below.

Structure   The *original* implements a particular service. Such a service may range from simple actions like returning or displaying data to complex data-retrieval functions or computations involving further components.

The *client* is responsible for a specific task. To do its job, it invokes the functionality of the original in an indirect way by accessing the proxy. The client does not have to change its calling behavior and syntax from that which it uses to call local components.

---

2. 'Component' is used very vaguely here intentionally. It can mean anything to which you do not want to give direct access for the above reasons. Some examples of such components are ordinary local objects, an external database, an HTML page on the Web or an image embedded in a text document.

Therefore, the *proxy* offers the same interface as the original, and ensures correct access to the original. To achieve this the proxy maintains a reference to the original it represents. Usually there is a one-to-one relationship between the proxy and the original, though there are exceptions to this rule for Remote and Firewall proxies, two variants of this general pattern. See the Variants section for more information.

The *abstract original* provides the interface implemented by the proxy and the original. In a language like C++, with no notable difference between subtyping and inheritance, both the proxy and the original inherit from the abstract original. Clients code against this interface when accessing the original.

Class Client	Collaborators • Proxy
Responsibilities • Uses the interface provided by the proxy to request a particular service. • Fulfills its own task.	

Class *AbstractOriginal*	Collaborators -
Responsibilities • Serves as an abstract base class for the proxy and the original.	

Class Proxy	Collaborator • Original
Responsibilities • Provides the interface of the original to clients. • Ensures a safe, efficient and correct access to the original.	

Class Original	Collaborators -
Responsibilities • Implements a particular service.	

The following OMT diagram shows the relationships between the classes graphically:

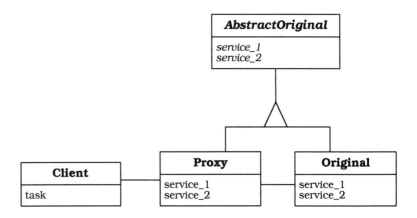

Dynamics   The following diagram shows a typical dynamic scenario of a Proxy structure. Note that the actions performed within the proxy differ depending on its actual specialization—see the Variants section for more information:

- While working on its task the client asks the proxy to carry out a service.

- The proxy receives the incoming service request and pre-processes it. This pre-processing involves actions such as looking up the address of the original, or checking a local cache to see if the requested information is already available.

- If the proxy has to consult the original to fulfill the request, it forwards the request to the original using the proper communication protocols and security measures.

- The original accepts the request and fulfills it. It sends the response back to the proxy.

- The proxy receives the response. Before or after transferring it to the client it may carry out additional post-processing actions such as caching the result, calling the destructor of the original or releasing a lock on a resource.

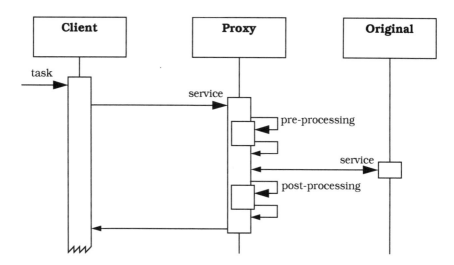

Implementation   To implement the Proxy pattern, carry out the following steps:

1 *Identify all responsibilities* for dealing with access control to a component. Attach these responsibilities to a separate component, the proxy. The details of this step are described in the Variants section.

2 If possible *introduce an abstract base class* that specifies the common parts of the interfaces of both the proxy and the original. Derive the proxy and the original from this abstract base. If identical interfaces for the proxy and the original are not feasible you can use an adapter [GHJV95] for interface adaptation. Adapting the proxy to the original's interface retains the client with the illusion of identical interfaces, and a common base class for the adapter and the original may be possible again.

3 *Implement the proxy's functions.* To this end check the roles specified in the first step.

4 *Free the original and its clients* from responsibilities that have migrated into the proxy.

5 *Associate the proxy and the original* by giving the proxy a handle to the original. This handle may be a pointer, a reference, an address, an identifier, a socket, a port and so on.

6 *Remove all direct relationships between the original and its clients.* Replace them by analogous relationships to the proxy.

Variants   We describe seven variants of the generic Proxy pattern below. We start by summarizing the situations to which the individual variants are best suited:

- *Remote Proxy.* Clients of remote components should be shielded from network addresses and inter-process communication protocols.

- *Protection Proxy.* Components must be protected from unauthorized access.

- *Cache Proxy.* Multiple local clients can share results from remote components.

- *Synchronization Proxy.* Multiple simultaneous accesses to a component must be synchronized.

- *Counting Proxy.* Accidental deletion of components must be prevented or usage statistics collected.

- *Virtual Proxy.* Processing or loading a component is costly, while partial information about the component may be sufficient.

- *Firewall Proxy.* Local clients should be protected from the outside world.

The paragraphs that follow detail the characteristics and implementation details of each variant.

A *Remote Proxy* encapsulates and maintains the physical location of the original. It also implements the IPC (inter-process communication) routines that perform the actual communication with the original. For every original, one proxy is instantiated per address space in which the services of the original are needed. For complex IPC mechanisms, you can refine the proxy by shifting responsibility for communication with the original to a forwarder component, as described in the Forwarder-Receiver pattern (307). Analogously, introduce a receiver component into the original.

For reasons of efficiency, we discern remote proxies into three cases:

- Client and original live in the same process.

- Client and original live in different processes on the same machine.

- Client and original live in different processes that run also on different machines.

The first case is simple: we do not need a proxy for talking to the original. For the second and third cases we put fields for a remote address into the proxy, usually consisting of machine ID, port or process number and an object ID. The second case obviously does not need the machine ID. If you want to save the few bytes that a machine ID occupies, bear in mind that the differentiation between the second and third cases complicates the code of the proxy. The effort of developing such differentiation logic is usually not justified, except in cases where the means of inter-process communication are different in both cases, enforcing such differentiation logic. Even then you can add a thin layer on top concealing the differences between the three cases, thus simplifying the code that uses the addressing scheme. The presence of an abstract original makes it completely transparent to the client which of the three cases is employed.

In high-performance applications, you often want to determine whether or not communication is expensive at the application level before committing to an off-board request. In such cases, a remote proxy reveals this information.

A *Protection Proxy* protects the original from unauthorized access. To achieve this the proxy checks the access rights of every client. You can most easily achieve this by using the access-control mechanisms your platform offers. If appropriate and possible, try to give every client its own set of permissions to other components. Access control lists are a widespread implementation of this concept.

To implement a *Cache Proxy*, extend the proxy with a data area to temporarily hold results. Develop a strategy to maintain and refresh the cache. When the cache is full and you need to free up space for new entries, there are several strategies you can use. For example, you can delete the least-frequently used cache entries, or implement a 'move-to-front' strategy—this is usually easier to implement and efficient enough. In this strategy, whenever a client accesses a cache entry, it is moved to the front of, say, a doubly-linked list. When new entries have to be added to the cache, entries can be deleted from the back of the list.

You must also take care of the 'cache invalidation' problem—when data in the original changes, copies of this data cached elsewhere become invalid. If it is crucial that your application always has up-to-date data, you can declare the whole cache invalid whenever the original copy of any of its entries is changed. Alternatively, you can use a 'write-through' strategy, well-known from microprocessor cache design, for finer-grained control. Whenever the original is modified all its copies are modified as well. Note that this becomes complicated when there is more than one copy, or when the copies are remote, in contrast to a microprocessor cache where the situation is simpler. If your clients can accept slightly outdated information, you can label individual cache entries with expiration dates. Examples of this strategy include World Wide Web browsers.

A *Synchronization Proxy* controls multiple simultaneous client accesses. If it is important that only one client—or a specified number of clients—can access the original at a time, the proxy can implement mutual exclusion via semaphores [Dij65]. Alternatively, it can use whatever means of synchronization your operating system offers. You may also differentiate between read or write access. In the former case, you can adopt more liberal policies, for example by allowing an arbitrary number of reads when no write is active or pending. The operating system literature is a good source for studying these mechanisms.

A *Counting Proxy* can be used for collecting usage statistics, or to implement a well-known technique for automatically deleting obsolete objects—reference counting. To achieve this the counting proxy maintains the number of references that exist to the original, and deletes the original when this number becomes zero. You need to ensure that there is exactly one counting proxy for every original, and that every access to an original goes through a defined interface of the respective proxy. Also keep in mind that reference counting alone does not help with the problem of finding cycles of otherwise isolated components that refer to each other's proxies.

The Counted Pointer idiom (353) illustrates a different way to implement a counting proxy in C++. It also discusses why some C++ implementations employ another level of handle to refer to the counting proxy, and to update the reference counter whenever a handle object is created or deleted.

A *Virtual Proxy*, also known as *lazy construction*, assumes that an application references secondary storage, such as the hard disk. This proxy does not disclose whether the original is fully loaded or whether only skeletal information about it is available. Loading missing parts of the original is performed on demand.

When a service request arrives and the information present in the proxy is not sufficient to handle the request, load the required data from disk and forward the request to the freshly-created or expanded original. If the original is already fully loaded, just forward the request. This forwarding should be done transparently such that clients always use the same interface independent of whether the original is in main memory or not. It is the responsibility of the client or an associated module to notify the proxy when the original, or parts of it, are no longer needed. The proxy then frees the space allocated. When several clients reference the same original, it may be appropriate to add the capabilities of the Synchronization and Cache Proxy variants.

A *Firewall Proxy* subsumes the networking and protection code necessary to communicate with a potentially hostile environment. Usually the firewall proxy is implemented as a daemon process on a firewall machine, which can also be referred to as a 'proxy server'. All clients who pass requests to the outside world reference this proxy. The proxy works behind the scenes by checking outgoing requests and incoming answers for compliance with internal security and access policies. It denies access when a request does not comply with such policies, or when its resources are exhausted. Clients are provided with an almost complete illusion of unhindered access to the outside, and do not need to go to the inconvenience of logging in to the firewall machine. Similarly, security is maintained, as user accounts are protected from attack from outside. Servers on the Internet are given the illusion that the proxy is the client. This allows the internal structure of the network behind the firewall to be hidden.

A notable characteristic of firewall proxies is that the user needs 'proxied' versions of client software. For example, the standard `ftp` software must be replaced by another version that contacts the proxy instead of the directly accessing the destination machine. A consequence of this can be that new services can only be used when equivalent proxied versions of these services are available.

Because all communication flows through the firewall proxy, it constitutes a potential bottleneck and provides an ideal place for optimizations such as caching. It also provides an ideal location for additional tasks like logging and accounting. For more information on firewall design, see [CZ95].

Example Resolved
You may often need to use more than one of the above Proxy variants —you may want the proxy to play several of the above roles and fulfill the corresponding responsibilities. Make your choice by first picking the desired roles, for instance virtual and cache, then thinking about combining these roles into one proxy.

If combining them bloats the resulting proxy too much, split it into smaller objects. One example of this is factoring out complicated networking code into a forwarder-receiver structure—see the Forwarder-Receiver pattern (307). In this case the proxy is left only with the location information of the original and the local-versus-remote decision.

You can solve remote data access problems by using proxies with the properties of both Remote and Cache Proxy variants. Implementing such a mixed-mode proxy can be accomplished by using the Whole-Part pattern (225).

One part is the cache. It contains a storage area and strategies for updating and querying the cache. By using the 'least frequently used' strategy and tuning the cache size, you can cut down the cost of external accesses. How you solve the cache invalidation problem depends on whether you have control over the database or not. If you have, you can arrange for individual cache entries to be invalidated when the corresponding original database entries are modified. If not, each access to the cache of the combined proxy has to check whether an entry found is still valid.

The other part of the combined proxy maintains the name and address of the original and performs the actual IPC. If the original is, say, a relational data base, it translates the client request into SQL queries and translates results into the required format. If it is another type of component, use the Forwarder-Receiver pattern (307).

Known Uses   The Proxy pattern is often used in combination with the Forwarder-Receiver pattern (307) to implement the 'stub' concept [LPW94].

NeXTSTEP. The Proxy pattern is used in the NeXTSTEP operating system to provide local stubs for remote objects. Proxies are created by a special server on the first access to the remote object. The responsibilities of a proxy object within the NeXTSTEP operating system are to encode incoming requests and their arguments, and forward them to their corresponding remote original.

OMG-CORBA [OMG92] uses the Proxy pattern for two purposes. So-called 'client-stubs', or IDL-stubs, guard clients against the concrete implementation of their servers and the Object Request Broker. IDL-skeletons are used by the Object Request Broker itself to forward requests to concrete remote server components.

Orbix [Iona95], a concrete OMG-CORBA implementation, uses remote proxies. A client can bind to an original by specifying its unique identifier. In the example of C++ language support, the bind() call returns a C++ pointer that the client can use to invoke the remote object using normal C++ function invocation syntax.

World Wide Web Proxy [LA94] describes aspects of the CERN HTTP server that typically runs on a firewall machine. It gives people inside the firewall concurrent access to the outside world. Efficiency is increased by caching recently transferred files.

OLE. In Microsoft OLE [Bro94] servers may be implemented as libraries dynamically linked to the address space of the client, or as separate processes. Proxies are used to hide whether a particular server is local or remote from a client. When the client calls a server located in its own address space, it directly invokes that server's implementation. If the server is not located in the client's address space, a proxy takes the arguments, packages them, and generates a remote procedure call to the remote server. In the server process another proxy—referred to as a 'stub' in OLE terminology—receives the request, unpacks the arguments, pushes them on the stack and invokes the appropriate server method. If the method invocation returns a result, this result is packaged and transmitted back to the client proxy. The client proxy unpacks the result and returns it to the client, which remains ignorant of whether the server was local or remote.

Consequences   One problem with the Proxy pattern as it is described here is that not all forces are equally well resolved. The traditional focus is on easy handling and achieving a certain degree of efficiency, as stated in the first and second forces. But what happens when the user or programmer needs to retain explicit control for fine-tuning, as requested by force three? One possibility is to mirror this at the level of the source code by doing away with the abstract superclass. The programmer is then always aware of whether the object at hand is 'the real thing' [U2] or just a surrogate. However, this violates forces one and two.

The Proxy pattern provides the following **benefits**:

Enhanced efficiency and lower cost. The Virtual Proxy variant helps to implement a 'load-on-demand' strategy. This allows you to avoid unnecessary loads from disk and usually speeds up your application. A similar argument holds for the Cache Proxy variant. Be aware, however, that the additional overhead of going through a proxy may have the inverse effect, depending on the application—see liabilities below.

Decoupling clients from the location of server components. By putting all location information and addressing functionality into a Remote Proxy variant, clients are not affected by migration of servers or changes in the networking infrastructure. This allows client code to become more stable and reusable. Note however that a straight-forward implementation of a remote proxy still has the location of the original hard-wired into its code. The advantage of this is that it usually provides better run-time performance. If this loss of flexibility is important, you can think about introducing a dynamic lookup scheme in addition to the proxies, as described in the Client-Dispatcher-Server pattern (323).

Separation of housekeeping code from functionality. In more general terms, this benefit applies to all Proxy variants. A proxy relieves the client of burdens that do not inherently belong to the task the client is to perform.

Two **liabilities** of the Proxy pattern can be identified:

Less efficiency due to indirection. All proxies introduce an additional layer of indirection. This loss of efficiency is usually negligible compared with the cleaner structure of clients and the gain of efficiency through caching or lazy construction that is achieved by using proxies. You should however check such impacts on efficiency thoroughly for every application of the Proxy pattern.

Overkill via sophisticated strategies. Be careful with intricate strategies for caching or loading on demand—they do not always pay. An example of this occurs when originals are highly dynamic, for example in an airline reservation or other ticket booking system. Here complex caching with invalidating may introduce overhead that defeats the intended purpose due to the rate at which the original's data changes. Usually, only coarse-grained entities justify the resultant cache maintenance effort.

See Also The *Decorator* pattern [GHJV95] is very similar in structure to Proxy. ConcreteComponent—the original in the Proxy pattern—implements some behavior that is invoked via a decorator—the proxy in the Proxy pattern. Both classes inherit from a common base. The major difference between the Decorator and Proxy patterns is one of intent. The decorator adds functionality or, more generally, gives options for dynamically choosing functionality in addition to the core functionality of ConcreteComponent. The proxy frees the original from very specific housekeeping code.

Credits [GHJV95] also describe the Proxy design pattern. Specifically, they describe four variants: the Remote, Virtual, and Protection Proxies, as well as 'Smart Reference', which is a combination of aspects of our Counting, Virtual, and Synchronization Proxies.

We thank the members of PLoP'95 Working Group 3 for their valuable criticism and suggestions for improvement of an earlier version of this pattern. Ken Auer, as assigned 'shepherd' for this pattern, gave key advice on re-factoring the pattern into a two-level pattern language, as described in [PLoP95].

3.5 Management

Systems must often handle collections of objects of similar kinds, of services, or even of complex components. One example is incoming events from users or other systems, which must be interpreted and scheduled appropriately. Another example occurs when interactive systems must present application-specific data in a variety of different ways. Such views must be handled appropriately, both individually and collectively.

In well-structured software systems, separate 'manager' components are often used to handle such homogeneous collections of objects. We describe two design patterns of this type:

- The *Command Processor* pattern (277) separates the request for a service from its execution. A command processor component manages requests as separate objects, schedules their execution and provides additional services such as the storing of request objects for later undo.

- The *View Handler* pattern (291) helps to manage views in a software system. A view handler component allows clients to open, manipulate and dispose of views, coordinates dependencies between views and organizes their update.

The Command Processor pattern and the Command pattern [GHJV95] both use the concept of encapsulating service requests into command objects. However, Command Processor embeds the Command pattern into a structure that deals with the management of command objects. [GHJV95] also describes a management pattern, Memento:

- The *Memento* pattern allows you to capture and externalize an object's internal state without violating encapsulation, so that its state can be restored later.

Memento helps you to manage the state of a particular component. For example, the state of a component may need to be restored when a previously-executed operation is undone. Another example occurs when a client needs to access the state of a component, but the component's encapsulation must not be violated. Memento allows you to provide the client with a copy of its current state.

Command Processor

The *Command Processor* design pattern separates the request for a service from its execution. A command processor component manages requests as separate objects, schedules their execution, and provides additional services such as the storing of request objects for later undo.

Example A text editor usually provides a way to deal with mistakes made by the user. A simple example is undoing the most recent change. A more attractive solution is to enable the undoing of multiple changes. We want to develop such an editor. For the purpose of this discussion let us call it TEDDI.

The design of TEDDI includes a multi-level undo mechanism and allows for future enhancements, such as the addition of new features or a batch mode of operation.

The user interface of TEDDI offers several means of interaction, such as keyboard input or pop-up menus. The program has to define one or several *callback* procedures that are automatically called for every human-computer interaction.

Context Applications that need flexible and extensible user interfaces, or applications that provide services related to the execution of user functions, such as scheduling or undo.

Problem   An application that includes a large set of features benefits from a well-structured solution for mapping its interface to its internal functionality. This allows you to support different modes of user interaction, such as pop-up menus for novices, keyboard shortcuts for more experienced users, or external control of the application via a scripting language.

You often need to implement services that go beyond the core functionality of the system for the execution of user requests. Examples are undo, redo, macros for grouping requests, logging of activity, or request scheduling and suspension.

The following *forces* shape the solution:

- Different users like to work with an application in different ways.

- Enhancements of the application should not break existing code.

- Additional services such as undo should be implemented consistently for all requests.

Solution   The *Command Processor* pattern builds on the Command design pattern in [GHJV95]. Both patterns follow the idea of encapsulating requests into objects. Whenever a user calls a specific function of the application, the request is turned into a *command* object. The Command Processor pattern illustrates more specifically how command objects are managed. The See Also section discusses further differences between the Command pattern and the Command Processor pattern.

A central component of our pattern description, the *command processor*, takes care of all command objects. The command processor schedules the execution of commands, may store them for later undo, and may provide other services such as logging the sequence of commands for testing purposes. Each command object delegates the execution of its task to *supplier* components within the functional core of the application.

Structure   The *abstract command* component defines the interface of all command objects. As a minimum this interface consists of a procedure to execute a command. The additional services implemented by the command processor require further interface procedures for all command objects. The abstract command class of TEDDI, for example, defines an additional undo method.

For each user function we derive a *command component* from the abstract command. A command component implements the interface of the abstract command by using zero or more *supplier components*. The commands of TEDDI save the state of associated supplier components prior to execution, and restore it in case of undo. For example, the delete command is responsible for storing the text deleted and its position in the document.

Class Abstract Command	*Collaborators*
Responsibility • Defines a uniform interface to execute commands. • Extends the interface for services of the command processor, such as undo and logging.	

Class Command	*Collaborators* • Supplier
Responsibility • Encapsulates a function request. • Implements interface of abstract command. • Uses suppliers to perform a request.	

The *controller* represents the interface of the application. It accepts requests, such as 'paste text,' and creates the corresponding command objects. The command objects are then delivered to the command processor for execution. The controller of TEDDI maintains the event loop and maps incoming events to command objects.

The *command processor* manages command objects, schedules them and starts their execution. It is the key component that implements additional services related to the execution of commands. The command processor remains independent of specific commands because it only uses the abstract command interface. In the case of our TEDDI word processor, the command processor also stores already-performed commands for later undo.

The *supplier* components provide most of the functionality required to execute concrete commands (that is, those related to the concrete command class, as opposed to the abstract command class). Related commands often share supplier components. When an undo mechanism is required, a supplier usually provides a means to save and restore its internal state. The component implementing the internal text representation is the main supplier in TEDDI.

Class	Collaborators
Controller	• Command Processor • Command
Responsibility	
• Accepts service requests. • Translates requests into commands. • Transfers commands to command processor.	

Class	Collaborators
Command Processor	• Abstract Command
Responsibility	
• Activates command execution. • Maintains command objects. • Provides additional services related to command execution.	

Class	Collaborators
Supplier	-
Responsibility	
• Provides application specific functionality	

The following diagram shows the principal relationships between the components of the pattern. It demonstrates undo as an example of an additional service provided by the command processor.

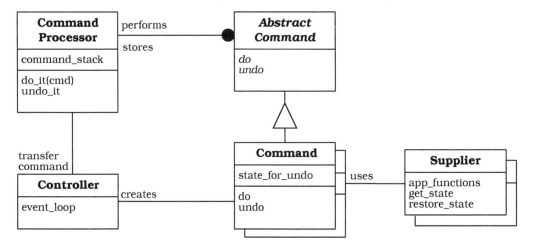

Dynamics The following diagram shows a typical scenario of the Command Processor pattern implementing an undo mechanism. A request to capitalize a selected word arrives, is performed and then undone. The following steps occur:

- The controller accepts the request from the user within its event loop and creates a 'capitalize' command object.

- The controller transfers the new command object to the command processor for execution and further handling.

- The command processor activates the execution of the command and stores it for later undo.

- The capitalize command retrieves the currently-selected text from its supplier, stores the text and its position in the document, and asks the supplier to actually capitalize the selection.

- After accepting an undo request, the controller transfers this request to the command processor. The command processor invokes the undo procedure of the most recent command.

- The capitalize command resets the supplier to the previous state, by replacing the saved text in its original position

- If no further activity is required or possible of the command, the command processor deletes the command object.

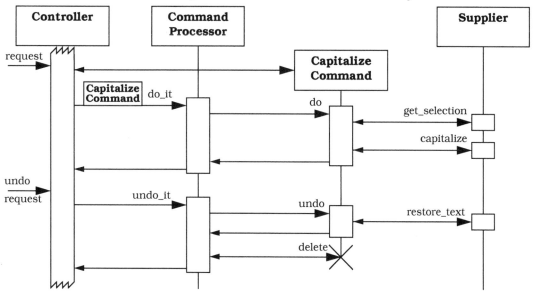

Implementation To implement this pattern, carry out the following steps:

1 *Define the interface of the abstract command.* The abstract command class hides the details of all specific commands. This class always specifies the abstract method required to execute a command. It also defines the methods necessary to implement the additional services offered by the command processor. An example is a method 'getNameAndParameters' for logging commands.

➡   For the undo mechanism in TEDDI we distinguish three types of commands. They are modeled as an enumeration, because the command type may change dynamically, as shown in step 3:

No change. A command that require no undo. Cursor movement falls into this category.

Normal. A command that can be undone. Substitution of a word in text is an example of a normal command.

No undo. A command that cannot be undone, and which prevents the undo of previously performed normal commands.

If we want our text to become 'politically correct' and replace all occurrences of 'he' by 'he/she', TEDDI would need to store all corresponding locations in the document to enable later undo. The potentially high storage requirement of global replacements is the main reason why commands belong to the category 'no undo'.

```
class AbstractCommand {
public:
    enum CmdType { no_change, normal, no_undo };
    virtual ~AbstractCommand();
    virtual void doit();
    virtual void undo();
    CmdType getType() const { return type;}
    virtual String getName() const { return "NONAME";}
        // gives name of command for selection
        // in undo/redo menu
protected:
    CmdType type;
    AbstractCommand(CmdType t=no_change): type(t){}
};
```

The method getName() is used to display the most recent command to the user when he selects 'undo'.   ❏

2 *Design the command components* for each type of request that the application supports. There are several options for binding a command to its suppliers. The supplier component can be hard-coded within the command, or the controller can provide the supplier to the command constructor as a parameter. An example of the second situation is a multi-document editor in which a command is connected to a specific document object.

➥ The 'delete' command of TEDDI takes the object representing the text as its first parameter. The range of characters to delete is specified by two additional parameters:

```
class DeleteCmd : public AbstractCommand {
public:
    DeleteCmd(TEDDI_Text *t, int start, int end)
        : AbstractCommand(normal) , mytext(t) ,
            from (start) , to (end) {/*...*/}
    virtual ~DeleteCmd();
    virtual void doit();
        // delete characters in mytext
        // between from and to and save them in delstr
    virtual void undo();
        // insert delstr again at position from
    String getName() const { return "DELETE " + delstr;}
protected:
    TEDDI_Text *mytext;// plan for multiple text buffers
    int from,to;      // range of characters to delete
    String delstr;    // save deleted text for undo
};
```

The implementation of the method `doit()` calls the method `deleteText()` of the `TEDDI_Text` supplier object. ❏

A command object may ask the user for further parameters. The TEDDI 'load text file' command, for example, activates a dialog to request the name of the file to be loaded. In this situation the event-handling system must deliver user input to the command, rather than to the controller. Commands that require user interaction during their creation or execution therefore call for additional care. The design of the event-handling system—which is outside the scope of this pattern—must be able to handle such situations.

Undoable commands can use the Memento pattern [GHJV95] to store the state of their supplier for later undo without violating encapsulation.

3 *Increase flexibility by providing macro commands* that combine several successive commands. Apply the Composite pattern [GHJV95] to implement such a macro command component.

➤ In TEDDI we implement a macro command class, to allow user-defined shortcuts to frequently-used command sequences:

```
class MacroCmd : public AbstractCommand {
public:
    MacroCmd(String name, AbstractCommand *first)
        : AbstractCommand( first->getType()),
                            macroname(name) {/*...*/}
    virtual ~MacroCmd();
    virtual void doit();
        // do every command in cmdlist
    virtual void undo();
        // undo all commands in cmdlist in reverse order
    virtual void finish(); // delete commands in cmdlist
    void add(AbstractCommand *next) {
        cmdlist.append(next);
        if (next->getType() == no_undo) type = no_undo;
        /*... */}
    String getName() const { return macroname;}
protected:
    String macroname;
    OrderedCollection<AbstractCommand*> cmdlist;
};
```

The command type of a MacroCmd depends on the commands that are added to the macro. An appended command of type no_undo will prevent the undo of the complete macro command. The undo function otherwise iterates through cmdlist in reverse order undoing all normal commands and skipping all commands of type no_change. ❑

4 *Implement the controller component.* Command objects are created by the controller, for example with the help of the 'creational' patterns Abstract Factory and Prototype [GHJV95]. However, since the controller is already decoupled from the supplier components, this additional decoupling of controller and commands is optional. A generic menu controller provides an example of the application of the Prototype pattern. Such a controller contains a command prototype object for each menu entry, and passes a copy of this object to the command processor whenever the user selects the menu entry. If such a menu controller can be dynamically configured with macro command objects, we can easily implement user-defined menu extensions.

➡ In TEDDI user interaction is handled by callback procedures in the controller. A callback creates the corresponding command object and passes it to the command processor. TEDDI uses a global variable `theCP` that refers to the single command processor component.

```
void TEDDI_controller::deleteButtonPressed() {
    AbstractCommand *delcmd =
        new DeleteWordCommand(
            this->getCursor(),// pass cursor position
            this->getText());  // pass text
    theCP->perform(delcmd);
}
```

On start-up the callback `deleteButtonPressed()` is registered with the event-handling system. ❏

5 *Implement access to the additional services of the command processor.* A user-accessible additional service is normally implemented by a specific command class. The command processor supplies the functionality for the 'do' method. Directly calling the interface of the command processor is also an option. Other intrinsic services such as logging of commands are performed automatically by the command processor.

➡ The class `UndoCommand` provides access to the undo mechanism of TEDDI. The implementation of this class cooperates with the internals of the command processor and is thus declared a friend to it. Note that `UndoCommand` objects must not be stored by the command processor, and fall in the category `no_change`.

```
class UndoCommand : public AbstractCommand {
public:
    UndoCommand()
        : AbstractCommand(no_change) {}
    virtual ~UndoCommand();
    virtual void doit() { theCP->undo_lastcmd(); }
};
```

The method `doit()` of `UndoCommand` asks the command processor to undo the last normal command executed. A class `RedoCommand` provides the inverse functionality. Its method `doit()` makes the command processor re-execute the undone command. ❏

6 *Implement the command processor component.* The command processor receives command objects from the controller and takes responsibility for them. For each command object, the command processor starts the execution by calling the do method. A command processor implemented in C++, for example, is responsible for deleting command objects that are no longer useful.

Apply the Singleton design pattern [GHJV95] to ensure that only one command processor exists.

➥ For TEDDI we implement a multi-level undo/redo with two stacks, one for performed commands and one for undone commands:

```cpp
class CommandProcessor {
public:
    CommandProcessor();
    virtual ~CommandProcessor();
    virtual void do_cmd(AbstractCommand *cmd){
        // do cmd and push it on donestack
        cmd->doit();
        switch(cmd->getType()){
        case AbstractCommand::normal:
            donestack.push(cmd); break;
        case AbstractCommand::no_undo:
            donestack.make_empty();
            undonestack.make_empty();
            // Fall through:
        case AbstractCommand::no_change:
            // take responsibility for command objects:
            delete cmd;
            break;
        }
    }
    friend class UndoCommand; // special relationship
    friend class RedoCommand; // special relationship
private:
    // this method is only used by UndoCommand
    virtual void undo_lastcmd();
        // pop cmd from donestack,
        // undo it, and push it on undonestack
    // this method is only used by RedoCommand
    virtual void redo_lastundone(){
        AbstractCommand *last = undonestack.pop();
        if (last) this->do_cmd(last);
    }
private:
    Stack<AbstractCommand*> donestack,undonestack;
};
```
❏

Variants *Spread controller functionality.* In this variant the role of the controller can be distributed over several components. For example, each user interface element such as a menu button could create a command object when activated. However, the role of the controller is not restricted to components of the graphical user interface.

Combination with Interpreter pattern. In this variant a scripting language provides a programmable interface to an application. The parser component of the script interpreter takes the role of the controller. Apply the Interpreter pattern [GHJV95] and build the abstract syntax tree from command objects. The command processor is the client in the Interpreter pattern. It carries out interpretation by activating the commands.

Known Uses **ET++** [WGM88] provides a framework of command processors that support unlimited, bounded, and single undo and redo. The abstract class Command implements a state machine to track the execution state of each command. This state machine is used to check if a command is performed or undone. The controller role is distributed over the event-handler object hierarchy of an ET++ application.

MacApp [App89] uses the Command Processor design pattern to provide undoable operations.

InterViews [LCITV92] includes an action class that is an abstract base class providing the functionality of a command component.

ATM-P [ATM93] implements a simplified version of the Command Processor pattern. It uses a hierarchy of command classes to pass command objects around, sometimes across process boundaries. The receiver of a command object decides how and when to execute it. Each process implements its own command processor.

SICAT [SICAT95] implements the Command Processor pattern to provide a well-defined undo facility in the control program and the graphical SDL editors.

Consequences   The Command-Processor pattern provides the following **benefits**:

Flexibility in the way requests are activated. Different user interface elements for requesting a function can generate the same kind of command object. It is thus easy to remap user input to application functionality. This helps to create an application interface that can be adapted to user preferences. An example is a text editor that provides different control modes such as a WordStar or an emacs keyboard.

Flexibility in the number and functionality of requests. The controller and command processor are implemented independently of the functionality of individual commands. Changing the implementation of a command or introducing new command classes does not affect the command processor or other unrelated parts of the application. For example, it is possible to build more complex commands from existing ones. In addition to a macro mechanism, such compound commands can be pre-programmed, and thus extend the application without modifying the functional core.

Programming execution-related services. The central command processor easily allows the addition of services related to command execution. An advanced command processor can log or store commands to a file for later examination or replay. A command processor can queue commands and schedule them at a later time. This is useful if commands should execute at a specified time, if they are handled according to priority, or if they will execute in a separate thread of control. An additional example is a single command processor shared by several concurrent applications that provides a transaction control mechanism with logging and rollback of commands.

Testability at application level. The command processor is an ideal entry point for application testing. If combined with the Interpreter pattern [GHJV95] as in the second variant above, regression tests can be written in the scripting language and applied after changes to the functional core. Furthermore, logging of command objects executed by the command processor allows you to analyze error situations. If the sequence of executed commands is stored persistently, it can be re-applied after error correction, or reused for regression testing.

Concurrency. The Command Processor design pattern allows commands to be executed in separate threads of control. Responsiveness improves, because the controller does not wait for the execution of a command to finish. However, this calls for synchronization when the global variables of the application, for example in a supplier component, are accessed by several commands executing in parallel.

The Command Processor pattern imposes some **liabilities**:

Efficiency loss. As with all patterns that decouple components, the additional indirection costs storage and time. A controller that performs a service request directly does not impose an efficiency penalty. However, extending such a direct controller with new requests, changing the implementation of a service, or implementing an undo mechanism all require more effort.

Potential for an excessive number of command classes. An application with rich functionality may lead to many command classes. You can handle the complexity of this situation in a number of ways:

- By grouping commands around abstractions.

- By unifying very simple command classes by passing the supplier object as a parameter.

- By pre-programmed macro-command objects that rely on the combination of few low-level commands.

Complexity in acquiring command parameters. Some command objects retrieve additional parameters from the user prior to or during their execution. This situation complicates the event-handling mechanism, which needs to deliver events to different destinations, such as the controller and some activated command object.

See also The Command Processor pattern builds on the *Command* design pattern in [GHJV95]. Both patterns depict the idea of encapsulating service requests into command objects. Command Processor contributes more details of the handling of command objects. The controller of the Command Processor pattern takes the role of the client in the Command pattern. The controller decides which command to use and creates a new command object for each user request.

In the Command pattern, however, the client configures an invoker with a command object that can be executed for several user requests. The command processor receives command objects from the controller and takes the role of the invoker, executing command objects. The controller from the Command Processor pattern takes the role of the client. The suppliers of the Command Processor pattern correspond to receivers, but we do not require exactly one supplier for a command.

Credits   Studying the CommandProcessor classes of ET++ [WGM88] initially motivated this pattern description. The Siemens SICAT team [SICAT95] pointed out the problems with event handling that occur when a command acquires additional parameters from the user during execution.

View Handler

The *View Handler* design pattern helps to manage all views that a software system provides. A view handler component allows clients to open, manipulate and dispose of views. It also coordinates dependencies between views and organizes their update.

Example Multi-document editors allow several documents to be worked on simultaneously. Each document is displayed in its own window.

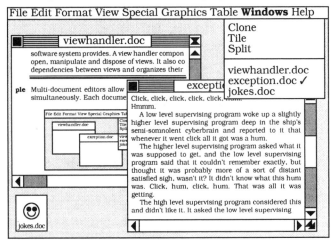

To use such editors effectively, users need support for handling windows. For example, they might want to clone a window to work with several independent views of the same document. Users also often do not close open windows before quitting the editor. It is the task of the system to keep track of all open documents and to close them carefully. Changes in one window may affect other windows as well. We therefore need an efficient update mechanism for propagating changes between windows.

Context A software system that provides multiple views of application-specific data, or that supports working with multiple documents.

Problem Software systems supporting multiple views often need additional functionality for managing them. Users want to be able conveniently to open, manipulate, and dispose of views, such as windows and their contents. Views must be coordinated, so that an update to one of them is propagated automatically to related views. Several *forces* drive the solution to this problem:

- Managing multiple views should be easy from the user's perspective, and also for client components within the system.

- Implementations of individual views should not depend on each other or be mixed with the code used to manage views.

- View implementations can vary, and additional type of view may be added during the lifetime of the system.

Solution   Separate the management of views from the code required to present or control specific views.

A *view handler* component manages all views that the software system provides. It offers the necessary functionality for opening, coordinating and closing specific views, and also for handling views— for example, a command to 'tile' all views, that is, arrange them in an orderly pattern.

Specific views, together with functionality for their presentation and control, are encapsulated within separate *view* components—one for each kind of view. *Suppliers* provide views with the data they must present.

The View Handler pattern adapts the idea of separating presentation from functional core, as proposed by the Model-View-Controller pattern (125). It does not provide an overall structure for a software system by itself—it only removes the responsibility of managing the entirety of views and their mutual dependencies from the model and view components. The pattern gives this responsibility to the view handler. For example, a view does not need to manage its subviews. The View Handler pattern, therefore, is of finer granularity than the Model-View-Controller pattern—it helps to refine the relationships between the model and its associated views.

You can consider the view handler component as an Abstract Factory [GHJV95] and as a Mediator [GHJV95]. It is an abstract factory because clients are independent of how specific views are created. It is a mediator because clients are independent of how views are coordinated.

➡ In the example of a document editor, we provide one view component for each type of document window. The system provides windows to edit documents, to preview printed output, and to see 'thumbnails' of document pages. A view handler manages these views. Besides creation and deletion of windows, the view handler offers functions to bring a specific window to the foreground, to clone the foreground window, and to tile all open windows so that they do not overlap. The suppliers of the windows are the documents to be displayed. There can be multiple simultaneous views of a document, and multiple documents can be displayed. ❑

Structure The *view handler* is the central component of this pattern. It is responsible for opening new views, and clients can specify the view they want. The view handler instantiates the corresponding view component, takes care of its correct initialization, and asks the new view to display itself. If the requested view is open already, the view handler brings this open view to the foreground. If the requested view is open but iconized, the view handler tells the view to display itself full size.

The view handler also offers functions for closing views, both individual ones and all currently-open views, as is needed when quitting the application.

The main responsibility of the view handler, however, is to offer view management services. Examples include functions to quickly bring a specific view into the foreground, to tile all views, to split individual views into several parts, to refresh all views, and to clone views to provide several views of the same document. Such management functionality would be hard to organize if its implementation were spread over many different view components.

Class	*Collaborators*
View Handler	• Specific View
Responsibility • Opens, manipulates, and disposes of views of a software system.	

An additional responsibility of the view handler is coordination. There may be dependencies between views such as occurs, for example, if several views display different parts of a compound document, such as VObjectText objects in ET++ [WGM88]. Such views should be placed next to each other when tiling them. If a user modifies one view of the document, it may be necessary to update the others in a predefined order. For example, views that show the most global information should be updated first.

An *abstract view* component defines an interface that is common to all views. The view handler uses this interface for creating, coordinating, and closing views. The platform underlying the system uses the interface to execute user events, for example the resizing of a window. The interface of the abstract view must offer a corresponding function for all possible operations that can be performed on a view.

Specific *view* components are derived from the abstract view and implement its interface. In addition, each view implements its own display function. This retrieves data from the view's suppliers, prepares this data for display, and presents them to the user. The display function is called when opening or updating a view.

Class Abstract View	*Collaborators*	*Class* Specific View	*Collaborators* • Supplier
Responsibility • Defines an interface to create, initialize, coordinate, and close a specific view.		*Responsibility* • Implements the abstract interface.	

Supplier components provide the data that is displayed by view components. Suppliers offer an interface that allows clients—such as views—to retrieve and change data. They notify dependent components about changes to their internal state. Such dependent components are individual views or, in the case where the view handler organizes updates, the view handler itself.

Class	Collaborators
Supplier	• Specific View
	• View Handler
Responsibility	
• Implements the interface of the abstract view—one class for each view onto the system.	

The following OMT class diagram shows the structure of the View Handler pattern:

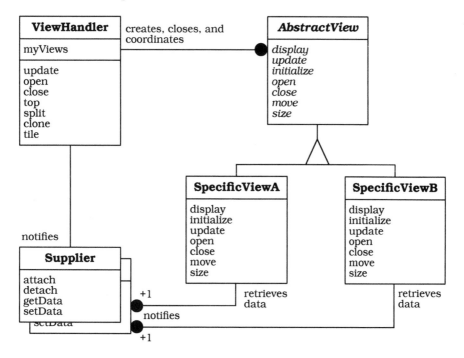

Dynamics We select two scenarios to illustrate the behavior of the View Handler pattern: view creation and tiling. Both scenarios assume that each view is displayed in its own window.

Scenario I shows how the view handler creates a new view. The scenario comprises four phases:

- A client—which may be the user or another component of the system—calls the view handler to open a particular view.

- The view handler instantiates and initializes the desired view. The view registers with the change-propagation mechanism of its supplier, as specified by the Publisher-Subscriber pattern (339).

- The view handler adds the new view to its internal list of open views.

- The view handler calls the view to display itself. The view opens a new window, retrieves data from its supplier, prepares this data for display, and presents it to the user.

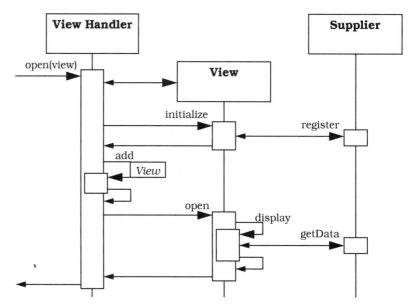

Scenario II illustrates how the view handler organizes the tiling of views. For simplicity, we assume that only two views are open. The scenario is divided into three phases:

- The user invokes the command to tile all open windows. The request is sent to the view handler.

- For every open view, the view handler calculates a new size and position, and calls its resize and move procedures.

- Each view changes its position and size, sets the corresponding clipping area, and refreshes the image it displays to the user. We assume that views cache the image they display. If this is not the case, views must retrieve data from their associated suppliers before redisplaying themselves.

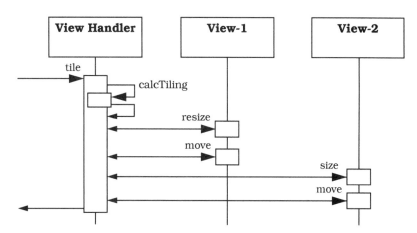

Implementation The implementation of a View Handler structure can be divided into four steps. We assume that the suppliers already exist, and include a suitable change-propagation mechanism.

1 *Identify the views.* Specify the types of views to be provided and how the user controls each individual view.

2 *Specify a common interface for all views.* This should include functions to open, close, display, update, and manipulate a view. The interface may also offer a function to initialize a view. This can be used, for example, to configure a view with data from a particular supplier. Encapsulate the interface in an abstract class. For some functions, for example view update, it is often possible to provide a default implementation.

➡ For our document editor example we specify the class `AbstractView`. The protected interface of the `AbstractView` class includes methods to display and delete a window, and to display the window's contents. The public interface includes methods to open, close, move, size, drag, and update a view, as well as an initialization method.

```
class AbstractView {
protected:
    // Draw the view
    virtual void displayData() = 0;
    virtual void displayWindow(Rectangle boundary) = 0;
    virtual void eraseWindow() = 0;

public:
    // Constructor and Destructor
    AbstractView() {};
    ~AbstractView() {};
    // Initialize the view
    void initialize() = 0;
    // View handling with default implementation
    virtual void open(Rectangle boundary) { /* ... */ };
    virtual void close() { /* ... */ };
    virtual void move(Point point) { /* ... */ };
    virtual void size(Rectangle boundary) { /* ... */ };
    virtual void drag(Rectangle boundary) { /* ... */ };
    virtual void update() { /* ... */ };
};                                                                   ❏
```

3   *Implement the views.* Derive a separate class from the AbstractView
    class for each specific type of view identified in step 1. Implement the
    view-specific parts of the interface, such as the displayData()
    method in our example. Override those methods whose default
    implementation does not meet the requirements of the specific view.

    If the view handler implements specific coordination and update
    policies, views must notify it about all events that may affect other
    views. For example, previously-hidden parts of other views can
    become visible when resizing a view. If the view handler coordinates
    the update of these views, it must be notified about the resizing. The
    Publisher-Subscriber pattern (339) helps with implementing such a
    change notification.

    ➥   In our example we implement three view classes: EditView,
    LayoutView, and ThumbnailView, as specified in the solution
    section. We do not need to override the default implementations
    inherited from the AbstractView class for their implementation.   ❏

4   *Define the view handler.* Implement functions for creating views as
    Factory Methods [GHJV95]. Clients can specify the view they want,
    but they do not control how it is created. The view handler is
    responsible for instantiating and initializing the correct view
    component.

The view handler maintains references to all open views internally. The Iterator pattern [GHJV95] can help you to implement this functionality. The view handler may also maintain additional information about views, such as the current position and size of a window on the screen. The view handler's management functionality, such as operations for cloning windows, uses this information.

Your view handler may need to implement application-specific view coordination policies. For example, one view may present information about another view, for example logging information about an animated simulation. Tiling should place these two dependent views next to each other or, if both views are iconized, opening one view should open the other as well.

Update strategies are another example of view coordination. It may be necessary, for example, to give a higher priority to the update of particular views. For instance, a view that displays alarms may need to be updated before other open views. In such a case, the suppliers notify the view handler about changes, rather than dependent views. The view handler forwards these requests to affected views using its update strategy. View handlers that coordinate the update of views usually offer an update function in their public interface.

To allow coordination strategies to be exchangeable they can be implemented with the Strategy pattern [GHJV95]. The Mediator design pattern [GHJV95] helps with implementing view coordination, for example by broadcasting a refresh request to all open views. Use the Singleton pattern [GHJV95] to ensure that the view handler class can only be instantiated once.

➡ The view handler in our example document editor provides functions to open and close views, as well as to tile them, bring them to the foreground, and clone them. Internally the view handler maintains references to all open views, including information about their position and size, and whether they are iconized.

```
class ViewHandler {
    // Data structures
    struct ViewInfo {
        AbstractView* view;
        Rectangle     boundary;
        bool          iconized;
    };
```

```
                Container<ViewInfo*> myViews;
                // The singleton instance
                static ViewHandler* theViewHandler;
                // Constructor and Destructor
                ViewHandler();
                ~ViewHandler();
            public:
                // Singleton constructor
                static ViewHandler* makeViewHandler();

                // Open and close views
                void open(AbstractView* view);
                void close(AbstractView* view);

                // Top, clone, and tile views
                void top(AbstractView* view);
                void clone(); // Clones the top-most view
                void tile();
            };
```

The following code illustrates the creation of new views.
defaultBoundary is an object of class Rectangle and defines the
default position and size for every new window. The code implements
Scenario I of the Dynamics section.

```
        void ViewHandler::openView(AbstractView* view) {
            ViewInfo*     viewInfo = new ViewInfo();

            // Add the view to the list of open views
            viewInfo->view        = view;
            viewInfo->boundary     = defaultBoundary;
            viewInfo->iconized     = false;
            myViews.add(viewInfo);

            // Initialize the view and open it
            view->initialize();
            view->open(defaultBoundary);
        };                                                      ❏
```

Variants   *View Handler with Command objects.* This variant uses command
objects [GHJV95] to keep the view handler independent of specific
view interfaces. Instead of calling view functionality directly, the view
handler creates an appropriate command and executes it. The
command itself knows how to operate on the view. For example, we
can specify a tile command that, when executed, first calls the size

and then the move function of a view. Another option is to create commands and pass them to a command processor (277) which takes care of their correct execution, but also allows for additional functionality such as undoing an executed command.

Known Uses **Macintosh Window Manager** [App85]. The Window Manager is the part of the Macintosh toolbox that can be compared to a view handler component. Its interface offers functions for window allocation, window display, mouse location, window movement and sizing, and update region maintenance. It also provides a data structure that underlies every Macintosh window. Parts of the interface for Pascal are as follows:

```
TYPE WindowRecord = RECORD
     port:          GrafPort;      {window's grafPort}
     windowKind:    INTEGER;       {window class}
     visible:       BOOLEAN;       {TRUE if visible}
     {more record elements ...}
     refCon:        LONGINT        {window's reference value}
END;

FUNCTION NewWindow( {lots of parameters} ) : WindowPtr;
PROCEDURE CloseWindow(theWindow: WindowPtr);

PROCEDURE SelectWindow(theWindow: WindowPtr);
PROCEDURE HideWindow(theWindow: WindowPtr);
PROCEDURE ShowWindow(theWindow: WindowPtr);

PROCEDURE BringToFront(theWindow: WindowPtr);
PROCEDURE SendBehind(theWindow, behindWindow: WindowPtr);

FUNCTION FindWindow(thePt: Point;
              VAR whichWindow: WindowPtr) : INTEGER;

PROCEDURE MoveWindow(theWindow: WindowPtr;
           hGlobal, vGlobal: INTEGER; front: BOOLEAN);
PROCEDURE DragWindow(theWindow: WindowPtr;
           startPt: Point; boundsRect: Rect);
PROCEDURE SizeWindow(theWindow: WindowPtr;
           w,h: INTEGER; fUpdate: BOOLEAN);

PROCEDURE BeginUpdate(theWindow: WindowPtr);
PROCEDURE EndUpdate(theWindow: WindowPtr);
```

The Macintosh Window Manager does not offer functions that operate on several or all windows, it only provides support for handling individual windows. The Macintosh Window Manager can therefore be viewed as a low-level view handler component.

Microsoft Word [Mic93b]. The Microsoft Word word-processing system offers functions for cloning, splitting, and tiling windows, and also for bringing an open window into the foreground. Quitting Word closes all open windows; dialogs are displayed requesting the desired action if a window contains data that has been changed but not saved. This provides an example of how a View Handler system can appear to the user, and the functionality it can provide.

Consequences The View Handler pattern provides the following **benefits**:

Uniform handling of views. All views share a common interface. The view handler and all other components of the system can therefore handle and manipulate all views uniformly, independent of what they display and how they are implemented.

Extensibility and changeability of views. The organization of view components in an inheritance hierarchy with an abstract base supports the integration of new views without changes to existing views and the view handler. Since individual views are encapsulated within separate components, changes to their implementation do not affect other components of the system.

Application-specific view coordination. Since views are managed by a central instance, it is possible to implement specific view coordination strategies.

The View Handler pattern also suffers from the following **liabilities**:

Restricted applicability. Using the View Handler pattern is only worthwhile if the system must support many different views, views with logical dependencies between each other, or views which can be configured with different suppliers or output devices. It is also useful if the system must implement specific view coordination strategies. If none of these apply, the View Handler pattern just introduces additional implementation effort and increases the internal complexity of the system.

Efficiency. The view handler component introduces a level of indirection between clients that want to create views, and also within the chain of propagation of change notifications, if the view handler is responsible to organizing view updating. This results in a loss of performance. In most cases these losses are negligible, however.

See also   The *Model-View-Controller* architectural pattern (125) provides an infrastructure for separating functionality from both input and output behavior. From the perspective of MVC the View Handler pattern is a refinement of the relationship between the model and its associated views.

The *Presentation-Abstraction-Control* architectural pattern (145) implements the coordination of multiple views according to the principles of the View Handler pattern. An intermediate level PAC agent that creates and coordinates views corresponds to the view handler. Bottom-level view PAC agents that present data to the user represent the view components.

Credits   Special thanks go to Dirk Riehle, who carefully reviewed an earlier version of this pattern.

3.6 Communication

Only few of today's medium and large-scale software systems run on a single computer—most of them use networks of computers. There are many reasons for this:

- Distributed systems allow better sharing and utilization of the resources available within the network.

- Fast but expensive server machines may host central services such as database management systems, while inexpensive workstations can access these services remotely.

- Work within corporations is inherently distributed, and therefore distributed software systems that implement the business logic match this organization of work.

The distribution of applications imposes an important requirement. Distributed subsystems must collaborate, and therefore need a means of communicating with each other. It is not possible to even think of distributed systems without having communication in mind. The problem with communication, however, is that there are so many mechanisms to choose from. Take UNIX as an example. Here, you might use TCP/IP, sockets, TLI (Transport Layer Interface) or RPCs (Remote Procedure Calls), to name only a few.

The use of communication facilities is often hard-wired into existing applications, leading to various problems. It may be difficult or even impossible to change the communication mechanism later, due to the fact that distributed systems depend directly on the communication mechanism used. Portability is another important issue. Finally, the migration of subsystems from one network node to another is only possible if the communication facility allows it.

There are several ways to loosen the coupling between components of a distributed system and the mechanism it uses for communication. Two of the most important aspects in this context are encapsulation and location transparency. Encapsulation of communication facilities means hiding the details of the underlying communication mechanism from its users. This is often done by providing an abstract programming interface on top of the low-level communication facilities. Location transparency allows your applications to access remote components without any knowledge of their physical location.

In this section we present two patterns that address these topics:

- The *Forwarder-Receiver* design pattern (307) provides transparent inter-process communication for software systems with a peer-to-peer interaction model. It introduces forwarders and receivers to decouple peers from the underlying communication mechanisms.

- The *Client-Dispatcher-Server* design pattern (323) introduces an intermediate layer between clients and servers, the dispatcher component. It provides location transparency by means of a name service, and hides the details of the establishment of the communication connection between clients and servers.

While the Forwarder-Receiver pattern provides encapsulation, Client-Dispatcher-Server offers location transparency. If you need to support both encapsulation and location transparency, you could combine these patterns.

Keeping cooperating components consistent is another problem in communication. This problem is independent of whether or not a system consists of distributed components. Consistency is a general issue you need to consider whenever several components cooperate to solve a particular task.

In this section we describe one pattern that addresses this issue:

- The *Publisher-Subscriber* pattern (339) pattern helps to keep the state of cooperating components synchronized. To achieve this it enables one-way propagation of changes: one publisher notifies any number of subscribers about changes to its state.

You may notice that our Publisher-Subscriber pattern is also described under the name Observer in [GHJV95]. Since it is not our intention to repeat existing work in yet another form and style, we only present a summary of the essence of this pattern. However, we also describe an important variant of Publisher-Subscriber that is not included in the Gang-of-Four version, the Event Channel. This variant is used in many distributed systems that use a Broker architecture (99), and is also used in infrastructures for distributed systems such as OMG-Corba [OMG92].

Forwarder-Receiver

The *Forwarder-Receiver* design pattern provides transparent inter-process communication for software systems with a peer-to-peer interaction model. It introduces forwarders and receivers to decouple peers from the underlying communication mechanisms.

Example   The company DwarfWare offers applications for the management of computer networks. In a new project a development team has defined an infrastructure for network management. Among other components, the system consists of agent processes written in Java that run on each available network node. These agents are responsible for observing and monitoring events and resources. In addition, they allow network administrators to change and control the behavior of the network, for example by modifying routing tables. To enable the exchange of information, as well as fast propagation of administration commands, each agent is connected to remote agents in a peer-to-peer fashion, acting as client or server as required. As the infrastructure needs to support a wide variety of different hardware and software systems, the communication between peers must not depend on a particular mechanism for inter-process communication.

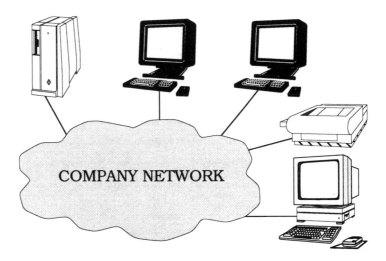

COMPANY NETWORK

Context Peer-to-peer communication.

Problem A common way to build distributed applications is to make use of available low-level mechanisms for inter-process communication (IPC) such as TCP/IP, sockets or message queues. These are provided by almost all operating systems, and are very efficient when compared to higher-level mechanisms such as remote procedure calls. These low-level mechanisms, however, often introduce dependencies on the underlying operating system and network protocols. By using a specific IPC mechanism, the resulting solution restricts portability, constrains the system's capability to support heterogeneous environments, and makes it hard to change the IPC mechanism later.

The Forwarder-Receiver pattern is useful when you need to balance the following *forces*:

- The system should allow the exchangeability of the communication mechanisms.

- The cooperation of components follows a peer-to-peer model, in which a sender only needs to know the names of its receivers.

- The communication between peers should not have a major impact on performance.

Solution Distributed *peers* collaborate to solve a particular problem. A peer may act as a client, requesting services, as a server, providing services, or both. The details of the underlying IPC mechanism for sending or receiving messages are hidden from the peers by encapsulating all system-specific functionality into separate components. Examples of such functionality are the mapping of names to physical locations, the establishment of communication channels, or the marshaling and unmarshaling of messages.

Structure The *Forwarder-Receiver* design pattern consists of three kinds of components, *forwarders*, *receivers*, and *peers*:

Peer components are responsible for application tasks. To carry out their tasks peers need to communicate with other peers. These may be located in a different process, or even on a different machine. Each peer knows the names of the remote peers with which it needs to communicate. It uses a forwarder to send messages to other peers and a receiver to receive messages from other peers. Such messages are either requests that a peer sends to remote peers, or responses that a peer transmits to the originators of requests.

➥   The peers in our DwarfWare example are the agents running on the network nodes. They continuously monitor network events and resources, and listen for incoming messages from remote agents. Each agent may connect to any other agent to exchange information and requests. The network management infrastructure connects the network administrator's console with all other agents. The administrator's task is to control network activities and events. For this purpose, administrators may send requests to network agents or retrieve messages from them by using available network administration tools.   ❏

Class	*Collaborators*
Peer	• Forwarder
	• Receiver
Responsibility	
• Provides application services.	
• Communicates with other peers.	

Forwarder components send messages across process boundaries. A forwarder provides a general interface that is an abstraction of a particular IPC mechanism, and includes functionality for marshaling and delivery of messages. It also contains a mapping from names to physical addresses. When a forwarder sends a message to a remote peer, it determines the physical location of the recipient by using its name-to-address mapping. In the transmitted message the forwarder specifies the name of its own peer, so that the remote peer is able to send a response to the message originator.

➥   In our example different kinds of messages exist:

• *Command messages* instruct the recipient to perform some activities such as changing the routing tables of its host machine.

• *Information messages* contain data on network resources and network events.

- *Response messages* allow agents to acknowledge the arrival of a message.

Forwarder components are responsible for forwarding all these messages to remote network agents without introducing any dependencies on the underlying IPC mechanisms.   ❏

Receiver components are responsible for receiving messages. A receiver offers a general interface that is an abstraction of a particular IPC mechanism. It includes functionality for receiving and unmarshaling messages.

➥   The receivers in our example wait for incoming messages on behalf of their agent process. As soon as a message arrives, they convert the received data stream into a general message format and forward the message to their agent process.   ❏

Class Forwarder	**Collaborators** • Receiver	**Class** Receiver	**Collaborators** • Forwarder
Responsibility • Provides a general interface for sending messages. • Marshals and delivers messages to remote receivers. • Maps names to physical addresses.		**Responsibility** • Provides a general interface for receiving messages. • Receives and unmarshals messages from remote forwarders.	

The static relationships in the Forwarder-Receiver design pattern are shown in the diagram below.

To send a message to a remote peer, the peer invokes the method sendMsg of its forwarder, passing the message as an argument. The method sendMsg must convert messages to a format that the underlying IPC mechanism understands. For this purpose, it calls marshal. sendMsg uses deliver to transmit the IPC message data to a remote receiver.

When the peer wants to receive a message from a remote peer, it invokes the receiveMsg method of its receiver, and the message is returned. receiveMsg invokes receive, which uses the functionality of the underlying IPC mechanism to receive IPC messages. After message reception `receiveMsg` calls `unmarshal` to convert IPC messages to a format that the peer understands.

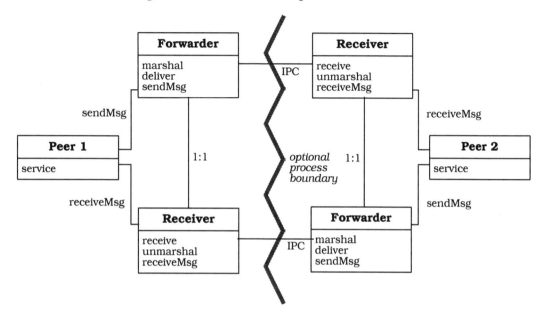

Dynamics The following scenario illustrates a typical example of the use of a Forwarder-Receiver structure. Two peers P1 and P2 communicate with each other. For this purpose, P1 uses a forwarder Forw1 and a receiver Recv1. P2 handles all message transfers with a forwarder Forw2 and a receiver Recv2:

- P1 requests a service from a remote peer P2. For this purpose, it sends the request to its forwarder Forw1 and specifies the name of the recipient.

- Forw1 determines the physical location of the remote peer and marshals the message.

- Forw1 delivers the message to the remote receiver Recv2.

- At some earlier time P2 has requested its receiver Recv2 to wait for an incoming request. Now, Recv2 receives the message arriving from Forw1.

- Recv2 unmarshals the message and forwards it to its peer P2.

- Meanwhile, P1 calls its receiver Recv1 to wait for a response.

- P2 performs the requested service, and sends the result and the name of the recipient P1 to the forwarder Forw2. The forwarder marshals the result and delivers it Recv1.

- Recv1 receives the response from P2, unmarshals it and delivers it to P1.

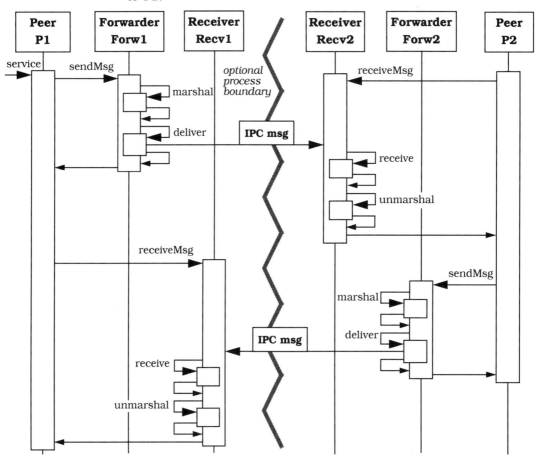

Implementation To implement a Forwarder-Receiver design pattern, iterate through the following steps:

1 *Specify a name-to-address mapping.* Since peers reference other peers by name, you need to introduce an appropriate *name space.* A name space defines rules and constraints to which names must conform in a given context. For example you could specify that all names consist of exactly fifteen characters and have to start with a capital letter, such as 'PeerVideoServer'. You may alternatively structure names as path names in an UNIX-like fashion, such as '/Server/VideoServer/AVIServer'.

   A name does not necessarily refer to a single address—it may refer to a group of addresses. When a peer sends a message with a destination name that represents a group of remote peers, the message is sent to each member of the group. You may even introduce hierarchical structures that allow a group to be a member of another group.

2 *Specify the message protocols* to be used between peers and forwarders. This protocol defines the detailed structure of message data a forwarder receives from its peer. Perform the same task for the message protocol to be used between receivers and their peers.

   ➥ Our DwarfWare example is over-simplified in that it does not cover the handling of errors, or further details of communication such as the partitioning of data into multiple packets. Peers use objects of the class Message when they invoke their forwarder. A receiver returns a Message object to its peer when it receives a message. In the example messages only contain the sender and the message data, both represented as Unicode strings. Messages do not contain the name of the recipient, because the sender passes this name as an extra argument to its forwarder. This allows us to send the same message to more than one recipient.

```
class Message {
    public String sender;
    public String data;
    public Message(String theSender, String rawData) {
        sender = theSender;
        data   = rawData;
    }
}
```

We also need a protocol for communication between the forwarders and the receivers of remote peers. A message sent from a forwarder to a remote receiver also includes the name of the sender.

Each message is transmitted as a sequence of bytes, in which the first four bytes specify the total length of the message. The succeeding bytes contain the sender of the message as well as the message data itself.   ❑

You often need to enable a system to cope with time-outs. For example, peers could specify time-out values to forwarders and receivers in order to prevent the whole system from becoming blocked should a receiver fail to respond to a message. Alternatively, time-outs could be specified by the user at run-time, or forwarders and receivers could free the user from having to specify such values by implementing internal time-outs.

You also need to consider what forwarders and receivers are expected to do in the case of communication failures. They may try to send or receive messages more than once, or they may immediately report an exception when the first communication attempt fails. All these aspects depend on the underlying IPC mechanism as well as the requirements of your application domain.

3   *Choose a communication mechanism.* This decision is driven mainly by the communication mechanisms available in the operating system you use. When specifying an IPC facility you need to consider the following aspects:

- If efficiency is important, a low-level mechanism such as TCP/IP [Ste90] may be the first choice. Such mechanisms are very efficient, and flexible in the communication protocols that may be built using them (see step 2).

- Low-level mechanisms such as TCP/IP require substantial programming effort, and are dependent on the platform you use, restricting portability. If your system must be portable between platforms, it is better to use IPC mechanisms such as sockets instead. Sockets are available on most operating systems and are efficient enough for almost all applications.

➡   For our DwarfWare application we decide to use sockets as the underlying communication mechanism.   ❑

4 *Implement the forwarder.* Encapsulate all functionality for sending messages across process boundaries in the forwarder. The forwarder provides its functionality through a public interface and encapsulates the details of a particular IPC mechanism.

Define a repository that maps names to physical addresses. The forwarder accesses this repository to retrieve the physical addresses of recipients before establishing a communication link to the remote peer. This repository may either be statically predefined or may be changeable at run-time. In the latter case the system is able to add, move or delete peers dynamically. Decide whether each forwarder should have its own private repository, or whether all forwarders should use a common repository that is local to their process. The first approach allows you to map the same name to different physical locations. For example, one peer could associate the name 'Printer' with a different physical location to that used by another peer. The structure of physical addresses is determined by the IPC mechanism you use. For example, if you implement communication using sockets, the physical address consists of the Internet address of the receiver, as well as its socket port. You could implement the repository using a hash table, for example.

➡   In our example forwarders make use of a repository class `Registry` for mapping names to addresses. The repository uses a hash table to manage all the address mappings. The implementation of the hash table is taken from the standard Java class libraries. A physical address of a remote peer denotes the combination of a target machine name and a socket port number. The class `Entry` thus has two data members: `destinationID` for specifying the target machine, and `portNr` for specifying the socket port number of the remote peer. The repository implementation maps strings to instances of the class `Entry`:

```
class Entry {
    private String destinationId; // target machine
    private int     portNr; // socket port
    public Entry(String theDest, int thePort) {
        destinationId = theDest;
        portNr = thePort;
    }
    public String dest() {
        return destinationId;
    }
```

```
                    public int port() {
                        return portNr;
                    }
            }
            class Registry {
                private Hashtable hTable = new Hashtable();
                public void put(String theKey, Entry theEntry) {
                    hTable.put(theKey,theEntry);
                public Entry get(String aKey) {
                    return (Entry) hTable.get(theKey);
                }
            }
```

We now introduce the Forwarder class. The constructor of the class
Forwarder expects a string argument theName that specifies the
logical name of the peer. When a peer calls the sendMsg method, the
following happens:

- The method sendMsg invokes unmarshal to convert the message
  theMsg to a sequence of bytes.

- deliver is called. This method looks up the physical location that
  is associated with the remote peer theDest in a local repository.

For this purpose, the global class fr contains a data member fr.reg
that is an instance of Repository. deliver opens a socket port,
connects with the remote peer, transmits the message, and closes all
sockets.

```
            class Forwarder {
                private Socket s;
                private OutputStream oStr;
                private String myName;
                public Forwarder(String theName) { myName = theName;}
                private byte[] marshal(Message theMsg) { /* ... */ }
                private void deliver(String theDest, byte[] data) {
                    try {Entry entry = fr.reg.get(theDest);
                        s = new Socket(entry.dest(),entry.port());
                        oStr = s.getOutputStream();
                        oStr.write(data);
                        oStr.flush();
                        oStr.close();
                        s.close();
                    }
                    catch(IOException e) { /* ... */ }
                }
                public void sendMsg(String theDest, Message theMsg) {
                    deliver(theDest, marshal(theMsg));
                }
            }
```

It is useful to separate the forwarder's responsibilities from each other, such as marshaling, message delivery and the repository. All this functionality can be decomposed to the concrete IPC mechanism. Use the Whole-Part design pattern (225) to encapsulate each responsibility in a separate part component of the forwarder.

5   *Implement the receiver.* Encapsulate all functionality for receiving IPC messages in the receiver. Provide the receiver with a general interface that abstracts from details of a particular IPC mechanism. The receiver needs to include functionality for receiving and unmarshaling IPC messages. With the Whole-Part design pattern (225) each of these responsibilities may be encapsulated in a separate part component of the receiver (see step 4).

Two other aspects need special consideration when you design the receivers. Since all peers run asynchronously, you need to decide whether the receivers should block until a message arrives:

- If so, the receiver waits for an incoming message. It only returns control back to its peer when it receives a message. In other words, the peer cannot continue until message reception is successful. This behavior is appropriate if the peer depends on the incoming message to continue its work.

- In all other cases, you should implement non-blocking receivers that allow peers to specify time-out values (see also step 2). If no message has arrived in the specified time period, the receiver returns an exception to its peer.

If the underlying IPC mechanism does not support non-blocking I/O, you could use a separate thread within the peer to handle communication.

The use of more than one communication channel within receivers is another important design issue. Such receivers are capable of de-multiplexing communication channels—they wait until a message arrives on one of the channels and return the message to their peer. If it is possible for more than one message to arrive at the same time, the receivers may provide an internal message queue for buffering messages. Whether demultiplexing is possible depends on the underlying IPC mechanism. For example, the UNIX system call `select` allows a process to wait for events on a set of file and socket descriptors. If the IPC mechanism does not support demultiplexing, you can provide multiple threads within the receiver, where each thread is responsible for a particular communication channel. For more details about demultiplexing events, see the Reactor pattern [Sch94].

➥ In our example the class `Receiver` provides the receiver's components. If a peer instantiates a receiver, it calls the constructor and passes its own name as argument. The receiver uses this name to determine which socket port to use for message reception. When a peer wants to retrieve a message, it calls the `receiveMsg` method of its `Receiver` object, which in turn invokes `receive`. The method `receive` does two things:

- After retrieving the socket port number from the global repository, it opens a server socket and waits for connection attempts from remote peers.

- As soon as a connection is established with a second socket, the incoming message and its size are read from the communication channel. `receive` returns the data to `receiveMsg`.

Finally, `receiveMsg` invokes `unmarshal` to convert the sequence of bytes into a `Message` object and returns this object to the peer.

```
class Receiver {
    private ServerSocket srvS;
    private Socket s;
    private InputStream iStr;
    private String myName;
    public Receiver(String theName) { myName = theName;}
    private Message unmarshal(byte[] anArray) { /* .. */ }
    private byte[] receive() {
        int val;
        byte buffer[] = null;
        try {
            Entry entry = fr.reg.get(myName);
            srvS = new ServerSocket(entry.port(), 1000);
            s = srvS.accept();iStr = s.getInputStream();
            val = iStr.read(); buffer = new byte[val];
            iStr.read(buffer);
            iStr.close(); s.close(); srvS.close();
        }
        catch(IOException e) { /* ... */ }
        return buffer;
    }
    public Message receiveMsg() {
        return unmarshal(receive());
    }
}
```

6 *Implement the peers of your application.* Partition the peers into two sets, *clients* and *servers.* The intersection of these sets does not need to be empty. If a peer acts as a client, it sends a message to a remote peer and waits for the response. After receiving the response, it continues with its task. Peers acting as servers continuously wait for incoming messages. When such a message arrives, they execute a service that depends on the message they received, and send a response back to the originator of the request. Note that servers may also be clients of other servers. It is even possible for servers and clients to change their roles dynamically.

The communication between two peers may not always be two-way. Sometimes it is sufficient for a peer to send a message to another peer without requiring a response—one-way communication. Here the peer sends a message and continues with its work. The recipient of the message retrieves the message from its receiver, but does not send a response to the message originator. You can use one-way communication to enable asynchronous communication between senders and recipients.

➥ Here is an example of a peer acting as a server:

```
class Server extends Thread {
    Receiver  r;
    Forwarder f;
    public void run() {
        Message result = null;
        r = new Receiver("Server");
        result = r.receiveMsg();
        f = new Forwarder("Server");
        Message msg = new Message("Server","I am alive");
        f.sendMsg(result.sender, msg);
    }
}                                                            ❏
```

7 *Implement a start-up configuration.* When your system starts up, forwarders and receivers must be initialized with a valid name-to-address mapping. Introduce a separate start-up routine that creates a repository and enters all name/address pairs. Such a configuration routine could read these pairs from an external file, removing the need to touch the source code when you changing the mapping.

If your software system allows different peers to have different name-to-address mappings, the start-up configuration must be capable of initializing the repositories according to this requirement (see step 4).

If you need the configuration to be able to change dynamically, implement additional functionality for modifying the repositories at run-time.

➡ In the DwarfWare example we introduce the following configuration class, allowing us to register a server and a client with the central repository:

```
class Configuration {
    public Configuration() {
        Entry entry = new Entry("127.0.0.1",1111);
        fr.reg.put("Client",entry);
        entry = new Entry("127.0.0.1",2222);
        fr.reg.put("Server",entry);
    }
}                                                              ❏
```

Example resolved   In our infrastructure for network management a common protocol determines the format of requests, information messages and responses. If an agent wants to retrieve information from a remote agent, such as current resource contention, for example, it sends a message to the recipient. The recipient retrieves the message from its receiver, packages the requested information into a response and sends the response back to the message originator. When an agent transmits a command message, the recipient receives the message, interprets it and performs the appropriate command. It then tells the sender whether or not it could successfully perform the command. All relevant information is displayed on the console of the network administrator using a graphical interface. To increase availability, every machine in the network is able to host the network administration console.

Variants   *Forwarder-Receiver without name-to-address mapping.* Sometimes performance issues are more important than being able to encapsulate all details of the underlying IPC mechanism. To achieve this, you can remove the mapping from names to physical locations within forwarders and receivers, for example. In such a configuration, peers need to tell their forwarder the physical location of the recipient. This variant, however, might significantly decrease the ability to change the IPC mechanism.

The software development toolkit **TASC** [TASC91] supports the implementation of Forwarder-Receiver structures within distributed applications for factory automation systems.

The material flow control software for flexible manufacturing that was developed as part of the **REBOOT** project [Kar95] uses Forwarder-Receiver structures to facilitate an efficient IPC.

The **ATM-P** switching system [ATM93] uses the Forwarder-Receiver design pattern to implement the IPC between statically-distributed components, for example between process-management and communication agents.

The Forwarder-Receiver design pattern is used to implement inter-process communication within the distributed Smalltalk environment **BrouHaHa** [Stee91].

Consequences The Forwarder-Receiver design pattern offers two **benefits**:

Efficient inter-process communication. The pattern enables you to provide very efficient inter-process communication. It structures communication between its components in a peer-to-peer fashion, in which every forwarder of an IPC message knows the physical locations of its potential receivers. A forwarder does not therefore need to locate remote components. However, the separation of IPC functionality from peers introduces an additional level of indirection. Compared to the time consumption of the actual IPC, however, this overhead should be negligible in most cases.

Encapsulation of IPC facilities. All dependencies on concrete IPC facilities are encapsulated within the forwarders and receivers. A change of the underlying IPC mechanism does not affect other components of the application, specifically the peers that communicate with each other through forwarders and receivers.

However, the Forwarder-Receiver design pattern has one significant **liability**:

No support for flexible re-configuration of components. Forwarder-Receiver systems are hard to adapt if the distribution of peers may change at run-time. Such a change potentially affects all peers collaborating with the 'migrated' peer. This problem can be solved by adding a central *dispatcher* component to the Forwarder-Receiver structure, as is described in the Client-Dispatcher-Server design pattern (323).

See also The *Client-Dispatcher-Server* design pattern (323) provides transparent inter-process communication for software systems in which the distribution of components is not known at compile-time, or may vary dynamically at run-time. You can apply this pattern in combination with the Forwarder-Receiver design pattern as described below.

The Client-Dispatcher-Server design pattern may be instantiated in such a way that the forwarder acts as the client and the receiver acts as the server. When a peer asks its forwarder to send a message, the forwarder causes the dispatcher to map the recipient's name to its physical location and to establish a communication channel with the remote receiver. Such an arrangement allows peers to migrate to other locations at run-time by unregistering and then re-registering with the dispatcher.

Client-Dispatcher-Server

The *Client-Dispatcher-Server* design pattern introduces an intermediate layer between clients and servers, the dispatcher component. It provides location transparency by means of a name service, and hides the details of the establishment of the communication connection between clients and servers.

Example   Imagine we are developing a software system ACHILLES for the retrieval of new scientific information. The information providers are both on our local network and distributed over the world. To access an individual information provider, it is necessary to specify its location and the service to be executed. When an information provider receives a request from a client application, it runs the appropriate service and returns the requested information to the client.

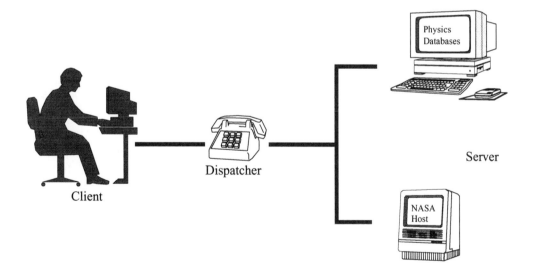

Context   A software system integrating a set of distributed servers, with the servers running locally or distributed over a network.

Problem   When a software system uses servers distributed over a network it must provide a means for communication between them. In many cases a connection between components may have to be established before the communication can take place, depending on the available communication facilities. However, the core functionality of the components should be separate from the details of communication mechanisms. Clients should not need to know where servers are located. This allows you to change the location of servers dynamically, and provides resilience to network or server failures.

We have to balance the following *forces*:

- A component should be able to use a service independent of the location of the service provider.

- The code implementing the functional core of a service consumer should be separate from the code used to establish a connection with service providers.

Solution   Provide a *dispatcher* component to act as an intermediate layer between *clients* and *servers*. The dispatcher implements a name service that allows clients to refer to servers by names instead of physical locations, thus providing location transparency. In addition, the dispatcher is responsible for establishing the communication channel between a client and a server.

Add servers to the application that provides services to other components. Each server is uniquely identified by its name, and is connected to clients by the dispatcher.

Clients rely on the dispatcher to locate a particular server and to establish a communication link with the server. In contrast to traditional Client-Server computing, the roles of clients and servers can change dynamically.

Structure   The task of a *client* is to perform domain-specific tasks. The client accesses operations offered by servers in order to carry out its processing tasks. Before sending a request to a server, the client asks the dispatcher for a communication channel. The client uses this channel to communicate with the server.

A *server* provides a set of operations to clients. It either registers itself or is registered with the dispatcher by its name and address. A server component may be located on the same computer as a client, or may be reachable via a network.

Class	Collaborators	Class	Collaborators
Client	• Dispatcher	Server	• Client
	• Server		• Dispatcher
Responsibility		**Responsibility**	
• Implements a system task.		• Provides services to clients.	
• Requests server connections from the dispatcher.		• Registers itself with the dispatcher.	
• Invokes services of servers.			

The *dispatcher* offers functionality for establishing communication channels between clients and servers. To do this, it takes the name of a server component and maps this name to the physical location of the server component. The dispatcher establishes a communication link to the server using the available communication mechanism and returns a communication handle to the client. If the dispatcher cannot initiate a communication link with the requested server, it informs the client about the error it encountered.

To provide its name service, the dispatcher implements functions for registering and locating servers.

Class	Collaborators
Dispatcher	• Client
	• Server
Responsibility	
• Establishes communication channels between clients and servers.	
• Locates servers.	
• (Un-)Registers servers.	
• Maintains a map of server locations.	

The static relationships between clients, servers and the dispatcher are as follows:

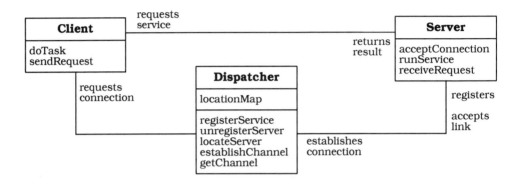

Dynamics   A typical scenario for the Client-Dispatcher-Server design pattern includes the following phases:

- A server registers itself with the dispatcher component.

- At a later time, a client asks the dispatcher for a communication channel to a specified server.

- The dispatcher looks up the server that is associated with the name specified by the client in its registry.

- The dispatcher establishes a communication link to the server. If it is able to initiate the connection successfully, it returns the communication channel to the client. If not, it sends the client an error message.

- The client uses the communication channel to send a request directly to the server.

- After recognizing the incoming request, the server executes the appropriate service.

- When the service execution is completed, the server sends the results back to the client.

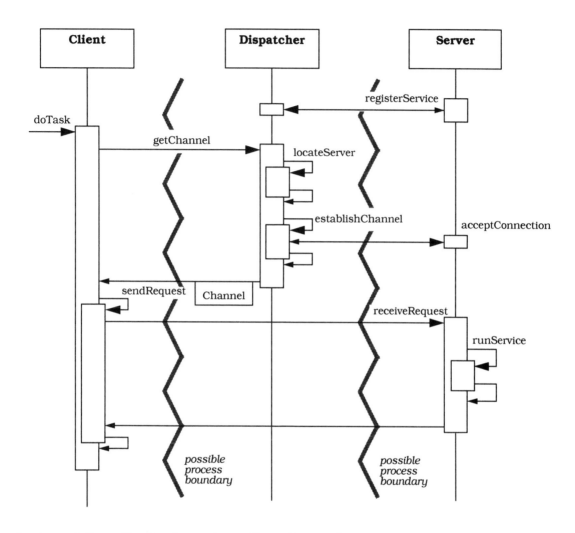

Implementation   To implement a Client-Dispatcher-Server structure, apply the following steps. You do not necessarily need to follow the steps in the order given, because some of them are interrelated.

1   *Separate the application into servers and clients.* Define which components should be implemented as servers, and identify the clients that will access these servers. This partitioning may be predefined, because the application under construction may have to

integrate existing servers. In such cases the separation into clients and servers may already be determined to some extent. Since clients may also act as servers, and vice-versa—their roles are not predefined and may change at run-time.

2   *Decide which communication facilities are required.* Select communication facilities for the interaction between clients and the dispatcher, between servers and the dispatcher and between clients and servers. You can use a different communication mechanism for each connection, or you can use the same mechanism for all three. Using a single communication facility decreases the complexity of the implementation. Sometimes, however, this approach is not possible or feasible. This may be because of performance issues. For example, if the dispatcher and the clients accessing it are on the same machine, shared memory is the fastest method of inter-process communication. In this example, clients may communicate with the dispatcher using shared memory, but the servers and the dispatcher, as well as clients and servers, could communicate using sockets. The servers may be distributed across different machines, making sockets a good choice for the communication between clients and servers.

Where existing servers have to be integrated into the application, the choice of an appropriate communication facility may be driven by the mechanisms already used by these servers.

If all components are located within the same address space, the interaction between components can rely on conventional procedure call interfaces.

3   *Specify the interaction protocols between components.* Consider the following diagram:

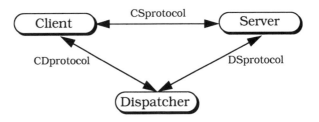

A protocol specifies an ordered sequence of activities for initializing and maintaining a communication channel between two components, as well as the structure of messages or data being transmitted. The Client-Dispatcher-Server pattern implies three different kinds of protocol.

We need an interaction protocol *DSprotocol* between a server and the dispatcher. This addresses two topics: it specifies how servers register with the dispatcher, and it determines the activities that are necessary to establish the communication channel to the server.

Between the client and the dispatcher *CDprotocol* defines the interaction that occurs when a client asks the dispatcher to establish a connection with a particular server. If communication establishment fails due to network or server problems, the dispatcher informs the client about the failure. The dispatcher may try to establish a communication link several times before it reports an error.

CSprotocol specifies how clients and servers talk to each other. This interaction could comprise the following steps:

- The client sends a message to the server using the communication channel previously established between them. To make this work, clients and servers need to share common knowledge about the syntax and semantics of messages they send and receive.

- The server receives the message, interprets it and invokes one of its services. After the service is completed, the server sends a return message to the client.

- The client extracts the service result from the message and continues with its task.

4   *Decide how to name servers.* The four-byte Internet IP address scheme is not applicable, because it does not provide location transparency. If IP addresses were used, a client would depend on the concrete location of the server. You need to introduce names that uniquely identify servers but do not carry any location information. For example, use strings such as 'ServerX' or predefined constants such as ID_SERVER_X. These location-independent names are mapped to physical locations by the dispatcher (see step 5).

5   *Design and implement the dispatcher.* Determine how the protocols you introduced in step 3 should be implemented using available communication facilities. If, for example, the dispatcher is located within the address space of the client, local procedure calls should be used for *CDprotocol*. For all other cases and protocols, you need to use facilities such as TCP ports or shared memory.

With some communication mechanisms the available communication channels may be a limited resource. For example, the number of socket descriptors is constrained by the size of descriptor tables in the operating system. There are several ways round this. For example, each server may allocate its own socket, limiting the number of possible servers. When a client request arrives, the dispatcher returns the server's socket descriptor to the client. Alternatively, the dispatcher could temporarily store client requests in an internal message queue. It would then provide a socket port where servers can ask whether new requests have arrived. When a service request arrives, the server opens a new socket and passes the new socket descriptor to the dispatcher. The dispatcher then forwards the information to the client. After the interaction between client and server is completed, the server closes its socket descriptor.

Define the detailed structure of requests, responses, and error messages based on your chosen communication mechanisms and the identification scheme you use for servers.

A dispatcher includes a repository for mapping server names to their physical locations. The representation of server locations depends on the underlying mechanism you use for Client-Server communication. For example, physical locations may be described in terms of socket ports, TCP ports, shared memory handles or some other suitable scheme.

You need to consider performance issues. When many clients access many servers using one dispatcher, the dispatcher obviously constitutes a bottleneck. Use multi-threading if possible to improve response and execution times. For example you can provide a pool of threads in the dispatcher. When a request arrives, one of the threads is then associated with the request, allowing you to handle many requests in parallel.

6 *Implement the client and server components* according to your desired solution and the decisions you make about the dispatcher interface. Configure the system and either register the servers with the dispatcher or let the servers dynamically register and unregister themselves. Follow the same strategies for optimizing performance that are described in step 5.

Example resolved

In our scientific information example ACHILLES, a TCP port number and the Internet address of the host machine are combined to uniquely identify servers. Clients connect to the dispatcher and ask for server locations by using identifiers such as 'NASA/ HUBBLE_TELESCOPE'. The system predefines the structure of all messages: a message header with a fixed size is followed by a random amount of raw data. All the information necessary to interpret the raw data, such as its size or format, is provided in the message header. Each header also contains the sender and the receiver of the message. Messages are tagged with sequence numbers to enable the receiver of a message to recombine the incoming packets into their correct order. When a server receives a request, it extracts information from the message such as the service to invoke. For example, a client may include the following information in its message: 'HUBBLE_DOC_RECEIVE, ANDROMEDA.jpg'. The server determines whether the requested file is available and sends a message containing the picture to the client.

Variants

Distributed Dispatchers. Instead of using a single dispatcher component in a network environment, distributed dispatchers may be introduced. In this variant, when a dispatcher receives a client request for a server on a remote machine, it establishes a connection with the dispatcher on the target node. The remote dispatcher initiates a connection with the requested server and sends the communication channel back to the first dispatcher. The channel is then returned to the client. Another possibility is to allow clients to communicate directly with the dispatcher on the remote machine. This constrains location transparency, however, since clients must know the network node of each server they want to access. Before using the Distributed Dispatchers variant, consider the use of the Broker architectural pattern (99).

Client-Dispatcher-Server with communication managed by clients. In this variant, instead of establishing a communication channel to servers, a dispatcher may only return the physical server location to the client. It is then the responsibility of the client to manage all communication activities with the server. You can use this variant to increase overall performance, or because the available communication facilities do not require you to establish an explicit communication link.

Client-Dispatcher-Server with heterogeneous communication. It is not always possible to implement the communication between clients and servers using only one communication mechanism. Some servers may use sockets, while others use named pipes. This leads to a variant of the Client-Dispatcher-Server pattern in which the dispatcher is capable of supporting more than one communication mechanism. In this variant, each server register itself with the dispatcher and specifies the communication mechanism it supports. When a client requests a communication channel to a particular server, the dispatcher establishes the communication using to the communication facility the server specified.

Client-Dispatcher-Service. In this variant, clients address *services* and not servers. When the dispatcher receives a request, it looks up which servers provide the specified service in its repository, and establishes a connection to one of these service providers. If it fails to establish the connection, it may try to access another server providing the same service instead, if one is available.

➡   The following sample Java code demonstrates the Client-Dispatcher-Service variant. All clients, servers and the dispatcher exist in the same address space.

The class `Dispatcher` uses a hash table of vectors as a name service repository. An entry in the hash table is available for each service name. Each entry consists of the vector of all servers providing the same kind of service. A server registers with the dispatcher by specifying a service name and the new server instance. When a client asks the dispatcher for a specific service, the dispatcher looks up all available servers in its repository. It randomly selects one of them and returns the server reference to the client.

```
import java.util.*;
import java.io.*;

// Exception thrown by the dispatcher:
class NotFound extends Exception {}
class Dispatcher {
    Hashtable registry = new Hashtable();
    Random rnd = new Random(123456); // for random access

    public void register (String svc, Service obj) {
        Vector v = (Vector) registry.get(svc);
        if (v == null) {
            v = new Vector();
            registry.put(svc, v);
        }
        v.addElement(obj);
    }
    public Service locate(String svc) throws NotFound {
        Vector v = (Vector) registry.get(svc);
        if (v == null) throw new NotFound();
        if (v.size() == 0) throw new NotFound();
        int i = rnd.nextInt() % v.size();
        return (Service) v.elementAt(i);
    }
}
```

The abstract class Service represents the available server objects. It registers server objects with the dispatcher automatically when the constructor is executed.

```
abstract class Service {
    String nameOfService; // service name
    String nameOfServer; // server name
    public Service(String svc, String srv) {
        nameOfService = svc;
        nameOfServer  = srv;
        CDS.disp.register(nameOfService,this);
    }
    abstract public void service(); // service provided
}
```

Concrete server classes are derived from the abstract class Service. They therefore have to implement the abstract method service. Instances of these concrete classes must call the base class constructor in their own constructors so that they are automatically registered.

```
class PrintService extends Service {
    public PrintService(String svc, String srv) {
        super(svc,srv);
    }
    public void service() { // test output
        System.out.println("Service " + nameOfService
                    + " by " + nameOfServer);
        // here the service code would be implemented
    }
}
```

Clients ask the dispatcher for object references, then use these references to invoke the appropriate method implementations.

```
class Client {
    public void doTask()
    {   Service s;
        try { s = CDS.disp.locate("printSvc");
            s.service();
        }
        catch (NotFound n) {
            System.out.println("Not available");
        }
        try { s = CDS.disp.locate("printSvc");
            s.service();
        }
        catch (NotFound n) {
            System.out.println("Not available");
        }
        try { s = CDS.disp.locate("drawSvc");
            s.service();
        }
        catch (NotFound n) {
            System.out.println("Not available");
        }
    }
}
```

The class CDS defines the main program of the application. It instantiates the dispatcher, some servers and a client. It then invokes the event loop of the client:

```
public class CDS {
    public static Dispatcher disp = new Dispatcher();
    public static void main(String args[]) {
        Service s1 = new PrintService("printSvc","srv1");
        Service s2 = new PrintService("printSvc","srv2");
        Client client = new Client();
        client.doTask();
    }
}
```

When the program is started, the following output is displayed:

```
Service printSvc by srv2
Service printSvc by srv1
Not available
```

When the user starts the application, the static method `main` of the class `CDS` is invoked. Two services `S1` and `S2` register with the dispatcher `disp` under the same name. The client is then created and started by calling `client.doTask()`. The client asks the dispatcher to locate the service 'PrintSvc' twice, and once to locate the service 'DrawSvc'. The dispatcher returns the service objects registered with a particular name by using a random number generator. The first service invocations of the client therefore refer to different service objects in the sample output. Since the service 'DrawSvc' is not available, an error occurs when the client asks the dispatcher to locate an appropriate server. ❑

Known Uses Sun's implementation of **Remote Procedure Calls** (RPC) [Sun90] is based upon the principles of the Client-Dispatcher-Server design pattern. It implements a combination of the variants *Distributed Dispatchers* and *Client-Dispatcher-Server with communication managed by clients*. The portmapper process takes the role of the dispatcher. A process initiating an RPC then becomes the client and the receiving process the server. When a client process invokes a remote procedure, it connects to the portmapper process on the target machine. This is possible because all portmappers use the same TCP/UDP port for receiving requests. The portmapper returns the TCP/UDP port of the requested service to the client, which then establishes a direct communication channel with the remote server.

The **OMG Corba** (Common Object Request Broker Architecture) specification [OMG92] uses the principles of the Client-Dispatcher-Server design pattern for refining and instantiating the Broker architectural pattern (99).

The Client-Dispatcher-Server design pattern has several **benefits**:

Exchangeability of servers. In the Client-Dispatcher-Server design pattern a software developer can change servers or add new ones without modifications to the dispatcher component or the clients becoming necessary. If a new implementation of a server is available, the server first unregisters itself. It then registers itself again with the new implementation.

Location and migration transparency. Clients do not need to know where servers are located—they do not depend on any location information. As a consequence, servers may be dynamically migrated to other machines. This does not work, of course, in the event of the server being migrated while it is connected to a client.

Re-configuration. The developer can defer decisions about which network nodes servers should run until the start-up time of the system, or even to run-time. The Client-Dispatcher-Server design pattern therefore allows you to prepare a software system for later conversion to a distributed system.

Fault tolerance. When network or server failures occur, new servers can be activated at a different network node without any impact to clients. This makes the system more robust and fault-tolerant.

The Client-Dispatcher-Server design pattern imposes some **liabilities**:

Lower efficiency through indirection and explicit connection establishment. The performance of a Client-Dispatcher-Server pattern depends on the overhead introduced by the dispatcher, due to its activities in locating and registering servers and explicitly establishing the connection. The alternative to this approach is to get rid of the dispatcher by hard-coding server locations into the clients. This leads to several disadvantages, however. For example, the clients would then depend directly on the server locations, thus loosing the exchangeability of servers.

Sensitivity to change in the interfaces of the dispatcher component. Because the dispatcher plays the central role, the software system is sensitive to changes in the interface of the dispatcher.

See also The *Forwarder-Receiver* design pattern (307) can be combined with the Client-Dispatcher-Server pattern to hide the details of inter-process communication. While the Client-Dispatcher-Server pattern allows you to decouple clients and servers by supporting location transparency, it does not encapsulate the details of the underlying communication facilities. To achieve this, you could introduce forwarders and receivers between clients and servers, clients and the dispatcher, and between servers and the dispatcher.

The *Acceptor and Connector* patterns [Sch96b] demonstrate a different way to decouple connection set-up from connection processing. Schmidt's patterns are more decentralized than our approach, which uses a centralized dispatcher. Every site that passively accepts connections in Schmidt's patterns can provide a family of Acceptor factories. These acceptors are responsible for constructing *service handlers*, which are entry points to the application-defined services.

Various Acceptors can be defined, to distinguish between different connection policies such as synchronous versus asynchronous, and to use different service policies, such as running concurrently in separate processes or threads or being demultiplexed reactively in a single process. The Connector pattern is the 'dual' of the Acceptor pattern—it is used by sites that actively initiate connection setup. Our Client-Dispatcher-Server pattern resembles a mini-Broker (99) that is equipped with a name service that also enables dynamic relocation of servers.

Credits We thank all participants of the writer's workshop at the PLoP'95 [PLoP95] for their valuable suggestions and comments.

Publisher-Subscriber

The *Publisher-Subscriber* design pattern helps to keep the state of cooperating components synchronized. To achieve this it enables one-way propagation of changes: one publisher notifies any number of subscribers about changes to its state.

Also known as Observer, Dependents

In this section we give an abbreviated pattern description based on the Observer pattern from [GHJV95], to allow us to present additional viewpoints and variants.

Problem A situation often arises in which data changes in one place, but many other components depend on this data. The classical example is user-interface elements: when some internal data element changes all views that depend on this data have to be updated. We could solve the problem by introducing direct calling dependencies along which to propagate the changes, but this solution is inflexible and not reusable. We are looking for a more general change-propagation mechanism that is applicable in many contexts.

The solution should balance the following *forces:*

- One or more components must be notified about state changes in a particular component.

- The number and identities of dependent components is not known a priori, or may even change over time.

- Explicit polling by dependents for new information is not feasible.

- The information publisher and its dependents should not be tightly coupled when introducing a change-propagation mechanism.

Solution One dedicated component takes the role of the *publisher* (called *subject* in [GHJV95]). All components dependent on changes in the publisher are its *subscribers* (called *observers* in [GHJV95]).

The publisher maintains a registry of currently-subscribed components. Whenever a component wants to become a subscriber, it uses the subscribe interface offered by the publisher. Analogously, it can unsubscribe.

Whenever the publisher changes state, it sends a notification to all its subscribers. The subscribers in turn retrieve the changed data at their discretion.

The pattern offers the following degrees of freedom in its implementation:

- You can introduce abstract base classes to let different classes be publishers or subscribers, as described in [GHJV95].

- The publisher can decide which internal state changes it will notify its observers about. It may also queue several changes before calling `notify()`.

- An object can be a subscriber to many publishers.

- An object can take both roles, that of a publisher as well as subscriber.

- Subscription and the ensuing notification can be differentiated according to event type. This allows subscribers to get messages only about events in which they are interested.

- The publisher can send selected details of the data change when it notifies its subscribers, or can just send a notification and give the subscribers the responsibility to find out what changed.

In more general terms we differentiate between the push and the pull model. In the *push model*, the publisher sends all changed data when it notifies the subscribers. The subscribers have no choice about if and when they want to retrieve the data—they just get it. In the *pull model*, the publisher only sends minimal information when sending a change notification—the subscribers are responsible for retrieving the data they need. Many variations are possible in the middle ground between these two extremes.

The push model has a very rigid dynamic behavior, whereas the pull model offers more flexibility, at the expense of a higher number of messages between publisher and subscribers.

For complex data changes, the push model can be a poor choice, especially when the publisher sends a large package to a subscriber that is not interested in it. Even pushing a package that just describes the nature of the data change can be too great an overhead. In such cases, use the pull model and make the subscribers find out what kind of data change occurred. The process of finding out successively great detail about data changes can be organized as a decision-tree.

Generally, the push model is a better choice when the subscribers need the published information most of the time. The pull model is used when only the individual subscribers can decide if and when they need a specific piece of information.

Variants   *Gatekeeper.* The Publisher-Subscriber pattern can be also applied to distributed systems. In this variant a publisher instance in one process notifies remote subscribers. The publisher may alternatively be spread over two processes. In one process a component sends out messages, while in the receiving process a singleton 'gatekeeper' demultiplexes them by surveying the entry points to the process. The gatekeeper notifies event-handling subscribers when events for which they registered occur. The Reactor pattern [Sch94] describes this scheme in detail.

The *Event Channel* variant was proposed by the OMG in its Event Service Specification [OMG95] and is targeted at distributed systems. This pattern strongly decouples publishers and subscribers. For example, there can be more than one publisher, and the subscribers only wish to be notified about the occurrence of changes, and not about the identity of the publisher—subscribers do not care which component's data has changed. Similarly, publishers are not interested in which components are subscribing.

In this variant, an event channel is created and placed between the publisher and the subscribers. To publishers the event channel appears as a subscriber, while to subscribers it appears as a publisher. A subscriber registers with the event channel, as illustrated in the figure below. It asks an administration instance to create a 'proxy publisher', and connects it over a process boundary with a local 'proxy subscriber'. Analogously, a 'proxy subscriber' is created between a publisher and an event channel and, on the event channel side, a 'proxy publisher'.

In this way publisher, event channel and subscriber can all exist in different processes. Providing the event channel with a buffer decouples publishers and subscribers even further. When messages

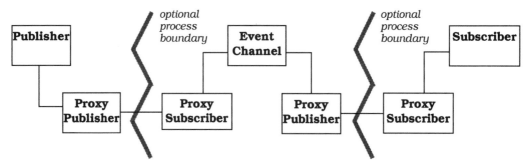

from a publisher arrive, the event channel does not have to notify the subscribers immediately, but can implement its own notification policies.

You can even chain several event channels. The reason for doing this is that event channels can provide additional capabilities, such as filtering events, or storing an event internally for a fixed period and sending it to all components that subscribe during that period. This is often referred to as 'quality-of-service'. A chain can then assemble all the capabilities necessary for a system—the chain sums the capabilities of the individual event channels of which it is composed, analogously to UNIX pipes.

The Event Channel variant is powerful enough to allow multiple publishers and typed events.

Another variant of the generic Publisher-Subscriber pattern uses the *Producer-Consumer* style of cooperation. In this a producer supplies information, while a consumer accepts this information for further processing. Producer and consumer are strongly decoupled, often by placing a buffer between them. The producer writes to the buffer without any regard for the consumer. The consumer reads data from the buffer at its own discretion. The only synchronization carried out is checking for buffer overflow and underflow. The producer is suspended when the buffer is full, while the consumer waits if it cannot read data because the buffer is empty. Another difference between the Publisher-Subscriber pattern and the Producer-Consumer variant is that in the latter producers and consumers are usually in a 1:1 relationship.

Only more complex patterns such as Event-Channel can simulate a Producer-Consumer relationship with more than one producer or consumer. Several producers can provide data by only allowing them to write to the buffer in series, either directly or indirectly. The case of more than one consumer is slightly more complicated. When one consumer reads data from the buffer, the event channel does not delete that data from the buffer, but only marks it as read by the consumer. The consumer is given the illusion that the data is consumed, and hence deleted, while other consumers will be given the illusion that the data is still present and unread. Iterators are a good way to implement this behavior. Each consumer has its own iterator on the buffer. The position of an iterator on the buffer reflects how far the corresponding consumer has read the buffer. The data in the buffer can be purged behind the lagging iterator, as all reads on it have been completed.

4 Idioms

Idioms are low-level patterns specific to a programming language. An idiom describes how to implement particular aspects of components or the relationships between them with the features of the given language.

In this chapter we provide an overview of the use of idioms, show how they can define a programming style, and show where you can find idioms. We refer mainly to other people's work instead of documenting our own idioms. We do however present the Counted Pointer idiom as a complete idiom description.

4.1   Introduction

Idioms represent low-level patterns. In contrast to design patterns, which address general structural principles, idioms describe how to solve implementation-specific problems in a programming language, such as memory management in C++. Idioms can also directly address the concrete implementation of a specific design pattern. We cannot therefore draw a clear line between design patterns and idioms. Idioms can address low-level problems related to the use of a language, such as naming program elements, source text formatting or choosing return values. Such idioms approach or overlap areas that are typically addressed by programming guidelines. To summarize, we can say that idioms demonstrate competent use of programming language features. Idioms can therefore also support the teaching of a programming language.

A programming style is characterized by the way language constructs are used to implement a solution, such as the kind of loop statements used, the naming of program elements, and even the formatting of the source code. Each of these separate aspects can be cast into an idiom, whenever implementation decisions lead to a specific programming style. A collection of such related idioms defines a programming style.

As with all patterns for software architecture, idioms ease communication among developers and speed up software development and maintenance. The collected idioms of your project teams form an intellectual asset of your company.

4.2   What Can Idioms Provide?

Learning a new programming language does not end after you have mastered its syntax. There are always many ways to solve a particular programming problem with a given language. Some might be considered better style or make better use of the available language features. You have to know and understand the little tricks and unspoken rules that will make you productive and your code of high quality.

A single idiom might help you to solve a recurring problem with the programming language you normally use. Examples of such problems are memory management, object creation, naming of methods, source code formatting for readability, efficient use of specific library components and so on.

There are several ways to acquire expertise in solving such problems. One is by reading programs developed by experienced programmers. This makes you think about their style and encourages you to try to reproduce it in your own code. This approach takes a long time, as trying to understand 'foreign' code is not always easy. If a set of idioms are available for you to learn, it is much easier to become productive in a new programming language, because the idioms can teach you how to use the features of a programming language effectively to solve a particular problem.

Because each idiom has a unique name, they provide a vehicle for communication among software developers. A team of experienced engineers who have been working together for some time might share experience by thinking in terms of their own idioms. It may be difficult for a newcomer to such a team to understand and learn these implicit idioms. It is therefore a good idea to make idioms and their use explicit—for example, try to document and name the idioms you use.

In contrast to many design patterns, idioms are less 'portable' between programming languages. For example, the design of Smalltalk's collection classes incorporates many idioms that are specific to the language. They depend on features not present in C++ such as garbage collection or meta-information. An early C++ class library, the NIHCL [GOP90], implemented collection classes for C++ programs by mimicking Smalltalk's collections. For example, every class that has objects stored in collections must inherit from the NIHCL root class `Object`. In addition, memory management relies completely on the programmer, which makes the NIHCL collections much harder to use than Smalltalk's collection classes. Modern C++ class libraries such as Generic++ [SNI94] abandon this approach and implement collection classes differently from NIHCL by using the C++ template mechanism. Such template collections can store any kind of data of a given type, even non-objects.

4.3   Idioms and Style

Experienced programmers apply patterns when doing their work, just as do other experts. A good program written by a single programmer will contain many applications of his set of patterns. Knowing the patterns a programmer uses makes understanding their programs a lot easier.

It may be difficult to follow a consistent style, however, even for an experienced programmer. If programmers who use different styles form a team, they should agree on a single coding style for their programs. For example, consider the following sections of C/C++ code, which both implement a string copy function for 'C-style' strings:

```
void strcopyKR(char *d, const char *s) {
    while (*d++=*s++);
}

void strcopyPascal(char d[], const char s[]){
    int i ;
    for (i = 0; s[i] != '\0'; i = i + 1)
    {
        d[i] = s[i];
    }
    d[i] = '\0'; /* always assign 0 character */
} /* END of strcopyPascal */
```

Both functions achieve the same result—they copy characters from string s to string d until a character with the value zero is reached. A compiler might even be able to create identical optimized machine code from both examples. The function strcopyKR() uses pointers as synonyms for array parameters, in the terse C style in the tradition of Kerninghan and Ritchie [KR88]. The strcopyPascal() function might have been written by a programmer with a background in a language such as Pascal, where pointers are intended for use with linked data structures. Both implementations follow their own style. Which version you prefer, or what your own version would look like, depends on your experience, background, taste and many other factors. A program that uses a mixture of both styles might be much harder to understand and maintain than a program that uses one style consistently. It is a prerequisite that we can understand the style of the program, such as the strange looking `while` loop in `strcopyKR()`.

Corporate style guides are one approach to achieving a consistent style throughout programs developed by teams. Unfortunately many of them use dictatorial rules such as 'all comments must start on a separate line'. This means that they are not in pattern form—they give solutions or rules without stating the problem. Another shortcoming of such style guides is that they seldom give concrete advice to a programmer about how to solve frequently-occurring coding problems.

We think that style guides that contain collected idioms work better. They not only give the rules, but also provide insight into the problem solved by a rule. They name the idioms and thus allow them to be communicated. For example, it is easier to say and memorize 'you should use an Intention Revealing Selector here' [Bec96] than 'apply rule §7-42 and change your method name accordingly'. However, not many such style guides exist yet. A further problem is that idioms from conflicting styles do not mix well if applied carelessly to a program.

Here is an example of a style guide idiom from Kent Beck's *Smalltalk Best Practice Patterns* [Bec96]:

Name   Indented Control Flow

Problem   How do you indent messages?

Solution   Put zero or one argument messages on the same lines as their receiver.

```
foo isNil
2 + 3
a < b ifTrue:[...]
```

Put the keyword/argument pairs of messages with two or more keywords each on its own line, indented one tab.

```
a < b
    ifTrue:[...]
    ifFalse:[...]
```

❏

Different sets of idioms may be appropriate for different domains. For example, you can write C++ programs in an object-oriented style with inheritance and dynamic binding. In some domains, such as real-time systems, a more 'efficient' style that does not use dynamic binding is required. A single style guide can therefore be unsuitable for large companies that employ many teams to develop applications in different domains. A style guide cannot and should not cover a variety of styles.

A coherent set of idioms leads to a consistent style in your programs. Such a single style will speed up development, because you do not have to spend a lot of time thinking about the simple problems covered by your set of idioms, like how to format a block of code. In addition a consistent style also helps during program evolution or maintenance, because it makes programs a lot easier to understand.

4.4   Where Can You Find Idioms?

It is beyond the scope of this book to cover a programming style for a programming language—such styles and idioms could easily fill an entire book by themselves. We suggest that you look at any good language introduction to make a start on collecting a set of idioms to use. As an exercise in documenting your own patterns, you can try to rephrase the guidelines given in such books to correspond to a pattern template. This will help you to understand when to apply the rules, so that you can easily determine which problem a guideline solves.

Some design patterns that address programming problems in a more general way can also provide a source of idioms. If you look at these patterns from the perspective of a specific programming language, you can find embedded idioms. For example, the Singleton design pattern [GHJV95] provides two idioms specific to Smalltalk and C++:

Name   Singleton (C++)

Problem   You want to implement the Singleton design pattern [GHJV95] in C++, to ensure that exactly one instance of a class exists at run-time.

Solution Make the constructor of the class private. Declare a static member variable `theInstance` that refers to the single existing instance of the class. Initialize this pointer to zero in the class implementation file. Define a public static member function `getInstance()` that returns the value of `theInstance`. The first time `getInstance()` is called, it will create the single instance with `new` and assign its address to `theInstance`.

Example

```
class Singleton {
static Singleton *theInstance;
Singleton();
public:
static Singleton *getInstance() {
        if (! theInstance)
            theInstance = new Singleton;
        return theInstance;
    }
};
//...
Singleton* Singleton::theInstance = 0;
```

❑

The corresponding Smalltalk version of Singleton solves the same problem, but the solution is different because Smalltalk's language concepts are completely distinct from C++:

Name Singleton (Smalltalk)

Problem You want to implement the Singleton design pattern [GHJV95] in Smalltalk, to ensure that exactly one instance of a class exists at run-time.

Solution Override the class method `new` to raise an error. Add a class variable `TheInstance` that holds the single instance. Implement a class method `getInstance` that returns `TheInstance`. The first time `getInstance` is called, it will create the single instance with `super new` and assign it to `TheInstance`.

Example

```
new
    self error: 'cannot create new object'

getInstance
    TheInstance isNil ifTrue: [TheInstance := super new].
    ^ TheInstance
```

❑

Idioms that form several different coding styles in C++ can be found for example in Coplien's *Advanced C++* [Cope92], Barton and Neckman's *Scientific and Engineering C++* [BN94] and Meyers' *Effective C++* [Mey92].

You can find a good collection of Smalltalk programming wisdom in the idioms presented in Kent Beck's columns in the *Smalltalk Report*. His collection of *Smalltalk Best Practice Patterns* is about to be published as a book [Bec96]. Beck defines a programming style with his coding patterns that is consistent with the Smalltalk class library, so you can treat this pattern collection as a Smalltalk style guide. Many of his patterns build on each other, so that in addition to being a style guide, his collection can be considered a pattern language.

You can also look at your own program code, or the code of your colleagues, read it and extract the patterns that have been used. You can use such 'pattern mining' to build a style guide for your programming language that becomes an intellectual asset of your team. By giving a name to each idiom, your style guide provides a language for communication between your developers. It can also provide a teaching aid for new developers who join your team.

Counted Pointer

The *Counted Pointer* idiom [Cope92] makes memory management of dynamically-allocated shared objects in C++ easier. It introduces a reference counter to a body class that is updated by handle objects. Clients access body class objects only through handles via the overloaded `operator->()`.

Example   When using C++ for object-oriented development, memory management is an important issue. Whenever an object is shared by clients, each of which holds a reference to it, two situations exist that are likely to cause problems: a client may delete the object while another client still holds a reference to it, or all clients may 'forget' their references without the object being deleted.

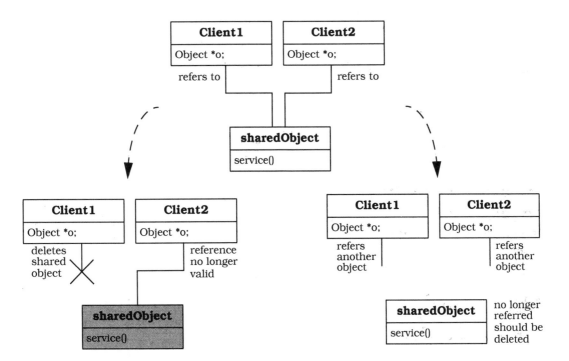

Context   Memory management of dynamically allocated instances of a class.

Problem   In every object-oriented C++ program you have to pass objects as parameters of functions. It is typical to use pointers or references to objects as parameters. This allows you to exploit polymorphism. However, passing object references around freely can lead to the situations shown in the diagram above—you do not know if references are still valid, or even still needed.

One approach to the problems arising from the use of pointers and references is to avoid them completely and pass objects by value, as is normally done with integers. C++ allows you to create programs that do this, and the compiler will automatically destroy value objects that go out of scope.

This solution does not work well for all kinds of program, however, for three reasons. Firstly, if the objects you pass by value are large, copying them each time they are used is expensive in run-time and memory consumption. Secondly, you might want to create dynamic structures of objects, such as trees or directed graphs, which is almost impossible to do in C++ using value objects alone. Lastly, you may want to share an object deliberately, for example by storing it in several collections.

If you have to deal with references or pointers to dynamically allocated objects of a class, you may need to address the following *forces*:

- Passing objects by value is inappropriate for a class.

- Several clients may need to share the same object.

- You want to avoid 'dangling' references—references to an object that has been deleted.

- If a shared object is no longer needed, it should be destroyed to conserve memory and release other resources it has acquired.

- Your solution should not require too much additional code within each client.

Solution   The *Counted Pointer* idiom eases memory management of shared objects by introducing reference counting. The class of the shared objects, called *Body*, is extended with a reference counter. To keep track of references used, a second class *Handle* is the only class allowed to hold references to Body objects. All Handle objects are passed by value throughout the program, and therefore are allocated and destroyed automatically. The Handle class takes care of the Body object's reference counter. By overloading `operator->()` in the Handle class, its objects can be used syntactically as if they were pointers to Body objects.

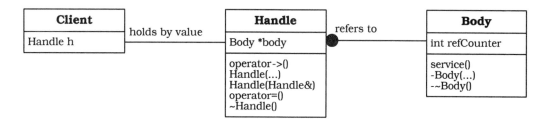

See the Variants section for a variation of this solution that applies when Body objects are only shared for performance reasons.

Implementation To implement the Counted Pointer idiom, carry out the following steps:

1 Make the constructors and destructor of the Body class private (or protected) to prohibit its uncontrolled instantiation and deletion.

2 Make the Handle class a friend to the Body class, and thus provide the Handle class with access to Body's internals.

3 Extend the Body class with a reference counter.

4 Add a single data member to the Handle class that points to the Body object.

5 Implement the Handle class' copy constructor and its assignment operator by copying the Body object pointer and incrementing the reference counter of the shared Body object. Implement the destructor of the Handle class to decrement the reference counter and to delete the Body object when the counter reaches zero.

6 Implement the arrow operator of the Handle class as follows:

```
Body * operator->() const { return body; }
```

and make it a public member function.

7 Extend the Handle class with one or several constructors that create
the initial Body instance to which it refers. Each of these constructors
initializes the reference counter to one.

Sample Code Applying the Counted Pointer idiom results in the following C++ code:

```
class Body {
public:
// methods providing the bodies functionality to the world
    void service() ;
    // further functionality...
private:
    friend class Handle;
    // parameters of constructor as required
    Body(/*...*/) { /* ... */ }
    ~Body() { /* ... */ }
    int refCounter;
};

class Handle {
public:
    // use Body's constructor parameters
    Handle(/*...*/) {
        body = new Body(/*...*/);
        body->refCounter = 1;
    }
    Handle(const Handle &h) {
        body = h.body;
        body->refCounter++;
    }
    Handle & operator=(const Handle &h) {
        h.body->refCoutner++;
        if (--body->refCounter) <= 0)
            delete body;
        body= h.body;
    }
    ~Handle() {
        if (--body->refCounter <= 0)
            delete body;
    }
    Body* operator->() { return body; }
private:
    Body *body;
};
```

```
// example use of handles ...
Handle h(/* some parameter */);
// create a handle and also a new body instance
{   Handle g(h); // create just a new handle
    h->service(); g->service();
} // g goes out of scope and is automatically deleted

h->service(); // still possible
// after h goes out of scope the body instance is
// automatically deleted.                                    ❑
```

Variants   A common application of reference counting, similar to Counted Pointer, is used for performance improvement with large Body objects. [Cope92] names this variant the *Reference Counting Idiom* or *Counted Body* in [Cope94a]. In this variant a client has the illusion of using its own Body object, even if it is shared with other clients. Whenever an operation is likely to change the shared Body object, the Handle creates a new Body instance and uses this copy for all further processing. To achieve this functionality it is not sufficient to just overload `operator->()`. Instead, the interface of the Body class is duplicated by the Handle class. Each method in the Handle class delegates execution to the Body instance to which it refers. Methods that would change the Body object create a new copy of it if other clients share this Body object.

See Also   Bjarne Stroustrup [Str91] discusses several ways of extending the Handle class. The Handle can be implemented as a template if the Body class, passed as a template parameter, cooperates with the Handle template class—for example, if the Body class provides the Handle class access to the reference counter.

The solution provided by the Counted Pointer idiom has the drawback that you need to change the Body class to introduce the reference counter. Coplien and Koenig give two ways to avoid this change.

James Coplien [Cope92] presents the Counted Pointer idiom and several variations. In cases where the Body class is not intended to have derived classes, it is possible to embed it in the Handle class. Another variation, shown in the diagram that follows, is to wrap existing classes with a reference counter class. This wrapper class then forms the Body class of the Counted Pointer idiom. This solution requires an additional level of indirection when clients access the Body object.

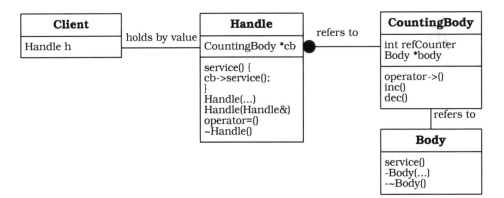

Andrew Koenig gives a further variation of the theme that allows you to add reference counting to classes without changing them [Koe95]. He defines a separate abstraction for use counts. Then the Handle holds two pointers: one to the body object, the other to the use-count object. The use-count class can be used to implement handles for a variety of body classes. The Handle objects of this solution require twice the space of the other Counted Pointer variants, but the access is as direct as with a change to the Body class.

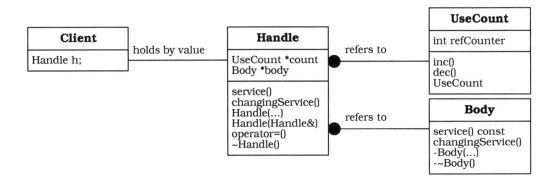

5 Pattern Systems

No pattern is an island.
Richard Helm, personal communication

A *pattern system* ties individual patterns together. It describes how its constituent patterns are connected with other patterns in the system, how these patterns can be implemented, and how software development with patterns is supported. A pattern system is a powerful vehicle for expressing and constructing software architectures.

In this chapter we specify a pattern system that includes the patterns we describe in this book, and that is open for the integration of other patterns, for example those from [GHJV95], [PLoP94] and [PLoP95], as well as your own patterns.

5.1   What is a Pattern System?

Patterns do not exist in isolation—there are many interdependencies between them. A plain catalog-like list of all patterns, however, does not reflect these manifold relationships. Instead, patterns should be interwoven in *pattern systems*.

A pattern system ties its constituent patterns together. It describes how the patterns are connected and how they complement each other. A pattern system also supports the effective use of patterns in software development.

Christopher Alexander uses the term 'language' instead of 'system' to describe the same concept [Ale79] p. 185:

> The elements [of a pattern language] are patterns. There is a structure on the patterns, which describes how each pattern is itself a pattern of other smaller patterns. And there are also rules, embedded in the patterns, which describe the way that they can be created, and the way that they must be arranged with respect to other patterns.

> However, in this case, the patterns are both elements and rules, so rules and elements are indistinguishable. The patterns are elements. And each patterns is also a rule, which describes the possible arrangements of the elements—themselves again or other patterns.

Indeed, a pattern system can be compared with a language. The patterns make the vocabulary of the language, and the rules for their implementation and combination make up its grammar.

We prefer the term 'pattern system' to 'pattern language'. A pattern language implies that its constituent patterns cover every aspect of importance in a particular domain. A pattern language for software architecture must be computationally complete: at least one pattern must be available for every aspect of the construction and implementation of software systems—there must be no gaps or blanks. Such pattern languages exist for some small and well-known domains. Two examples are Crossing Chasms [PLoP95] for connecting object-oriented applications to relational databases, and CHECKS [Cun94] for information integrity. However, the patterns we describe only cover certain aspects of the construction of software architectures. Their entirety is not computationally complete, even when extended with all the other related patterns we know about. We however have more than just a catalog of patterns, since we describe how our patterns are tied together, but we have far less than a pattern language.

We define the term 'pattern system' as follows:

A *pattern system for software architecture* is a collection of patterns for software architecture, together with guidelines for their implementation, combination and practical use in software development.

The main objective of a pattern system for software architecture is to support the development of high-quality software systems. By 'high-quality', we mean systems that fulfill both their functional and non-functional requirements. To achieve this objective, a pattern system must meet the following requirements:

- *It should comprise a sufficient base of patterns.* We need patterns that support specification of the basic architecture of a system, patterns that help with refining this basic architecture, and patterns that help with implementing a software architecture in a specific programming language.

- *It should describe all its patterns uniformly.* The form of description must capture both the essence of a pattern and a precise depiction of its details. The form must further support the comparison of a pattern with other patterns.

- *It should expose the various relationships between patterns.* The pattern system must identify which other patterns a pattern refines, which other patterns it exposes, with which patterns it can be combined, and what alternatives are available.

- *It should organize its constituent patterns.* Users should be able to find a pattern quickly that helps them solve their concrete design problem, and they should be able to explore alternative solutions that are addressed by different patterns.

- *It should support the construction of software systems.* A pattern system should show how to apply and implement its constituent patterns.

- *It should support its own evolution.* With evolving technology, a pattern system will evolve as well. Existing patterns will change, their description will improve, new or missing patterns will be added and existing ones may even 'die'.

The patterns in this book, and patterns written by others, already fulfill the first requirement—we are able to provide a sufficiently large and useful set of patterns. These patterns cover all ranges of scale, and address many problems in software architecture.

Our pattern description template is also adjusted to the needs of a pattern system (see Chapter 1, *Patterns*). It allows us to draw the 'big picture' for a pattern, to detail its concrete structure and dynamics, and to guide the implementation of the pattern described. Most importantly for pattern systems, our description template shows how a pattern is connected with other patterns, with which other patterns it can be refined and combined, which variants it exposes and which other patterns solve the same problem in a different way.

However, a pattern system is more than just a collection of patterns described with a template. We must specify a useful organization scheme for patterns, and guide users in selecting patterns and building software systems with patterns. Finally, we must ensure that the pattern system is open to its own evolution.

5.2   Pattern Classification

The more patterns a pattern system includes, the more difficult it becomes to understand and use. If software developers must read, analyze and understand every pattern in detail to find the one they need, the pattern system as a whole is useless, even if its constituent patterns are useful. To handle the entirety of all patterns conveniently within a pattern system it is therefore helpful to classify them into groups of related patterns. A pattern classification schema that supports the development of software systems using patterns should have the following properties:

- *It should be simple and easy to learn*, rather than complex, hard to understand, and use.

- *It should consist of only a few classification criteria*, rather than of a multi-dimensional pattern space that organizes patterns according to every theoretically-possible pattern property.

- *Each classification criterion should reflect natural properties of patterns*, for example the kinds of problems the patterns address, rather than artificial criteria such as whether patterns belong to a pattern language or not.

- *It should provide a 'roadmap'* that leads users to a set of potentially-applicable patterns, rather than a rigid 'drawer-like' schema that tries to support finding the one 'correct' pattern.

- *The schema should be open to the integration of new patterns* without the need for refactoring the existing classification.

We keep our classification schema simple. It is build upon two classification criteria: *pattern categories* and *problem categories*.

Pattern Categories

The most fundamental classification criteria in our classification schema are the pattern categories. We distinguish *architectural patterns*, *design patterns* and *idioms* (see Chapter 1, *Patterns*). All three categories are related to important phases and activities in software development:

- *Architectural patterns* can be used at the beginning of coarse-grained design, when specifying the fundamental structure of an application.

- *Design patterns* are applicable towards the end of coarse-grained design, when refining and extending the fundamental architecture of a software system, for example deciding on the basic communication mechanisms between subsystems. Design patterns are also applicable in the detailed design stage for specifying local design aspects, such as the required support for multiple implementations of a component.

- *Idioms* are used in the implementation phase to transform a software architecture into a program written in a specific language.

Note that although the above guidelines work well in most cases, they are not an immutable rule. Exceptions occur for example if you want to instantiate a singleton layered abstraction of a subsystem. The Singleton pattern [GHJV95] should be thought about first, then you can go on to think about how to structure the subsystem with the Layers pattern (31).

Problem Categories

Our second classification criterion provides a problem-oriented view of a pattern system. Every pattern addresses a specific problem that may arise in the development of software systems. For example, the Forwarder-Receiver pattern (307) describes how to implement peer-to-peer communication between distributed components, and the Client-Dispatcher-Server pattern (323) how to achieve location transparency in a distributed system. Abstracting from specific problems leads to problem categories that expose several related problems. Forwarder-Receiver and Client-Dispatcher-Server, for example, address problems that arise when implementing inter-process communication, or more generally, communication between components. Problem categories correspond directly to concrete design situations. They are therefore a useful pattern classification criterion for patterns. We define the following problem categories:

- *From Mud to Structure* includes patterns that support a suitable decomposition of an overall system task into cooperating subtasks.

- *Distributed Systems* includes patterns that provide infrastructures for systems that have components located in different processes or in several subsystems and components.

- *Interactive Systems* includes patterns that help to structure systems with human-computer interaction.

- *Adaptable Systems* includes patterns that provide infrastructures for the extension and adaptation of applications in response to evolving and changing functional requirements.

- *Structural Decomposition* includes patterns that support a suitable decomposition of subsystems and complex components into cooperating parts.

- *Organization of Work* includes patterns that define how components collaborate to provide a complex service.

- *Access Control* includes patterns that guard and control access to services or components.

- *Management* includes patterns for handling homogenous collections of objects, services and components in their entirety.

- *Communication* includes patterns that help to organize communication between components.

- *Resource Handling* includes patterns that help to manage shared components and objects.

Some patterns cannot be assigned to a single problem category, however. These patterns address several problems—one main problem and several secondary ones. We assign these patterns to all the relevant problem categories. For example, we assign the Pipes and Filters pattern (53) to the problem categories *From Mud to Structure* and *Distributed Systems*.

The Classification Schema

Both pattern categories and problem categories interweave to form a two-dimensional pattern classification schema—for every pattern we can define its corresponding pattern and problem categories.

The schema itself is very simple, expressive and easy to learn. There are only two classification criteria. These correspond to two major aspects in software development: the general development activity that must be performed, and the concrete problem that must be solved. Both criteria also reflect natural properties of patterns—range of scale and the problem addressed.

You may have noticed that the structure of this book reflects our classification schema. Chapters 2–4 correspond to the pattern categories, and each chapter is further structured according to different problem categories. The following table gives an overview of the classification of our patterns.

	Architectural Patterns	Design Patterns	Idioms
From Mud to Structure	Layers (31) Pipes and Filters (53) Blackboard (71)		
Distributed Systems	Broker (99) Pipes and Filters (53) Microkernel (171)		
Interactive Systems	MVC (125) PAC (145)		
Adaptable Systems	Microkernel (171) Reflection (193)		
Structural Decomposition		Whole-Part (225)	
Organization of Work		Master-Slave (245)	
Access Control		Proxy (263)	
Management		Command Processor (277) View Handler (291)	
Communi-cation		Publisher-Subscriber (339) Forwarder-Receiver (307) Client-Dispatcher-Server (323)	
Resource Handling			Counted Pointer (353)

Other patterns fit into this classification schema as well. Reactor and Client-Server [PLoP94], for example, are architectural patterns for structuring distributed systems. Composite Message [SC95b] is a design pattern that addresses communication aspects. Handle-Body [Cope92] is an idiom that guards access to services.

Our classification schema is also extensible—see Section 5.5, *The Evolution of Pattern Systems*. We can add new pattern and problem categories to classify patterns that cannot be assigned to existing categories. Extending the schema in this way does not violate our existing pattern classification.

Comparison

Our classification schema is not the only one to be defined for organizing patterns. Probably the best-known schema is described in [GHJV95]. Like our schema, the Gang-of-Four's schema has two dimensions: *purpose* and *scope*. The following paragraphs are an excerpt from the Gang-of-Four book.

> The first criterion, called purpose, reflects what a pattern does. Patterns can have either creational, structural, or behavioral purpose. Creational patterns concern the process of object creation. Structural patterns deal with the composition of classes or objects. Behavioral patterns characterize the ways in which classes or objects interact and distribute responsibility.

> The second criterion, called scope, specifies whether the pattern applies primarily to classes or to objects. Class patterns deal with relationships between classes and their subclasses. These relationships are established through inheritance, so they are static—fixed at compile-time. Object patterns deal with object relationships, which can be changed at run-time and are more dynamic.

According to this classification schema, for example, Composite [GHJV95] and Whole-Part (225) are structural object patterns, while Interpreter [GHJV95] is a behavioral class pattern.

We believe, however, that a distinction between structural and behavioral patterns is too vague. Problem categories are more expressive. They explicitly name specific problem areas with which developers must deal when building software systems. Furthermore, the Gang-of-Four's scope criterion will not help software developers when selecting a pattern. This is because it does not relate to any specific design situation or activity, and also does not fit with non-object-oriented patterns such as Layers (31) or Pipes and Filters (53).

Other organizational schemes for patterns are presented in [EKM+94], [Zim94] and [BM94]. [EKM+94] builds on problem categories, such as transactions or bridging the gap between object-oriented applications and relational databases, in the same way that our schema does. [Zim94] focuses on relationships between patterns, such as 'pattern A uses pattern B' or 'pattern A is similar to pattern B' in its solution.

[BM94] is the predecessor of the schema we present in this book. It is three-dimensional. The first two dimensions—called 'granularity' and 'functionality'—correspond directly to our pattern and problem categories. The third dimension, 'structural principles', depicts the technical principles that underlie the solutions the patterns propose. For example, the Whole-Part pattern (225) is based on the separation of policy and implementation [RBPEL91]. However, as with the scope criterion of the Gang-of-Four's schema, the structural principle criterion is of less importance when selecting a pattern—we therefore dropped it when defining our new classification schema.

5.3 Pattern Selection

Based on our classification schema, our pattern description template (see Chapter 1, *Patterns*) and the relationships between patterns, we can define the following simple procedure for selecting a specific pattern. It includes seven steps:

1 *Specify the problem.* To be able to find a pattern that helps you solve a concrete problem, you must first specify the problem precisely: what is the general problem, and what are its forces? If the general problem has several aspects, such as specifying the basic architecture of a system that is both distributed and interactive, split the problem into subproblems. Describe each subproblem and its forces separately. For each subproblem, try to find a pattern that helps to solve it.

Let's assume, for example, that your problem is to define the fundamental structure of an interactive text editor. The system should be portable to different user-interface libraries and different customer-specific style guides. We will use this example to illustrate the remaining pattern selection steps.

2 *Select the pattern category* that corresponds to the design activity you are performing. For our example, we need to specify the basic architecture of the text editor. We therefore select the architectural pattern category.

Although this step does not require detailed knowledge about the design problem involved, it already significantly limits the number of patterns that are potentially applicable to the design problem.

3   *Select the problem category* that corresponds to the general nature of the design problem. Every problem category broadly summarizes the types of problems addressed by the patterns it contains. In our text editor example, we would select the problem category Interactive Systems, where we find the Model-View-Controller pattern (MVC) (125) and the Presentation-Abstraction-Control pattern (PAC) (145). If no problem category matches the concrete design problem, select an alternative problem category if possible (step 7).

4   *Compare the problem descriptions.* Each pattern in your selected problem category may address a particular aspect of your concrete problem, and either a single pattern or a combination of several can help to solve it. Select the patterns whose problem descriptions and forces best match your design problem. This step is the first that requires specific knowledge about the design problem to be solved. For a text editor, for example, we would probably select Model-View-Controller. Both MVC and PAC support changing the user interface of a system. However, since the domain of text editing mainly consists of a set of closely-related functions rather than of several independent subdomains, there is no need for our editor to have the agent-based architecture proposed by PAC.

   If the patterns in the selected problem category do not address aspects of the concrete design problem, select an alternative problem category if possible (step 7).

5   *Compare benefits and liabilities.* This step investigates the consequences of applying the patterns selected so far. Pick the pattern that provides the benefits you need and whose liabilities are of least concern to you. Since we have already selected a particular pattern for the architecture of our text editor, we skip this step.

6   *Select the variant* that best implements the solution to your design problem. In the case of our text editor example, the view and controller functionality is usually strongly interwoven. We therefore select the Document-View variant of MVC to specify the basic architecture of our editor.

Unless you encountered problems with step 3 or step 4, you have now completed your pattern selection.

7   *Select an alternative problem category.* If there is no appropriate problem category, or if the selected problem category does not include patterns you can use, try to select a problem category that further generalizes your design problem. This category may include patterns that, when specialized, can help you to solve the problem. Then return to step 4, *Compare the problem descriptions.*

Many patterns are specializations of other patterns from different problem categories. For example, the Composite Message pattern [SC95b], which addresses communication aspects, is basically a specialization of the Composite pattern [GHJV95], which is assigned to the problem category Structural Decomposition. If you are facing the problem that is addressed by Composite Message, but do not have it available, you could perhaps use the Composite pattern instead.

If steps 2, 3 and 4 provide no result, even after trying to select alternative problem categories, you should stop searching—the pattern system does not contain a pattern that can help you to solve your design problem. You may decide to look at other pattern languages, systems or catalogs to see whether they contain a pattern you can use, or you can solve your design problem without applying patterns.

You do not need to apply the search procedure when implementing or refining a pattern you have already selected. The implementation section of our pattern descriptions refers directly to those patterns that naturally complement the pattern being implemented.

5.4   Pattern Systems as Implementation Guidelines

All our pattern descriptions provide steps and guidelines that specify their implementation. They help with the task of transforming a given software architecture that does not include the pattern into one that includes it. The implementation steps can be seen as a *micro-method* for solving the specific problem addressed by the pattern.

Like the patterns themselves, the steps for their implementation are interwoven—they often refer to other patterns that complement the pattern being described. Whenever another pattern is referenced, its implementation steps can be applied.

Example   Implementing a Model-View-Controller architecture (125)

The implementation section of Model-View-Controller refers to seven other patterns:

- Step 2: 'Implement the change-propagation mechanism' suggests the use of the Publisher-Subscriber design pattern (339).

- Step 4: 'Design and implement the controllers' refers to the Command Processor design pattern (277).

- Step 5: 'Design and implement the view-controller relationship' refers to the Factory Method design pattern [GHJV95].

- Step 7: 'Dynamic view creation' builds upon the View Handler design pattern (291).

- Step 9: 'Infrastructure for hierarchical views and controllers' uses the Composite [GHJV95] and Chain of Responsibility [GHJV95] patterns.

- Step 10: 'Further decoupling from system dependencies' suggests the application of the Bridge pattern [GHJV95].

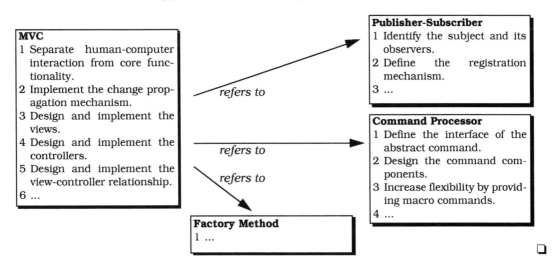

The above example reveals that the implementation steps of all patterns collectively form an extensible set of guidelines for software design and implementation. The implementation steps for individual patterns are its building-blocks. They can be plugged with the implementation steps of other patterns, namely those that refer to the pattern you are implementing. You can therefore solve complex problems by recursively applying the implementation steps of all patterns that are involved in its solution.

This focus on solving specific problems distinguishes the implementation guidelines for patterns from existing analysis and design methods, such as Booch [Boo94], Coad/Yourdon [CY91], Object Modeling Technique [RBPEL91] or Shlaer/Mellor [SM88]. These only provide general and problem-independent guidelines for software development such as 'Identify the objects/classes required to model the system' [Kar95]. The construction of a specific architecture, for example a Model-View-Controller architecture, is still based on your own experience and intuition.

You may wonder how complete the guidelines are that you can derive from the implementation steps of individual patterns. Examining our pattern system shows that the support for software development in general is fairly incomplete and small. We cover only those problem areas of software architecture for which the system includes at least one pattern. For many problem areas, however, our guidelines give no support, because we do not provide patterns that address these problems. Examples include component creation, event handling, transactions, connecting object-oriented applications with relational databases, extensibility of an application with new functionality and so on.

However, we designed our pattern system to be extensible (see Section 5.5, *The Evolution of Pattern Systems*)—it can be extended with patterns for problem areas that are not yet covered. When integrating a new pattern in this way, we also specify its relationships to other patterns. This integrates the implementation steps for the new pattern with the implementation steps of related existing patterns. Every new pattern therefore extends the guidelines provided by the whole pattern system—they become more powerful, more specific, and cover more of the problem areas of software architecture.

Even the most comprehensive pattern system, however, will not and should not cover every problem area of software architecture. There will always be blank spots—design problems for which no pattern is available. [Cope96] maintains that 'the broader design space lends itself well to the common techniques of well-known paradigms'. For example, there is no need for patterns that describe the general use of modules, interfaces or procedures. Our implementation guidelines for individual patterns also do not address general aspects of software development, such as providing overall process and software life cycle models. Patterns do not therefore define a new method for software development that replaces existing ones. Instead, they complement general but problem-independent analysis and design methods with guidelines for solving specific and concrete problems.

We therefore suggest the following pragmatic approach to the development of software systems using patterns:

1 Use any method you like to define an overall software development process and the detailed activities to be performed in each development phase, such as Booch [Boo94], Coad/Yourdon [CY91], Object Modeling Technique [RBPEL91], Shlaer/Mellor [SM88], Responsibility-Driven-Design [WBWW90] or the Unified Method [BR95].

2 Use an appropriate pattern system to guide your design and implementation of solutions to specific problems. Whenever this pattern system includes a pattern that addresses a design problem you are faced with, use the implementation steps associated with that pattern to solve the problem. If these refer to other patterns, recursively apply these patterns and their associated implementation steps to complement your implementation of the original pattern.

3 If the pattern system does not include a pattern for your design problem, try to find a pattern from other pattern sources you know.

4 If no pattern is available, apply the analysis and design guidelines of the method you are using. These guidelines provide at least some useful support for solving the design problem at hand.

This simple approach avoids defining yet another design method. It combines the experience in software development captured by exist-

ing analysis and design methods with the specific solutions to concrete design problems described by patterns.

5.5   The Evolution of Pattern Systems

Even the most mature pattern systems will not remain static.
Knowledge evolves over time—new technologies are developed and
existing technologies are enhanced or become outdated. New patterns
will therefore emerge and existing patterns may 'die'. Every new
pattern to emerge must be integrated into the pattern system to keep
it up-to-date. Outdated patterns must be removed if they are no
longer used. Even individual pattern descriptions will change over
time—specific aspects will be clarified and further known uses added.
Whenever a new pattern is integrated into the system, or an existing
pattern is removed, the relationships between existing patterns must
be updated.

Within the context of pattern system evolution, several issues must
be considered: the evolution of pattern descriptions, 'pattern-mining',
the integration of new patterns into the system, the removal of
outdated patterns and the extension of the organization schema. The
following sections discuss these issues.

The Evolution of Pattern Descriptions

It is important to improve and stabilize the description of every
pattern in a pattern system continuously for the system to remain
useful. The more mature a pattern is, the longer it will stay in a
pattern system and the greater is the chance of its successful
application. Whenever a pattern is applied, the experience gained
from its application should be used for a critical review of the pattern
and its description.

Such a review may lead to the recognition of additional benefits that
are provided by the pattern, but also to further potential liabilities
and limitations. You may also recognize the need for a slight

modification of the structure and dynamics of the pattern, or for the integration of a new variant in the pattern description.

Example   Proxy (263)

Proxy is a good example of the evolution of a pattern and its description. The original description in [GHJV95] lists three variants: Remote Proxy, Virtual Proxy and Protection Proxy, whose specific details were also interwoven with the description of the general principle. In [PLoP95] we presented an alternative description, which separated the general principle of the Proxy pattern from the details of its concrete uses. We also presented four additional kinds of proxies: Cache Proxy, Firewall Proxy, Counting Proxy and Synchronization Proxy. Based on the feedback we received from many reviews of our Proxy description, we improved the pattern description further. We sharpened the phrasing of the essentials and added more technical information about the various variants. The result of this improvement process is the Proxy pattern to be found in this book (263).   ❑

You can stabilize a pattern further by extending the list of its known uses whenever you apply it successfully. The more known uses that are listed, the greater is the chance that users will identify a similar design situation to those described. In such a case there is 'reference-application' of the pattern and users can directly benefit from previous experience with it.

Writer's Workshops

Every pattern review should follow a structured format. The objective is to acquire as much feedback for constructive improvement as possible. Unstructured reviews tend to be insufficiently systematic—points are raised in an arbitrary and unrelated order, and many aspects for improvement are not discussed or are discussed only briefly.

The format we suggest for pattern reviews is adapted from one used for the review of written works, specifically poetry. It is called a *writer's workshop* and—when used for the review of patterns—follows the following format:

- The pattern is discussed by a group of people that includes its author and a group of reviewers familiar with the contents of the pattern description. A moderator is also present to help the participants follow the conventions of the workshop.

- The author of the pattern description reads a paragraph of their choice from the pattern description.

- Two reviewers summarize the description from their personal viewpoints.

- In separate stages the strong points of the pattern description are first discussed, then its deficiencies, and finally every other aspect. Within this discussion, the author of the pattern description is only 'virtually' present—the author does not participate actively in the discussion, nor do the reviewers address the author directly. The reviewers should discuss the pattern description as if its author were not present. The author is, however, allowed to take notes about the discussion.

- After this discussion, the author may question the reviewers to clarify particular statements made.

- The author concludes the session with a final comment on the discussion.

The pattern description can be improved on basis of the results from the writer's workshop. All patterns in [PLoP94] and [PLoP95], and most of our patterns, were reviewed in writer's workshops.

Pattern-Mining

There is not always a suitable pattern for solving a concrete design problem. In such a case it is often useful to 'mine' new patterns that address such problems, especially if you face them frequently. The following rules of thumb have proved to be practical:

1 *Find at least three examples* where a particular recurring design or implementation problem is solved effectively by using the same solution schema. The examples should all be from different real-world systems, and all systems should have been developed by different teams.

2 *Extract the solution schema.* Abstract the general solution schema from the specific details of its concrete applications. Describe the problem that the solution schema addresses, and the forces that are associated with the problem—use an appropriate pattern description template. List the examples from which you derived the solution schema as 'known uses'.

3 *Declare the solution schema to be a 'pattern-candidate'.*

4 *Run a writer's workshop* to improve the description of the candidate pattern and to share it with your colleagues.

5 *Apply the candidate pattern* in a real-world software development project.

6 *Declare the candidate pattern to be a pattern* if its application is successful, and integrate it into your pattern system. Improve its description by running another writer's workshop. Add the new application to the list of known uses of the pattern.

If the application of the candidate pattern failed, improve its description from the lessons learned and try to apply it again. Alternatively, consider abandoning the candidate completely and looking for a better solution to the original problem.

The Integration of New Patterns

When integrating a new pattern into a pattern system, either an existing pattern or a pattern you have 'mined', you need to perform two activities:

1 *Specify the relationships* of the new pattern to other patterns in the pattern system, and all relationships from existing patterns to the new pattern.

2 *Classify the pattern* by assigning it to appropriate pattern and problem categories. If you cannot assign the new pattern to existing categories, extend your organization schema appropriately (see below).

Removing Outdated Patterns

With evolving technology, patterns can become outdated. There are several reasons for this:

- *Disappearance of the problem.* A problem that in the past had to be explicitly addressed might now be handled by the programming languages or system environments in use. For example, introducing garbage collection in C++ makes several C++-specific idioms superfluous, namely those that address the handling of shared objects.

- *Better alternatives.* A new solution to a particular design problem might become available which is preferable to existing patterns that address the same problem.

- *Technology evolution.* A new paradigm, the evolution of programming languages and styles, or a change in the kinds of system that are developed can cause existing patterns to become outdated.

Main Program and Subroutines [PLoP95] is an example of an outdated pattern. This suggests the decomposition of an application's functionality into a set of 'nested collections of procedures'. When structural programming was new and programs were small, Main Program and Subroutines was a useful pattern, as it helped programmers to think about system decomposition. A program that was not a large 'chunk' of code was thought of as well-structured.

Today almost all programs use subroutines—even badly-structured ones. It is no longer a sign of quality if Main Program and Subroutines is the main architectural principle of a system. The reason for this is that systems grow continuously both in size and functional complexity. They become more and more distributed, and most of them provide graphical user interfaces. Complex systems, however, call for architectural principles other than the one described by Main Program and Subroutines—this once useful pattern has become outdated.

When should you remove a 'dying' pattern from a pattern system? Certainly it should not be used when developing new software systems. It may, however, still be necessary to apply it, for example when maintaining legacy systems. Such systems may follow programming practices of the past. The application of 'up-to-date' patterns often does not make sense—they may break the architectural vision underlying these systems. We must apply 'old-fashioned' patterns that fit with the existing architecture. Patterns that become outdated should therefore only be removed from a pattern system if it is unlikely that they will ever be used in any future software development, or during system maintenance.

Extending the Organization Schema

With the evolution of a pattern system it may be necessary to modify its organization schema. We may need to add new pattern categories, for example. Our pattern system as specified in this book only covers patterns that are of general applicability in software development. We do not provide domain-specific patterns that specify the organization of work in a particular application domain and which can be applied in the analysis phase.

To integrate such patterns, we could add an Analysis Patterns category. Alternatively, we may define new problem categories, for example for component creation. New problem categories are necessary to extend our pattern system with the patterns from [GHJV95]:

- *Creation* includes patterns that help with instantiating objects and recursive object structures.

- *Service Variation* comprises patterns that support changing the behavior of an object or component.

- *Service Extension* includes patterns that help to add new services to an object or object structure dynamically.

- *Adaptation* provides patterns that help with interface and data conversion.

All the other Gang-of-Four patterns can be assigned to existing problem categories. The following table shows the integration of their patterns into our pattern system. To distinguish the Gang-of-Four patterns from ours, they are shown in italics.

	Architectural Patterns	Design Patterns	Idioms
From Mud to Structure	Layers (31) Pipes and Filters (53) Blackboard (71)	*Interpreter*	
Distributed Systems	Broker (99) Pipes and Filters (53) Microkernel (171)		
Interactive Systems	MVC (125) PAC (145)		
Adaptable Systems	Microkernel (171) Reflection (193)		
Creation		*Abstract Factory* *Prototype* *Builder*	*Singleton* *Factory Method*
Structural Decomposition		Whole-Part (225) *Composite*	
Organization of Work		Master-Slave (245) *Chain of Responsibility* *Command* *Mediator*	
Access Control		Proxy (263) *Facade* *Iterator*	
Service Variation		*Bridge* *Strategy* *State*	*Template Method*
Service Extension		*Decorator* *Visitor*	
Management		Command Processor (277) View Handler (291) *Memento*	
Adaptation		*Adapter*	
Communi- cation		Publisher-Subscriber (339) Forwarder-Receiver (307) Client-Dispatcher-Server (323)	
Resource Handling		*Flyweight*	Counted Pointer (353)

Another possible extension is the addition of new classification criteria, for example Scope as defined by [GHJV95], or Enabling Technique as described in [BM94], which specifies the principles that underlie specific patterns. Is this really useful, however? We do not believe so. Firstly, a multi-dimensional schema becomes overloaded. Users are confronted with a variety of different classification criteria that make a pattern system hard to understand and use. Secondly, more criteria require a knowledge of more details about the current design problem when selecting a pattern.

The introduction of further, finer-grained criteria for grouping patterns should only be considered if the existing pattern groups become very large and thus hard to handle. Your goal should always be to help users to get an overview of the patterns in a pattern system, and to guide the selection of patterns, rather than providing a complete and detailed classification that covers every property that patterns can expose.

5.6   Summary

Patterns for software architecture exist in many ranges of scale and abstraction. They can be applied in different phases of software development and address a variety of different problems. They also exhibit different relationships with each other. The benefits of a set of related patterns is more than the sum of the benefits of each individual pattern in the set.

To take advantage of such sets of patterns, we need to organize them into pattern systems. A pattern system helps to handle a significant number of patterns in a convenient way. It describes all patterns uniformly. It supports an overview of the patterns it includes by classifying them. It supports the selection of a pattern by providing an appropriate search strategy. It provides a set of guidelines to support the development of software systems with patterns. Finally, a pattern system supports its own evolution.

Our pattern system includes patterns of general applicability in software development, from the specification of the basic architecture of a software system to the implementation of specific design aspects in a concrete programming language. The pattern system is extensible with patterns that address further aspects of the construction of software architectures, such as those from [GHJV95], [Sch95], [Cope92] and many of the patterns described in [PLoP94] and [PLoP95]. Extending our pattern system with these patterns provides concrete and practical support for solving many recurring design and implementation problems.

We can also extend our pattern system with domain-specific patterns, such as the switching system patterns in [PLoP95]. For particular application domains it then becomes possible to cover most of the software development process with patterns, from analysis to implementation. Such a pattern system becomes a powerful vehicle for constructing software systems.

6 Patterns and Software Architecture

The sign read:
'Hold stick near the centre of its length.
Moisten pointed end in mouth.
Insert in tooth space, blunt end next to gum.
Use gentle in-out motion.'

'It seemed to me,' said Wonko the Sane,
'that any civilization that had so far lost its head
as to need to include a set of detailed instructions
for use in a packet of toothpicks,
was no longer a civilization
in which I could live and stay sane.'

Douglas Adams, So Long, and Thanks for All the Fish

Patterns are an important vehicle for constructing high-quality software architectures. However, several other techniques, methods, and processes for software architecture already exist. How do patterns build on these techniques, methods, and processes, and how do patterns complement them? Do patterns even define the state of the art in software architecture?

In this chapter we discuss how patterns are integrated into the larger field of software architecture. The chapter is not intended to provide a complete survey of software architecture, however.

6.1   Introduction

Before discussing how patterns are integrated with software architecture, we need to characterize our understanding of this field. In this section we therefore briefly discuss some important aspects related to the discipline of software architecture. We give our definitions of the following terms:

- Software Architecture
- Component
- Relationship
- View
- Functional Property
- Non-functional Property
- Software Design

Software Architecture

Throughout our book we use the term 'software architecture' without any further explanation—we assume that you already have an intuitive understanding of its meaning. But what do we really mean by a software architecture?

A *software architecture* is a description of the subsystems and components of a software system and the relationships between them. Subsystems and components are typically specified in different views to show the relevant functional and non-functional properties of a software system. The software architecture of a system is an artifact. It is the result of the software design activity.

Component

A *component* is an encapsulated part of a software system. A component has an interface. Components serve as the building blocks for the structure of a system. At a programming-language level, components may be represented as modules, classes, objects or a set of related functions.

The following figure shows three different components:

```
DEFINITION MODULE
  CoreData;

FROM Sys IMPORT
 ObjType,
 ObjID;

EXPORT QUALIFIED
 PROCEDURE
  newObj():ObjType;

 PROCEDURE
  loadObj(ID:ObjID):ObjType;

 PROCEDURE
  storeObj(obj:ObjType);

END CoreData.
```

```
class Random {
private:
   int seedA;
   int seedB;
public:
   Random(int seed);
   ~Random();
   int random_card(int max);
};
```

```
float sin(float x) {
  // ...
};

float cos(float x) {
  // ...
};

float square(float x) {
  // ...
};

float square_root(float x) {
  // ...
};
```

MODULA-2 definition module   C++ class definition   C functions

Note that components can be of very different natures. In the Broker pattern (99), for example, we mention 'the Broker component'. Depending on the implementation of this pattern, the Broker component can be a linked library or a separate process. The term 'component' is—at least at first sight—independent of its eventual manifestation in source code.

We sometimes use the term 'component' even more loosely. For example, when we speak of the 'client component', we intentionally want to forget for the moment how the client will be implemented. We want instead to focus on a different problem, for example that of specifying how clients can exploit the services that a pattern offers.

But how can we categorize components in principle? Here we list two different ways. [PW92], for example, distinguishes three different kinds of components, called *elements*:

- Processing elements
- Data elements
- Connecting elements

Processing elements supply transformations of the data elements that contain the information that is transformed. Connecting elements—which at any time may be either processing elements, data elements or both—constitute the 'glue' that holds the different pieces together.

Another categorization of components developed for the object-oriented programming paradigm is as follows:

- Controller components
- Coordinator components
- Interface components
- Service provider components
- Information holder components
- Structuring components

Relationship

A *relationship*[1] denotes a connection between components. A relationship may be static or dynamic. Static relationships show directly in source code. They deal with the placement of components within an architecture. Dynamic relationships deal with temporal connections and dynamic interaction between components. They may not be easily visible from the static structure of source code.

---

1. Other definitions for software architecture use the term 'connector' instead of relationship [SG96].

Aggregation and inheritance are examples of static relationships. Object creation, communication between objects, and data transfer are usually dynamic relationships. An example of a temporal relationship is when an object is inserted into a container at some point in time and later deleted.

The following figure shows three static relationships in OMT notation [RBPEL91].

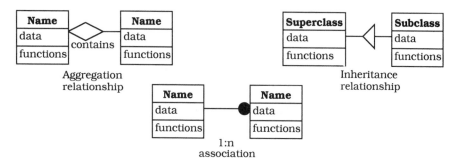

Relationships between components have a great impact on the overall quality of a software architecture. For example, changeability is much better supported by software architectures in which the relationships support the variation of the components, in contrast to architectures in which any change to a component affects the implementation of its clients and collaborators. This explicit exposition of the importance of relationships can be observed in many of the recent definitions and discussions of software architecture [SG96] [PW92] [KMS+92].

View

A *view* represents a partial aspect of a software architecture that shows specific properties of a software system[2].

Examples of views are the state view of a component, or the communication or data flow views of the relationships between components.

---

2. Note that the term 'view' as used here has no direct relationship to *view components* in several of our patterns.

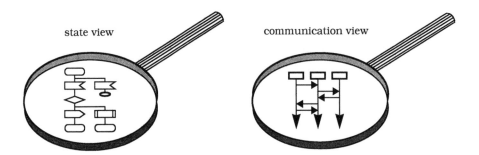

[SNH95] propose describing software architectures by taking the following four different views:

- *Conceptual architecture:* components, connectors...

- *Module architecture:* subsystems, modules, exports, imports...

- *Code architecture:* files, directories, libraries, includes...

- *Execution architecture:* tasks, threads, processes...

A similar approach is taken in [Kru95]. Four different views—enhanced by selected use cases—describe the software architecture.

- *Logical view:* the design's object model, or a corresponding model such as an entity relationship diagram.

- *Process view:* concurrency and synchronization aspects.

- *Physical view:* the mapping of the software onto the hardware and its distributed aspects.

- *Development view:* the software's static organization in its development environment.

There is obvious overlap between both approaches. For example, the conceptual architecture and the logical view seem very similar. Other views do not map well onto each other. For example, the module and code architectures together seem to cover the development view, but may also cover additional aspects. It would be interesting to see an example architecture described in both approaches.

Functional and Non-functional Properties

When discussing software architectures we often hear the term 'non-functional properties'. In contrast, the 'functional properties' are only assumed implicitly.

A *functional property* deals with a particular aspect of a system's functionality, and is usually related to a specified functional requirement. A functional property may either be made directly visible to users of an application by means of a particular function, or it may represent aspects of its implementation, such as the algorithm used to compute the function.

While developers were used in the past to concentrating on providing the stated functional properties for software, today non-functional properties are becoming increasingly important:

A *non-functional property* denotes a feature of a system that is not covered by its functional description. A non-functional property typically addresses aspects related to the reliability, compatibility, cost, ease of use, maintenance or development of a software system.

In Section 6.4, *Non-functional Properties of Software Architecture* we discuss the following non-functional properties at length:

- Changeability

- Interoperability

- Efficiency[3]

- Reliability

- Testability

- Reusability

---

3. In this book we consider efficiency as a non-functional property. However, efficiency constraints may also be part of the functional requirements, for example in real-time systems. Similar arguments hold for other non-functional requirements that may become functional requirements when explicitly required by the customer.

Non-functional properties are of explicit interest when designing a software architecture. Firstly, software systems evolve over time. They must respond to changing technology, requirements and system environments. It is therefore not enough merely to decompose the global task of an application appropriately—the system has to be prepared for changes, extensions and adaptations as well. If this is not done a software system, especially if it has a long life-span, becomes difficult and expensive to maintain. Secondly, the functionality of a software system must often obey certain general requirements, for example for its overall operability, reliability or efficiency. To satisfy such requirements, its software architecture has to be designed appropriately.

Software Design

Software design is the activity performed by a software developer that results in the software architecture of a system. It is concerned with specifying the components of a software system and the relationships between them within given functional and non-functional properties.

Conventional wisdom has been to use terms like 'software architecture', 'software architectural design', or 'coarse-grained design' for the high-level structural subdivision of the system, and 'design' or 'detailed design' for more detailed planning. As mentioned earlier, we denote the whole activity of constructing a software system as 'software design' and the resulting artifacts as 'software architecture'.

Many developers nowadays prefer the term 'software architecture' to 'software design' for denoting all the artifacts that result from design activities. In doing so, they want to express the fact that they do not just decompose the functionality of a system into a set of cooperating components, but rather that they construct a software architecture. They want to show that they focus explicitly on an appropriate construction of the components of a software system, their attached responsibilities, their functionality and interfaces, their inner structures, the manifold relationships that exist between them and the way they collaborate—all with explicit consideration of non-functional properties such as changeability and portability. They no longer agree that high-level design decisions can be made independently of lower-level decisions.

Summary

The brief discussion in this section already shows that the design of a software architecture is more than a simple activity within a limited scope. It comprises the technical, methodological and process aspects of software engineering. It explicitly addresses the needs of productive software development and maintenance, and has a great impact on the final quality of a software system.

In the following section we show how patterns address the needs of software architecture and how they relate to existing approaches.

6.2   Patterns in Software Architecture

Our work on patterns is closely related to much other work in software architecture, object-oriented or procedural analysis, design and programming.

Our patterns build on the immense practical experience in software development gathered by designers and programmers over the last three to four decades. None of the patterns we describe is artificially constructed, neither by us nor by anyone else—they evolved over time. Software developers recognized that particular solutions solved a problem better than others, and so they reused these solutions again and again. Some of the patterns we describe have existed for a long time. For example, the Pipes and Filters pattern (53) has been known since the 1960s, and the Model-View-Controller pattern (125) since the late 1970's [KP88]. Without this practical experience, no patterns would exist.

Patterns also build explicitly on the many principles that have been developed for structured programming—patterns are not dedicated solely to object technology. Many programming principles that were developed in the 1970's form the foundation of our patterns. We discuss the relationships of patterns to these principles in Section 6.3, *Enabling Techniques for Software Architecture*.

Another objective of patterns is to build software systems with predictable non-functional properties. Patterns therefore also build on the principles for developing software for and with reuse, design for change and so on. We also discuss the relationships of patterns to important non-functional properties for software systems in Section 6.4, *Non-functional Properties of Software Architecture*.

Methodologies

A common question asked about patterns is how they relate to existing analysis and design methods such as the Booch method [Boo94], Coad/Yourdon [CY91], Object Modeling Technique [RBPEL91] or Shlaer/Mellor [SM88]. Before we had patterns these methods were heralded as the solution to 'the design problem'. More recently, people have become increasingly critical of methodologies—or certainly towards the idea of relying on them too heavily. Michael Jackson, for example, writes in [Jac95]:

> Failure to focus on problems has harmed many projects. But it has caused even more harm to the evolution of development METHOD. Because we don't talk about problems we don't analyze them or classify them. So we slip into the childish belief that there can be universal development methods, suitable for solving all development problems. We expect methods to be panaceas—medicines that cure all diseases. This cannot be. It's a good rule of thumb that the value of a method is inversely proportional to its generality. A method for solving all problems can give you very little help with any particular problem.

It is not hard to foresee that people will voice similar complaints about patterns if we do not limit expectations. James Coplien recently wrote [Cope96]:

> One fear I harbor for patterns is that designers will look to them first for their design solutions. This happened when the object paradigm was young, too. Many design problems can be solved by well-known paradigms, and good designers should carry those in their toolkits—not always try to use the most recent tools, even if they are the most powerful.

In the recent past, we've tried to use object tools to solve everything. Patterns take us outside pedestrian object design methods, often into structures that are handled well by no existing paradigm. To me, that's where patterns shine—the dark corners of design. To me, patterns cover only small holes in the design space: the broader design space lends itself well to the common techniques of well-known paradigms, and we should seek to use those paradigms where they fit.

By curtailing our expectations, we can use both patterns and methodologies to our advantage. Methodologies provide many useful steps and guidelines for constructing high-quality software. The implementation sections of our patterns loosely follow these steps, adapted to the needs of the specific problems the patterns address. In addition, these methods define an overall process for software development that you can adapt and extend to integrate your use of patterns. Patterns complement the existing analysis and design methods with a set of concrete techniques for solving very specific but recurring design problems.

Bear in mind that neither patterns, methodologies nor their combination will provide you with the 'Yellow Brick Road' to a fine architecture. There will be plenty of design problems left that you will have to solve on your own.

Software Processes

The blanket application of methodologies tends to cause even worse problems for software processes. How much harm has been done by enforcing the waterfall process in projects? A defined process has its benefits, but becomes a liability when it causes organizational overheads or enforces a way of working that doesn't fit your project's goals. How can a process that tries to fit all projects also fit your own project's special circumstances? How can you use crucial insights gained during implementation to redesign defined parts of your system if you are not allowed to go back to the design stage? You should not allow any methodology or process to dictate strictly how design and implementation is to proceed.

How can patterns help here? We would like to integrate patterns into an incremental delivery process that gets rid of the strict separation of development phases. Object-oriented analysis and design methodologies tend to blur the boundaries between phases. We hope to contribute towards making this incremental and sometimes cyclic way of working more predictable. For example, if patterns help to produce better and more stable designs, we can limit the number of cycles through the phases and restrict redesign to well-defined parts of the system.

We are often asked at what point of development should patterns be used: during analysis, high- or low-level design, or even during implementation? There is no single correct answer, but a rule of thumb is that you should use the high-level architectural patterns earlier than medium-level design patterns, which are themselves used before idioms. Section 5.2, *Pattern Classification* discusses this issue in more detail.

Architectural Styles

In 1992 Dwayne E. Perry and Alexander L. Wolf introduced the notion of *architectural style*:

An *architectural style* defines a family of software systems in terms of their structural organization. An architectural style expresses components and the relationships between them, with the constraints of their application, and the associated composition and design rules for their construction.

Generally speaking, an architectural style expresses a particular kind of fundamental structure for a software system together with an associated method that specifies how to construct it. An architectural style also comprises information about when to use the architecture it describes, its invariants and specializations, as well as the consequences of its application.

Example Multi-phase architectural style [PW92]

The multi-phase architectural style consists of processing elements and data elements that are exchanged between processing elements. For example, the multi-phase style for a compiler includes:

- *Processing elements:* lexer, parser, semantor, optimizer, code generator.

- *Data elements:* characters, tokens, phrases, correlated phrases, annotated phrases, object code.

If the multi-phase architectural style is organized sequentially, it also uses the following connecting elements:

- *Connecting elements:* procedure calls and parameters.

The form of an architectural style is expressed by weighted properties and relationships among its architectural elements. For example, in a compiler the optimizer and the annotated phrases must be found together, but they are only preferred elements and not mandatory. Architectural elements are also constrained by various other important perspectives, such as that of processing.

For example, in a compiler the lexer is constrained to accept a sequence of characters C, to produce a sequence of tokens T, and to preserve the ordering correspondence between characters and tokens:

$$\text{lexer: } C \rightarrow T, \text{ where } T \text{ } preserves \text{ } C$$

The processing constraints must be specified for every element of a given architectural style. Further constraints are defined for the connections between components, the data flow, and the state of the computation. All constraints together strongly determine the concrete architecture of a software system that uses the multi-phase sequential architectural style. ❏

Architectural styles have also been proposed in [SG96] and [SNH95]. Architectural styles are very similar to our architectural patterns. In fact every architectural style can be described as an architectural pattern. For example, the Multi-phase architectural style corresponds to the Pipes and Filters pattern (53). On the other hand, architectural styles differ from patterns in several important respects:

- Architectural styles only describe the overall structural frameworks for applications. Patterns for software architecture, however, exist in various ranges of scale, beginning with patterns for defining the basic structure of an application (architectural patterns) and ending with patterns that describe how to implement a particular design issue in a given programming language (idioms).

- Architectural styles are independent of each other, but a pattern depends on the smaller patterns it contains, on the patterns with which it interacts, and on the larger patterns in which it is contained [Ale79].

- Patterns are more problem-oriented than architectural styles. Architectural styles express design techniques from a viewpoint that is independent of an actual design situation. A pattern expresses a very specific recurring design problem and presents a solution to it, all from the viewpoint of the context in which the problem arises.

Frameworks

Frameworks are another important approach to software architecture:

A *framework* is a partially complete software (sub-) system that is intended to be instantiated. It defines the architecture for a family of (sub-) systems and provides the basic building blocks to create them. It also defines the places where adaptations for specific functionality should be made. In an object-oriented environment a framework consists of abstract and concrete classes.

The instantiation of a framework involves composing and subclassing the existing classes. A framework for applications in a specific domain is called an *application framework*.

According to [Pree94] an application framework consists of *frozen spots* and *hot spots*. Frozen spots define the overall architecture of a software system—its basic components and the relationships between them. These remain unchanged in any instantiation of the application framework. Hot spots represent those parts of the application framework that are specific to individual software systems. Hot spots are designed to be generic—they can be adapted to the needs of the application under development.

When creating a concrete software system with an application framework, its hot spots are specialized according to the specific needs and requirements of the system. To achieve adaptability and changeability with an application framework, you are not restricted to object-oriented techniques such as inheritance and polymorphism—you can also use patterns [Tal94]. For example, the Abstract Factory pattern [GHJV95] is used in the InterViews framework [LCITV92] to create user-interface objects with a specific 'look and feel', and in the ET++ framework [WGM88] to achieve portability across different window systems. Unidraw [VL90] applies the Command pattern [GHJV95] to implement undoable commands.

From the perspective of application frameworks, patterns can be seen as their building blocks. From the perspective of patterns, an application framework can be seen as a pattern for complete software systems in a given application domain.

6.3 Enabling Techniques for Software Architecture

The construction of software is based on several fundamental principles. We call these principles *enabling techniques*, since the principles involved have become blurred over time. Techniques have been developed to realize these widely-accepted principles, to a degree that it becomes increasingly difficult to differentiate between principles and techniques. We therefore take the simple approach and use both terms as synonyms.

All enabling techniques are independent of a specific software development method, and most of them have been known for years. They were developed and proposed mainly in the 1970's in connection with publications on structured programming. Classical references are the papers by Parnas and colleagues—see for example [Par79] and [PCW85]. Although the importance of enabling techniques has been recognized for a long time, their significance for successful software development has increased over the last few years, strongly linked to the emerging discipline of software architecture. Patterns for software architecture are explicitly built on these principles, many of them with a special focus on a particular principle. The following sections summarize some of the most important enabling techniques for software architecture:

- Abstraction

- Encapsulation

- Information Hiding

- Modularization

- Separation of Concerns

- Coupling and Cohesion

- Sufficiency, Completeness and Primitiveness

- Separation of Policy and Implementation

- Separation of Interface and Implementation

- Single Point of Reference

- Divide-and-Conquer

Abstraction

Abstraction is one of the fundamental principles humans use to cope with complexity. Grady Booch defines abstraction as 'The essential characteristics of an object that distinguish it from all other kinds of objects and thus provide crisply defined conceptual boundaries relative to the perspective of the viewer.' [Boo94]. The word 'object' may be replaced with 'component' to achieve a more general definition of abstraction. Several forms of abstraction exist, such as entity abstraction, action abstraction, virtual machine abstraction and co-incidental abstraction [SS86]. This principle is addressed by several patterns such as the Layers pattern (31) and the Abstract Factory pattern [GHJV95].

Encapsulation

Encapsulation deals with grouping the elements of an abstraction that constitute its structure and behavior, and with separating different abstractions from each other. Encapsulation provides explicit barriers between abstractions. The Forwarder-Receiver pattern (307), for example, encapsulates the implementation details of inter-process communication mechanisms. Encapsulation fosters non-functional properties like changeability and reusability.

Information Hiding

Information hiding involves concealing the details of a component's implementation from its clients, to handle system complexity better and to minimize coupling between components. Any details of a component that clients do not need to know in order to use it properly should be hidden by the component. The Whole-Part pattern (225) addresses this principle explicitly. The principle of encapsulation is often used as a way to achieve information hiding. Information hiding can also be achieved using the principle of separation of interface and implementation, described later in this section.

However, what is to be hidden inside a component sometimes depends on the application. Aspects that clients do not need to know in one application may need to be externally visible in another. For example, in one system direct access to the internal data structures of a component may be necessary for performance tuning. Such access may not be necessary when the component is used in other systems for which its performance is already adequate.

The concept of reflection relaxes the principle of information hiding [Smi82]. The Reflection pattern (193) opens the implementation of a software system or a component in a defined way, to provide more flexibility for adaptation and change [Kee89]. However, information hiding is still one of the fundamental and most important principles of software engineering.

Modularization

Modularization is concerned with the meaningful decomposition of a software system and with its grouping into subsystems and components. The major task is to decide how to physically package the entities that form the logical structure of an application. The main objective of modularization is to handle system complexity by introducing well-defined and documented boundaries within a program. Modules serve as physical containers for functionalities or responsibilities of an application. Modularization is closely related to the principle of encapsulation. Examples of patterns that address modularity are the Layers pattern (31), the Pipes and Filters pattern (53) and the Whole-Part pattern (225).

Separation of Concerns

Different or unrelated responsibilities should be separated from each other within a software system, for example by attaching them to different components. Collaborating components that contribute to the solution of a specific task should be separated from components that are involved in the computation of other tasks. If a component plays different roles in different contexts, these roles should be independent and separate from each other within the component. Almost every pattern of our pattern system addresses this fundamental principle in some way. For example, the Model-View-Controller pattern (125) separates the concerns of internal model, presentation to the user and input processing.

Coupling and Cohesion

Coupling and cohesion are principles originally introduced as part of the structured design approach. Coupling focuses on inter-module aspects, whereas cohesion emphasizes intra-module characteristics.

Coupling is the measure of the strength of association established by a connection from one module to another. Strong coupling complicates a system, since a module is harder to understand, change, or to correct if it is highly interrelated with other modules. Complexity can be reduced by designing systems with weak coupling between modules.

Cohesion measures the degree of connectivity between the functions and elements of a single module. There are several forms of cohesion. The most desirable form is functional cohesion, in which the elements of a module or component 'all work together to provide some well-bounded behavior' [Boo94]. The worst form is coincidental cohesion, in which entirely unrelated abstractions are thrown into the same module. Other types of cohesion—logical cohesion, temporal cohesion, procedural cohesion, communicational cohesion, sequential cohesion and informal cohesion—are described by [Bal85].

This principle is addressed by all our design patterns for organizing communication between components, such as the Client-Dispatcher-Server pattern (323) and the Publisher-Subscriber pattern (339).

Sufficiency, Completeness and Primitiveness

[Boo94] states that 'Every component of a software system should be sufficient, complete, and primitive'. 'Sufficient' means that the component should capture those characteristics of an abstraction that are necessary to permit a meaningful and efficient interaction with the component. 'Completeness' means that a component should capture all relevant characteristics of its abstraction. By 'primitiveness', Booch means that all the operations a component can perform can be implemented easily. It is a major goal of every pattern to be sufficient and complete with respect to the solution of a given problem. Many patterns are also relatively primitive and easy to implement, for example the Strategy pattern [GHJV95].

Separation of Policy and Implementation

A component of a software system should deal with policy or implementation, but not both:

- A *policy* component deals with context-sensitive decisions, knowledge about the semantics and interpretation of information, the assembly of many disjoint computations into a result or the selection of parameter values.

- An *implementation* component deals with the execution of a fully-specified algorithm in which no context-sensitive decisions have to be made. The context and interpretation are external, and are normally supplied by arguments to the component.

Because of their independence from a certain context, pure implementation components are easier to reuse and maintain, whereas policy components are often application-specific and subject to change.

If it is not possible to separate policy and implementation into different components within a software architecture, there should at least be a clear separation of policy and implementation functionality within a component. The Strategy pattern [GHJV95] focuses on this principle.

Separation of Interface and Implementation

Any component should consist of two parts:

- An *interface* part that defines the functionality provided by the component and specifies how to use it. This interface is accessible by the clients of the component. An exported interface of this type usually consists of function signatures.

- An *implementation* part that includes the actual code for the functionality provided by the component. The implementation part may also comprise additional functions and data structures that are only used internally to the component. The implementation part is not accessible by the component's clients.

The main objective of this principle is to protect a component's clients from its implementation details, and only to provide clients with the component's interface specification and guidelines for use. In addition, this principle allows you to implement the functionality of a component independently of its use by other components. Separation of interface and implementation is, like encapsulation, a technique to achieve information hiding, the principle that states that 'A client should only know what it needs to know'.

Separation of interface and implementation also supports change-ability—a component is much easier to change if its interface is separated from its implementation. This separation prevents clients from being directly affected by a change. The principle especially eases the task of changing a component's behavior or representation, for example for performance tuning, in cases where the change does not necessitate a change to its interface. The separation of interface and implementation is addressed, for example, by the Bridge pattern [GHJV95].

Single Point of Reference

Any item within a software system should be declared and defined only once. The main objective of this principle is to avoid problems of inconsistency.

Due to their design principles and implementations, however, many programming languages such as C++ [ES90] require a single point of definition, but allow or even mandate several points of declaration. In the case of C++ this is mainly due to the limitations of traditional compiler and linker technologies. The consequence for the programmer is an increased workload in manually maintaining consistency.

Divide-and-Conquer

This principle is well-known, both from the politics of the ancient world as well as from combinatorial algorithms such as Merge-sort. We use this principle heavily in software architecture. Top-down design, for example, divides a task or component into smaller parts that can be designed independently. The Whole-Part pattern (225) approaches this technique at the pattern level. Other patterns also concentrate on such subdivision, although more specifically than the generic Whole-Part. The Microkernel pattern (171), for example, subdivides what once might have been a monolithic block of code. Divide-and-Conquer also often provides a way to realize the principle of separation of concerns.

Summary

This list of principles may be extended further, for example to include the general principles for object-oriented software development proposed by Trygve Reenskaug [Ree92]. However, these are basically variations of the principles presented in this section.

It is important to note that not all general principles are complementary—some are contradictory. Examples of this are the principle of separating interface and implementation and that of single point of reference. The first principle—when realized with traditional technology—requires at least two points of reference for a particular function, one in the interface part of a component and the other in its implementation part. This is in contradiction to the strict interpretation of the principle of a single point of reference. Generating interfaces from implementations could be a solution, of course, and this is used in more modern approaches.

Other principles are closely related, such as abstraction and encapsulation. A proper abstraction for a particular entity within a software system also requires encapsulation of all the elements that constitute its structure in a single component or module.

6.4   Non-functional Properties of Software Architecture

Non-functional properties of a software system have a great impact on its development and maintenance, its general operability and its use of computer resources. They have an equal impact on the quality of an application and its architecture as do the system's functional properties. The larger and more complex a software system and the longer its lifetime, the more important its non-functional properties become. Patterns for software architecture explicitly consider these non-functional aspects.

In this section we discuss some of the most important non-functional properties of software architecture in relation to patterns:

- Changeability

- Interoperability

- Efficiency

- Reliability

- Testability

- Reusability

Changeability

Large-scale industrial and commercial software systems usually have a long life-span, sometimes twenty years or more. Many such applications do not remain static after their original development phase—they tend to evolve continuously during their lifetime. Existing requirements change and new ones are added. To reduce maintenance costs and the workload involved in changing an application, it is important to prepare its architecture for modification and evolution.

Parnas writes very vividly about software aging [Par94]:

> Programs, like people, get old. We can't prevent aging, but we can understand its causes, take steps to limit its effects, temporarily reverse some of the damage it has caused, and prepare for the day when the software is no longer viable.

He lists two reasons why software ages:

- Lack of movement—software ages if it is not frequently updated.

- Ignorant surgery—changes made by people who do not understand the original design gradually destroy the architecture.

In another publication, Parnas adds two further reasons:

- The software is inflexible from the start.

- The documentation is inadequate, allowing understanding of the system to be eroded over time.

The costs of software aging, as described in [Par94], are a growing inability to keep up with the market by introducing new features, reduced performance and decreased reliability. These can be prevented by accurate documentation, preserving structure when introducing changes, intense reviewing, and of course designing for change a priori.

We consider that changeability has four aspects:

- *Maintainability.* This deals mainly with problem fixing, 'repairing' a software system after errors occur. A software architecture that is well-prepared for maintainability tends to localize changes and minimize their side effects on other components.

- *Extensibility.* This focuses on the extension of a software system with new features, as well as the replacement of components with improved versions and the removal of unwanted or unnecessary features and components. To achieve extensibility a software system requires loosely-coupled components. The aim is a structure that allows you to exchange components without affecting their clients. Support for integrating new components into an existing architecture is also necessary.

- *Restructuring.* This deals with the reorganization of the components of a software system and the relationships between them, for example when changing the placement of a component by moving it to a different subsystem. Support for the restructuring of a software system needs careful design of the relationships between components. They should ideally allow you to configure components flexibly without affecting major parts of their implementation.

- *Portability.* This deals with adapting a software system to a variety of hardware platforms, user interfaces, operating systems, programming languages or compilers. To be portable, a software system needs to be organized in such a way that dependencies on hardware, other software systems and environments are factored out into special components such as system and user interface libraries.

A software system designed for change also supports the construction of variants for different customers better than a software system that is not so designed. Many patterns address changeability, for example the Reflection pattern (193) and the Bridge pattern [GHJV95].

Finally, a word of caution on designing for change. With the growing use of patterns we have seen people overdo it. Classes are no longer simple. Every 'chunk' of code is highly flexible and can adapt to many different contexts. Such flexibility, however, comes at a price. Flexible software often consumes more resources by using more levels of indirection or increasing storage consumption. It also requires more thought and more work in coding. Good designers therefore try to decide in advance which parts of the software should be highly flexible to cope with foreseeable changes, and which parts will probably remain fairly static. If they prove wrong, there are still ways to introduce additional flexibility by carefully restructuring parts of the system, or by using a pattern that supports design for change. This approach is more economical than engineering in total changeability from the start.

Interoperability

Software that formspart of a system does not exist independently. It is frequently interacting with other systems or its environment. To support interoperability, a software architecture must be designed to offer well-defined access to externally-visible functionality and data structures. The interaction of a program with software systems written in other programming languages is an aspect of interoperability that also impacts the software architecture of an application. The Broker architecture (99) is probably the most prominent example of a pattern that addresses interoperability.

Efficiency

Efficiency deals with the use of the resources available for the execution of software, and how this impacts response times, throughput and storage consumption. Efficiency is not only a matter of using sophisticated algorithms. The appropriate distribution of responsibilities to components, as well as their coupling, are important architectural activities for achieving efficiency in a given application.

Efficiency also plays a significant role in distributed software systems. The IPC (inter-process communication) mechanisms underlying a distributed application must be fast enough to transfer messages and data with sufficient speed. Patterns like Forwarder-Receiver (307) address issues of efficiency. Many patterns, however, introduce an additional level of indirection to solve a problem, which may decrease rather than increase efficiency.

Reliability

Reliability deals with the general ability of a software system to maintain its functionality, both in the face of application or system errors and in situations of unexpected or incorrect usage. Two aspects of reliability can be distinguished:

- *Fault tolerance.* This aims at ensuring correct behavior in the event of errors, and their internal 'repair', such as losing a connection to a remote component in a distributed software system and subsequently reconnecting to it. After repairing such an error, the software system should resume or repeat the execution of the operation in progress when the error occurred.

- *Robustness.* This deals with protecting an application against incorrect usage and degenerate input, and keeping it in a defined state in the event of unexpected errors. Note that in contrast to fault tolerance, robustness does not necessarily mean that the software is able to continue computation in the event of errors—it may only guarantee that the software terminates in a defined way.

Software architecture has a major impact on the reliability of a software system. Examples of the way in which software architecture supports reliability include the intentional inclusion of redundancy in an application, or the integration of monitoring components and exception handling. The Master-Slave pattern (245) provides an example of how patterns can support specific aspects of reliability.

Testability

With the increasing size and complexity of software systems, especially industrial ones, testing is becoming more difficult and expensive. A software system needs support from its architecture to ease the evaluation of its correctness—proving correctness is unluckily still out of reach in most cases. Software structures that support testability allow for better fault detection and fixing, and also for temporary integration of debugging code and debugging components.

Although the patterns we describe do not address testing explicitly, many of them have a major impact on the testability of a software system. The Command Processor pattern (277), for example, facilitates testability on the level of user interaction by allowing the logging and replay of user command objects. The Broker pattern (99) eases testing of individual client and server components in a distributed system. This architecture frees components from dependencies on their communication partners and the communication mechanisms they use.

The Broker pattern, however, complicates testing the collaboration between clients and servers, because it introduces additional components to support their independence. In contrast to implementations in which clients and servers are more strongly coupled, debugging an error in the delivery of a message from a client to a server is much harder. This is because several other components are involved in marshaling and unmarshaling data and sending messages across process boundaries.

Reusability

Reusability is currently one of the most discussed topics in software engineering. It promises a reduction of both cost and development time for software systems, as well as better software quality [Kar95]. Adele Goldberg once defined reuse as 'the act of achieving what is desired with the help of what already exists' [Gol91]. Reusability has two major aspects—software development with reuse and software development for reuse:

- Software development *with reuse* means reusing existing components and results from previous projects or commercial libraries, design analyses, design specifications or code components. These reusable artifacts are integrated into the application under development, either as they are or with modifications. Practising software development with reuse requires the construction of software architectures that allow you to 'plug in' prefabricated structures and code components. Software development with reuse aims to support software composition, which means composing an application out of existing components by adapting them to the needs of the development and implementing 'glue' components to connect them.

- Software development *for reuse* focuses on producing components that are potentially reusable in future projects as part of the current software development. This requires software architectures that allow self-contained parts to be taken from the application under development and reused in other systems without significant modification.

Although patterns do not address reusability explicitly, almost every pattern that supports changeability also supports reusability. For example, the Model-View-Controller pattern (125) supports the exchange of views and controllers and the reusability of the model.

Some non-functional properties require similar architectural techniques for their achievement, for example design reusability and changeability. Others serve a similar overall purpose: for example, design portability and interoperability deal with the integration of a software system into its environment, while reliability and efficiency deal with its general usability [Bal85].

Non-functional properties may contradict as well as complement each other. For example, when replicating the functionality of an application to achieve fault tolerance, the resulting structure is usually less efficient and more expensive than a structure without such redundancy. When specifying non-functional requirements for a software architecture, you need explicitly to consider the interdependencies and trade-offs that exist between them. You also need to specify an ordering priority between different non-functional requirements, to define a preference of one requirement against another in case of conflict.

Although non-functional properties are very important in software architecture, their achievement is hard to measure. The detailed criteria a software architecture must satisfy has only been specified for a few such properties, for example reusability and changeability [Kar95]. For this reason, estimating the degree to which a software architecture achieves a given non-functional property is still mainly based on the experience of software engineers.

6.5 Summary

Patterns fit in well with existing approaches to software architecture:

- They explicitly build on enabling techniques for constructing well-defined software systems, such as information hiding and the separation of interface and implementation.

- They stress the importance of non-functional properties, such as changeability and reliability.

- They complement existing problem-independent software development processes and methods with guidelines for solving specific recurring design and implementation problems.

Patterns also provide an important contribution to the benefits you can gain from software architecture:

- They help with the recognition of common paradigms, so that high-level relationships between software systems can be understood and new applications built as variations on old systems.

- They provide support for finding an appropriate architecture for the software system under development.

- They provide support for making principled choices among design alternatives.

- They help with the analysis and description of high-level properties of complex software systems.

- They provide support for change and evolution of software systems.

Patterns provide a big step forward in supporting the systematic construction of high-quality software systems with defined functional and non-functional properties. Patterns provide a pragmatic method- and process-independent way to solve the many design and implementation problems that software developers face every day.

7 The Pattern Community

Every great movement must experience three stages:
ridicule, discussion, adoption

John Stuart Mill

Many software developers document patterns with which they are familiar and share them with colleagues world-wide. Together they form a community that shares a common interest in software patterns. But who makes up this pattern community? Where does it come from and who are its leading figures?

This chapter gives an overview of 'who's who' in the pattern community.

7.1 The Roots

The architect Christopher Alexander laid the foundations on which many of today's pattern approaches are built. He, and members of the Center for Environmental Structure in Berkeley, California, spent more than twenty years developing an approach to architecture that used patterns. This 'entirely new attitude in architecture and planning' is published in a series of books [Ale79] [AIS77] [ASAIA75] [ANAK87]. Alexander describes over two hundred and fifty patterns that span a wide range of scale and abstraction, from structuring towns and regions down to paving paths and decorating individual rooms. He also defined the fundamental Context-Problem-Solution structure for describing patterns, the so-called 'Alexander form'. Recently, some pattern writers have started to distance themselves a little from Alexander, since they feel that his view on patterns does not translate directly into software patterns. They acknowledge the importance of Alexander's work, but would like to go their own way. Despite this discussion, however, Alexander's work is well worth reading by everybody who is interested in patterns.

The pioneers of patterns in software development are Ward Cunningham and Kent Beck. They read Alexander's books and were inspired to adapt his ideas to software development. Ward and Kent's first five patterns deal with the design of user interfaces—their patterns Window per Task, Few Panes, Standard Panes, Nouns and Verbs and Short Menus mark the birth of patterns in software engineering [Cope95]. Since their publication Ward and Kent have written many more patterns. Ward captured his experience in the development of business systems, principally of accounting applications. The CHECKS pattern language for information integrity [Cun94] is one result of this work. Kent focused on idioms in Smalltalk. His patterns will be published as a series of books, of which the first volume *Smalltalk Best Practice Patterns, Volume 1: Coding* [Bec96] is about to be released. Kent is also a regular columnist on Smalltalk idioms in the *Smalltalk Report*.

The first published work about the use of patterns in software development was Erich Gamma's 1991 doctoral thesis [Gam91]. Written in German, this work did not achieve much recognition outside central Europe. Erich was the first to describe how to use object-oriented mechanisms in an elegant way to solve typical design problems encountered in the development of application frameworks. You can find early versions of about half of the patterns described in [GHJV95] in his thesis.

7.2 Leading Figures and their Work

Four software design experts—known as the 'Gang-of-Four' in the pattern community—paved the way for the wide acceptance of patterns in software engineering. Erich Gamma, Richard Helm, Ralph Johnson and John Vlissides are the authors of the seminal work *Design Patterns – Elements of Reusable Object-Oriented Software* [GHJV95]. Our patterns often build on the Gang-of-Four's patterns, although we initially collected them independently, in parallel to the compilation of the first Gang-of-Four catalog. We also share many aspects of our general view of patterns with the Gang-of-Four, for example about pattern systems versus pattern languages. We describe our patterns in a similar way to theirs, and try to integrate their patterns into our pattern system.

James O. Coplien is another leading expert on patterns. In 1991 he published the widely recognized C++ text-book *Advanced C++ Programming Styles and Idioms* [Cope92]. Although he does not use the term 'pattern', nor describe his ideas in a pattern form, he is one of the pioneers of idioms specific to C++. He is currently working on patterns that address the structuring of organizations and software development projects, as well as people's roles in them [PLoP94]. He recently started a column on patterns with John Vlissides in the *C++ Report*.

Douglas C. Schmidt is another noteworthy figure in the pattern community. Several years ago, as a Ph.D. student, he started working on the ACE (Adaptive Communication Environment) framework. ACE supports the construction of distributed applications [Sch96]. He is the author of many patterns, mainly on the subject of distribution and high-speed networking [Sch94] [Sch95]. Doug's patterns are widely used in many industrial communication software systems.

Robert Martin describes patterns that are suitable for use with C++. They can be categorized somewhere between design patterns and idioms [PLoP94]. He derived these patterns from applications he developed, but without prior knowledge of the existence of the pattern movement—he just knew that they represented good solutions to the problems he was solving.

Peter Coad also works on patterns, and recently published his work as a book [Coad95]. This contains about two hundred patterns, most of which are intended to help with analyzing a given application domain and using object-oriented technology to build applications. Some of his patterns also fall into our category of design patterns. Peter Coad was one of the first people to present the subject of patterns to the public [Coad92].

Wolfgang Pree has looked at the structural principles of design patterns for framework development [Pree94]. Wolfgang categorizes these structural principles into seven so-called 'meta-patterns'. His views on design patterns focus more on the structural principles that are available for framework development, rather than on the concrete solutions that help to solve specific design and implementation problems.

You can see from the above that much published work about patterns is available. Many more publications on patterns exist which we cannot list here for reasons of space. In the near future even more will be published—papers, conference proceedings, special issues of various magazines and journals, and books.

7.3   The Community

We and all the people mentioned in this chapter are working on and with patterns. Many software engineers from all over the world are documenting their experience in patterns and sharing it with others. Sharing our patterns with them was both helpful and enjoyable for us.

This pattern community recently found its own forum, the PLoP (Pattern Languages of Programming) conference. Its proceedings are published as a series of books. The PLoP'94 [PLoP94] and PLoP'95 [PLoP95] proceedings are already available. PLoP also has a European arm, EuroPLoP, and its proceedings will also be part of the series. PLoP and EuroPLoP differ from other conferences in the following respects:

- *Focus on practicability.* The conference looks for pattern descriptions of proven solutions to problems, rather than on presenting the latest scientific results.

- *Aggressive disregard of originality.* Pattern authors do not need to be the original developers of the solutions they describe.

- *Non-anonymous review.* Submissions are 'shepherded' rather than reviewed. The 'shepherd' contacts the authors of submitted papers and discusses the submissions with them. The goal is to improve the paper such that it can be accepted for review at the conference and suffer as little rejection as possible.

- *Writer's workshops instead of presentations.* All patterns are discussed in writer's workshops made up of conference attendees, rather than being presented by their authors in open forum.

- *Careful editing.* Authors get the chance to include the feedback from the writer's workshops, and all patterns are copy-edited before they appear in the final conference proceedings.

To discuss patterns and pattern-related issues, the pattern community offers several mailing lists and a World Wide Web page. The URL of the pattern home page is:

```
http://st-www.cs.uiuc.edu/users/patterns/patterns.html
```

This page provides useful information about forthcoming pattern events and available books on patterns, and offers references to other Web pages about patterns, such as the Portland Pattern Repository at `http://c2.com/ppr`, which is maintained by Ward Cunningham.

There are also several Internet mailing lists on patterns. For example, `patterns@cs.uiuc.edu` discusses concrete patterns that people want to share and `patterns-discussion@cs.uiuc.edu` hosts discussions of aspects related to patterns, such as 'What is a pattern?' and 'How should patterns be described?'. Several other relevant mailing lists exist, among them a list for discussing the Gang-of-Four patterns and a list for discussing our patterns. You can find details about available mailing lists and how to subscribe to them on the patterns home page.

The unofficial steering committee of the pattern community is Hillside Incorporated, also known as the 'Hillside Group'. Hillside Inc. is a non-profit organization made up of several individuals, among them Ward Cunningham and Kent Beck, the Gang-of-Four, Grady Booch and James O. Coplien. The main goal of the Hillside Group is to propagate the use of patterns in software development, to lead the pattern community, and to give support to newcomers in this new discipline of software engineering. The 'spiritual father' of the Hillside Group is Kent Beck. The Hillside Group also organizes and sponsors the PLoP and EuroPLoP conferences.

As you can see, there is a large pattern community worldwide, and many leading figures in software engineering and software erchitecture are part of it. Most members of the pattern community work in the software industry, and are software developers with experience in designing and building large-scale applications. Academic members are mainly involved in industrial projects—they do not just teach how to build software systems, they also *do* it. By joining the pattern community you can take advantage of all this experience, captured in many well-documented patterns that are ready for practical use. You will also be able to share your own experience in software development with other experts by writing your own patterns.

The pattern community is the only community in computer science that is based on interest in a literal form, the pattern form for describing well-proven knowledge. This brings people with different backgrounds and fields of expertise together. Most interestingly, the pattern form makes it possible to discuss and share such knowledge with people who are expert in other domains, or even with newcomers and novices in software engineering.

We invite you to join the pattern community if you are not already part of it. Visit the pattern home page, subscribe to the pattern mailing lists, look at the various pattern books, attend the PLoP or EuroPLoP conferences, capture your own experience as patterns and share them with experts from all over the world. You will certainly be rewarded by many positive 'aha!' effects.

8 Where Will Patterns Go?

These are the voyages of the Starship Enterprise.
Its five-year mission: to explore strange new worlds.
To seek out new life and new civilizations.
To boldly go where no man has gone before...

Star Trek: The Original Series
© Paramount Pictures 1966–1968

At the time that this book is being written, patterns are in the forefront of everybody's mind. People speak enthusiastically about patterns and the benefits they will bring to software development. But where will patterns go? What are the directions for future research?

This chapter describes our view of the future of patterns.

8.1   Pattern Mining

Although a lot of patterns are already available, of all scales and degrees of abstraction and for many domains, mining new patterns will remain an important activity for the future.

Patterns for Software Architecture

Several specific areas of software, such as object-oriented design in general, user interface programming and distributed computing, are well described by a variety of different patterns. Other areas, however, are not yet covered by patterns, or by only a few patterns. Examples include security and transaction-processing systems, parallel and scientific computing and fault tolerance. Filling these blank spots will be an important activity in the future.

Considering patterns as a mental tool, some experienced developers suggest first looking at patterns that do not fit directly into the domain of the application under design. Sometimes it is possible to generalize the key idea of a pattern and transfer it to another domain, resulting in a new pattern or a variant of the original.

Capturing experience with common programming languages as idioms will be another important activity. Today, an adequate set of idioms only exists for Smalltalk and C++. Filling this gap for languages such as Pascal or C will help many programmers to use these languages more effectively.

An exciting and certainly a widely-recognized activity will be writing idioms for Java. This relatively new programming language is touted by many software development experts as the language of the future. Java must be learned first, however, and understanding its details is not easy. Idioms that reflect the growing programming experience with Java will be of great help for all who want to learn its proper use efficiently. Such idioms would form an excellent teaching course to help developers avoid stumbling into Java's pitfalls.

In addition to the use of a programming language, programmer productivity relies on the use of libraries, frameworks such as the Microsoft Foundation Classes, or so-called 'middleware' platforms such as object brokers. Understanding and using these platforms efficiently can and should be supported by appropriate pattern collections. Not many of them exist in published form today. However, as the advantages of patterns become known to more and more developers, we hope to see such collections of patterns emerge from practical experience. It may be that future framework documentation will contain patterns that describe how to use the framework effectively.

Organizational Patterns

Patterns are already used to cover aspects of software development other than just design and implementation. One example is the collection of organizational patterns produced by James O. Coplien [Cope94b]. These describe how to structure organizations and projects to provide appropriate support for the management of software development projects.

An example of an organizational pattern is Architect Controls Product [Cope94b]. This addresses the fact that a product designed by many individuals lacks elegance and cohesiveness. The pattern states that in larger projects you should create an architect role. The architect should advise and control the developers and communicate closely with them, as well as maintaining close contact with the customer.

Other areas, such as how to organize requirements analysis, are not covered by many patterns yet. Mining patterns for such activities can help to make the whole software development process more effective and productive.

Domain-specific Patterns

Application domains such as telecommunications are a potentially large field for patterns. Specific domain knowledge is increasingly being documented in pattern form. Such patterns capture the structure of a domain, namely its constituting entities, their relationships, and, very importantly, how work is organized.

Development staff at AT&T, for example, have started to collect patterns for switching systems in the telecommunication domain. They developed more than hundred patterns, eight of which are published in [PLoP95]. Another example is the Internet mailing list for publishing and discussing patterns in business applications (business-patterns@cs.uiuc.edu). Other domain-specific patterns are being written for factory automation, warehouse management, accounting, medical health and telecommunication network management.

However, most domain-specific patterns are confidential—they represent a company's knowledge and expertise about how to build particular kinds of applications, so references to them are not available. We believe however that more and more of this knowledge will become public over time. In the long term, sharing experience is usually more effective for everyone than trying to hold onto secrets.

Pattern Languages

The development of complete pattern languages is an optimistic but worthwhile goal. Such languages provide solutions to all design problems that can occur in the respective domains. Christopher Alexander claims to have done this for areas in architecture [AIS77]. Pattern languages already exist for small sub-domains of software design, for example the CHECKS pattern language for information integrity [Cun94]. It will be exciting to see how far the pattern community travels along this road.

Even if we do not reach completeness in a strict sense, it would be very beneficial to have pattern languages that cover a substantial part of the design space of the respective domains. The Gang-of-Four book [GHJV95], for example, may be considered as covering a substantial amount—perhaps as much as half—of the general-purpose design patterns that occur in object-oriented design on the granularity level of a small number of cooperating classes.

8.2 Pattern Organization and Indexing

Most of today's work focuses on developing patterns and pattern languages. Over recent years, the pattern community has produced a large range of patterns for software architecture, design, and implementation. The books on patterns that are available, and the many patterns that are discussed on mailing lists and at the PLoP conferences, reflect this growing volume of documented expertise.

The more this repository of available patterns grows, the harder it will be to handle the patterns in their entirety, and to find and use a particular pattern. We therefore need an appropriate organization method to cover all patterns. The relationships between the patterns must be made explicit, patterns must be categorized, and multiple descriptions of the same patterns must be unified—such as the Proxy pattern, which exists in both the Gang-of-Four's version and our own.

We hope that our work on pattern systems will provide a useful starting point for organizing patterns. Another such starting point is Ward Cunningham's Portland Pattern Repository. This provides pattern languages for various aspects of software development, such as CHECKS [Cun94] and many Smalltalk programming patterns originating from Kent Beck [Bec94].

A very interesting approach was taken by the pattern community at PLoP'95—the 'pattern map'. Authors linked the patterns they wrote to related patterns from other authors. They wrote the pattern names on paper, placed these sheets somewhere on the floor of the main conference room, and connected each pattern to related patterns with string. A first picture of the pattern universe was thus drawn, although in a very informal, ad hoc and uncoordinated way. Nevertheless, about three hundred different patterns were connected in this way.

The Hillside Group used this map as input to a more serious attempt at linking patterns. At a mountain lodge in Canada in early 1996, the group wrote more than one hundred and fifty so-called 'pattlets'—pattern abstracts that include the pattern name, a short problem description, the key ideas of its solution and a reference to the pattern's full-length description. Most importantly, all these pattlets were linked together using several different relationship types. Most of these directly corresponded to the relationships we define in our book, such as the refinement relationship. Other relationships were new, such as the 'contrasts' relationship that describes the differences between two completely distinct patterns that at first glance look similar.

All the Hillside Group's pattlets will be available on the World Wide Web. Unfortunately the Web page was not available when we finished writing this book. For specific details about this interesting pattern index we therefore refer you to the pattern home page, which you can find at:

`http://st-www.cs.uiuc.edu/users/patterns/patterns.html`

The Hillside Group also defined a procedure for extending their pattern index with new pattlets. This allows you to write your own pattlet, connect it with other pattlets and integrate it into the index. Over time the index will grow, and with the addition of every new pattlet will draw a more complete picture of the pattern universe.

Despite all this promising and interesting work, however, there is still much to be done before we can build really mature pattern systems that support the development of high-quality software effectively. We need much more concrete experience of applying patterns, and also more research into ways of organizing them.

8.3 Methods and Tools

More and more people are working on pattern tools. Examples include the Re-Engineering Tool SUS (Software Understanding System) [THG94], or the software development environment FACE (Framework Adaptive Composition Environment) [ME96]. Others work on libraries of prefabricated code frameworks for particular patterns [Sou94]. The objective of all these approaches is to provide CASE tool support for patterns and to automate the use of patterns as much as possible. Work on such tools will continue in the future.

Software development methods that support the use of patterns are also under discussion. Their goal is to guide software developers in selecting the patterns that should be applied in a specific development activity. Other work focuses on specifying general guidelines for selecting, applying and combining patterns, and for integrating them into an existing software architecture.

Many experienced software developers, however, are sceptical about the usefulness of such tools and methods. Their first argument is that if you do not understand the patterns themselves, no method and tool will help you. Secondly, they argue that patterns are mental building blocks and leave blank spaces intentionally, to be filled out by the developer. Each pattern must be adjusted to the needs of the application under development. As a result, no two implementations of a pattern are likely to be the same. You cannot therefore provide fully-fledged prefabricated code for a pattern, nor can you completely automate its instantiation.

Combining several patterns into a heterogeneous structure is even more complicated. It does not just consist of connecting the components of different patterns in a particular order. You often need to merge the responsibilities of components from different patterns into a single component, and to attach the responsibilities of pattern components to existing components in your design. If combined wrongly, the resulting structure may introduce additional complexity and lose the properties each individual pattern supports. Finally, whether a pattern can be applied or not depends on the specific design problems and their associated forces.

In conclusion, using patterns successfully still requires the intellectual skills of the software developer. We believe that a well-designed pattern browser or World Wide Web tool can be much more efficient in helping a developer to find and use patterns than a fully integrated 'pattern-supporting' software development environment ever could be.

Despite this argument, however, many people are convinced of the usefulness of pattern tools and methods. Such tools and method issues will be discussed further, and no doubt more research work will be done and more tools and methods developed.

8.4   Algorithms, Data Structures and Patterns

Patterns help to capture the existing knowledge of experts and to use it to find solutions to recurring problems in software design. A similar goal once lead to an intensive search for fundamental algorithms and data structures. Whereas patterns focus primarily on architectural issues, algorithms and data structures address computational problems such as searching and sorting. Unfortunately, software developers have to deal with both finding an appropriate architecture and solving computational problems. Only a combined use of patterns, abstract data types and algorithms helps developers to solve their specific problems.

There is a twofold relationship between patterns and algorithms. On one hand, when we instantiate a particular pattern, we have to implement all the services of its participants as well as their collaborations. Some of these services may be very complex. This is where algorithms and data structures come into play—they provide a means for implementing such services. On the other hand, design patterns and idioms can support the instantiation of algorithms and data structures.

We expect that future research will further clarify the combined usage of patterns and algorithms. As a first step, existing algorithms and data structures may be described in pattern form. A format derived from that which we introduced for describing patterns can be used. This would need some modifications and extensions when compared to pattern descriptions. For example, an additional section on complexity analysis is required. Other sections such as Structure should be changed or removed.

Nevertheless, algorithms and data structures fit well into similar description schemes. For example, both address problems in a given context. The same algorithm may lead to several variants. Like pattern instantiations, the use of particular algorithms implies specific consequences. An algorithm may refine other algorithms. It may also be useful to group algorithms into systems and associate them with specific problem categories. Overall, algorithm descriptions reveal many properties that also apply to pattern descriptions. We hope new algorithm catalogs will appear that describe algorithms and data structures in a uniform and systematic way.

Although you can use the same scheme for describing algorithms and patterns, algorithms and patterns are not different sides of the same coin—algorithms help to solve computational problems, while patterns describe architectural elements.

8.5   Formalizing Patterns

The academic world especially is involved in discussions about how to formalize patterns. Supporters of such formalization argue that it allows more precise pattern descriptions, especially with respect to their structure, dynamics and concrete semantics. Formalized patterns would support the development of pattern tools much better than the informal pattern descriptions of today. In the near future we therefore expect to see a lot of work in formalizing patterns.

However, as with tools and methods, many practitioners do not agree with these arguments. Formalizing the problem statement makes it harder to match a pattern to a specific design problem, which is usually not formalized. Formalizing the solution makes it harder to grasp the key ideas of the pattern and to create valid variants. A formalized solution may thus narrow the applicability of a pattern unnecessarily. Conversely, it may make it too general to be of any use. In addition, we do not know of a formalism suitable for describing the benefits and liabilities of a pattern.

All these aspects are of fundamental importance to the understanding of a pattern and the decision about whether it helps to solve a specific design problem. Similar arguments hold for the implementation guidelines for a pattern. Programmers need concrete information that they can understand and transfer directly into their own code, not an impressive formula. Patterns are mental building-blocks whose concrete appearance can show countless different faces. Formalisms, however, tend to describe particular issues very precisely, but do not allow for the variation that is inherently embedded into every pattern. Formal methods have their place in software development—we just think that they do not apply to patterns.

8.6   A Final Remark

Patterns expose knowledge about software construction that has been gained by experts over many years. All work on patterns should therefore focus on making this precious resource widely available. Every software developer should be able to use patterns effectively when building software systems. When this is achieved, we will be able to celebrate the human intelligence that patterns reflect, both in each individual pattern and in all patterns in their entirety.

Notations

Class-Responsibility-Collaborator Cards

Class-Responsibility-Collaborators (CRC-) cards [BeCu89] help to identify and specify objects or components of an application in an informal way—especially in the early phases of software development.

Class Name	*Collaborators* • Partner • Components
Responsibility • Operations may go across several lines.	

A CRC-card describes a component, an object or a class of objects. The card consists of three fields that describe the name of the component, its responsibilities, and the names of other collaborating components. The use of the term 'class' is historical [Ree92], and we use CRC cards for other kinds of components or single objects as well.

Object Modeling Technique

The Object Modeling Technique (OMT) [RBPEL91] is a widely-used object-oriented analysis and design method. OMT consists of three models, the object model, the dynamic model and the functional model. We adopt the notation only for the object model, to show the static structure of interacting components. The object model describes objects or classes, their attributes, methods, and relationships. We also use the boxes that represent classes in OMT for other kinds of components. OMT represents association, aggregation, and inheritance relationships between components by lines that connect the components. The basic concepts of OMT's object model notation are illustrated below:

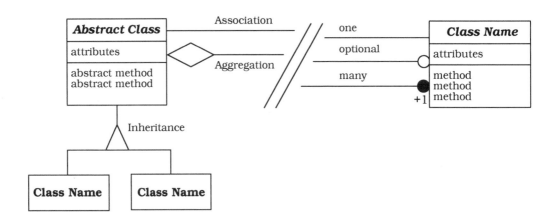

Component A rectangular box, denoting the name of the component and optionally its attributes and operations. Abstract components are labeled in *italics* as well as their corresponding abstract methods.

Methods Method names are written in the component boxes. They denote the operations of components. We show abstract methods, that is, those that only provide the interface for polymorphism, in *italics*.

Association A line that connects components. Associations can be optional (shown with a hollow circle) or multiple (shown with a black circle). A number at the end of an association may denote its cardinality. Association of components is used to show any kind of component relationship except aggregation and inheritance. Transitive relationships are typically not drawn.

Aggregation A diamond shape at the termination of an association line denotes that the partner component(s) at the other end of the association are contained within the component.

Inheritance This relationship is denoted by a triangle in the middle of the association line. The apex of the triangle points to the superclass.

Object Message Sequence Charts

Message Sequence Charts (MSC) are a standard notation for designing and specifying protocols among concurrently-operating entities such as processes or hardware elements [GR92][GGR93]. The MSC notation is standardized in the telecommunication domain and integrated into the SDL language. It specifies a scenario that shows the signal flow between the entities of a given domain. We do not follow the SDL/MSC standard notation, however, and adapt the MSC notation to demonstrate object or component interaction among the participants of a pattern. We refer to this adaptation as Object Message Sequencing Chart notation (OMSC).

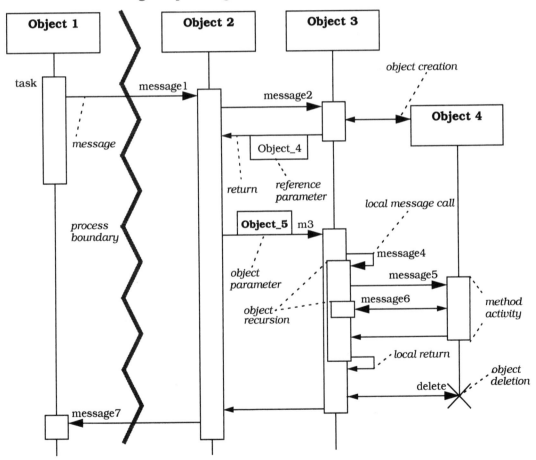

Object

An object or component in an OMSC is drawn as a rectangular box. The box is labeled with the name of the component in the pattern. An object that sends or receives messages in the OMSC has a vertical bar attached to the bottom of the box.

Time

Time flows from top to bottom. The time axis is not scaled.

Messages

Messages between objects are denoted by arrows. These arrows are labeled with the method name at the head, if applicable. To show the return of the control flow to the sender we extend the standard MSC notation by using arrows with a smaller head. Both types of arrows are combined to a single double-headed arrow if the activated method does not send other relevant messages.

Object Activity

To denote the activity of objects that perform a specific function, procedure, or method, rectangular boxes are placed on the vertical bar attached to the object. An object may also send messages to itself to activate other methods. This situation is represented by nested boxes offset slightly to the right.

Parameter

Parameters are only noted explicitly when they are necessary for the understanding of an OMSC. Parameters of a message are shown as a box on top of the arrow, and return parameters below the returning arrow. If responsibility for a parameter object is passed along the arrow the name of the object is shown in **boldface**. If only a reference to the object is passed as a parameter, its name is shown in *italics*.

Object Life cycle

In most cases we assume that all relevant objects already exist, and the corresponding boxes are drawn at the top of the OMSC. If an OMSC shows object creation, this is denoted by an unlabeled arrow to a box placed within the OMSC. If an object ceases to exist, this is denoted by a cross that terminates the vertical bar. This notation corresponds to the constructor and destructor calls in C++.

Address Space

A thick angled line shows an address space or process boundary. Messages that cross this boundary are transferred by a means of an IPC mechanism. Typically those messages are treated asynchronously and processing continues within the sending and the receiving object concurrently. Remote procedure calls across process boundaries that block the sender until the remote procedure returns are an exception to this.

Glossary

The glossary our use of many of the terms that are used frequently throughout the book. All the terms are related to specific aspects of software architecture. We have omitted many terms that we only use in one context, for example the terms borrowed from Artificial Intelligence in the Blackboard pattern. When we felt that such terms needed an explanation we gave it context rather than including them in the Glossary. We have also omitted central terms such as 'pattern', 'software architecture' or 'idiom'—these are explained in length in dedicated sections of the book.

Abstract Class A class that does not implement all the methods that are defined in its interface. An abstract class defines a common abstraction for its subclasses.

Abstract Component A *component* that specifies an interface for other components. An abstract component can either be given explicitly, like an *abstract class*, or implicitly by using its interface within another component, such as a class parameter of a C++ template function. Abstract components form the basis for exploiting polymorphism and implementing flexible *systems*. This term is used in the same way as abstract class, to avoid restricting the pattern to an object-oriented implementation.

Abstract Method An interface for an operation of a class that must be defined by a subclass.

API Application programming interface. The external interface of a software *platform*, such as an operating system, that is used by *systems* or applications built on top of it.

Application A program or collection of programs that fulfills a customer's requirements.

Application Framework	A *framework* for complete applications in a specific *domain*.
Associative Array	An array indexed via arbitrary key values rather than integers. Hash tables demonstrate one way of implementing associative arrays.
Class	A fundamental building block in object-oriented languages. A class specifies and encapsulates its internal data structure as well as the functionality of its *instances* or *objects*. A class' description may build on one or more other classes by *inheritance*.
Client	In our descriptions *client* denotes a *component* or subsystem that exploits functionality offered by other components.
Collaborator	A *component* that cooperates with another component. An element of a *CRC card*.
Component	An encapsulated part of a software *system*. A component has an interface that provides access to its services. Components serve as building blocks for the structure of a system. On a programming language level components may be represented as *modules*, *classes*, *objects* or a set of related functions. A component that does not implement all the elements of its interface is called an *abstract component*.
Concrete Class	A *class* from which objects can be *instantiated*. In contrast to *abstract classes*, all methods are implemented in a concrete class. The term is used to distinguish derived concrete classes from their abstract superclass.
Concrete Component	A *component* that implements all elements defined in its interface. Used to distinguish components from the *abstract component* that defines their interface, in the same way that a *concrete class* is distinguished from an *abstract class*.
Container	The common name for data structures that hold a number of elements. Examples of containers are lists, sets, and arrays.
CRC Card	Class-Responsibility-Collaborator card. A design tool and notation (see page 429). We also use CRC cards to describe *components* that are not *classes*.

Demultiplexing   A mechanism that routes incoming data from an input port to its intended receivers. There is a 1:N relationship between input port and receivers. Demultiplexing is commonly applied to incoming events and data streams. The reverse operation is known as multiplexing.

Design   The activity performed by a software developer that results in the software architecture of a *system*. Very often the term design is also used as a name for the result of this activity.

Domain   Denotes concepts, knowledge and other items that are related to a subject. Often used as 'application domain' to denote the problem area an application addresses.

Drag and Drop   User activity supported by modern *GUIs*. Drag and drop allows a user to perform an operation on a graphical object by selecting it and dragging it to another place on the screen. For example, a document can be printed by selecting it and dragging it to a printer icon.

Dynamic Binding   A mechanism that defers the association of an operation name (a *message*) to the corresponding code (a *method*) until run-time. It is used to implement *polymorphism* in object-oriented languages.

Framework   A semi-finished software (sub-) system intended to be *instantiated*. A framework defines the architecture for a family of (sub-) systems and provides the basic building blocks to create them. It also defines the parts of itself that must be adapted to achieve a specific functionality. In an object-oriented environment a framework consists of *abstract* and *concrete classes*. Instantiation of such a framework consists of composing and subclassing the existing classes.

Functional Property   A particular aspect of a system's functionality, usually related to a specified functional requirement. A functional property may be either made directly visible to users of an *application* by means of a particular function, or it may represent aspects of its implementation, such as the algorithm used to compute the function.

GUI   Graphical user interface.

Hardwiring   Coding in a very inflexible way, for example by using a literal number or a string instead of a variable. Such literal numbers are also known as 'magic numbers' since the number itself may give no clue to understanding where it came from and what it is for.

Inheritance A feature of object-oriented languages that allows new *classes* to be derived from existing ones. Inheritance defines implementation reuse, a subtype relationship, or both. Depending on the programming language, single or multiple inheritance is possible.

Inlining Code expansion at compile time that inserts the code of a function or procedure body instead of the code used to call the function. Inlining long function bodies can lead to code 'bloat', with negative effects on storage consumption and paging effects.

Instance An *object* originated from a specific *class*. Often used as a synonym for object in an object-oriented environment. This term may also be used in other contexts (see *Instantiation*).

Instantiation A mechanism that creates a new *instance* from some template. The term is used in several contexts. *Objects* are instantiated from *classes*. C++ templates are instantiated to create new classes or functions. An *application framework* is instantiated to create an *application*. The phrase 'instantiating a pattern' is sometimes used to refer to taking the pattern as described and filling in the necessary details to fit a specific application.

Intercession The addition to, or modification of, the structure, behavior or state of a *system* by the system itself.

Intranet A wide-area network of computers within a company. Such a network may be secured from outside access, and provides a platform for company-wide information exchange. cooperative work and work flow.

Introspection The examination of selected aspects of the structure, behavior and state of a *system* by the system itself.

IPC Inter process communication. Examples of IPC mechanisms are shared memory, pipes, message queues and network communication.

Message Messages are used for the communication between *objects* or processes. In an object-oriented *system* the term message is used to describe the selection and activation of an operation or *method* of an object. This kind of message is synchronous, which means that the sender waits until the receiver finishes the activated operation.

Processes typically communicate asynchronously, in which the sending process continues its execution without waiting for the receiver to reply. Remote procedure calls (RPC) are a means of synchronous inter-process communication.

Method Denotes an operation performed by an *object*. A method is specified within a *class*. The term is also used in 'software development method', which consists of a set of rules, guidelines and notations to be used by engineers during the development process.

Mix-In A 'small' *class* that defines an additional interface or functionality to be added to classes by multiple *inheritance*. Mix-In also denotes the mechanism for adding such functionality by *inheriting* from classes.

Module A syntactical or conceptual entity of a software *system*. Often used as a synonym for *component* or *subsystem*. Sometimes, 'modules' also denote compilation units or files. Other writers use the term as an equivalent to 'package' when referring to a code body with its own name space. We use the term as stated in the first sentence.

Multiple Inheritance *Inheritance* in which a *class* can have many *superclasses*.

Non-functional Property A feature of a *system* not covered by its *functional* description. A non-functional property typically addresses aspects related to the reliability, compatibility, efficiency, cost, ease of use, maintenance or development of a system.

Object An identifiable entity in an object-oriented *system*. Objects respond to messages by performing a *method* (operation). An object may contain data values and references to other objects, which together define the state of the object. An object therefore has state, behavior, and identity.

Off-board Communication Communication that crosses machine boundaries. Note that the term 'inter-process communication' depicts different types of communication, depending on whether the communicating processes exist on the same machine or on different machines. Such communication types may differ in latency, throughput and error probability.

On-the-wire Protocol An 'on-the-wire' protocol' defines how higher-level communication toolkits (such as DCE, CORBA, or Network OLE) transform messages, objects, data and other entities into buffers that can be passed 'across the wire'. The term 'wire' today also includes transmission media such as microwave, fiber, and radio transmissions.

Peer-to-peer In a distributed *system* peers are the processes that communicate with each other. In contrast to *components* in Client-Server architectures, peers may act as *clients*, as servers or as both, and may change these roles dynamically.

Platform The sum of hardware and/or software a *system* uses for its implementation. Software platforms include operating systems, libraries, and *frameworks*. A platform implements a virtual machine with *applications* running on top of it.

Polymorphism A concept in which a single name may denote different things. A function name may be bound over time to several different operations, or a variable may be bound to objects of different types. This concept makes it possible to implement flexible systems based on abstractions. In object-oriented languages polymorphism is implemented by the *dynamic binding* mechanism of operations. This implies that a fixed portion of code may behave differently depending on its collaborating objects.

Relationship A connection between *components*. A relationship may be static or dynamic. Static relationships show directly in source code. They deal with the placement of components within an architecture. Dynamic relationships deal with the interaction between components. They may not be easily visible from source code or diagrams.

Responsibility The functionality of an *object* or a *component* in a specific context. A responsibility is typically specified by a set of operations. The responsibility section is an element of a *CRC card*.

Role The responsibility of *component* within a context of related components. An implemented component may take different roles, even within a single pattern.

S.E.P. Somebody Else's Problem, Software Engineering Process, or Software Engineering with Patterns—whatever you want it to be.

Server A *component* or subsystem triggered by *client* requests. When a client request arrives the server attempts to fulfill it, either on its own, or by delegating subtasks to other components.

Single Inheritance *Inheritance* in which a *class* can have at most one direct *superclass*.

Subsystem A set of collaborating *components* performing a given task. A subsystem is considered a separate entity within a software architecture. It performs its designated task by interacting with other subsystems and components.

Superclass A *class* from which another class inherits.

System A collection of software and/or hardware performing one or several tasks. A system can be a *platform*, an *application* or both.

System Family A set of related *systems* solving similar tasks. Systems in a system family share a great part of their architecture and implementation, often because every system is derived from the same *framework*. When a single system evolves over time, its delivered releases also build a system family.

Unicode A standard for character representation using 16-bit coding. Unicode includes characters for almost all written languages, as well as representations for punctuation, mathematical and other symbols.

References

[Ada79]   D. Adams: *The Hitchhiker's Guide to the Galaxy*, page 2^6, Pan Books Ltd., London, 1979

[Ada84]   D. Adams: *So long, and Thanks for All the Fish*, Chapter 31, Pan Books Ltd., London, 1984

[AG96]   K. Arnold, J. Gosling: *The Java Programming Language*, Addison-Wesley, 1996, see also http://java.sun.com

[Ale79]   C. Alexander: *The Timeless Way of Building*, Oxford University Press, 1979

[ANAK87]   C. Alexander, H. Neis, A. Anninou, I. King: *A New Theory of Urban Design*, Oxford University Press, 1987

[ASAIA75]   C. Alexander, M. Silverstein, S. Angel, S. Ishikawa, D. Abrams: *The Oregon Experiment*, Oxford University Press, 1975

[AIS77]   C. Alexander, S. Ishikawa, M. Silverstein with M. Jacobson, I. Fiksdahl-King, S. Angel: *A Pattern Language – Towns·Buildings·Construction*, Oxford University Press, 1977

[ASU86]   A. Aho, R. Sethi, J. Ullman: *Compilers – Principles, Techniques, and Tools*, Addison Wesley, 1986

[ATM93]   Siemens AG: *ATM-P: Komplexspezifikation*, internal document, 1993

[App85]   Apple Computer Inc.: *Inside Macintosh, Volume I*, Cupertino, CA, 1985

[App89]   Apple Computer Inc.: *Macintosh Programmers Workshop Pascal 3.0 Reference*, Cupertino, CA, 1989

[Bac86]   M.J. Bach: *The Design of the UNIX Operating System*, Prentice Hall, 1986

[BaCo91]   L. Bass, J. Coutaz: *Developing Software for the User Interface*, Addison-Wesley, 1991

[Bal85] H. Balzert: *Die Entwicklung von Software-Systemen*, B·I· Wissenschaftsverlag, Mannheim Wien Zürich, 1985

[Bec94] K. Beck: *Patterns and Software Development*, Dr. Dobb's Journal, 19(2), pp. 18–23, February 1994

[Bec96] K. Beck: *Smalltalk Best Practice Patterns, Volume 1: Coding*, Prentice-Hall, to be published, see also his column on Smalltalk idioms in *The Smalltalk Report* by SIGS Publications and ftp://st.cs.uiuc.edu/pub/patterns/sbpp/

[BeCu89] K. Beck, W. Cunningham: *A Laboratory For Teaching Object-Oriented Thinking*, Proceedings of OOPSLA '89, N. Meyrowitz (Ed), Special Issue of SIGPLAN Notices, Vol. 24, No. 10, pp. 1–6, October 1989

[BI93] A.P. Black, M.P. Immel: *Encapsulating Plurality*, Proceedings of ECOOP '93, pp. 57–79, [ECOOP93]

[BJ94] K. Beck, R. Johnson: *Patterns Generate Architectures*, Proceedings of ECOOP '94, pp. 139–149, [ECOOP94]

[BKSP92] F. Buschmann, K. Kiefer, M. Stal, F. Paulisch: *The Meta-Information-Protocol: Run-Time Type Information for C++*, Proceedings of IMSA '92, pp. 82–87, [IMSA92]

[BM94] F. Buschmann, R. Meunier: *A System of Patterns*, Proceedings of PLoP '94, pp. 325–343, [PLoP94]

[BM95] F. Buschmann, R. Meunier: *Building a Software System*, Electronic Design, February 20, 1995

[BN94] J.J. Barton, L.R. Nackman: *Scientific and Engineering C++ – An Introduction with Advanced Techniques and Examples*, Addison-Wesley, 1994

[Boo94] G. Booch: *Object-Oriented Analysis and Design With Applications*, Second Edition, Benjamin/Cummings, Redwood City, California, 1994

[BR95] G. Booch: *Unified Method for Object-Oriented Development*, Version 0.8, Rational Software Corporation

[Bro94] K. Brockschmidt: *Inside OLE 2*, Microsoft Press, 1994

[Bro96] Phil Brooks: *Master-Slave Pattern for Parallel Compute Services*, submitted to the 1996 Conference on Object-Oriented Technologies and Systems (COOTS)

[BuCa96] R.J.A. Buhr, R.S. Casselman: *Use Case Maps for Object-Oriented Systems*, Prentice Hall, 1996

[Cam94]   F.R. Campagnoni: *IBM's System Object Model*, Dr. Dobb's Journal, Special Report, #225 Winter 1994/95, pp. 24–28

[Cho90]   Chorus systemès: *Chorus Kernel v3.2, Implementation Guide*, CS/TR-90-5

[CNS95]   J. Coutaz, L. Nigay, D. Salber: *Agent-Based Architecture Modelling for Interactive Systems*, The Amodeus Project, ESPRIT Basic Research Action 7040, System Modelling/WP53, April 1995

[CM93]   S. Chiba, T. Masuda: *Designing an Extensible Distributed Language with a Meta-Level Architecture*, Proceedings of ECOOP '93, pp. 482–501, [ECOOP93]

[Coad92]   P. Coad: *Object-Oriented Patterns*, Communications of the ACM, Vol. 35, No. 9, September 1992

[Coad95]   P. Coad with D. North and M. Mayfield: *Object Models – Patterns, Strategies, & Applications*, Yourdon Press, Prentice Hall, 1995

[Cope92]   J.O. Coplien: *Advanced C++ – Programming Styles and Idioms*, Addison-Wesley, Reading, MA, 1992

[Cope94a]   J.O. Coplien: *The Counted Body Idiom*, Pattern Mailing List Reflector, Feb 1994

[Cope94b]   J.O. Coplien: *Generative pattern languages: An emerging direction of software design*, C++ Report, SIGS Publications, July-August 1994

[Cope94c]   J.O. Coplien: *A Generative Development-Process Pattern Language*, Proceedings of PLoP '94, pp. 183–237, [PLoP94]

[Cope95]   J.O. Coplien: *The History of Patterns*, see http://c2.com/cgi/ wiki?HistoryOfPatterns

[Cope96]   J.O. Coplien: Pattern Mailing List Reflector, V96 #35, April 1996

[Cou87]   J. Coutaz: *PAC, an Object Oriented Model for Dialog Design*, Human-Computer Interaction – INTERACT '87 proceedings, H.-J. Bullinger and B. Shackel (Eds), pp. 431–436, Stuttgart, Germany, Elsevier Science Publishers B.V. (North-Holland), 1987

[Cra95]   Iain Craig: Blackboard Systems, Ablex Publishing Corporation, Norwood, New Jersey, 1995

[Cro85]   J. Crowley: *Navigation for an Intelligent Mobile Robot*, IEEE Journal of Robotics and Automation, Vol. RA-1, No. 1, pp. 31–41, March 1985

[Cun94]   W. Cunningham: *The CHECKS Pattern Language of Information Integrity*, Proceedings of PLoP '94, pp. 145–155, [PLoP94]

[Cus93]   H. Custer: *Inside Windows NT*, Microsoft Press, 1993

[CY91]   P. Coad, E. Yourdon: *Object-Oriented Analysis*, Prentice Hall, second edition, 1991

[CZ95]   D. Chapman, E. Zwicky: *Building Internet Firewalls*, O'Reilly & Associates, 1995

[Dij65]   E.W. Dijkstra: *Solution of a Problem in Concurrent Programming Control*, CACM, Vol. 8, No. 9, p. 569, Sept. 1965

[DWP95]   ANSI document X3J16/95 0088 WG21/N0688: *Programming Language C++*, draft working paper, July 1995

[ECOOP92]   O. Lehrmann Madsen (Ed.): *ECOOP '92 – European Conference on Object-Oriented Programming*, Proceedings of 6th European Conference, Utrecht, The Netherlands, June/July 1992, Lecture Notes in Computer Science 615, Springer-Verlag, Berlin Heidelberg New York, 1992

[ECOOP93]   O. Nierstrasz (Ed.): *ECOOP '93 – Object-Oriented Programming*, Proceedings of 7th European Conference, Kaiserslautern, Germany, July 1993, Lecture Notes in Computer Science 707, Springer-Verlag, Berlin Heidelberg New York, 1993

[ECOOP94]   M. Tokoro, R. Pareschi (Eds.): *ECOOP '94 – Object-Oriented Programming*, Proceedings of 8th European Conference, Bologna, Italy, July 1994, Lecture Notes in Computer Science 821, Springer-Verlag, Berlin Heidelberg New York, 1994

[ECOOP95]   W. Olthoff (Ed.): *ECOOP '95 – Object-Oriented Programming*, Proceedings of 9th European Conference, Åarhus, Denmark, August 1995, Lecture Notes in Computer Science 952, Springer-Verlag, Berlin Heidelberg New York, 1995

[EHLR88]   L.D. Erman, F. Hayes-Roth, V.R. Lesser, D.R. Reddy: *The Hearsay-II Speech-Understanding System: Integrating Knowledge to Resolve Uncertainty*, ACM Computing Surveys 12 (2), pp. 213–253, 1980, reprinted in *Blackboard Systems*, pp. 31–86, [EM88]

[EKM+94]   R. Eisenhauer, S. Kumsta, F. Miralles, K. Möbius, U. Steinmüller, P. Stobbe, C. Vester: *Architektur-Handbuch für Software-Architekten*, Siemens Nixdorf Informationssysteme AG, internal report, 1994

[EM88]   R. Engelmore, T. Morgan (Eds): *Blackboard Systems*, Addison-Wesley, 1988

[ES90]   M.A. Ellis, B. Stroustrup: *The Annotated C++ Reference Manual*, Addison-Wesley, 1990

[Etz64]   A. Etzioni: *Modern Organizations*, Prentice-Hall, 1964

[Fel84]   K. Fellbaum: Sprachverarbeitung und Sprachübertragung, Springer-Verlag, Berlin Heidelberg New York Tokyo,1984

[FMcD77]   C. Forgy, J. McDermott: *OPS: a domain-independent production system language*, Proceedings of the Fifth International Joint Conference on Artificial Intelligence IJCAI-77, pp. 933-939

[Fow96]   M. Fowler: *Object Blueprints: Patterns in Systems Analysis*, Addison-Wesley, to appear

[Gam91]   E. Gamma: *Objektorientierte Software-Entwicklung am Beispiel von ET++: Klassenbibliothek, Werkzeuge, Design*, Dissertation, Universität Zürich, 1991

[Gel85]   D. Gelernter: *Generative Communication in LINDA*, ACM Transactions on Programming Languages and Systems, Vol. 7, No. 1, pp. 80–112, Jan. 1985

[GGR93]   J. Grabowski, P. Graubmann, E. Rudolph: *The Standardization of Message Sequence Charts*, in Software Engineering Standards Symposium, Brighton, UK, 1993

[GR92]   J. Grabowski, E. Rudolph: *Message Sequence Charts (MSC) – A Survey of the new CCITT Language for the Description of Traces within Communication Systems*, 1992

[GHJV93]   E. Gamma, R. Helm, R. Johnson, J. Vlissides: *Design Patterns: Abstraction and Reuse of Object-Oriented Design*, Proceedings of ECOOP '93, pp. 406–431, [ECOOP93]

[GHJV95]   E. Gamma, R. Helm, R. Johnson, J. Vlissides: *Design Patterns – Elements of Reusable Object-Oriented Software*, Addison-Wesley, 1995

[GJ79]   M. Garey, D. Johnson: *Computers and Intractability – A Guide to the Theory of NP-Completeness*, W.H. Freeman and Company, New York, 1979

[Gol91]   A. Goldberg: *Object-Oriented Project Management*, Tutorial TOOLS Europe, Paris, 1991

[GOP90]   K. Gorlen, S. Orlow, P. Plexico: *Data Abstraction and Object-Oriented Programming in C++*, John Wiley & Sons, 1990

[GR83]	A. Goldberg, D. Robson: *Smalltalk-80: the language and its implementation*, Addison-Wesley, 1983
[HAJ90]	X.D. Huang, Y. Ariki, M.A. Jack: *Hidden Markov Models for Speech Recognition*, Edinburgh University Press, Edinburgh, 1990
[HHS94]	R. Händel, M.N. Huber, S. Schröder, *ATM Networks – Concepts, Protocols, Applications*, 2nd Edition, Addison-Wesley, 1994
[HRV95]	J. Hartmann, C. Reichetzeder, M. Varian: *CMS Pipelines*, http://www.akh-wien.ac.at/pipeline.html
[HT92]	Y. Honda, M. Tokoro: *Soft Real-Time Programming through Reflection*, Proceedings of IMSA '92, pp. 12–23, [IMSA92]
[IEEE88]	IEEE: *Portable Operating System Interface for Computer Environments (POSIX)*, 1003.1, Sept. 1988
[IMSA92]	A. Yonezawa, B.C. Smith (Eds.): Proceedings of the *International Workshop on New Models for Software Architecture '92 – Reflection and Meta-Level Architecture*, Tokyo, Japan, 1992
[IMY92]	Y. Ichisugi, S. Matsuoka, A. Yonezawa: *RbCl: A Reflective Object-Oriented Concurrent Language without a Run-time Kernel*, Proceedings of IMSA '92, pp. 24–35, [IMSA92]
[Iona95]	IONA Technologies Ltd: *Orbix Programmer's Guide*, compare also http://www.iona.ie/, Dublin, Ireland, 1995
[Jac95]	M. Jackson: *Software Requirements & Specifications – a lexicon of practice, principles and prejudices*, Addison-Wesley, 1995
[Joh94]	R. Johnson: *An Introduction to Patterns*, Report on Object Analsysis & Design, Vol.1, No. 1, SIGS Publications, May-June 1994
[Joh95]	R. Johnson: private communication
[Joh96]	R. Johnson: private communication
[Kar95]	E-A. Karlsson (Ed.): *Software Reuse – A Holistic Approach*, John Wiley & Sons, 1995
[Kee89]	S.E. Keene, *Object-Oriented Programming in Common Lisp – A Programmer's Guide to CLOS*, Addison-Wesley, 1989

[Kic92]   G. Kiczales: *Towards a New Model of Abstraction in Software Engineering*, Proceedings of IMSA '92, pp. 1–11, [IMSA92]

[KLLM95]   G. Kiczales, R. DeLine, A. Lee, C. Maeda: *Open Implementation – Analysis and Design™ of Substrate Software*, Tutorial #21 of OOPSLA '95, October 1995

[KMS+92]   A. Kausche, M. van Meegen, A. Schappert, P. Sommerlad, K. Bergner, B. Rumpe: *Exploration Field Automated Software Development – State-of-the-Art Report*, Siemens AG, internal technical report, Munich, 1992

[Koe95]   A. Koenig: *Another handle variation*, Journal of Object-Oriented Programming (JOOP), SIGS Publications, November-December 1995

[KP88]   G.E. Krasner, S.T. Pope: *A cookbook for using the Model-View-Controller user interface paradigm in Smalltalk-80*, Journal of Object-Oriented Programming, 1(3), pp. 26–49, August/September 1988, SIGS Publications, New York, NY, USA, 1988

[KR88]   B. W. Kerninghan, D.M. Ritchie, *The C Programming Language*, 2nd edition covering ANSI-C, Prentice Hall, 1988

[KR96]   J. Knopp, M. Reich: *A Data Model For Architecture Independent Parallel Programming*, Workshop on High-Level Programming Models and Supportive Environments at the IEEE International Parallel Processing Symposium, Honolulu, 1996

[KRB91]   G. Kiczales, J. des Rivières, D. Bobrow: *The Art of the Metaobject Protocol*, MIT Press, 1991

[Kru95]   P.B. Kruchten: *The 4 + 1 View Model of Architecture*, IEEE Software, November 1995, pp. 42–50

[Kru96]   D. Kruglinski: *Inside Visual C++*, Microsoft Press, 1995

[KSS96]   S. Kleiman, D. Shah, B. Smaalders: *Programming with Threads*, SunSoft Press, Prentice Hall, 1996

[LA94]   A. Luotonen, K. Altis: *World-Wide Web Proxies*, WWW94 Conference, 1994, see also http://www.w3.org/pub/WWW/Daemon/

[LCITV92]   M. Linton, P. Calder, J. Interrante, S. Tang, J. Vlissides: *InterViews Reference Manual*, CSL, Stanford University, 3.1 edition, 1992

[Lea96]   D. Lea: *Collections, a Java package*, http://g.oswego.edu/dl/, 1996

[LeEr88]   V.R. Lesser, L.D. Erman: *A Retrospective View of the Hearsay-II Architecture,* in *Blackboard Systems,* Proc. of IJCAI-77, pp. 790–800 and Technical Report CMU-CS-78-117, reproduced in *Blackboard Systems,* pp. 87–121, [EM88]

[Lim93]   C.-C. Lim: *A Parallel Object-Oriented System for Realizing Reusable and Efficient Data Abstractions,* PhD dissertation, TR-93-063, International Computer Science Institute, Berkeley, CA, 1993, see also http://www.icsi.berkeley.edu/~sather/psather.html

[LP91]   W.R. LaLonde, J.R. Pugh: *Inside Smalltalk, Volume II,* Prentice-Hall, 1991

[LPW94]   K.-P. Löhr, I. Piens, T. Wolff: *Verteilungstransparenz bei der objektorientierten Entwicklung verteilter Applikationen,* OBJEKTspektrum 5/1994, pp. 8–14, SIGS Publications, München, Germany, 1994

[Mae87]   Pattie Maes, *Concepts and Experiments in Computational Reflection,* in Proceedings of OOPSLA '87, pp. 147–155, 1987

[Maf96]   S. Maffeis: *The Object Group Design Pattern,* 2nd USENIX Conference on Object-Oriented Technologies and Systems (COOTS), Toronto, Ontario, Canada, 1996

[Mar95]   J. Markowitz: *Talking to Machines,* Byte, December 1995, pp. 97–104

[McA95]   J. McAffer: *Meta-level Programming with CodA,* Proceedings of ECOOP '95, pp. 190–214, [ECOOP95]

[ME96]   T.D. Meijler, R. Engel: *Making Design Patterns explicit in FACE, a Framework Adaptive Composition Environment,* submitted to EuroPLoP '96

[Mes94]   G. Meszaros: *Pattern: Half Object + Prototocol (HOPP),* Proceedings of PLoP '94, pp.129–132, [PLoP94]

[Mey92]   S. Meyers: *Effective C++ – 50 Specific Ways to Improve Your Programs and Designs,* Addison-Wesley, 1992

[MFL93]   S. Murer, J. Feldman, C. Lim: *pSather: Layered Extensions to an Object-Oriented Language for Efficient Parallel Computation,* International Computer Science Institue, TR-93-028, Berkeley, CA, 1993

[Mic93b]   Microsoft Corporation: *Microsoft Word,* User's Guide, 1993

[Mic95]   Microsoft Corporation: *Microsoft Visual Basic,* Programmer's Guide, 1995

[Nii86]   H.P. Nii: *Blackboard Systems, Part I and II,* The AI Magazine, vol. 7, nos 2 (pp. 38–53) and 3 (pp. 82–106), 1986

[NS72]   A. Newell, H.A. Simon: *Human Problem Solving*, Prentice-Hall, 1972

[OIT92]   H. Okamura, Y. Ishikawa, M. Tokoro: *AL-1/D: A Distributed Programming System with Multi-Model Reflection Framework*, Proceedings of IMSA '92, pp. 36–47, [IMSA92]

[OMG92]   Object Management Group: *The Common Object Request Broker: Architecture and Specification*, OMG Document Number 91.12.1, Revision 1.1, 1992

[OMG95]   Object Management Group: *CORBAservices: Common Object Services Specification*, OMG Document Number 95-3-31, 1995

[Omo93]   S.M. Omohundro: The Sather programming language, Dr. Dobb's Journal, 18(11):42–48, October 1993, see also http://www.icsi.berkeley.edu/Sather/

[Par79]   D.L. Parnas: *On the criteria to be used in decomposing systems into modules*, CACM, Vol. 15, pp.1053–1058, Dec. 1972

[Par94]   D.L. Parnas: *Software Aging*, IEEE Proceedings of the 16th International Conference on Software Engineering, 1994

[PCW85]   D.L. Parnas, P.C. Clements, D.M. Weiss: *The Modular Structure of Complex Systems*, IEEE Transactions on Software Engineering, Vol. SE-11, No. 3, March 1985

[PLoP94]   J.O. Coplien, D.C. Schmidt (Eds.): *Pattern Languages of Program Design*, Addison-Wesley, 1995 (a book publishing the reviewed Proceedings of the First International Conference on Pattern Languages of Programming, Monticello, Illinois, 1994)

[PLoP95]   J.O. Coplien, N. Kerth, J. Vlissidis (Eds.): *Pattern Languages of Program Design*, Addison-Wesley, 1996 (a book publishing the reviewed Proceedings of the Second International Conference on Pattern Languages of Programming, Monticello, Illinois, 1995)

[PP90]   ParcPlace Systems Inc.: *Objectworks\Smalltalk Release 4.1 User's Guide*, ParcPlace Systems, 1992

[Pree94]   W. Pree: *Meta Patterns – A Means For Capturing the Essentials of Reusable Object-Oriented Design*, Proceedings of ECOOP '94, pp 150–162, [ECOOP94]

[Pree95]   W. Pree: *Design Patterns for Object-Oriented Software Development*, Addison-Wesley, 1995

[PST96]   G. Parulkar, D. Schmidt, J. Turner: a^It^Pm: *a Strategy for Integrating IP with ATM*, Proceedings of SIGCOMMM, ACM, Aug/Sep 1996, see also http://siesta.cs.wustl.edu/~schmidt/

[PW92]   D.E. Perry, A.L. Wolf: *Foundations for the Study of Software Architecture*, ACM SIGSOFT, Software Engineering Notes, Vol. 17, No. 4, pp. 40–52, October 1992

[Rab86]   L.R. Rabiner et al: *An Introduction to Hidden Markov Models*, IEEE ASSP Magazine, Vol 3, pp. 4–16, January 1986

[Rab89]   L.R. Rabiner: *A Tutorial on Hidden Markov Models and Selected Applications in Speech Recognition*, Proceedings IEEE, Vol 77, No 2, pp 257–285, 1989

[RBPEL91]   J. Rumbaugh, M. Blaha, W. Premerlani, F. Eddy, W. Lorensen: *Object-Oriented Modeling and Design*, Prentice Hall, 1991

[Ree92]   T. Reenskaug: *Intermediate Smalltalk, Practical Design and Implementation*, Tutorial, TOOLS Europe '92, Dortmund, 1992

[RWL96]   T. Reenskaug, P. Wold, O.A. Lehne: *Working with Objects: The OOram Software Engineering Method*, Manning Publications Company, 1996

[SC95a]   A. Sane, R. Campbell: *Detachable Inspector/Removable cout: A Structural Pattern for Designing Transparent Layered Services*, Proceedings of PLoP '95

[SC95b]   A. Sane, R. Campbell: *Composite Messages: A Structural Pattern For Communication Between Components*, OOPSLA '95 Workshop on Concurrent, Parallel, and Distributed Object-Oriented Systems, Austin TX, 1995, see also http://siesta.cs.wustl.edu/~schmidt/OOPSLA-95/index.html

[Sch86]   K.J. Schmucker: *Object-Oriented Programming for the Macintosh*™, Hayden Book Company, Hasbrouck Heights, New Jersey, 1986

[Sch94]   D.C. Schmidt: *Reactor: An Object Behavioral Pattern for Concurrent Event Demultiplexing and Event Handler Dispatching*, Proceedings of PLoP '94, pp. 529–545, [PLoP94]

[Sch95]   D.C. Schmidt: *A System of Reusable Design Patterns for Communication Software*, Theory and Practice of Object Systems, Special Issue on Patterns and Pattern Languages, S.P. Berczuk (Ed), John Wiley and Sons, 1995

[Sch96]   D.C. Schmidt: *ACE – The ADAPTIVE Communication Environment*, see http://siesta.cs.wustl.edu/~schmidt/ACE.html

[Sch96b]   D.C. Schmidt: *Acceptor and Connector – Design Patterns for Initializing Network Services*, submitted to EuroPLoP '96

[Set95]   J. Sethna: *LASSPTools: Graphical and Numerical Extensions to Unix*, http://www.lassp.cornell.edu/LASSPTools/LASSPTools.html

[SG96]   M. Shaw, D. Garlan: *Software Architecture – Perspectives on an Emerging Discipline*, Prentice Hall, 1996

[SHA96]   D. C. Schmidt, T. Harrison, E. Al-Shaer: *Object-Oriented Components for High-speed Network Programming*, Department of Computer Science, Washington University, 1996, see also http://siesta.cs.wustl.edu/~schmidt/

[SICAT95]   Siemens AG: *SICAT Steuerprogramm: Entwurfsspezifikation*, internal document no. P30308-A6331-A000-02-D8

[SL92]   B. Stroustrup, D. Lenkov: *Run-Time Type Identification for C++*, ANSI C++ standards document No. X3J16/92-0028, 1992

[SM88]   S. Shlaer, S.J. Mellor: *Object-Oriented Systems Analysis – Modeling the World In Data*, Yourdon Press, Prentice Hall, 1988

[Smi82]   Brian C. Smith, *Reflection and Semantics in a Procedural Language*, PhD thesis, Massachusetts Institute of Technology, 1982

[SNH95]   D. Soni, R. Nord, C. Hofmeister: *Software Architecture in Industrial Applications*, in Proceedings of the 17th International Conference on Software Engineering, pp. 196–207, Seattle, Washington, ACM Press, April 1995

[SNI94]   Siemens Nixdorf Informationssysteme AG: *Generic++ 2.0, Portable C++ Foundation Class Library*, User manual, October 1994

[Sou94]   J. Soukup: Implementing Patterns, Proceedings of PLoP '94, pp.395–412, in [PLoP94]

[SRC84]   J. Saltzer, D. Reed, D. Clark: *End-To-End Arguments in System Design*, ACM Transactions on Computer Systems, Vol. 2, No. 4, pp. 277–288, Nov. 1984

[SS86]   E. Seidewitz, M. Stark: *Towards a General Object-Oriented Software Development Methodology*, Proceedings of the First International Conference on Ada Programming Language Applications for the NASA Space Station, Lyndon B. Johnson Space Center, Texas, NASA, 1986

[Stee91]   D. Steel: *Distributed Object Oriented Programming: Mechanisms & Experience*, Proceedings of TOOLS USA '91, pp. 27–35, Prentice Hall, 1991

[Ste90]   W.R. Stevens: *UNIX Network Programming*, Prentice Hall Software Series, 1990

[Ste94]   W.R. Stevens: *TCP/IP Illustrated, Volume 1, The Protocols*, Addison-Wesley, 1994

[Str91]   B. Stroustrup: *The C++ Programming Language*, Second Edition, Addison-Wesley, 1991

[Sun90]   Sun Microsystems, Inc.: *Sun OS Documentation Tools, Formatting Documents*, March 1990

[SW95]   R.J. Stroud, Z. Wu: *Using Metaobject Protocols to Implement Atomic Data Types*, Proceedings of ECOOP '95, pp. 168–189, [ECOOP95]

[Tal94]   Taligent Inc.: *Taligent's Guide To Designing Programs – Well-Mannered Object-Oriented Design in C++*, Addison-Wesley, 1994

[Tan92]   A.S. Tanenbaum: *Modern Operating Systems*, Prentice Hall, 1992

[TASC91]   Siemens AG: *Toolkit for Autonomous Software Components Communication*, Systemdokumentation, internal document, 1991

[Ter88]   A. Terry: *Using Explicit Strategic Knowledge to Control Expert Systems*, originally published in 1985, reproduced in *Blackboard Systems*, pp. 159–188, [EM88]

[THG94]   R. Thomson, K.E. Huff, J.W.Gish: *Maximizing Reuse During Reengineering*, Proceedings of the Third International Conference on Software Reuse, Rio de Janeiro, Brazil, pp. 16–23, IEEE Computer Society Press, 1994

[THP94]   W.F. Tichy, J. Heilig, F. Newbery Paulisch: *A Generative and Generic Approach to Persistence*, C++ Report, SIGS Publications, January 1994

[TS93]   C. Traving, H. Stadtherr: *Building a Traffic Management System with C++*, Proceedings of the C++ User Group Technical Conference, Munich, 1993

[U2]   U2: *even BETTER than the REAL THING*, Island Records Ltd., 1991

[VBT95]   Allan Vermeulen, Gabe Beged-Dov, Patrick Thompson: *The Pipeline Design Pattern*, OOPSLA '95 Workshop on Design Patterns for Concurrent, Parallel and Distributed Object-Oriented Systems, see also

             http://siesta.cs.wustl.edu/~schmidt/OOPSLA-95/html/papers.html

[VL90]   J. Vlissides, M. A. Linton: *Unidraw – A framework for building domain-specific graphical editors*, acm Transactions on Information Systems, Vol. 8, No. 3, pp. 237–268, July 1990

[WBWW90]   R. Wirfs-Brock, B. Wilkerson, L. Wiener: *Designing Object-Oriented Software*, Prentice Hall, 1990

[WGM88]   A. Weinand, E. Gamma, R. Marty: *ET++ – An Object-Oriented Application Framework in C++*, in Proceedings of OOPSLA '88, pp. 46–57, San Diego, 1988

[Wil84]   M.A. Williams: *Hierarchical Multi-expert Signal Understanding*, Technical Report ESL-IR201, ESL Inc, Sunnyville, CA, 1984. Reproduced in *Blackboard Systems*, pp. 387–415, [EM88]

[Woo96]   D.W. Woodward: *Ein Microkernel für die Datenbank*, Software-Entwicklung, AWi Verlag, April 1996, S. 28–31

[Yok92]   Y. Yokote: *The New Mechanism for Object-Oriented System Programming*, Proceedings of IMSA '92, pp. 88–93, [IMSA92]

[ZEWH95]   S.H. Zweben, S.H. Edwards, B.W. Weide, J.E. Hollingsworth: *The Effects of Layering and Encapsulation on Software Development Cost and Quality*, IEEE Transactions on Software Engineering, Vol. 21, No. 3, pp. 200–208, 1995

[Zim94]   W. Zimmer: *Relationships Between Design Patterns*, Proceedings of PLoP '94, pp. 345–364, [PLoP94]

[Zim96]   C. Zimmermann: *Objektorientierte Konzepte: Entscheidungsschichten zwischen Anwendung und Betriebssystemkern—Zwischenspiele*, iX, Februar 1996, S.146–151

Index of Patterns

Abstract Factory 206, 211, 284, 292, 380, 397, 398
Acceptor 206, 337
Active Object 162, 257
Adapter 49, 158, 267, 380

Blackboard 26, 29, **71**-**95**, 366, 380
Bridge 40, 49, 140, 206, 211, 371, 380
Broker 26, 98, **99**-**122**, 191, 306, 331, 335, 337, 366, 380, 385
Builder 380

Chain of Responsibility 139, 244, 371, 380
Client-Dispatcher-Server 106, 121, 163, 182, 222, 256, 274, 306, 322, **323**-**337**,
    364, 366, 380
Client-Server 366
Command 41, 244, 276, 278, 289, 300, 380
Command Processor 136, 142, 158, 222, 276, **277**-**290**, 301, 366, 371, 380
Composite 51, 129, 139, 224, 234, 238, 240, 241, 284, 367, 370, 371, 380
Composite Message 51, 152, 160, 161, 366, 370
Connector 206, 337
Counted Body 357
Counted Pointer 14, 15, 234, 270, **353**-**358**, 366, 380

Decorator 275, 380
Dependents 339
Detachable Inspector 206
Document-View 17, 140, 141, 369

Envelope-Letter 211
Event Channel 223, 341
Exceptional Value 255, 256

Facade. 40, 86, 158, 159, 208, 242, 261, 380
Factory Method 137, 298, 371, 380
Flyweight. 380
Forwarder-Receiver 18, 121, 162, 182, 222, 232, 256, 268, 272, 273, 306, **307**-**322**, 337, 364, 366, 380, 399

Half-Sync/Half-Async 162
Handle-Body 15, 366

Indented Control Flow 349
Interpreter. 287, 288, 367, 380
Iterator 261, 299, 380

Layers . . .26, 29, **31**-**51**, 69, 70, 85, 120, 183, 192, 199, 364, 366, 367, 380, 398, 400

Main Program and Subroutines 378
Master-Slave 222, 243, 244, **245**-**260**, 366, 380
Mediator 121, 160, 233, 244, 292, 299, 380
Memento 276, 283, 380
Meta-Level Architecture 193
Microkernel 26, 38, 47, 51, 98, 169, **171**-**192**, 219, 366, 380
Model-View-Controller 3, 9, 10, 12, 16, 17, 22, 26, 123, **125**-**143**, 167, 292, 303, 366, 369, 371, 380, 391, 400
MVC see Model-View-Controller

Object Group. 260
Objectifier 206
Observer 13, 223, 306, 339
Open Implementation 193

PAC see Presentation-Abstraction-Control
Pipes and Filters 26, 29, 41, **53**-**70**, 86, 98, 365, 366, 367, 380, 391, 400
Presentation-Abstraction-Control. . . . 26, 51, 123, 143, **145**-**168**, 303, 366, 369, 380
Prototype. 284, 380
Proxy. .18, 23, 104, 105, 113, 121, 162, 186, 222, 256, 261, **263**-**275**, 366, 375, 380
Publisher-Subscriber. 13, 16, 41, 127, 132, 160, 161, 223, 298, 306, **339**-**343**, 366, 371, 380

Reactor 41, 186, 318, 341, 366
Reference Counting Idiom 357
Reflection 26, 40, 85, 112, 115, 169, 191, **193**-**219**, 366, 380, 399

Singleton 208, 253, 286, 299, 364, 380
Singleton (C++) 350
Singleton (Smalltalk) 351
State 206, 380
Strategy 23, 40, 84, 206, 209, 211, 252, 259, 299, 380

Template Method 380

View Handler 138, 157, 222, 276, **291-303**, 366, 371, 380
Visitor 206, 211, 380

Whole-Part 208, 222, 224, **225-242**, 272, 317, 366, 367, 368, 380, 399, 400
Window Place 2